Oxford Word Skills

牛津英语词汇

—— 初 级（第 2 版）——

Learn to use the most important words and phrases in English topic by topic

〔英〕鲁思·盖尔恩斯 〔美〕斯图亚特·雷德曼 著 孙欣祺 译

上海译文出版社

ACKNOWLEDGEMENTS

Cover illustration by Carol Verbyst

Although every effort has been made to trace and contact copyright holders before publication, this has not been possible in some cases. We apologize for any apparent infringement of copyright and, if notified, the publisher will be pleased to rectify any errors or omissions at the earliest possible opportunity.

Disclaimer: This book includes some words which have or are asserted to have proprietary status as trademarks or otherwise. Their inclusion does not imply that they have acquired for legal purposes a non-proprietary or general significance nor any other judgement concerning their legal status. In cases where editorial staff have some evidence that a word has proprietary status this is indicated in the listing of that word in the Word List but no judgement concerning the legal status of such words is made or implied thereby.

The publisher would like to thank the following for their permission to use the following photographs: **Alamy Stock Photo** pp. 64 (receptionist/Zoonar GmbH), 66 (police/Martin Brayley), 112 (post office/Kumar Sriskandan), 129 (history/Ian Dagnall), (literature/CBW), 158 (Vanessa May/ITAR-TASS News Agency), (Jonas Kaufmann/dpa picture Alliance), 159 (Glastonbury/Roger Cracknell 01), 160 (Mr Bean/United Archive GmbH), (Dunkirk/Moviestore Collection Ltd), (Bond/Entertainment Pictures), (cartoon/MARKA), (science fiction/Sportsphoto), 165 (Mary Shelley/Heritage Image Partnership Ltd), 177 (information office/EDU Vision); **Metropolitan Museum of Art** p. 129 The Mr. and Mrs. Henry Ittleson Jr. Purchase Fund, 1956 © Metropolitan Museum, New York; **OUP** pp. 65 (mobile phone/Maxx Studio), 80 (monkey, snake, whale, cow, spider), 92 (milk, bread, chocolates), 94 (apple, grapes, pineapple), 95 (cucumber), 96 (cow, beef, lamb), 102 (bike), 140 (computer), 154 (TV), 171 (plane); **Shutterstock** pp. 17 (spoon/Alex Staroseltev), 24 (seasons/mandritoiu), 28 (woman/JP Chretian), (man/Studioloco), 30 (tall/Asier Romero), (average/pikselstock), (short/mimagephotography), (slim/Ebitkar), (average build/AlexNastya), (overweight/Gelpi), 31 (beard/Cookie Studio), (blonde hair/nakaridore), (straight hair/Roman Samborskyi), (grey hair/AJP), 34 (reception/SeventyFour), 36 (damon/aastock), (Elsie/India Picture), (Alf/Pathdoc), (Dave/kurhan), (Maggie/Djomas), (Paul/eurobanks), (Jane/natu), (Luke/Spectral Design), (Karen/Heather Shimmin), (James/Gelpi), (Jessica/all-about people), 37 (couple/Spectral Design), (Damon/aastock), 38 (laughing/WAYHOME Studio), 39 (Gemma, Sophie/WAYHOME Studio), 40 (couple/Bobex-73), 41 (Sophie, Gemma/WAYHOME Studio), 51 (Caroline/Artem Varnitsin), 53 (tennis/imtmphoto), 56 (scarf/Yuri Gulakov), (hat/FoodTravelStockforlife), (belt/Jian Zhongyan), (handbag/specnaz), (umbrella/Scrudje), (watch/Olga Popova), (shoes/Kutlavev Dmitry), (leather boots/Hlemedida Ivan), (trainers/Den Rozhnovsky), (socks/valkoinen), (tights/Kajonsak Tui), (glasses/Ajintai), (sunglasses/yod67), (gloves/Andrey Armyagov), (rings/AOME1812), (jewellery/Alina MD), (necklace/Alpay Erdem), 57 (Shoes/glamour/(necklace/superphoto65), (watch/Hugh Adams), (boots/Hlemdida Ivan), (trainers/Harry Cabance), (gloves/TinasDreamworld), (belt/AlenKadr), (tights/Spinsv), (plastic ring/Nikos Andreou), 58 (red skirt/Velvet Eye), (blue skirt/lev radin), (orange handbag/Nadia Korel), (green handbag/Khmelnitskaia Evgeniia), (tie/Sandratsky Dmitriy), (purple tie/bg_knight), (shoes/Ivan Popelyshko), (red shoes/azure), 59 (shop assistant/Zoriana Zaitseva), (large shirt/EveniiAnd), 60 (bank notes & coins/Ubermensch Matt), (bank notes/Andrew Baker), (coins/UKRID), (debit car/robertindiana), (brown wallet/Ekaterina43), (purse/Bayanova Svetlana), (wallet/LomdetP), 61 (table setting/allstars), (hair products/Maria Francesca Moccia), (car/White Vector), 62 (toys/Billion Photos), 64 (diary/Panya Anusami), (old camera/finwal89), (cassette/Ensuper), 65 (fan/ScriptX), (electric fan/Ratthaphong Ekariyasap), (old phone/Adrio Communications Ltd), 68 (headache/Makistock), (toothache/PARIN.PSA), (stomach ache/napatsor aungsirochinda), (backache/Obprod), (cold/Samo Trebizan), (cough/Stockbakery), (flu/kryzhov), (temperature/Ermolaev Alexander), (sick/New Africa), 69 (ill/Rawpixel.com), 71 (rocks/Tatiana Popova), 72 (logging/Sheryl Watson), 73 (coal/Pail Oleg), (petrol/Novikov Alex), (electricity/TW Stock), (gas/Happyhunt), 78 (sunny/traXX), (cloudy/Suzanne Tucker), (raining/Inga Neilson), (windy/Rainer Fuhrmann), (snow/Alexander Demyanov), 79 (stormy/diamond), 80 (lion/Eric Isselee), (tiger/nattanan726), (elephant/Rich Carey), (bear/Alexander Cher), (bird/Dennis Jacobsen), (horse/mariait), (sheep/Aaron Amat), (pg/photomaster), (dog/Dora Zett), (cat/Timmary), (mouse/Eric Isselee), (fly, bee/irin-k), 89 (painting/Olena Yakobchuck), (timetable/PR Image Factory), (family/Iakov Filimonov), (cinema/Nikolay Antonov), (holding up hands/fizkes), 90 (fighting/Anton Watman), (phone call/WAYHOME Studio), (waking up/YAKOBCHUK VIACHESLAV), (smelling rose/Arthit Premprayot), (asleep/Golubovy), (smiling/Antonio Guillem), 92 (butter/akf ffm), (cheese/Hong Vo), (eggs/nechaevkon), (sugar/Kasabutskaya Nataliya), (cake slice/ninikas), (cake/Brittny), (jam/Alter-ego), (biscuits/TairA), (olive oil/Agorohov), (olives/Africa Studio), (rice/RVillalon), (spaghetti/jamakosy), (chocolate/etorres), 93 (grocers/Iakov Filimonov), (btuchers/Minerva Studio), (bag/Pitchayarat Chootai), 94 (banana/vandycan), (orange/Valentyn Volkov), (peach/Svetlana Serebryakova), (pear/Ines Behrens-Kunkel), (lemon/Valery121283), (strawberry/Maks Narodenko), (nuts/Svetlana Verbitckaia), 95 (potato/grey_and), (beans /ConstantinosZ), (onion/Lubava), (carrot/VictoriaKH), (peas /AmyLv), (cabbage/jamakosy), (mushroom/bergamot), (garlic/Artem Kutsenko), (lettuce/Gavran333), (tomato/Tim UR), (red pepper/SOMMAI), (peas/Africa Studio), (cooked peas/stevemart), 96 (sheep/Aaron Amat), (lamb/Tanya Sid), (chicken/Olhastock), (duck/Aksenova Natalya), (pig/Tsekhmister), (chicken/JIANG HONGYAN), (duck/bonchan, (pork/Mirek Kijewski), (ham/sripfoto), (bacon/Richard Griffin), (sausages/kzww), (salmon/TheFarAwayKingdom), (tuna/picturepartners), (squid/demarco), (prawns/aperturesound), (crab/LAURA_VN), 99 (waiter/Iakov Filimonov), 100 (coffee/Photoongraphy), (black coffee/amenic181), (tea/Pavol Lys), (hot chocolate/Lilya Kandrashevich), (orange juice/r.classen), (cola/StudioBy The Sea), (sandwich/gowithstock), (brown bread/Richard M Lee), (toasted sandwich/Drozhzhina Elena), (roll/Ninetechno), (crisps/Mettus), (cakes/V_L), 102 (car/Rawpixel.com), (us/Sanit Fuangnakhon), (coach/Mikbiz), (van/TeamDaf), (lorry/Sunday Stock), (motorbike/Dimitris Leonidas), (taxi/maradon 333), (underground/MirasWonderland), 105 (information/SIHASAKPRACHUM), 107 (pointing/tofumax), 108 (directions/Haelen Haagen), 110 (closed sign/AOFTO), (toilets/Thas Pol Sangsee), (exit/Piotr Zajda), (sale/Sundry Photography), (no smoking/Lester Balajadia), (keep left/Focus Dzign), (no dogs/Britain), (out of order/Junpinzon), (no exit/Eddie H S Cho), (no parking/Mike Kuhlman), (do not feed/Richard Johnson), (no vacancies/Chiycat), (danger/AC Rider), (entrance/Stripped Pixel), (queue/imrankadir), (mind the gap/Joseph Maguire), (keep off the grass/emattil), 112 (castle/Daniela Miglionrisi), (palace/Fulcanelli) (church/Caron Badkin), (museum/Anton_Ivanov), (art gallery/Sofia Voronkova), (market/Epel), (park/EarthScape ImageGraphy), (library/Ermolaev Alexander), (tower/prasit jmkajornkiat), (square/PHOTOCREO Michael Bednarek), (bridge/Carlos Bruzos Valin), 129 (chemistry/Picel-Shot), (physics/Science Photo), (biologyNew Africa), (maths/Billion Photos), (computer science/Aleksey Khilko), (geography/TonelloPhotography), (languages/Aysezgicmeli), (exercise/Summersky), (design and technology/RomanR), 130 (uniform/Rawpixel.com), 131, 132 (man/AJR_Photo), 133 (doctor/Monkey Business Images), (plans/asobov), (hard hat/Nattanan Zia), (scales of justice/Billion Photos), (newspaper/DONOT6_Studio), (computer/Stanisic Vladimir), (businessman/michaeljung), 134 (police/betto Rodrigues), (business people/gigsy25), (dentist/djrandco), (model/FashionStock.com), (shop assistant/Lstock Studio), (nurse/Monkey Business Images), (fashion designer/Nenad Aksic), (soldier/Misha Belly), (pilot/Angelo Giampiccolo), (builder/ALPA PROD), (teacher/Asia Images Group), (chef/Wavebreak Media), (cleaner/RossHelen), (lorry driver/Kzenon), (hairdresser/Iakov

Filimonov), 136 (secretary/Dragon Images), (office/Africa Studio), (factory/You Touch Pix of Eu Toch), (hospital/Tyler Olsen), 138 (interview/Blue Planet Studio), 140 (computer screen/Russian Ivantsov), (keyboard/On_Ter), (mouse/AG-Photos), (printer/cigdem), (laptop/Sergey Peterman), (tablet/Umberto Shtanzman), (computer programme/Morrowind), (drop down menu/Semenchenko), 144 (mobile phone/Ellica), (phone charger/2Ban), 147 (sightseeing/Rosshelen), (tent/Alexlukin), (painting/Syda Productions), 150 (bathroom/Artazum), (dining room/roakoma), (bus stop/den-arcticman), (DJ/FabrikaSimf), (railway station/CapuletBK), (art gallery/Anton_Ivanov), (address book/Photology1972), (dishwasher/Leszek Glasner), 151 (phone/jeka), 153 (man/Africa Studio), (two people/Rommel Canlas), 154 (tent/Alexlukin), (fishing rod/Rvector), (weights/Valerii Ivaschenko), (guitar/Andrej Valadzenkou), (golf clubs/Sean Locke Photography), (computer game/Gorodenkoff), (suitcase/omnimoney), (sketch pad/Nastya Sokolova), (cooking/Creativa Images), (stamp albu/279Photo Studio), (friends/Monkey Business Images), (DVDs/Ingrid Balabanova), 155 (ballet/Flamingo Images) 156 (goalkeeper/FOTOKITA), (baseball/zsolt_uveges), (basketball/Fabrizio Andrea Bertani), (swimming/jeep2499), (American football/Brocreative), (tennis/Q Stock), (table tennis/Stefan), (ice hockey/Sergey Mironev), (running/EverenKalinbacak), (motor racing/Ev.Safronov), (skiing/Andrey Nikulin), (football/Herbert Kraty), 158 (orchestra/Ferenc Szelepcsenyi), 158 (Lang Lang/Maria Laura Antonelli/AGF), 159 (CD/Arkadi Bulva), 160 (love story/Bogolijubb), (horror/Studio Canal), 161 (movie poster/Universal Pictures), 164 (reading/Motortion Films), 166 (passport/Ray Morgan), 167 (double room/Nasimi Babaev), (single room/Ruslana Maskenskaia), 168 (hotel/alexkatov), 169 (key card/Pressmaster), (key/Zelikjo Radojko), 170 (ticket machine/illpazphotomatic), (check in desk/Tyler Olsen), 171 (businessman/Maridav), (seat belt/inewsfoto), (flight attendant/Sorbis), (plane/tzuky333), (passport official/FrameStockFootages), (carousel/fizkes), 173 (taking photos/Stokkete), 179 (teacher/Dean Drobot), 180 Dean Drobot, 184 (wedding/Olya64), (Sonya/ProStockStudio), 188 (café/pickingpok), 191 (taking off jacket/Cecilia Tomio), (light switch/Svetlana Cherkasova), (putting on shoes/BOKEH STOCK).

All illustrations by: CCS Digital Education.

Contents 目录

Spotlight boxes 词汇聚光灯

关于《牛津英语词汇》（第二版）

《牛津英语词汇》（第二版）系列一套三册，供学生学习词汇使用，并配以练习。

初级：

初级［对应欧洲语言共同参考框架（CEFR）的A1、A2水平］

中级：

中级［对应欧洲语言共同参考框架（CEFR）的B1水平］

高级：

高级［对应欧洲语言共同参考框架（CEFR）的B2、C1水平］

每册收录新词或短语2000余个，可供课堂教学或自学使用。

丛书结构

《牛津英语词汇》（第二版）每册分100个单元，每单元包括两部分：词汇学习与配套练习。"词汇学习"篇幅适中，"配套练习"紧随其后，通常在同一页面。根据话题所涉内容的长短，每单元1至2页不等。

每3至10个单元组成一个模块。多数模块围绕日常话题，如"人""食物与饮料""学习与工作"。部分模块聚焦语言本身，如"介词""形容词与副词""动词"。

本册还包括：

- "词汇聚光灯"索引
- 词性转换表
- 不规则动词表
- 参考答案
- 单词总表，其中包括词汇索引，并根据"牛津英语3000词表"（Oxford 3000™）、"牛津英语5000词表"（Oxford 5000™）或"牛津英语短语表"（Oxford Phrase List™）标注了单词或短语的欧框等级。

所收词汇

本册词汇涉及：

- 广泛的日常话题，例如：服装、闲暇、机场；
- 社交场合使用的单词和短语，例如：邀请他人、见面与问候；
- 各类词法，例如：介词、动词、形容词、副词。

本丛书主要收录日常英语口语中的高频词汇。在此基础上，中级、高级两册收录了更多不同文体的用语和词汇的比喻用法。

本丛书依据使用频率和实用价值选取词汇，以"牛津英语3000词表"（下简称"牛津3000"）或"牛津英语5000词表"（下简称"牛津5000"）为参考标准。这两份词表由牛津大学出版社英语教学词典团队编制，分别收录英语学习者所需掌握的3000和5000个最重要的单词。根据欧洲语言共同参考框架（CEFR），"牛津3000"中的单词可由易至难划分为四级：A1、A2、B1、B2；"牛津5000"增收部分B2和C1级别的单词。

- 初级主要收录"牛津3000"中A2级别的词汇，也包含众多A1级别的词汇；
- 中级聚焦"牛津3000"中B1级别的词汇，并再现部分A2级别的词汇；
- 高级重点收录"牛津3000"中B2级别的词汇，兼及"牛津5000"中B2和C1级别的词汇。本丛书未收录C2级词汇，因为C2级别更切合"精通"（proficiency）程度的用词需求。

本丛书还参考了"牛津英语短语表"和牛津英语词典的话题列表。前者作为"牛津3000"和"牛津5000"词表的补充，涵盖近千个重要短语，能满足不同级别学生的需求，结合上述词表，可覆盖各级难度的单词和短语；后者选编自牛津大学出版社的各类学习型词典，以60个话题统摄核心词汇，结合"牛津3000"一同使用，使学生既注重高频词汇的学习，又掌握了一些虽不常用，但在特定语境中相当有意义的词条，例如：与饭店相关的main course，与机场相关的hand luggage。

书中提供了大量精确的插图、简洁的释义及实用的例证，尽可能确保学习者掌握所有新单词与新短语的含义。此外，学习者应当注意，许多英语单词含有多义，如需了解这些单词的其他含义，可通过查阅词典获取相关信息。

我们默认学习者已经掌握"牛津3000"A1级别中的部分高频词汇，因此未在本册书中作详细解释，仅在书后将它们统一列出。

一些关键词有时会在书的后半部分重复出现，但未标粗。如果学生不认识，可以对照书后的单词总表，找出该词在书中的出处和释义，温故知新，有益学习。

写给教师的话

教师如何运用本书开展课堂教学？

本书中的新词汇通过以下方式呈现：

- 视觉材料

| | sit down
pt sat down | stand up
pt stood up | walk | run
pt ran | fall over
pt fell over | ride
pt rode |

- 表格

	a day	a date
on	**on** Tuesday **on** Friday evening **on** Tuesday**s** = every Tuesday **on** my birthday **on** Christmas Day	**on** September 10 **on** 6th May

- 不同类型的拓展文本

B Friends 朋友

WHY WE LIKE
each other
· ·
Sophie: I **get on very well with** Gemma – she's great. I don't know why, because we've got

GLOSSARY	
each other	She likes me and I like her. = We like **each other**.
get on (well) with sb	have a good relationship with sb
personality	what a person is like that makes them different from other people
meet *pt* met	**1** see and speak to sb for the first time **2** go to a place and wait for sb: *We're **meeting** them at 7.30.*
become	begin to be sth: ***become friends/flatmates***
flatmate	a person you live with, but not in a romantic relationship
advice [U]	an opinion or information that you give to help sb with a problem **give (sb) advice**
see sb	talk to or visit sb

视觉材料（即照片和插图）能清晰直观地诠释词汇含义，表格和拓展文本呈现了词汇的地道用法，单词释义则归纳总结在单词表（GLOSSARY）中。词汇输入（input）部分大多仅占一页，且通常不超过15项，可在课堂教学中直接使用。以下使用步骤仅供参考：

- 让学生学习"词汇学习"部分的视觉材料或文本，至少10分钟。在此期间，他们能够巩固视觉性输入材料和单词含义之间的关联，或者能够精读单词表，查看例句、对话或拓展文本中的新词含义。提醒学生注意单词表（GLOSSARY）中的其他内容，包括反义词、近义词、派生词、搭配、其他例证，这种方法在很多情况下有助于事半功倍地拓宽词汇面。同样需要关注的还有"词汇聚光灯"（SPOTLIGHT）。这一部分是本书特色，精选了价值较高的内容。以下为"词汇聚光灯"展示的"else的用法"和"flat、house、home之间的区别"。

SPOTLIGHT *else*

You can use **else** to mean 'different' after words like **everyone**, **somewhere** and **nothing**.

- *I didn't like it, but everyone else did.* (= all the other people)
- *The restaurant was full so we went somewhere else.* (= to another place)
- *We had bread because there was nothing else to eat.* (= no other thing)

SPOTLIGHT *flat, house, home*

A **flat** is a number of rooms on one floor of a building. SYN **apartment**

A **house** is a building that is made for people to live in. It can have more than one floor.

Home is where you live (in a flat or a house).

- 学生在学习"词汇学习"部分时，可提出任何有关词汇的问题。教师可以答疑，也可以提供发音示范，让学生跟读，以免课堂冷场。可以示范朗读课文，也可以让学生朗读片段。

- 等学生学完"词汇学习"部分，让他们完成第一个练习。可以让他们自行核对答案，也可以在课堂上讲解。后一种方法更好，因为这样既能分析答错的原因，也能关注、练习发音。最好按顺序完成习题，因为从"接受性练习"（receptive practice）过渡到"半开放练习"（controlled productive practice），再到 ABOUT YOU 或 ABOUT YOUR COUNTRY 这样的"开放练习"（freer productive practice），是一个循序渐进的过程。

- 第一个练习完成后，监督学生独立或结对完成其他练习，教师可适时提供帮助。许多题目适合进行口语练习，尤其是"将对话填写完整"和"将句子填写完整"。学生可以结对练习对话或互相朗读完整的句子。

- 完成书面习题后，学生可以进行新词自测。本书的设计编排便于学生用纸张等物品遮住图片下的新词，然后对照视觉材料进行自测。这一方法也适用于部分表格和单词表：遮住新词，只看释义；或者遮住释义，只看新词。这一方法简单易行，适合反复操练，所以无需不断寻找各种类型的习题。课堂演示"遮书自测"也便于学生效仿，在课余时间用此方法复习词汇。

- ABOUT YOU 和 ABOUT YOUR COUNTRY 是个性化习题，让学生有机会结合各自生活的语境，自由发挥，使用新学的词汇。做这些习题时，学生可以自己写下答案，但更理想的方式是两两结对，运用新学的词汇来练习口语。如果让学生进行口语练习，也可以让他们在练习之余将自己或搭档的答案写下来。"参考答案"中，答题者既包括以英语为母语的人，也包括来自非英语国家或地区、但英语说得非常流利的人。通过比较答案，自学者受益良多。

学生如何运用本书进行自学？

本书在编写时，就考虑到要同时适用于课堂教学和自学。自学者应从第一模块开始学习，以便更有效地使用本书。他们可以通过书后"参考答案"进行批改，也可以用上文介绍的"遮书自测法"进行自测，还可以选择感兴趣的话题或希望拓展知识面的话题自主学习，这就是本书用作自学的一大优势。

1 Classroom vocabulary 课堂词汇

1   whiteboard (ALSO board)
2   board pen
3   noticeboard
4   notice
5   desk
6   chair
7   bag
8   pen
9   coursebook
10 pencil
11 table
12 dictionary
13 CD
14 CD player
15 piece of paper
16 exercise book / notebook

1 Tick (✓) the things you can put in a bag. Put a cross (✗) by the things you can't.
以下物品能否放进包里? 可以的打钩 (√) , 不能的打叉 (×)。

▶ pen ✓   2 desk ☐   5 table ☐   8 noticeboard ☐
▶ board ✗   3 notice ☐   6 coursebook ☐   9 dictionary ☐
1 pencil ☐   4 CD player ☐ 7 chair ☐   10 piece of paper ☐

2 Complete the words or phrases. 将单词或短语填写完整。

▶ notebook

1 board _____   3 notice _____   5 piece of _____
2 course _____   4 exercise _____   6 CD _____

3 Write your answers. 填写相应物品。

▶ You sit on one of these.   a chair
1 The teacher writes on this.   _____
2 You find the meaning of words in this. _____
3 You sit behind one of these.   _____
4 You write in one of these.   _____
5 The teacher puts information on this. _____
6 The teacher can play one of these. _____
7 You can put your books in this.   _____
8 You study from one of these.   _____

4 ABOUT YOU Write four things you've got at home, and four things you haven't got.
分别写出4件你家里有和没有的物品。

▶ I've got a dictionary. _____   ▶ I haven't got a CD player. _____

_____   _____
_____   _____
_____   _____

Read this short text.

> An old woman walked slowly up the hill.
> On the way, she spoke to a little boy.
> 'Good morning', she said.

- There are eight **words** in the first **sentence**.
- *Walk* is a **regular** verb. The **past simple** is *walked*.
- *Speak* is an **irregular** verb. The past simple is *spoke*, and the **past participle** is *spoken*. (The past participle is used to form the present perfect: *Have you spoken to the doctor today?*)

Look at the different **parts of speech**.

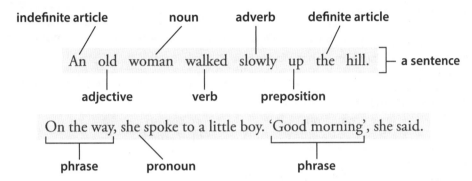

1 Circle the correct answer. 圈出正确答案。

▶ *A* and *the* are *adjectives* / (*articles.*)

1 *A* and *an* are *definite* / *indefinite* articles.
2 *Woman* is *a noun* / *an adjective*.
3 *Up* is a *preposition* / *pronoun*.
4 *Have* is *a regular* / *an irregular* verb.

5 *He* and *she* are *nouns* / *pronouns*.
6 *Go* and *do* are *verbs* / *nouns*.
7 *Badly* and *happily* are *adverbs* / *adjectives*.
8 *Gone* is the *past simple* / *past participle* of the verb *go*.

2 Find the answers for each sentence. 从句中找出相应部分。

I have an English lesson now.	▶	a verb _have_	**2**	an indefinite article ....
	1	a pronoun	**3**	a noun ....
There's a young man from Rome in the class.	**4**	an adjective	**6**	an indefinite article ....
	5	a preposition		
This morning, he asked a question, and he spoke very quietly.	**7**	an adverb	**9**	a regular past simple ....
	8	an irregular past simple	**10**	a phrase ....
I think he's in the wrong class.	**11**	a noun	**14**	a pronoun ....
	12	a verb	**15**	a sentence ....
	13	an adjective		

3 What are the parts of speech for the other words in the text at the top of the page?
写出上文中其他单词的词性。

▶ hill   _noun_

1 on   ....
2 the   ....
3 way   ....
4 spoke   ....
5 to   ....

6 a   ....
7 little   ....
8 boy   ....
9 she   ....
10 said   ....

Learn these words. You need to understand them to do the exercises. 学习下列单词和短语，为练习做好准备。

tick	✓ (= *yes* OR *correct*)
underline	<u>word</u>
cross out	~~word~~
circle	(word)
complete	I <u>like</u> ice cream.
correct/wrong	2 + 2 = 4 is **correct** (ALSO **right**). 2 + 2 = 5 is **wrong**.
mistake	If sth is a **mistake**, it's wrong. e.g. ~~Inglish~~. SYN **error**
correct	make sth right, e.g. ~~Inglish~~ (wrong), *English* (right); tell sb what mistakes they are making
true/false	'Paris is in France.' That's **true**. 'Paris is in Italy.' That's **false**.
the same/different	*Small* and *little* are **the same** (*small = little*). *Small* and *big* are **different**.
match sth (with sth)	**Match** 1–3 with a–c. 1 I come from _c_ . a) English 2 I speak a little .... b) married 3 I'm .... c) Japan ✓
missing	If sth is **missing**, it is not there. e.g. *He comes Tokyo.* (The word *from* is **missing**.) *He comes* <u>from</u> *Tokyo.*
cover	put one thing over another thing
test sb OR yourself	If you **test yourself**, you ask yourself questions to find what you know and understand, e.g. *When I **test myself** on English verbs, I look at the verb, then say the meaning in my language.*
table	This is a **table**: | Question	Answer
What does *awful* **mean?** (NOT ~~What means 'awful'?~~)	**I don't know.** OR **It means** 'terrible'.	
column	The table above has got two **columns**: one for questions and one for answers.
put sth in order	put things in the right place or position: **Put** these words **in order** to make a sentence. *bed / I / early / to / went* <u>I went to bed early.</u>

Short forms and symbols 缩写与符号

- *TV* is a **short form** of *television*.
- A **symbol** is a sign or picture with a special meaning. e.g. **=** is a symbol that means **equals** OR **is the same as**: 2 + 2 = 4.

e.g.	is short for **for example**: *fruit*, **e.g.** *apples and bananas*.
OPP	is short for **opposite**: *Big* is **the opposite of** *small*.
SYN	is short for **synonym** (= a word that means the same as another): *small* SYN *little*.
etc.	You use **etc.** at the end of a list to show there are more things, but you don't want to say them all: *We bought apples, oranges, bananas,* **etc.** We can say **etc.** as 'etcetera' or **and so on**.
inf	means **informal**. If a word is **informal**, you use it when you are speaking to friends or people you know well, but not in serious writing or important letters. OPP **formal**
sth	is a short form of **something**.
sb	is a short form of **somebody/someone**.

1 **Read the sentences and write your answers.** 阅读句子，按要求圈划或填写答案。

▶ Put a tick at the end of this sentence. ✓

1 Underline the third word in this sentence.

2 Circle the first word in this sentence.

3 Cross out the last word in this sentence.

4 What's the opposite of *big*? ....

5 What's a synonym for *fantastic*? ....

6 Correct the mistak in this sentence. ....

7 What's a more informal word for *thank you*? ....

8 Is it *true* or *false* that London is in Scotland? ....

9 What word missing in this sentence? ....

10 Is eight thirty the same as half past eight? ....

11 Fourteen and twenty-seven is forty-three. Is that right or wrong? ....

12 Complete the next sentence. *Where* .... *you live?* ~ I live near the park.

2 **Match the opposites.** 反义词配对。

▶	formal	*c*	**a**	wrong
1	the same	....	**b**	opposite
2	correct	....	**c**	informal ✓
3	true	....	**d**	different
4	synonym	....	**e**	false

3 **What do these short forms and symbols mean? Write your answers.** 写出下列缩写和符号的含义。

▶ **OPP** *opposite*

1 e.g. ....   **4** **SYN** ....

2 ✓ ....   **5** = ...

3 *inf* ....   **6** etc. ....

4 **Complete the sentences.** 将句子填写完整。

▶ Do days of the week have a capital letter? Yes, that's *correct/right* .

1 You use .... at the end of a list to show that there are other things but you are not going to say them all.

2 What word is .... in the next sentence? *I went bed early.*

3 If you put something in .... , you put it in the correct place or position.

4 12 and 12 is 26, isn't it? No, that's ....

5 = is a .... , and it means 'equals' or 'is ....'

6 I make lots of .... when I speak, but my teacher usually .... me.

7 After each page, I always .... myself on all the new words. I often look at the words, ... the meanings, and then try to remember and say the meanings.

8 *US* is a .... of the United States of America.

9 In this exercise, you have to .... *a* to *e* with *1* to *5*.

10 *Hi* is a more .... way of saying *hello*.

11 San Francisco is the capital of America. True or .... ?

12 .... is a synonym for *mistake*.

13 How many .... has this table got? ~ Three.

Word	Synonym	Example
family name	surname	Rodriguez
first name(s)	forename(s)	Maria Helena

14 We have to .... the correct answer, e.g. I looked <u>at</u>/in the board.

15 We have to .... the wrong answer, e.g. I looked at/ⓘn the board.

A How to learn words 如何学习单词

Here are some **things** to **help** you when you are learning new words:

- Repeat words **out loud** two or three times to practise the **pronunciation**.
- **Write down** new words in a **notebook**. It's important to **keep a record** of them because it will help you to remember them.
- Write the **meaning** in English or your own language.
- Write an example sentence with the new word. This helps you to understand how to **use** the new word.
- Think of **situations** where you can use this word, and perhaps write them down.

GLOSSARY

help	do sth good for sb; make their life easier
out loud	so that other people can hear it
pronunciation	how to say a word **pronounce** v
write sth down	write sth on paper so you can remember it
notebook	a book that you can write in
record	notes of things that have happened, e.g. a **record** of money that you have spent **keep a record (of sth)**
meaning	The **meaning** of *small* is 'little'.
use	do a job with sth: *I use a key to open my door.*
situation	things that are happening at a certain time or in a certain place: *I was in a difficult **situation** at work today because my computer wasn't working.*

SPOTLIGHT *thing(s)*

We often use **thing(s)** to talk about an idea or a subject. It means we don't need to find the exact name for something.

- *We talked about lots of **things**.*
- *Art is the **thing** that interests me most.*

1 Complete the dialogues with one word. 将对话填写完整，每空格只填一词。

▶	What's this word?	~ *Beige*, but I don't know the correct __pronunciation__ .
1	Was the homework easy?	~ No, it wasn't, but my father _____ me.
2	Did the others hear you?	~ Yes, I said his name out _____ .
3	How do you know you've read that book?	~ Because I keep a _____ .
4	How did you remember her phone number?	~ I wrote it _____ .
5	Do you know the meaning of *awful*?	~ Yes, but I don't know how to _____ it.
6	I've broken my mother's favourite cup. I don't know what to say to her.	~ What a difficult _____ !
7	Have you got a new computer?	~ Yes, but I don't know how to _____ it yet.
8	Did you talk about the holiday?	~ Yes, and lots of other _____ .

2 Complete the sentences. First, cover the text at the top of the page. 遮住上文，将句子填写完整。

Here are some ▶ __things__ to help you when you are learning new words.
1 Repeat words _____ two or three times to practise the pronunciation.
2 Write down new words in a _____. It's important to _____ a record of them.
3 Write the _____ in English or your own language.
4 If you write an example sentence, it helps you to remember how to _____ a new word.
5 Think of _____ where you can use this word.

3 Answer the questions. 回答问题。

▶ Why do you do lots of different things when you are learning new words?
   To help me to understand and remember them.
1 Why do you repeat words out loud? _____
2 Where can you write down new words? _____
3 Why is it important to do that? _____
4 How can you write the meaning? _____
5 Why do you write an example sentence? _____
6 What can you do after that? _____

B Questions about words 与单词相关的提问

Question	Answer
What does *awful* **mean?** (NOT ~~*What means awful?*~~)	**I don't know.** OR **It means** 'terrible'.
What's this called in English? **How do you say** *fils* **in English?**	**I can't remember.** OR **It's a** spoon. *Son.* OR *Fils* is French for *son.*
Could you explain 'No vacancies'? (NOT ~~*Could you explain me ...?*~~)	Yes. You see it in a hotel window. It means the hotel is full. There are no free rooms.
What's the difference between *hello* and *hi*?	The **meaning** is the same, but *hi* is informal.
What's the opposite of *big*?	Small.
How do you pronounce *tie*?	**It's like** *my*.
Eight is pronounced like *night*. **Is that right/correct?**	**No, that's wrong.** OR **That's not right.** It's pronounced like *wait*.
How do you spell *apple*? **I'm not sure.** (Is it one 'p' or two?)	**It's** A-**double** P-L-E. (double P = two Ps)

4 **Match 1–6 with a–g.** 配对题。

▶ How do you *spell* your name? ....*c*....
1 How do you say *cup* in German? ....
2 What's the opposite of *closed*? ....
3 What does *tiny* mean? ....
4 How do you pronounce *weight*? ....
5 Could you explain *hello*? ....
6 *Come* and *go* mean the same thing. ....

a Very small.
b It's what you say when you meet a friend.
c A-double N-A. ✓
d It's like *wait*.
e No, they don't. That's wrong.
f I don't know. I only speak French.
g Open.

5 **Complete the dialogues.** 将对话填写完整。

▶ What does *awful* ....*mean*.............. ? ~ Terrible.
1 What's this .... in English? ~ It's a frying pan.
2 How do you pronounce *what*? ~ It's .... *hot*.
3 .... you spell *eye*? ~ I'm not sure. I think it's E-Y-E.
4 What's the difference .... *bye* and *goodbye*? ~ *Bye* is more informal.
5 *Pen* is the same as *pencil*. Is that right? ~ No, that's ....
6 What's the .... of *interesting*? ~ Boring.
7 What .... *enormous* mean? ~ It means 'very big'.
8 Could you .... *EXIT*? ~ You see it on a door. It means you can go out there.

6 **Write a question using each word.** 用下列单词提问。

▶ pronounce ...*How do you pronounce*............ *vegetable*?
1 mean .... ?
2 spell .... ?
3 say .... ?
4 explain .... ?
5 opposite .... ?
6 called .... ?

5 Classroom activities 课堂活动

A Teacher instructions 教学用语

OK, **repeat** after me.

When you finish, **compare** your answers **with** a partner.

I want you to write a **description** of someone you know.

Please **pay attention**.

Practise new words every day.

I'd like you to **make up** a story.

Listen to the conversation. Then answer the questions.

Listen, then **follow the instructions** in the book.

If you don't know the meaning, try to **guess**.

And don't **forget** to **do** the **homework**.

GLOSSARY

repeat	say or do sth again
compare sth (with sth)	think about things or people to see how they are different
description	words that tell what sb or sth is like or what happened **describe** v
pay attention	look or listen carefully
practise	do sth many times so that you do it well **practice** n
make sth up	say sth that is not true SYN **invent**
instructions	words that tell you what you must do or how to do sth. You **follow (the) instructions**.
guess	give an answer when you do not know if it is right **guess** n SYN **have a guess**
forget	If you **forget** to do sth, you don't remember to do it.
homework	work that a teacher gives you to do at home: I'm doing my **homework**. (NOT I'm making my homework.)

SPOTLIGHT word building

Many nouns in English are formed from verbs, and -(t)ion is a common noun ending:
- instruct (verb) → instruction (noun)

There is often a spelling change:
- describe → description
- explain → explanation
- educate → education

① Match 1–8 with a–i. 配对题。

▶ repeat it _c_

1 make something up ....
2 follow the instructions ....
3 pay attention ....
4 I forget. ....
5 compare with another student ....
6 describe it ....
7 practise it ....
8 have a guess ....

a talk to another student about it
b listen carefully
c say it again ✓
d do it a few more times
e invent something
f say what it's like
g If you don't know, just think of an answer.
h I don't remember.
i do what it tells you

② Complete the table. If you don't know the answer, have a guess. 将表格填写完整。不会的地方，试着猜一猜。

VERB	NOUN	VERB	NOUN
▶discuss	discussion	instruct	....
explain	....	invent	....
describe	....	practise	....
guess	....	educate	....

③ Complete the dialogues. 将对话填写完整。

▶ Were you listening? ~ No, the teacher told me to pay _attention_ .

1 Can you say that again, please? ~ Yes, I'll .... it.
2 Did you remember your .... ? ~ No, I'm afraid I forgot to do it.
3 Did you know the answer? ~ No, but I had a ....
4 How can I get better? ~ You have to .... more.
5 How do you know they're different? ~ We .... them.
6 Did you .... the homework? ~ No, I .... it. I'm sorry.
7 Did you invent that story? ~ Yes, I .... it ....
8 Did you write a description? ~ No, I just .... it to her.

B Student activities 学生活动

Here are **activities** that students do in the classroom:

* read a **text**
* guess the meaning of new words from the **context**
* listen to **dialogues**
* **look up** the meaning of new words in a dictionary
* write a **paragraph** about something
* write a short **essay** on something
* **revise vocabulary** from another lesson
* do written **exercises**
* have a **conversation** about something in English
* have a **discussion** about something

GLOSSARY	
activity	sth you do, perhaps often
text	a short piece of writing that you read
context	the words that come before or after another word or sentence
dialogue	words that people say to each other, often in a book or film
look sth up	try to find information in a book
paragraph	a group of lines of writing
essay	a short piece of writing about sth. It usually has three or more paragraphs.
revise	look at or do sth again
vocabulary	all the words that sb knows or uses
simple	easy to do or understand
exercise	work that you do to learn sth
conversation	a talk between two or more people
discussion	talking about sth seriously **discuss** *v*

4 **Underline the correct answer.** 在正确答案下划线。

▶ I like to *revise* / *look up* the vocabulary after I've studied it.
1 We read a *text* / *context* in class about pop music in the 1970s.
2 I don't need to write a lot – just one *context* / *paragraph*.
3 We practised the *essay* / *dialogue* in pairs, and the teacher listened to us.
4 The teacher sometimes asks us what *contexts* / *activities* we want to do.
5 I have to write *a discussion* / *an essay* for homework.
6 You can understand the meaning from the *text* / *context*.
7 We had a *discussion* / *conversation* in class about politics.
8 Everyone understood because it was quite *simple* / *difficult*.

5 **Complete the sentences.** 将句子填写完整。

▶ We started the ___exercise___ in class and finished it for homework.
1 We studied the past tense last week and we're going to _____ it this week.
2 I didn't understand so I _____ it _____ in my dictionary.
3 Yesterday, I had a _____ in English with my American friend.
4 Yesterday in class we did three _____ on irregular verbs.
5 We listened to a _____ , then practised it in pairs.
6 Speaking is my favourite _____ in class.
7 I'm sure you can understand this text: it's very _____ .
8 We had to write an _____ in English about our holidays for homework.

6 ABOUT YOU **Write your answers, or ask another student.** 根据自身情况回答问题，也可以向同学提问。
1 How often do you read texts in English? What do you read? _____
2 Do you often use the context to help you understand the meaning of a new word? _____

3 How often do you write an essay in English? _____
4 Do you often revise vocabulary? Why? / Why not? _____
5 What's your favourite activity when you are studying English, inside or outside class? _____

6 Do you like listening to dialogues? Do you think listening to them helps you to learn vocabulary? _____

6) Numbers 数字

A 1–100

1	one	11	eleven	21	twenty-one	40	forty
2	two	12	twelve	22	twenty-two	50	fifty
3	three	13	thirteen	23	twenty-three	60	sixty
4	four	14	fourteen	24	twenty-four	70	seventy
5	five	15	fifteen	25	twenty-five	80	eighty
6	six	16	sixteen	26	twenty-six	90	ninety
7	seven	17	seventeen	27	twenty-seven	100	a/one hundred
8	eight	18	eighteen	28	twenty-eight		
9	nine	19	nineteen	29	twenty-nine		
10	ten	20	twenty	30	thirty		

GLOSSARY

count When you count, you say numbers one after another, e.g. *1–2–3–4–5. I* **counted** *the chairs – there were 15. I can* **count** *in German.*

equal be the same as sth: *2 + 2* **equals** (=) *4*

minus less; when you take away: *6* **minus** (–) *4 = 2*

plus and; added to: *4* **plus** (+) *4 = 8*

SPOTLIGHT *about* and *around*

about/around = a bit more or a little less than
- How many students are there? ~ **Around/about** *20.* (= 18? 19? 20? 21? 22?)
- How much is it? ~ It's **about/around** €100.
- How long is the programme? ~ **About/around** half an hour.

1 Write the middle number in words. 用英语写出两数之间的数。

▶ 24 _twenty-five_ 26

1	7	9	6	5		7
2	19	21	7	12		14
3	66	68	8	71		73
4	49	51	9	23		25
5	34	36	10	88		90

2 Write the number in words using *about* or *around*. 用about或around表达概数。

▶ sixty-eight people _about/around seventy people_

1 ninety-seven euros ....   5 forty-nine dollars ....
2 nine lessons ....   6 seventy-eight people ....
3 thirty-one years ....   7 sixty-eight pounds ....
4 forty-one students ....   8 nineteen chairs ....

3 Do the maths. Write your answers in words. 计算后填写答案。

▶ three plus nine equals _twelve_   ▶ ten minus six equals _four_

1 twelve and seventeen equals ....
2 forty-three plus thirty-four equals ....
3 eighty-seven minus twenty-four equals ....
4 seventeen plus fourteen equals ....
5 sixty minus thirty-six equals ....
6 seventeen plus twenty-eight equals ....

4 Close your book and count from 1 to 20. Then count from 30 to 100 in tens.
合上书本，从1数到20。再从30开始，以10为间隔，数到100。

B Large numbers 较大的数字

101	a/one **hundred and** one	2,000	two thousand (NOT *two thousands*)
140	a/one hundred **and** forty	100,000	a/one hundred thousand
200	two hundred (NOT *two hundreds*)	1,000,000	a/one **million**
1,000	a/one **thousand**	2,000,000	two million (NOT *two millions*)
1,050	a/one thousand **and** fifty	1,000,000,000	a/one **billion**
1,250	a/one thousand **two hundred and** fifty		

In numbers over 999, write a comma (,) between:
- *thousands* and *hundreds*, e.g. 11,000
- *millions* and *thousands*, e.g. 3,000,000

SPOTLIGHT *hundreds, thousands, millions*

We use **hundreds**, **thousands**, and **millions** (with an 's') when we don't use a specific number.
- *We saw **hundreds of** animals.* (OR *We saw **three hundred** animals.*)
- *There were **thousands of** people at the concert.*
- *The new shopping centre will cost **millions**.*

5 **Correct the mistakes in the spoken or written number.** 改正数字的读法或写法。

▶ one hundred two   <u>one hundred and two</u>
1 two hundreds
2 three hundred forty
3 one thousand and five hundred
4 two thousand six hundred fifty
5 seven thousands
6 42500

6 **Write the next number in words.** 用英语写出下一个数。

▶ 243   <u>two hundred and forty-four</u>
1 999
2 5055
3 11,300
4 999,999
5 2,499
6 324,999
7 999,999,999
8 1,999

7 **Write the sentences in a more general way. Use** *hundreds/thousands/millions* **or** *about/around*.
改写句子，用hundreds/thousands/millions或about/around表达概数。

▶ There are four hundred flats. <u>There are hundreds of flats.</u>
1 They said it was three thousand dollars.
2 It's forty-eight minutes.
3 There are six thousand of them.
4 I bought seventeen books.
5 We want to grow four hundred trees.
6 There are about ten to twelve million people with this problem.

A What's the time? 现在几点?

What's the time?	What time is it?
It's **four o'clock**.	It's **five past six**.
It's **(a) quarter past four**. It's **four fifteen**.	It's **twenty past six**. It's **six twenty**.
It's **half past four**. It's **four thirty**.	It's **twenty to seven**. It's **six forty**.
It's **(a) quarter to five**. It's **four forty-five**.	It's **three minutes to seven**. It's **six fifty-seven**.

> **SPOTLIGHT** *minutes to* or *past*
>
> We use **minutes to** or **minutes past** with numbers which are not *five, ten, fifteen, twenty* or *twenty-five*.
> - *eight **minutes to** two* (NOT *eight to two*)
> - *three **minutes past** six* (NOT *three past six*)

1 Write the times in words. Don't use *past* or *to*. 用英语表达时间, 不用past或to。

▶	3.10	three ten	▶	6.15	six fifteen
1	9.15	....	**5**	5.50	....
2	10.25	....	**6**	7.20	....
3	3.35	....	**7**	2.30	....
4	6.45	....	**8**	4.40	....

2 Write the times in words. Use *past* and *to*. 用英语表达时间, 使用past或to。

▶	12.30	half past twelve	▶	6.40	twenty to seven
1	7.15	....	**5**	8.55	....
2	9.30	....	**6**	1.03	....
3	11.35	....	**7**	2.45	....
4	3.50	....	**8**	4.17	....

3 Look at the timetable and answer the questions. Write your answers in words.
浏览时刻表后回答问题, 并用英语写下答案。

Bath Spa	7.25 ▾	7.45 ▾	8.05 ▾	8.35 ▾	9.05 ▾
Swindon	7.57 ▾	8.17 ▾	8.45 ▾	9.07 ▾	9.42 ▾
Didcot Parkway	8.15 ▾		9.02 ▾		9.58 ▾
Reading	8.35 ▾	8.55 ▾	9.15 ▾	9.45 ▾	10.10 ▾
London Paddington	8.55	9.15	9.35	10.05	10.35

▶	When does the first train leave Bath?	At seven twenty-five.
1	When does the first train after 8.00 leave Bath?	....
2	You want to be in London before 10.00. What time is the best train from Swindon?	....
3	When does the 8.05 train from Bath get to Didcot Parkway?	....
4	When does the 8.05 from Bath get to London Paddington?	....
5	When does the 9.05 from Bath get to Reading?	....

4 ABOUT YOU AND YOUR COUNTRY Write your answers, or ask another student.
根据自身情况回答问题, 也可以向同学提问。

1 What time do banks open and close in your country? ....
2 What time do most shops open and close? ....
3 What time do most restaurants open and close? ....
4 When do most people start and finish school/work? ....
5 When do you have lunch? ....
6 When do you have dinner? ....

B Exact times and periods of time 时间点与时间段

9.00 **a.m.**	nine o'clock **in the morning**
12.00 **p.m.**	(at) **midday / noon**
9.00 a.m. – 1.00 p.m.	**all morning**
1.58	**just before / nearly / almost** two
5.00 p.m.	five o'clock **in the afternoon**
2.00 – 5.30 p.m.	**all afternoon** (ALSO **all day** from 9.00 – 5.00)
7.00 p.m.	seven o'clock **in the evening**
8.02	**just after** eight
11.30 p.m.	eleven thirty **at night**
12.00 a.m.	(at) **midnight**

sun

moon

5 **Same or different? Write *S* or *D*.** 两者是否相同？相同填S，不同填D。

▶ 8.45 p.m. / 8.45 in the evening   S
1 12.00 at night / midnight   ....
2 4.00 a.m. / 4.00 in the afternoon   ....
3 6.27 / nearly 6.30   ....
4 11.45 p.m. / 11.45 at night   ....
5 almost 7 o'clock / just before 7.00   ....
6 9 a.m. – 1.00 p.m. / all day   ....

▶ 3.00 p.m. / nearly 3.00   D
7 8.43 / nearly quarter to nine   ....
8 2.17 / quarter past two   ....
9 12.03 p.m. / just after midday   ....
10 2.00 p.m. – 5.30 p.m. / all afternoon   ....
11 8.30 / just before 9.00   ....
12 3.00 a.m. / three o'clock   ....

6 **Complete the sentences.** 将句子填写完整。

▶ I can meet you _in_ the morning.
1 She usually leaves .... before three.
2 Our train was late, and it was .... eight thirty when we arrived.
3 The party ends .... midnight, and then I'll get a taxi home.
4 It starts to get really hot around ....
5 We got there at about five o'clock .... the afternoon.
6 I usually go to bed around 11 o'clock .... night.
7 They are very busy, so they'll be at work .... day.
8 It was .... 7 o'clock when we got home.
9 The train leaves .... after 8.00, at 8.03.
10 She's there .... morning, from nine until lunchtime.

7 **One word is missing in each sentence. What is it, and where does it go?**
在句中相应位置补上遗漏的单词。

▶ I get up just/seven o'clock.   before / after
1 I'm meeting my friend midday.   ....
2 I only drink coffee the morning.   ....
3 I work day in a bank.   ....
4 I see my friends the evening.   ....
5 I watch television evening.   ....
6 I go to bed midnight.   ....
7 I don't get home before 10.00 night.   ....
8 It's three minutes to 8.00 – it's 8.00.   ....
9 I always get up before 7.00, at 6.55.   ....

A Days, months and dates 天、月份、日期

DAYS of the WEEK	Monday Tuesday Wednesday Thursday Friday Saturday Sunday
MONTHS of the YEAR	January February March April May June July August September October November December
SEASONS (in Britain)	spring (March–May) summer (June–August) autumn (September–November) winter (December–February)
SPECIAL DAYS	Christmas Day (25 December) New Year's Day (1 January) your birthday (the day you were born)

spring

summer

autumn

winter

SPOTLIGHT capital letters

Days and months have a capital letter.
Monday (NOT ~~monday~~); **January** (NOT ~~january~~)

1 **Put the words in the correct order. Write the numbers in the boxes.** 单词排序，在方框内填写数字。

1 Wednesday ☐   Saturday ☐   ▶ Monday [1]   Friday ☐   Tuesday ☐   Sunday ☐   Thursday ☐

2 autumn ☐   spring ☐   winter ☐   summer ☐

3 December ☐   March ☐   June ☐   February ☐   November ☐   January ☐
   October ☐   April ☐   July ☐   September ☐   May ☐   August ☐

2 **Say the days of the week and the months in the correct order. Practise saying the words.**
用英语从星期一数到星期日，从一月数到十二月，并练习发音。

3 **Write the next day, month or season.** 写出后一天、下一月或下个季节。

▶ May   June   ▶ Sunday   Monday
1 Monday   ....   6 March   ....
2 August   ....   7 January   ....
3 spring   ....   8 autumn   ....
4 November   ....   9 Wednesday ....
5 Friday   ....   10 June   ....

4 **ABOUT YOU** **Write your answers, or ask another student.** 根据自身情况回答问题，也可以向同学提问。

1 Which month is your birthday? ....
2 Which season do you like best? Why? ....
3 Which day of the week do you like best? Why? ....
4 What do you do on Christmas Day? ....
5 What do you do on New Year's Day? ....
6 What are two other special days in the year, and when are they? ....
....

B Ordinal numbers and dates 序数词与日期

1st	first	11th	eleventh	21st	twenty-first
2nd	second	12th	twelfth	22nd	twenty-second
3rd	third	13th	thirteenth	23rd	twenty-third
4th	fourth	14th	fourteenth	30th	thirtieth
5th	fifth	15th	fifteenth	31st	thirty-first
6th	sixth	16th	sixteenth		
7th	seventh	17th	seventeenth		
8th	eighth	18th	eighteenth		
9th	ninth	19th	nineteenth		
10th	tenth	20th	twentieth		

> **SPOTLIGHT** saying and writing dates and years
>
> We can write the date like this:
> - **10 March** OR **10th March** OR **March 10** OR **3.10.07** OR **3/10/07**
>
> We say the date like this:
> - **What's the date today?** ~ It's **March the tenth**.
>   ~ It's **the tenth of March**.
>
> Say the year like this:
> - 1995 **nineteen ninety-five** ■ 2006 **two thousand and six**
> - 2020 **twenty twenty** OR **two thousand and twenty**

5 **Complete the words.** 将单词填写完整。

▶ ni_n_th

1 th___rd
2 twent___eth
3 fi___th

4 f___rst
5 eig___th
6 si___teenth

7 fo___rteenth
8 th___rteenth
9 s___cond

6 **Answer the questions below, then practise saying the dates you wrote.**
根据日历回答问题，并练习日期的发音。

CALENDAR	
MARCH	**APRIL**

S	M	T	W	T	F	S		S	M	T	W	T	F	S
				1	2	3		1	2	3	4	5	6	7
4	5	6	7	8	9	10		8	9	10	11	12	13	14
11	12	13	14	15	16	17		15	16	17	18	19	20	21
18	19	20	21	22	23	24		22	23	24	25	26	27	28
25	26	27	28	29	30	31		29	30	31				

What's …

▶ the first Saturday in March? *March the third / the third of March.*

1 the second Tuesday in April? ....
2 the first Sunday in March? ....
3 the third Tuesday in April? ....
4 the third Wednesday in March? ....

5 the second Wednesday in April? ....
6 the first Friday in April? ....
7 the fifth Saturday in March? ....
8 the fourth Monday in April? ....

7 **Write the dates/years as we say them.** 写出下列日期/年份的读法。

▶ 6.9   *the sixth of September*

1 3.2 ....
2 4.7 ....
3 10.12 ....
4 12.8 ....
5 15.1 ....
6 2022 ....

7 21.5 ....
8 30.11 ....
9 22.4 ....
10 2015 ....
11 today's date ....
12 the date next Tuesday ....

A The past, the present and the future 过去、现在、将来

Look at the **diary** and read the sentences below. It's midday on Thursday, 11 April.

APRIL		
MON 1 Moscow	MON 8 Jonah & Charlotte 7.30	MON 15 London
TUES 2	TUES 9 pay phone bill	TUES 16 dinner with Scott 8.00
WED 3	WED 10 lunch with Ella 1.00 / meet Logan 7.45	WED 17 ▾
THUR 4 ↓	THUR 11 (TODAY) cinema 7.15	THUR 18 Dr Holton 10.45
FRI 5 Bath	FRI 12 meeting 9.00–12.00 / Wheeler's café 7.30	FRI 19 theatre 8.00
SAT 6	SAT 13 stay at Will's	SAT 20 Callum's birthday
SUN 7	SUN 14 ↓	SUN 21 to Mum and Dad's for lunch

I was in Moscow **last week**.

I saw Jonah and Charlotte three days **ago**.

I had lunch with Ella **yesterday**.

I went out with Logan **last night**.

I'm going to the cinema **this evening**.

I have a meeting **tomorrow morning**.

I'm staying at Will's **this weekend**.

I'm going to London for three days **next week**.

I have a doctor's **appointment next Thursday**.

I'm seeing my parents **in** ten days.

GLOSSARY			
diary	a book where you write what you're going to do	**last night**	(NOT *yesterday night*)
last week	(the past) = 1–7 April	**yesterday evening**	(NOT *last evening*)
this week	(the present) = 8–14 April	**appointment**	a meeting at a fixed time, often with one person, for work or with a doctor/dentist, etc.
next week	(the future) = 15–21 April		
ago	before now; in the past	**in ten days, etc.**	ten days, etc. from now

1 True or false? Write *T* or *F*. 判断正误，正确填T，错误填F。

▶ I was in Moscow last week.   T

1 I got back from Moscow two days ago. ....

2 I saw Jonah and Charlotte this week. ....

3 I paid the phone bill three days ago. ....

4 I met Logan yesterday. ....

5 I was in London last week. ....

6 I'm going to the cinema this afternoon. ....

7 I'm going out tomorrow evening. ....

8 I'm seeing Scott in four days. ....

9 I'm seeing the doctor in a week. ....

10 I'm going to the theatre next Friday. ....

2 Complete the sentences. 将句子填写完整。

▶ We saw them at the cinema yesterday _evening_ .

1 She saw Paul about three days ....

2 I won't forget Pedro's birthday – I wrote it in my ....

3 She called me at 10 o'clock last ....

4 He wants to come .... week, not next week.

5 She can't come tomorrow morning. She's got a dentist's ....

6 I'm going to Italy .... week.

3 Look at the diary again. It is now Wednesday, 17 April. Write three more things about last week and three things about this week. 对照日记，假设今天是4月17日星期三，分别写出上周和本周做的三件事情。

▶ _I had lunch with Ella_ a week ago.

1 .... last Thursday evening.

2 .... five days ago.

3 .... last weekend.

4 .... tomorrow morning.

5 .... in three days.

6 .... this weekend.

B Time words and tenses 与时间相关的单词和时态

There are some words about time in English that we often use with particular tenses.

ever	Do you **ever** swim in the winter? (present) Have you **ever** been to Moscow? (present perfect)
while	He often phones **while** I'm eating. (present continuous) They arrived **while** I was watching TV. (past continuous)
already	I was **already** there when they arrived. (past) Do you want lunch? ~ No thanks. I've **already** eaten. (present perfect)
recently	I went to the dentist **recently**. (past) I haven't seen Tom **recently**. (present perfect)
yet	I haven't done my homework **yet**. (present perfect) Have you seen Almodovar's new film **yet**? (present perfect)
just	Where are the girls? ~ They've **just** left. (present perfect)
for	I've been in this job **for** three years. (present perfect)
since	We've lived here **since** we got married. (present perfect)

GLOSSARY

ever	at any time (any time now with the present tense, or any time before now with the present perfect)
while	during the time that (sth else is/was happening)
already	before now or before then (but we don't know exactly when). In negative sentences, we use **yet**, not **already**.
recently	not long ago (with the past simple), or in a short period of time before now (with the present perfect)
yet	used for talking about sth that hasn't happened, but you think it will
just	a very short time before now

SPOTLIGHT *for* and *since*

We use **for** with a period of time.
- **for** *two weeks, six months,* etc.

We use **since** with a point in time in the past:
- **since** *2003,* **since** *last year,* **since** *I came to England,* etc.

We often use these words with the present perfect.
- *I've been at university* **for** *two years.*
- *I've known Joe* **since** *2018.*

4 Complete the sentence with *for* or *since*. 用for或since填空。

I've known her …

▶	_for_	a year	▶	_since_	last year.
1		2010	4		a couple of years
2		a long time	5		I got married
3		about three months	6		I was at university

5 Circle the correct answer. 圈出正确答案。

▶ My girlfriend wants to go to Ibiza, but I've (already) / yet been there.

1 Paolo is in the classroom. I've *just / yet* seen him.
2 Lily arrived *while / ever* we were having lunch.
3 Do you *just / ever* go to concerts?
4 We haven't seen them *since / for* yesterday.
5 I haven't been to Turkey *recently / already*.
6 I want to work abroad, but I haven't found a job *already / yet*.
7 Have you *ever / yet* driven a bus?
8 I went to Spain *just / recently*. I stayed in Seville *since / for* two weeks.

6 Complete the sentences. 将句子填写完整。

▶ He's been in that flat _for_ three months.

1 Have you finished your English course _____? ~ No, I've got another two weeks.
2 I was _____ awake when Mum came into my bedroom this morning. I was reading.
3 Where's Sophia? ~ She has _____ gone out. She was here a minute ago.
4 I haven't been to the dentist's _____. I must make an appointment.
5 Do you _____ go to that café when you're in town?
6 I haven't had lunch _____. I'm really hungry.
7 George tried to phone me _____ I was in the meeting.
8 We haven't seen Joe _____ he left school.

7 Translate the words in **bold** on this page into your own language. 将本页中粗体的单词翻译成汉语。

1   head
2   face
3   hair
4   eye
5   ear
6   nose
7   mouth
8   tooth
    (*pl* **teeth**)
9   chin
10 neck
11 shoulder

Head

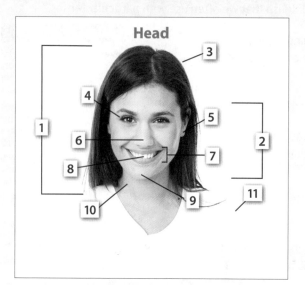

Inside the body

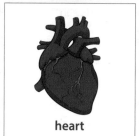

heart

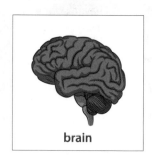

brain

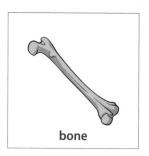

bone

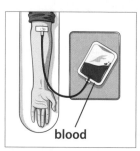

blood

Body

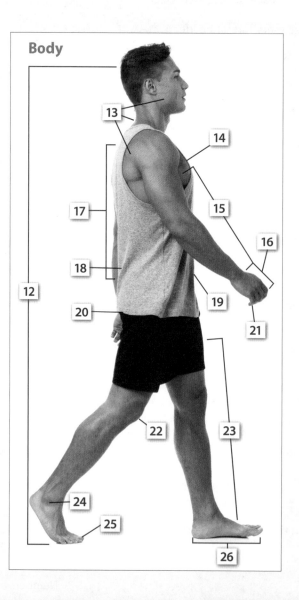

12 body
13 skin
14 chest
15 arm
16 hand
17 back
18 waist
19 stomach
20 bottom
21 finger
22 knee
23 leg
24 ankle
25 toe
26 foot
    (*pl* **feet**)

GLOSSARY	
body	the total physical form of a person or an animal
hair [U]	*My **hair** is long.* (NOT ~~*My hairs are long.*~~)
skin [U]	It covers the outside of a person or an animal's body.
blood [U]	It is pronounced like *sun*.

1 **Tick (✓) the words which are correct. Put a cross (✗) by the words which are wrong.**
下列表述是否正确? 正确的打钩 (√) , 错误的打叉 (×)。

I've got two ... ► eyes ✓   ears ☐   backs ☐   ankles ☐
 ► necks ✗   waists ☐   legs ☐   heads ☐
 noses ☐   knees ☐   hands ☐   arms ☐
 feet ☐   shoulders ☐   mouths ☐   teeth ☐

2 **Which word is different? Circle it.** 圈出各组中与其他三个不同的单词。

►	finger	arm	(waist)	hand	**4**	nose	bottom	chin	hair
1	foot	shoulder	toe	ankle	**5**	shoulder	chest	neck	blood
2	arm	hand	shoulder	stomach	**6**	teeth	legs	knees	ankle
3	neck	ears	nose	eyes	**7**	bone	brain	heart	finger

3 **Complete the words.** 将单词填写完整。

► h a i r
1 s___ ___n
2 n___ ___e
3 b___ ___k
4 c___ ___n

5 f___ ___e
6 h___ ___d
7 te___ ___h
8 ch___ ___t

9 bl___ ___d
10 br___ ___n
11 bo___ ___ ___m
12 st___ ___ ___ ___h

4 **Is the pronunciation of the underlined vowels the same or different? Write *S* or *D*, and practise saying the words.** 划线部分的元音发音是否相同? 相同填S, 不同填D, 并练习发音。

► chest   leg   S
1 bone   toe   ....
2 hand   back   ....
3 head   heart   ....
4 knee   feet   ....
5 tooth   soon   ....

► arm   ankle   D
6 blood   foot   ....
7 foot   took   ....
8 stomach   bottom   ....
9 shoulder   mouth   ....
10 stomach   blood   ....

5 **Which part of the body comes between the other two parts?** 写出位于两者之间的部位。

► eyes   nose   mouth
1 hand   ....   shoulder
2 waist   ....   leg
3 ankle   ....   toes
4 chest   ....   head
5 hair   ....   nose
6 bottom   ....   ankle

6 **Complete the sentences with a part of the body.** 用表示身体部位的单词将句子填写完整。

► I put the soap in my hand .
1 I can't see – there's something in my ....
2 People have five .... at the end of each foot.
3 I have a problem with the middle .... of my left hand.
4 You sit on your ....
5 I usually wash my .... every two or three days.
6 I had a problem with my .... so I went to the dentist.
7 My .... is about 80 cm. It could be about 77 cm if I eat less.
8 We had a lot of sun and now the .... on my hands is a bit red, and they feel hot.
9 Can you stand on one .... ?
10 I cut my finger with a knife, and there was a lot of ....
11 When my aunt was in hospital, she nearly died: her .... stopped for several minutes.
12 If you want to make good decisions, you have to use your ....
13 My brother broke a .... in one of his fingers.
14 Your skin covers the whole of your ....

A Height and weight 身高与体重

How tall is she? She's …   Is he **thin** or **fat**? He's …   How much does he **weigh**?

tall

average height

short

slim

average weight

overweight

GLOSSARY	
height	(sounds like *white*) how tall sb is: *She's 175 cm **tall**.* OR *She's 175 cm **in height**.* **cm** = **centimetres**
weigh	*He **weighs** 60 kg.* OR *He's 60 kg **in weight**.* **kg** = **kilos**
slim	thin, but **slim** is more positive
weight	(sounds the same as *wait*) describes how heavy sb or sth is
put on weight	become heavier/fatter OPP **lose weight**

SPOTLIGHT *quite*

Quite is a very common word, and it means 'not very'.
- *She's **quite** tall.* (= not very tall but more than average height)
- *He plays the piano **quite** well.* (= not very well but better than OK)

1 **True or false? Write *T* or *F*.** 判断正误，正确填T，错误填F。

▶ If you are *overweight*, you aren't slim. .... T

1 *Average height* means not fat and not slim. ....

2 *Quite thin* and *very thin* are the same. ....

3 *Put on weight* and *lose weight* are opposites. ....

4 If someone is *fat*, they are *overweight*. ....

5 The answer to *How much does he weigh?* is *200 cm*. ....

6 *How tall are you?* is a correct question. ....

7 *Average weight* means quite slim. ....

8 *Thin* and *slim* mean the same, but *thin* is more positive. ....

9 If you *lose weight*, you get thinner. ....

10 *Average height* and *average weight* are the same. ....

2 **Complete the dialogues. Don't use the words in *italics* in your answer.** 将对话填写完整，替换斜体单词。

▶ Is he quite short? ~ No, he's very _tall_.

1 She's not tall or short, really. ~ No, she's average ....

2 Are they quite *thin*? ~ Yes, they're both very ....

3 Is he *overweight*? ~ Yes, he's getting a bit ....

4 Is she very slim? ~ No, but she's .... slim.

5 Max is looking a bit fat. ~ I know. He has .... 10 kilos.

6 Is he about average weight? ~ I think so. He .... 75 kg.

7 Scarlet isn't very tall, is she? ~ No, actually she's quite ....

8 Ben is looking very slim. ~ Yes, he has .... a lot of weight.

9 This box is very heavy. ~ Is it? How .... does it weigh?

10 Is Willie very tall? ~ No, but he's .... tall.

B Features 容貌

beard

smile

1 a **good-looking man**
with **dark curly** hair
and a **beard**

2 a **pretty teenager**
with **long blonde** hair
and a **lovely smile**

3 a very **attractive**
woman with **straight
fair** hair

4 a **middle-aged** man
with s**hort grey** hair

GLOSSARY	
feature(s)	an important part of sth, e.g. *your face, your eyes*
teenager	a person between the ages of 13 and 19 **teenage** *adj*
lovely	beautiful or very nice: *a lovely smile/dress*
smile	(*see picture 2*) **Smile** is also a verb: *He **smiled at** me.*
middle-aged	about 45 to 60 years old

SPOTLIGHT *good-looking, beautiful,* etc.

For a woman, we can say **beautiful** or **(very) good-looking/
attractive**. For a man, we usually say **good-looking** or
handsome. For girls especially, we can say **beautiful**, but we
often use **pretty**.

3 Look at the pictures. True or false? Write *T* or *F*. If false, correct the mistake.
根据以上图片判断正误，正确填T，错误填F，并改正错误的句子。

▶ The girl isn't a teenager. *F – She is a teenager.*

1 She's got a lovely smile. ....

2 She's got dark hair. ....

3 It's also quite short. ....

4 The young man isn't handsome. ....

5 He's got dark hair. ....

6 The woman has got blonde hair. ....

7 Her hair is straight. ....

8 She's beautiful. ....

9 The other man is old. ....

10 His hair is dark. ....

4 Complete the words in the texts. 将文中的单词填写完整。

My sister (15):	▶is a teenager........... . She's very **(1)** pr.................... , with **(2)** d.............. brown hair, and she has a lovely **(3)** sm................... , which is one of her best **(4)** fe................... .
My brother (18):	is also a **(5)** te............... . He's very **(6)** g............-l............... and he knows it. He's got short **(7)** st................ hair, and no **(8)** be................... .
My father (52):	is **(9)** m................-a................ now. I think he's still a **(10)** ha.................. man, but his hair is quite **(11)** gr................ .
My mother (50):	has short **(12)** bl................ hair. She was **(13)** be................... when she was young and she is still very **(14)** at................... .
Me (20):	I am no longer a **(15)** t................... boy. I'm different from my sister because I've got **(16)** f................ hair, and different from my brother because my hair is **(17)** cu................ . And I'm also different from them because, unfortunately, I'm not very **(18)** g................-................... .

5 ABOUT YOU Write two or three sentences describing yourself using some of the vocabulary from
this page. Then look at the pictures again. Do <u>you</u> think the four people are beautiful/handsome/
attractive? If possible, talk to someone else about them. 用两到三句话描述自己，需要用到上文所学单词。观察
图片中的四人，你认为他们漂亮/帅气/有魅力吗? 如有条件，可与同学互相交流。

A Using your body 运用身体

sit down
pt **sat down**

stand up
pt **stood up**

walk

run
pt **ran**

fall over
pt **fell over**

bike

ride *pt* **rode**

climb

jump

lie down
pt **lay**

dance

get on
pt **got on**

get off
pt **got off**

> **SPOTLIGHT** irregular verbs
>
> Many of the verbs above are **irregular**: the past simple is not formed by adding *-ed*. There is a list of the past simple and past participle forms of all the irregular verbs in the book on page 198. See also Unit 39.

1 **Write the present form of the verbs.** 写出动词的现在式。

▶ walked   walk ....
1 lay down   ....
2 fell over   ....
3 rode   ....

4 stood up   ....
5 sat down   ....
6 got on   ....
7 ran   ....

2 **Complete these sentences with verbs from above.** 用上题中的动词或短语填空。

▶ When you go to bed, you do this.   lie down ....
1 When you hear music and you're happy, you do this. ....
2 When you're tired, you do this. .... or ....
3 When you don't see something on the floor in front of you, you could do this. ....
4 When you go on a bike, you do this. ....
5 When you're waiting at the bus stop and the bus arrives, you do this. ....

3 **Complete the sentences. You need the past simple in sentences 6–9.**
将句子填写完整，6–9句需用动词的一般过去式。

▶ I   sat down .... at my desk and worked for two hours.
1 The children have to .... when the teacher comes into the classroom.
2 I often .... to work in the summer – it's only twenty minutes on foot.
3 I want to .... Mount Kilamanjaro next year.
4 Do you often .... when you go to clubs?
5 The doctor asked me to .... on the bed.
6 The boys .... into the swimming pool.
7 She .... her bike to school this morning.
8 I was late, so I .... to the bus stop, but I .... over and hurt my leg.
9 She .... the bus, went into the station and got .... a train.

B Using your hands 运用双手

push

pull

carry

hold *pt* **held**

pick sth **up**

put sth **down** *pt* **put**

break *pt* **broke**

give *pt* **gave**

close/shut *pt* **shut**
OPP **open**

drop

throw *pt* **threw**

catch *pt* **caught**

4 **Cover the pictures and underline the correct answers.** 遮住上图，在正确答案下划线。

▶ You can drop *a glass* / *a house*.
1 You can open *a door* / *a light*.
2 You can catch *a car* / *a ball*.
3 You can throw *a book* / *a house*.
4 You can push *the sky* / *a person*.
5 You can hold *a dictionary* / *a country*.
6 You can break *some juice* / *a pencil*.
7 You can pick up *a car* / *a bicycle*.

5 **Do you need two hands to do these things? Or can you do them with one hand?**
完成下列动作，你需要单手还是双手？

▶ shut a dictionary ..1..
▶ give someone five dictionaries ..2..

1 pick up a cup ....   drop a cup ....
2 pick up a TV ....   turn on a TV ....
3 break a bottle ....   open a bottle ....
4 pull a person ....   carry a person ....

5 throw a ball ....   catch a ball ....
6 drop a ruler ....   break a ruler ....
7 carry a door ....   close a door ....
8 pick up a baby ....   hold a baby ....

6 **Complete the sentences with suitable verbs from above.** 用恰当的动词或短语填空。

▶ I _opened_ the garage door and then three of us _pushed_ the car out.
1 It was cold, so he _____ the window.
2 She _____ the cat and _____ it _____ in its bed.
3 I'm afraid I _____ your best glass and it broke. I'm really sorry.
4 Four of us _____ the boat out of the sea and then _____ it along the beach.
5 I _____ the baby to Mum and she _____ it in her arms.
6 I _____ the ball to my brother but he dropped it on the floor.
7 The box is very heavy. I can't _____ it to the car.

13 Personal information 个人信息

A Facts 实际情况

Sandro is studying English in Cambridge. The **receptionist** needs some **information**.

receptionist

reception

Receptionist	**What's your family name?** (OR **What's your surname?**)
Sandro	Bertoli.
Receptionist	And **your first name?**
Sandro	Sandro.
Receptionist	OK, Sandro. **What's your address** and **postcode?**
Sandro	45 Alfred Road, CB2 4TX.
Receptionist	So, Sandro, **where are you from?** (OR **Where do you come from?**)
Sandro	Italy.
Receptionist	**Whereabouts** in Italy? (OR **Where** in Italy **exactly?**)
Sandro	Pisa.
Receptionist	**What do you do** in Pisa? (OR **What's your job?**)
Sandro	I'm a doctor.
Receptionist	And **are you married** or **single?**
Sandro	I'm married. My wife is German.
Receptionist	And **how old** are you?
Sandro	I'm 34.

> **SPOTLIGHT** *information*
>
> **Information** [U] means facts about people or things, e.g. *name, address*, etc. **Information** is uncountable. Don't say *an information* OR *informations*.
> **Personal information** is information about one person.

1 In each sentence, one word is in the wrong place. **Correct it.** 调整一个单词的位置，使句子通顺。

▶ Are married you?

1 I need some information personal.   3 Do what you do?   5 How old you are?
2 Where do come from you?   4 What your postcode is?   6 Where the receptionist is from?

2 Write the questions with different words but with the same meaning. 改写问句，保持句意不变。

▶ What's your family name?   What's your surname ?
1 Where are you from?   Where do ?
2 Whereabouts in Poland?   Where in Poland ?
3 What's your job?   What do ?
4 Where do you live?   What's your ?
5 What's your age?   How ?

3 Complete the questions in the table. 将表格填写完整。

	QUESTIONS	ANSWERS	ABOUT YOU
▶	What's your name ?	Kovács.	
1	And your name?	Zsuzsa.	
2	Where are you ?	Hungary.	
3	in Hungary?	The capital, Budapest.	
4	your address?	Tarcali utca 27.	
5	And the ?	1113.	
6	And what you do?	I'm an engineer.	
7	Are you ?	No, I'm single.	
8	How are you?	I'm 27.	

4 ABOUT YOU Write your answers to the questions in the table, or ask another student.
根据自身情况回答表格中的问题，也可以向同学提问。

B Talking about your English course 谈论英语课

Sandro has been in Cambridge now for two months and is talking to the receptionist again.

Receptionist	So, Sandro. What's your English **level** now?
Sandro	I'm intermediate.
Receptionist	Yes, you **communicate** very well.
Sandro	Thank you, but I still need to **improve**.
Receptionist	Why's that?
Sandro	Because I want to work **abroad** and **help** people in other countries. For that, my English has to be **perfect**.
Receptionist	So **how long are** you **planning to** stay here?
Sandro	I don't know.
Receptionist	But you're enjoying your **course**?
Sandro	Yes, it's **great**. I've made a lot of **progress**.

GLOSSARY	
level	how high sth is, e.g. *an elementary/ intermediate/advanced* **level** *of English*
communicate (with sb)	be able to say what you mean, or have a conversation with other people
improve	become better **improvement** n
abroad	in another country
help	do sth good for sb so their life is easier
perfect	so good it can't be better
how long?	how much time? (NOT *how long time?*)
plan (to do) sth	decide what you are going to do and how you are going to do it
course	a number of lessons
great	very good or nice SYNS **fantastic**, **wonderful**
progress	improvement

5 **True or false? Write *T* or *F*.** 判断正误，正确填T，错误填F。

▶ If you *help* someone, you make their life easier. ....T....
1 *Perfect* means the same as good. ....
2 *Plan to do something* is the same as decide what to do and how to do it. ....
3 *Improve* means to make something different. ....
4 *Abroad* means in another country. ....
5 *A language course* means the same as *a language level*. ....
6 If you *communicate* something, you are able to say what you mean. ....
7 *How long?* means the same as *how far?* ....
8 *Great* means the same as *fantastic*. ....

6 **Agree with the first speaker, but replace the words in *italics* with different words.**
用其他单词替换斜体部分，表示同意对方观点。

▶ The course is *really good*.   ~ Yes, it's ..*great*.............. .
1 She's *getting better*.   ~ Yes, she's ....
2 Her English is *very good* now.   ~ Yes, it's at a high ....
3 She can *express ideas* very well.   ~ Yes, she ....
4 She wants to work *in another country*. ~ Yes, she wants to go and work ....
5 They're *thinking about* going to Spain. ~ Yes, they're .... to go there.
6 I thought it was *fantastic*.   ~ Yes, it was ....
7 He's really *improving*.   ~ Yes, he's making a lot of ....
8 He wants to *make* people's *lives better*. ~ Yes, he wants to ....

7 **ABOUT YOU** **Write your answers, or ask another student.** 根据自身情况回答问题，也可以向同学提问。

1 What's your English level? ....
2 How well do you communicate in English? ....
3 Do you want or need to improve? ....
....
4 Are you making progress? ....
....
5 Are you planning to go to an English-speaking country? If so, where? ....
....
6 Would you like to work abroad? ....
....

A Damon's family tree 达蒙的家谱

Elsie
Damon's
grandmother

Alf
his
grandfather

grandparents

Dave
his **father**

Maggie
his **mother**

Paul
his **uncle**

Jane
his **aunt**

Luke
his **brother**

Damon

Karen
his **sister**

James
his **cousin**

Jessica
his **cousin**

All the people here are Damon's **relatives**.
Luke is Dave and Maggie's **son**.
Karen is Dave and Maggie's **daughter**.
Maggie is Dave's **wife**.
Dave is Maggie's **husband**.
Elsie and Alf are Maggie's **parents**.

Dave is Paul's **brother-in-law**.
Jane is Maggie's **sister-in-law**.
James is Maggie's **nephew**.
Karen is Paul's **niece**.
Luke is Elsie's **grandson**.
Jessica is Elsie's **granddaughter**.

1 **Complete the sentences about Damon's family.** 根据达蒙的家庭关系填空。

▶ Paul is Elsie and Alf's   son   .
1 Maggie is Elsie's ....
2 Luke is Paul's ....
3 Jessica is Maggie's ....
4 Maggie is Jane's ....
5 Karen is Jessica's ....

6 Elsie and Alf are Damon's ....
7 Paul is Jane's ....
8 Elsie is Jessica's ....
9 Paul is Luke's ....
10 Maggie is Jessica's ....
11 James, Dave and Alf are Damon's ....

2 **Complete the table.** 将表格填写完整。

MALE	FEMALE	MALE	FEMALE
▶ father	mother	brother-in-law	....
brother	....	grandfather	....
husband	....	grandson	....
nephew	....	cousin	....
relative	....	parent	....
son	....	uncle	....

3 ABOUT YOU **Draw your family tree. Write the names and** *brother, sister, uncle,* **etc.**
绘制自己的家谱，填写人名和相应称谓。

B Family history 家史

My parents **got married** 25 years ago. Two years later, my brother Luke **was born**. Then I was born a year after that. I've also **got** a sister, Karen, who is two years younger than me, so **there are five of us** in my family. Luke has got a **girlfriend**, Amy, and they live in a small flat. Karen and I still live with **Mum** and **Dad**. We **spend** a lot of **time together**.

GLOSSARY	
get married	become husband or wife with sb OPP **get divorced** stop being husband or wife with sb
be born	start your life
have got	have
there are five of us	(NOT ~~We are five.~~)
girlfriend	a girl or woman who sb has a romantic relationship with ALSO **boyfriend**
mum *inf*	mother
dad *inf*	father
spend time with sb	be with sb and do things with them
together	with each other: *My family all live **together** in the same house.*

SPOTLIGHT comparatives and superlatives

- *Damon **is 22 (years old)**.* (NOT ~~Damon is 22 years.~~)
- *His brother **is older than** him. He's 23.*
- *His sister **is younger than** him. She's 20.*
- *Luke is **the oldest in the family**.*
- *Karen is **the youngest** in the family.*

Luke   Amy

4 **True or false? Write *T* or *F*.** 判断正误，正确填T，错误填F。

▶ Damon is Luke's older brother.   F

1	Damon's parents are divorced.	....	**6** Damon is Amy's boyfriend.	....
2	Damon was born after Luke.	....	**7** There are four in Damon's family.	....
3	Luke is younger than Karen.	....	**8** Karen is the youngest in the family.	....
4	Luke and Amy live together.	....	**9** Damon and Karen are often together.	....
5	Luke's mum has three children.	....	**10** Luke is Damon's dad.	....

5 **Write the words in the correct order.** 连词成句。

▶ his / divorced / are / parents   His parents are divorced.
1 born / I / 2001 / in / was   ....
2 spend / of / together / we / lot / time / a   ....
3 older / my / than / girlfriend / me / is   ....
4 in / six / my / of / are / family / there / us   ....
5 the / family / I / youngest / in / my / am   ....
6 brother / older / younger / an / 've got / I / a / and / sister   ....

6 ABOUT YOU **Write your answers, or ask another student.** 根据自身情况回答问题，也可以向同学提问。

1 How many people are there in your family? ....

2 When were you born? ....

3 Have you got any brothers and sisters? If yes, are they older or younger than you? ....

4 In your family, who do spend a lot of time with? ....

5 Do you all live together? ....

A What's he/she like? 他/她是个怎样的人?

Word	Example	Meaning
friendly	The students in my class are all really **friendly**. It's great.	happy to meet and talk to other people OPP **unfriendly**
kind	He visited me in hospital, which was really **kind**.	friendly and good to other people
nice	I met Charlie on holiday, and he's a really **nice** guy.	kind and friendly (a very common word in spoken English)
fun	I love Caitlin; she's **great fun**.	sb or sth that makes you happy **Good/great fun** is common.
funny	Josh makes me **laugh** – he's a really **funny** man.	making you **laugh**
relaxed	I felt very **relaxed** after my holiday.	calm and not worried
clever	Tom is really **clever** – the best student in our class.	quick at learning and understanding things SYN **intelligent** OPP **stupid**
patient	My boyfriend is often late, but I'm very **patient**.	able to stay calm and not get angry when you are waiting
strange	He's a **strange** man – I never know what he's thinking.	unusual or surprising

---

SPOTLIGHT *What's he/she/it like?*

We use this question to find out more about somebody/something.
- **What's** Jack **like**? ~ He's very nice. (NOT *He's like very nice.*)
- **What was** the teacher **like**? ~ She was **good fun**.

---

1 **Complete the words.** 将单词填写完整。

▶ f u n
1 n___ ___e
2 f___ ___ ___y

3 c l___ ___ ___r
4 s t___ ___ ___ ___e
5 f___ ___ ___ ___ ___ ___y

6 p___t___ ___ ___t
7 la___ ___h
8 r___l___x___d

2 **Cover the table, then answer the questions.** 遮住表格，回答问题。

What's ...

▶ a synonym for nice?   friendly
1 the opposite of friendly?   ....
2 a synonym for clever?   ....
3 the opposite of clever?   ....

What do you call someone who ...

4 is able to learn quickly?   ....
5 makes you laugh?   ....
6 is able to wait for things?   ....
7 is calm and doesn't worry?   ....

3 **Complete the conversations.** 将对话填写完整。

1 What ▶ 's .... Alex like? ~ Oh, he's very funny. We .... a lot when we're together.
2 What are Ana's parents .... ? ~ Well, her mother's great .... I like her very much. But I never know what to say to her father – he's very ....
3 .... was your grandmother like? ~ She was very .... : she always helped everyone. And she was .... too: she went to university.

4 **ABOUT YOU** **Write the names of people you know who are:** 根据自身情况填写相应人名。

kind ....
good fun ....

very friendly ....
intelligent ....

patient with you ....
strange ....

B We like each other 相亲相爱

Gemma

Sophie

WHY WE LIKE
each other

Gemma: I met Sophie at university. I was **on my own** in the café, and she came and talked to me. She's like that. What's interesting is that we're **completely different.** She has a very **active social life** and meets lots of new people. I'm very **quiet** and **serious.** But it didn't **matter.** We became friends and **shared a flat** for two years. I'm **tidy** and did most of the housework. Sophie's quite **lazy,** but she is a great cook and a **really** nice person.

GLOSSARY

each other	She likes me and I like her. = We like **each other.**
on my own	not with other people SYN **alone**
completely different	totally different; different in every way
active	busy and able to do a lot of things
social life	going out with friends
quiet	Somebody who is **quiet** doesn't say very much.
serious	A **serious** person thinks a lot and doesn't laugh much.
matter	be important; **it doesn't matter** = it's not important
share a flat	live in the same flat as another person
tidy	A **tidy** person likes everything to be in the right place. OPP **untidy**
lazy	A **lazy** person doesn't like working. OPP **hard-working**

SPOTLIGHT *really*

Really is important in spoken English. It means 'very', and you can use it before most adjectives.

- *I'm in a **really** nice class.* ▪ *She was **really** lazy.*

---

5 **Is the pronunciation of the <u>underlined</u> sound the same or different? Write S or D. Practise saying the words.** 划线部分的发音是否相同？相同填S，不同填D，并练习发音。

- ▸ <u>so</u>cial / <u>doe</u>sn't .... D
- 1 <u>o</u>ther / <u>ow</u>n ....
- 2 hardw<u>or</u>king / d<u>oe</u>sn't ....
- 3 al<u>o</u>ne / s<u>o</u>cial ....
- 4 compl<u>e</u>tely / <u>o</u>ther ....
- 5 complet<u>e</u>ly / s<u>e</u>rious ....

6 **Read the text again. True or false? Write T or F.** 再读一遍课文并判断正误，正确填T，错误填F。

- ▸ Sophie likes cooking. .... T
- 1 Gemma was alone when she met Sophie. ....
- 2 Gemma and Sophie are similar. ....
- 3 Gemma doesn't say very much. ....
- 4 They lived together at university. ....
- 5 Gemma is really lazy. ....
- 6 Sophie goes out a lot. ....
- 7 Gemma's untidy. ....
- 8 It was a problem that they were completely different. ....

7 **Complete the sentences.** 将句子填写完整。

- ▸ I never put things away. I'm very _untidy_ .
- 1 When we met, I was on my .... and wanted someone to talk to.
- 2 I've always had an active social .... : I go out most nights.
- 3 We wanted to .... a flat together.
- 4 Do you want me to help? ~ No, it doesn't ....
- 5 My sister and I are .... different.
- 6 We've always liked each ....

8 **ABOUT YOU** **Write your answers, or ask another student.** 根据自身情况回答问题，也可以向同学提问。

Questionnaire

What are you like?

1 Are you tidy or untidy? _____
2 Are you hard-working or a bit lazy? _____
3 Are you quiet? _____
4 Are you serious? _____
5 Do you have an active social life? _____
6 Do you like being on your own? _____

16) Relationships 人际关系

A Romantic relationships 恋爱关系

Max is my **partner**, and we have a very good **relationship**. We'**ve been together** for about two years. I started to **go out with** him after I came to London. We met at my **ex-boyfriend's** house, and because Max lived near me, it was easy for us to **get to know** each other. Now Max wants us to **get married** and **have a baby**, but I'm not sure. I have friends who are happily married, but I also know married **couples** who have **separated** and **are** now **divorced**. I don't want that to happen to us.

GLOSSARY

partner	sb you have a romantic relationship with (your *boyfriend*, *girlfriend*, *wife* or *husband*)	**get to know sb**	learn more about sb and become friends
		get married	become husband or wife with sb
be together	be in a romantic relationship	**have a baby**	become a new mother/father
go out with sb	have a romantic relationship with sb	**couple**	two people, often in a romantic relationship
ex-boyfriend	a person who was your boyfriend in the past ALSO **ex-girlfriend**, **ex-husband**, etc.	**separate**	stop being together
		be divorced	married in the past but not now

SPOTLIGHT *relationship*

You have a **relationship** with somebody. It can be good or bad.
- *I have a **good relationship** with my classmates.*
- *He has a **difficult relationship** with his father.*

We often talk about **romantic relationships** with wives, boyfriends, etc.

1 Make six more phrases using words from the box. 用方框内的词组成六个短语。

| get to | ex- | be ✓ | get | go out | have | romantic | a baby | relationship |
| together ✓ | know somebody | | boyfriend | with somebody | married | | | |

▶ be together
....
....
....
....

2 Write the words in the correct order. 连词成句。
▶ get / to / they / married / want They want to get married .
1 baby / last / had / a / year / they ....
2 separated / January / they / in ....
3 have / good / a / very / relationship / we ....
4 boyfriend / you / how / your / get / did / to / know ....?
5 three / together / for / they / years / were ....
6 with / six / went / him / months / I / for / out ....

3 Complete the sentences with a single word. 将句子填写完整, 每空格只填一词。
▶ They _have_ a very good relationship.
1 Tom .... married last summer, but I don't know his new ....
2 We .... to know each other at university, and we've been .... now for a year.
3 I know Tom and Lucy very well. They're a lovely ....
4 She went .... with him last year, but they .... in January.
5 Sonia is his .... girlfriend, but they still talk to each other.
6 My parents were married for twenty years, but now they're .... My father has a new .... , but I don't think they're going to .... married.

B Friends 朋友

WHY WE LIKE
each other

Sophie: I **get on very well with** Gemma – she's great. I don't know why, because we've got very different **personalities**. We first **met** at university about six years ago, and then we **became flatmates**. If I have a problem, Gemma is the first person I go to her for **advice**. And she always gives me good advice. We don't **see** each other very often now because we live in different cities, but I**'ve known** her for quite a long time, and she will always be my **best friend**.

GLOSSARY

each other	She likes me and I like her. = We like **each other**.
get on (well) with sb	have a good relationship with sb
personality	what a person is like that makes them different from other people
meet *pt* **met**	**1** see and speak to sb for the first time **2** go to a place and wait for sb: *We're **meeting** them at 7.30.*
become	begin to be sth: *become friends/ flatmates*
flatmate	a person you live with, but not in a romantic relationship
advice [U]	an opinion or information that you give to help sb with a problem **give (sb) advice**
see sb	talk to or visit sb
know *pt* **knew** *pp* **known**	If you **know sb**, you have met them. If you **have known sb** for a long time, you are often friends.

SPOTLIGHT *friend*

A **friend** is a person that you like and know well. Your **best friend** is your most important friend. You can also have a **close friend** (= a very good friend) or an **old friend** (= somebody you have known a long time).

4 **Are the sentences the same or different? Write *S* or *D*.** 两句句子的含义是否相同？相同填S，不同填D。

▶ We met last year. / I have known her for a year. .....S....
1 We live near each other. / We are flatmates. ....
2 We get on very well. / We have a very good relationship. ....
3 I see her every Saturday. / I visit her every Saturday. ....
4 She's my best friend. / She's a close friend. ....
5 We became friends. / We stopped being friends. ....
6 She gives me advice. / She helps me with my problems. ....

5 **Complete the sentences.** 将句子填写完整。

▶ Abigail and I soon _became_ friends.
1 My best friend often gives me good ....
2 Charles and Ed are good friends – they see .... other almost every day.
3 Mia is an .... friend – I've .... her for many years.
4 Sammy seems to .... on well with everyone – he's very popular.
5 I first .... my wife when we were at university – we were only twenty.
6 I've .... Olivia for a long time, but we don't .... each other very much now.
7 I'm .... my friends outside the cinema at 7 o'clock.
8 Emma was just my .... – we shared a flat for a year. Now she's my .... friend, but we have very different ....

6 **ABOUT YOU** **Write your answers, or ask another student.** 根据自身情况回答问题，也可以向同学提问。

1 Who is your best friend? ....
2 How long have you known him/her? ....
3 How and where did you first meet? ....
4 How often do you see each other? ....
5 Why do you get on well with him/her? ....
6 Do you often give each other advice? ....

A Feelings and emotions 感受与情绪

1 She's **happy.**

2 She's **sad.** SYN **unhappy**

3 They're **excited.**

4 He's **bored.**

5 He's **angry.**

6 She's **scared/afraid** (of sth/sb).

7 She's **embarrassed.**

8 She's **surprised.**

9 He's **in love.**

10 She's **worried.**

> **SPOTLIGHT** *feelings* and *emotions*
>
> **Feelings** or **emotions** are what you have inside yourself.
> We use adjectives after the verb **be** to describe our feelings,
> e.g. I'm **happy/sad/angry/afraid**, etc.
> We can also use many of these adjectives after the verb
> **feel** (*pt* **felt**): I feel **happy/sad/angry**, etc.

1 Complete the words. 将单词填写完整。

▶ ha p p y

1 ang___ ___
2 wor___ ___ ___ ___
3 bo___ ___ ___

4 sc___ ___ ___ ___
5 emb___ ___ ___ ___ ___ ___ ___
6 unh___ ___ ___ ___

7 af___ ___ ___ ___
8 sur___ ___ ___ ___ ___ ___
9 ex___ ___ ___ ___

2 Answer the questions. 回答问题。

▶ What's the opposite of *sad*? happy
1 What's another word for *feelings*? ....
2 What's the opposite of *excited*? ....
3 What's another word for *unhappy*? ....
4 What's another word for *afraid*? ....

5 If two people love each other, how can we say it another way? They are ....
6 If you do something stupid, how do you feel? ....

3 Complete the sentences. 将句子填写完整。

▶ The teacher got ...angry... because the children were running round the classroom.
1 I got very .... yesterday because I couldn't find my credit card. I found it this morning.
2 I got 100% in my English exam. I was happy but also very ....
3 My brothers get very .... when they're watching football on TV.
4 I made a mistake and everyone laughed. I .... stupid and a bit ....
5 My sister and Jake are getting married. My parents are .... because they like Jake.
6 I didn't like the film and I was .... after half an hour.
7 My aunt never travels by plane. She's .... of flying.
8 Oliver and Marcia met on holiday. I think they're in ....
9 I had different .... when I first flew in a plane: I was excited but also a bit scared.

B How did you feel? 你感受如何?

> How did you **feel** ...

when you went to bed last night?	~ Quite **tired**.
on your walk when it got hot?	~ I was **thirsty**.
after you had nothing to eat for hours?	~ I was **hungry**.
when everyone came to your party?	~ I was very **pleased**.
when you forgot a friend's birthday?	~ I was very **sorry**.
before your important exam today?	~ I was **nervous**.
when you broke your finger?	~ I was **in pain**.
when your dog died?	~ I was very **upset**, and I **cried**.
when you **argued with / had an argument with** your best friend?	~ I felt **bad** and **unhappy** about it.

She's crying.

4 **How do you feel? Write your answers.** 写下你的感受。
- ▶ It's the end of a working day. — tired
- 1 Your best friend hasn't invited you to his party. — ....
- 2 You are meeting your boyfriend or girfriend's parents for the first time. — ....
- 3 You've had nothing to drink for hours. — ....
- 4 It's lunchtime and you didn't have breakfast. — ....
- 5 You walked into a door and hit your head. — ....
- 6 A friend wrote a letter to thank you for something. — ....
- 7 A friend asked you to do something, and you forgot. — ....

5 **Complete the dialogues.** 将对话填写完整。
- ▶ When's lunch? ~ I don't know. Are you __hungry__ ?
- 1 I've got my driving test tomorrow. ~ Oh, are you .... ?
- 2 I'm going to bed. ~ OK. Are you .... ?
- 3 Did Dan finally pass his exam? ~ Yes, he's so ....
- 4 Did Amelia fall down the stairs? ~ Yes, she was in a lot of ....
- 5 Steph looked very angry. ~ I know. She's just had an .... with her boyfriend.
  Really? What about? ~ I don't know, but they often ....
- 6 I'm really .... I couldn't come last night. ~ That's OK.
- 7 I'm .... ~ OK. What would you like to drink?
- 8 Julia's mother was in hospital and died last week, so Julia is very ....
  ~ Oh, that's probably why she was .... when I saw her.

6 ABOUT YOU **Write your answers, or ask another student.** 根据自身情况回答问题，也可以向同学提问。

Questionnaire

When was the last time you ...

1 felt tired? _____

2 felt nervous? _____

3 felt hungry? _____

4 felt thirsty? _____

5 argued with somebody? _____

6 were in pain? _____

7 cried? _____

8 felt pleased? _____

18 Prepositions: time 表示时间的介词

at	**a time** **at** six o'clock **at** midday/midnight	**a mealtime** **at** breakfast **at** lunch / lunchtime **at** dinner / dinner time

on	**a day** **on** Tuesday **on** Friday evening **on** Tuesdays = every Tuesday **on** my birthday **on** Christmas Day	**a date** **on** September 10 **on** 6th May

in	**a part of a day** **in** the morning **in** the afternoon **in** the evening	**a season** **in** (the) spring/summer/ autumn/winter	**a month, year or century** **in** July/December **in** 1990/2050 **in** the 21st **century** (= 2000–2099)

SPOTLIGHT *at*

We also use **at** in these time phrases:
- *I relax **at the weekend**.*
- *What are you doing **at Christmas** / **at New Year**?*
- *Some doctors work **at night**.* (NOT ~~in the night~~)
- *He's not here **at the moment**.* (= now).

---

1 **Cross out the word or phrase which is not correct.** 划掉错误的单词或短语。

▶ **in** the spring / ~~February 15th~~ / the evening

1 **at** lunchtime / 2020 / the weekend
2 **in** August / summer / Friday
3 **on** April / your birthday / Saturdays
4 **at** night / the morning / half past seven
5 **in** autumn / the 20th century / 4.00

6 **on** midnight / June 2nd / Sunday afternoon
7 **at** breakfast / midday / the autumn
8 **on** winter / Christmas Day / 5th May
9 **in** the afternoon / lunchtime / 2018
10 **at** New Year / the evening / six o'clock

2 **Write the correct preposition.** 用介词填空。

We went to Brighton for a few days last week. We left ▶ _on_____ Thursday morning **(1)** _____ about nine o'clock and got there **(2)** _____ lunchtime. We found a nice hotel, and then **(3)** _____ the afternoon we went to the beach. The weather can be quite cold **(4)** _____ spring, but it was great – really sunny. **(5)** _____ Friday, we had lunch with an old friend. I first met her at university **(6)** _____ 2007. Then **(7)** _____ the evening, we went to a restaurant and got home **(8)** _____ midnight. **(9)** _____ the weekend, we went shopping and then went back to the beach. We'd like to go back for the Brighton Festival, which starts **(10)** _____ May 6th.

3 **ABOUT YOU** **Write answers using a preposition and a time phrase from the table, or ask another student.** 根据自身情况，用表格中的介词和与时间相关的短语回答问题，也可以向同学提问。

When do you …
get up? ....
study English? ....
go swimming? ....
usually go out with friends? ....
watch TV? ....
go to bed? ....

When …
is your birthday? ....
were you born? ....
are there public holidays
in your country? ....
....

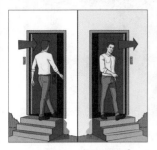

go **into**   go **out of**
(the house)

go **across** the road

go **up**   go **down**
(the stairs)

go **along** the road

go **past** the church

go **through** the gate

go **under**   go **across/over**
(the bridge)

go **towards** the hill

1 **Circle the correct word.** 圈出正确答案。
- ▶ Don't run down the *hill* / *town*.
- **1** Walk under the *trees* / *field*.
- **2** Drive along the *city* / *motorway*.
- **3** Don't go across the *river* / *gate*.
- **4** Go into the *beach* / *shop*.
- **5** Go towards the *church* / *clouds*.
- **6** Walk through the *gate* / *stairs*.
- **7** Go up the *floor* / *mountain*.
- **8** We flew over the *sky* / *field*.
- **9** Walk out of the *building* / *hill*.

2 **Complete the sentences with a preposition. Use a different one in each sentence.**
用介词填空，每词限用一次。
- ▶ Go straight on, _along_ this road.
- **1** We shouted hello as the boat went _____ the bridge.
- **2** She went _____ the hotel and spoke to the receptionist.
- **3** They drove _____ the hill to look at the view from the top.
- **4** I walked _____ the village, which was about a kilometre away.
- **5** We drove _____ a restaurant on the way to the station.
- **6** He came _____ the door and fell over. It was very funny.
- **7** I came _____ the bank and saw the accident.
- **8** We went _____ the hill, into the valley below.
- **9** The dog saw a cat in one of the gardens, and he just ran _____ the road.

3 **Complete the sentences with a preposition.** 用介词填空。   ABOUT YOU
- ▶ What do you see when you go _out of_ the building where you live?
- **1** Do you ever walk _____ a bridge near your home?
- **2** Do you ever drive _____ a river or a railway line?
- **3** Do you walk _____ a gate when you leave your home?
- **4** Have you ever walked _____ the River Thames?
- **5** When you walk to work, do you go _____ any interesting buildings?

4 ABOUT YOU **Write answers to the questions in Exercise 3, or ask another student.**
根据自身情况回答练习3中的问题，也可以向同学提问。

A *at, in, on*

| at | **a place where something happens**
Let's meet **at** the bank / **at** the bus stop.
I saw him **at** the match / **at** the party / **at** home
at work / **at** school. |

| in | **something with walls or sides**
in a box / **in** a cupboard
in a room / **in** an office / **in** a flat
in a garden / **in** a park | **a big area**
in a village / **in** a town / **in** a city
in the countryside
in London/Spain/Asia/the world |

| on | **something long**
on the road / **on** the coast
on a river | **something flat**
on the table / **on** the wall
on the first floor | **in** OR **on**
He's **in** the river.
She's **on** the river. |

1 Underline **the correct preposition.** 在正确的介词下划线。

▶ I live *in* / *on* Canada.

1 She's not *in* / *on* her office.
2 The photos are *in* / *on* the wall.
3 We met *in* / *at* a golf match.
4 We stayed *in* / *on* a lovely village.
5 He's swimming *in* / *on* the pool.
6 Barcelona is *in* / *on* the coast.
7 We live *at* / *in* the countryside.

8 There is a white line *at* / *on* the road.
9 Dinner is *on* / *at* the table.
10 They're sitting *in* / *at* the garden.
11 The books are *on* / *in* the table.
12 I saw her *in* / *at* the bus stop.
13 The number is *in* / *on* the door.
14 I spoke to her *in* / *at* the party.

2 Complete **the questions with** *at, in* **or** *on.* 用at、in或on填空。

▶ Which country do you live __in__ ?

1 Do you live .... a village, a town or a city?
2 Do you live .... a flat or a house?
3 Is your town .... a river?
4 Which floor is your bedroom .... ?

5 What's .... the walls in your living room?
6 Do you like walking .... the countryside?
7 Do you ever meet new people .... parties?
8 Did you learn English .... school, ... work,
or .... an English-speaking country?

3 ABOUT YOU **Write your answers to Exercise 2, or ask another student.**
根据自身情况回答练习2中的问题，也可以向同学提问。

B Other prepositions 其他介词

The people are **in front of** the garage.
The postman is **between** Mum and Dad.
The adults are **behind** the children.
The tree is **near** the house.

The office is **above** the garage.
The garage is **below** the office.
The seat is **next to** the bus stop.
The bus stop is **opposite** the house.

4 **True or false? Write *T* or *F*.** 判断正误，正确填T，错误填F。
▶ The tree is opposite the house.　_F_
1 The blue car is near the house.　........
2 The big window is above the door.　........
3 The seat is opposite the garage.　........
4 The people are opposite the garage.　........
5 The postman is next to Mum.　........

6 The gate is between the house and the tree.　........
7 The children are behind Mum and Dad.　........
8 The girl is in front of the postman.　........
9 The front door is below the big window.　........
10 The green car is next to the bus stop.　........

5 **Complete the sentences.** 将句子填写完整。
▶ The tree's _behind_ the blue car.
1 The bus stop is .... the seat.
2 The blue car is .... the tree.
3 The boy is standing .... Dad.
4 The gate is .... the house and the garage.

5 The blue car is .... the house.
6 The people are .... the garage.
7 The postman is .... Dad.
8 The garage is .... the people.

6 ABOUT YOU **Write your answers, or ask another student.** 根据自身情况回答问题，也可以向同学提问。
1 What's opposite the building where you live? ....
2 What's behind your building? ....
3 What's next to your building? ....
4 Are there any shops near it? ....
5 What's above your living room? ....
6 What's below your bedroom? ....
7 What's next to your bedroom? ....
8 Is there anything between your building and the street? If so, what? ....

21 Prepositions: phrases 介词短语

A Position 表示位置

1 **at the front of** the car
2 **on the side of** the car
3 OPP **on the other side**
4 **at the back of** the car
5 **in the back of** the car

at the beginning/start of the book

in the middle of the book

at the end of the book

at the top of the mountain

at the bottom of the staircase

SPOTLIGHT *at first* and *in the end*

We often talk about time using **at first** (= at the beginning of the time) and **in the end** (= finally) when we tell stories.

- **At first**, I didn't like being in the water, but I soon learned how to swim.
- It was a long journey. **In the end**, we arrived at our hotel.

---

1 **Cross out the wrong answer.** 划掉错误的单词。

▶ at the front of the *cinema / bread / house*
1 at the back of the *night / bus / classroom*
2 at the beginning of the *story / meal / pencil*
3 at the top of the *stairs / book / building*
4 at the bottom of the *glass / river / apple*
5 in the middle of the *book / road / milk*
6 on the other side of the *sky / house / river*
7 at the end of the *film / morning / mountain*

2 **Complete the sentences with a phrase.** 用介词短语填空。

▶ There's a murder __at the beginning__ of the film.
1 There's a great view .... of the hill.
2 I always sit .... of the class where the teacher can't see me.
3 They found an old boat .... of the lake.
4 .... I didn't enjoy learning English, but now I like it.
5 When I go and see a film, I like to sit .... of the cinema, where I can see easily.
6 What happens .... of the book? I didn't finish it.
7 They put a big sign .... of the square so everyone could see it.
8 We had a lot of problems, but .... it was OK.
9 The problem is not on this side of the wall – it's ....
10 .... of the film I couldn't understand their English, but it got better.
11 .... the restaurant was empty, but a few customers arrived about 6.30. Then a large group came in at about seven, followed by several more smaller groups. .... , it was almost full and really busy.

B Fixed phrases 固定短语

Did you like London when you went there?	~ I don't remember. I was only 8 **at the time**.
How many people came?	~ **At least** 25.
What are Liam and Yasmin doing **at the moment**?	~ I think they're **on holiday**.
Did you know Ellie **at university**?	~ Yes, we were there **at the same time**.
Is Ethan here?	~ Yes, but he's **on the phone**.
Were you late?	~ No, I'm always **on time**.
When will you finish painting the house?	~ Oh, **by the end of** the week.
Is Xav working now?	~ No. **In fact**, he's **in hospital** with a broken leg.

SPOTLIGHT *at university, in hospital,* etc.

If you are **at university**, you are studying in a university.
If you are **at school**, you are a pupil/student.
If you are **in hospital**, there is something wrong with you and you must stay there.
If you are **in prison**, you have done something wrong/illegal and you must stay there for a period of time.

GLOSSARY

at the time	then: *I worked there in 2016. I was 24 **at the time**.*
at least	not less than
at the moment	now or around now: *I'm busy **at the moment**.* (NOT ~~in this moment~~)
on holiday	not working/studying and often away from home
at the same time	used to say that two or more things happen together
on the phone	using the phone and speaking to sb ALSO **on his/her phone** (= mobile phone)
on time	not early or late
by the end of sth	not later than sth
in fact	used to say that sth is true (often the opposite of what sb says or thinks): *She looks English, but **in fact**, she's Spanish.* SYN **actually**

3 Make phrases using the words in the box. 用方框内的词组成短语。

least	holiday	university ✓	fact	the same time	the time
the phone	the moment	prison	time	hospital	

AT ▶ university _____ _____ _____

ON _____ _____ _____

IN _____ _____ _____

4 Complete the dialogues in a suitable way. 以恰当的方式将对话填写完整。

▶ Is he at university? ~ No, he's still _at school_ .
1 Did they arrive together? ~ Yes, _____ .
2 Are they away? ~ Yes, they're _____ .
3 What are you doing _____ ? ~ Now? Nothing. Why?
4 Is he ill? ~ Yes, he's _____ .
5 Were there many people there? ~ _____ 50.
6 Were you late? ~ No, I was _____ .
7 Is she still studying? ~ Yes, she's _____ .

5 Complete the sentences with a suitable phrase from above. 选取文中恰当的短语，将句子填写完整。

▶ I was _on time_ , but Max was late, as usual.
1 We came here in 2012, but I was only nine _____ .
2 My father has been _____ with a heart problem.
3 The hotel is quite expensive: a room is _____ $200.
4 She's on holiday at the moment, but she'll be back _____ the week.
5 He's been _____ for two years for stealing money.
6 I know she looks Swedish, but _____ she's English.
7 My sister has been _____ for two years. She finishes at the end of next year.
8 He's always _____ . He never stops sending texts.

22) Word + preposition 介词搭配

A Verb or adjective + preposition 动词或形容词+介词

You will find the meaning of some of the verbs and adjectives in this unit in other parts of the book.

Questionnaire
ABOUT YOU AND YOUR FAMILY

Do you still **live with** your parents?
Do you still **depend on** your parents?
Do you ever **ask** them **for** money?
Do you usually **agree with** your parents?
Do you **spend** a lot of money **on** clothes?
Do you **care about** making money?
Do you always **thank** people **for presents**?
What are you **interested in**?
What are you **good at**?
Do you get **bored with** things quickly?

GLOSSARY	
depend on sb/sth	need sb or sth
agree with sb	have the same view or opinion as sb (NOT ~~I'm agree.~~) OPP **disagree with sb**
spend money (on sth) *pt* spent	pay money for sth
care about sb/sth	think that sb or sth is important
thank sb (for sth)	tell sb you are pleased or happy because they gave you sth or helped you
present	sth that you give to sb or get from sb SYN **gift**

SPOTLIGHT preposition + *-ing* form

A preposition can be followed by a noun or an *-ing* form.
- *I'm **good at** maths.*
- *I'm **interested in** art.*
- *I'm **good at** drawing.*
- *I'm **interested in** learning languages.*

1 **Correct the mistakes.** 改错题。
▶ I spend a lot of money ~~in~~ food. _on_
1 I'm good in playing chess. ....
2 We must stop now. ~ Yes, I'm agree. ....
3 My brother depends of me. ....
4 I am bored for my job: it's always the same. ....
5 Do you ask for money your parents? ....
6 Do you care at the clothes you wear? ....
7 I live by two friends – we have a flat together. ....
8 I'm not interested in speak other languages. ....

2 **Complete the sentences with the correct verb or adjective.** 用动词或形容词填空。
▶ I'm not very _good_ at English. I make lots of mistakes.
1 I must .... my aunt for the .... she gave me for my birthday.
2 My boss is great. He really .... about his workers and wants them to do well.
3 He's new in the job so he still .... on other people for help and advice.
4 I .... $500 on a new tablet.
5 I know you used to take lots of photos. Are you still .... in photography?
6 If you can't do this, why don't you .... the teacher for help?

3 **Complete the sentences with the correct preposition.** 用介词填空。
▶ She spent all her money _on_ that computer.
1 I quickly get bored .... housework.
2 Did you ask them .... help?
3 I'm not interested .... cooking.
4 I forgot to thank him .... helping me.
5 They all depend .... Maxine for help.
6 My mother cares .... other people.
7 Why are you so good .... maths?
8 Does she live .... her family?
9 I disagree .... the others – I think it's a wonderful book.

4 ABOUT YOU Write answers to the questionnaire above, or ask another student. Use the new vocabulary in your answers. 根据自身情况，用新学的词汇填写以上问卷，也可以向同学提问。
▶ _I don't live with my parents because I'm married. I live with my wife._

B Verb + preposition 动词+介词

Read about Caroline, and some of the things she does and thinks.

> I often **listen to** the radio in the morning.
> I usually **hear about** things for the first time on social media.
> When I **look at** people, I don't **notice** what they're wearing.
> I like films that are **based on** true stories.
> I like furniture **made of** wood.
> I hate **waiting for** buses and trains, but don't like **paying for** taxis.
> I haven't **applied for** a job yet.
> I don't **think about** the future very much.

GLOSSARY

hear about sth	If you **hear about** sth, sb tells you sth or you read about it.
notice	see or pay attention to sb or sth
base sth on sth	make sth using another thing as the beginning: *We **based** the book **on** her diaries and letters. The book is **based on** her letters and diaries.*
apply for sth	write to ask for sth, e.g. for a job

SPOTLIGHT *think about* and *think of*

- *I always **think about** my grandmother when I see that photo.* = I have thoughts about her in my head.
- *What did you **think of** the film?* = What was your opinion of the film?

5 Match 1–6 with a–g. 配对题。

▶	Have you listened to	_c_	**a**	the photo I sent you?
1	Did you apply for	....	**b**	the new TV yet?
2	Have you looked at	....	**c**	their new song? ✓
3	Are you waiting for	....	**d**	leather?
4	Have you paid for	....	**e**	somebody to phone you?
5	Did you base your story on	....	**f**	the job?
6	Is the coat made of	....	**g**	something that happened to you?

6 Complete the sentences with the correct preposition. 用介词填空。

- ▶ I wasn't listening _to_ her.
- **1** What are you looking .... ?
- **2** Who paid .... the meal?
- **3** Did you apply .... a place on the course?
- **4** Why are you thinking .... Ali?
- **5** Is the film based .... a book?
- **6** Who are you waiting .... ?
- **7** How did you hear .... the party?
- **8** What did you think .... the book?
- **9** I think this is made .... plastic.

7 Complete the sentences with the correct verb. 用动词的正确形式填空。

- ▶ I'm _thinking_ about the weather. Is it warm enough to go swimming?
- **1** My story is .... on something I read in the newspaper.
- **2** Have you .... about Marta? She's getting married.
- **3** The food was free, but we had to .... for drinks.
- **4** I've just seen Mia, and I .... that she had a new hairstyle. It's very short.
- **5** I don't know why she .... for that job – it isn't very interesting.
- **6** I liked the film. What did you .... of it?

8 ABOUT YOU **Look at the sentences at the top of the page. Are they true for you? Write your answers or ask another student. Use the new vocabulary in your answers.**
上文中提到的情况是否与你相同？根据自身情况，用新学的词汇回答问题，也可以向同学提问。

- ▶ I never listen to the radio. In the morning I sometimes listen to music on my phone.

23) Routines 日常惯例

A Weekdays (Monday to Friday) 工作日 (星期一到星期五)

What's your **daily routine**?

I **wake up** at 7.00.
I **get up immediately**.

I **have a shower**.

I **get dressed**.

I **have breakfast**.

I **usually leave home** at 8.00.

I **get to work/arrive at work** at 8.30.

I **finish work/ go home** at 5.00.

I **have dinner** at 8.00.

I **normally go to bed** at about 11.30.

I **sleep** about seven hours a night.

GLOSSARY	
daily	happening every day
routine	your usual way of doing things
wake up	stop sleeping
immediately	now, without waiting
have + meal	e.g. *have breakfast*, *have lunch*, *have dinner*
usually	most often SYN **normally**

1 Is the meaning the same or different? Write *S* or *D*. 两者的含义是否相同? 相同填S, 不同填D。

▶ get dressed / get up   D

1 I go home at 6.00. / I leave home at 6.00. ....
2 I have lunch at 1.00. / I eat lunch at 1.00. ....
3 He finishes work early. / He gets to work early. ....

4 I get up immediately. / I get up daily. ....
5 We usually leave / We normally leave at 7.00. ....
6 Do you wake up early? / Do you get up early? ....

2 A word is missing in each line. What is it and where does it go? Write it after the sentence.
在句中相应位置补上遗漏的单词。

▶ I normally / up at 6.30.   wake

1 I usually get immediately. ....
2 I have a before breakfast. ....
3 I get after my shower. ....
4 I at work before 8.30. ....

5 I work and go home at 6.00. ....
6 I dinner with my family. ....
7 I go bed when I'm tired. ....
8 I usually six hours a night. ....
9 My daily is what I do every day. ....

3 Complete the questions with the correct verb. 用正确的动词或短语填空。 ABOUT YOU

▶ What time do you usually wake   up   in the morning?   I usually wake up early, at 6.00.
1 Do you .... dressed before or after breakfast? ....
2 Do you .... a shower in the morning? ....
3 Where do you usually .... breakfast? ....
4 What time do you .... home in the morning? ....
5 What time do you .... school/university/work? ....
6 Who do you have .... with in the evening? ....
7 What time do you normally .... to bed? ....
8 How many hours a night do you .... ? ....

4 ABOUT YOU Write your answers to the questions in Exercise 3, or ask another student.
根据自身情况回答练习3中的问题, 也可以向同学提问。

B Weekends (Saturdays and Sundays)
周末（星期六与星期日）

During the week I usually **stay in** after school and study, watch TV, or just talk to my family. **Once** or **twice** a week, my boyfriend **comes round** and we have dinner together or play video games. But **at the weekend**, I go out a lot more. On Saturday morning, I usually **go shopping** with a friend, and then my boyfriend and I go out in the evening. Sometimes we go to the cinema or a concert. On Sundays, I **always** get up **late**. We often **go for a walk**, and in the summer we **play tennis** or **go for a swim**.

GLOSSARY	
during the week	from Monday to Friday
stay in	stay at home OPP **go out**
once a week	one time in every week
twice a week	two times in every week
come round	visit sb at their home
at the weekend	on Saturday and Sunday
go shopping ALSO **do the shopping**	go to the shops to buy clothes, books, etc. buy food
late *adv*	after the usual time **late** *adj* OPP **early**
go for a walk/swim	have a short walk/swim to enjoy yourself
play tennis	(*see picture*)

5 **Write the words in the correct order.** 连词成句。

▶ twice / John / a / see / I / week I see John twice a week .
1 shopping / do / the / do / often / you ....?
2 school / never / late / is / he / for ....
3 early / up / we / tennis / get / play / sometimes / and ....
4 weekend / at / shopping / the / you / always / do / go ....?
5 the / goes / during / often / out / week / Martha ....
6 week / or / sister / a / once / see / my / I / twice ....

6 **Complete the phrases with one word.** 将短语填写完整，每空格只填一词。

▶ ..go.......... out = go to the cinema, a restaurant, etc.
1 not go out = ... in
2 buy clothes, books, etc. = ... shopping
3 have a game of tennis = ... tennis
4 have a short walk = ... for a walk
5 buy food = ... the shopping
6 on Saturday and Sunday = ... the weekend
7 from Monday to Friday = ... the week
8 on Tuesdays only = ... a week
9 on Mondays and Fridays only = ... a week

7 ABOUT YOU **True or false? Write *T* or *F*. If a sentence is false, change the word in bold to make it true.**
根据自身情况判断正误，正确填T，错误填F。通过替换粗体的单词或短语来改正句子。

▶ I **often** get to work or school late.   F – I never get to school late.
1 I **always** play tennis in the summer. ....
2 In my family, I **never** do the shopping. ....
3 I **often** go for a long walk during the week. ....
4 I **sometimes** play video games at the weekend. ....
5 I **never** have dinner with my family. ....
6 **During the week**, I go out a lot in the evenings. ....
7 I like to get up **early** at the weekend. ....
8 I **often** go shopping with a friend. ....

button

Milla

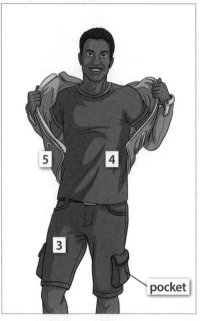

pocket

Enzo

Osman

1   dress
2   coat
3   shorts
4   T-shirt
5   jacket
6   suit
7   trousers
8   jacket
9   shirt
10   tie
11   jeans
12   jumper/sweater
13   uniform
14   skirt
15   top

These are all **items of clothing**.

Kim

Megan

GLOSSARY	
clothes	things like *trousers*, *shirts* and *coats* that you wear to cover your body
item of clothing	a thing that you wear, e.g. *a skirt*, *a tie*
wear *pt* **wore** *pp* **worn**	have clothes on your body
put sth on	take clothes and wear them: ***Put on*** your shoes. ***Put*** your coat ***on***. OPP **take sth off**
uniform	the special clothes that everybody in the same job, school, etc. wears

1 **Complete the words.** 将单词填写完整。

- s u i t
1 j___ ___ ___ t
2 t___ ___ ___ ___ ___ s
3 j___ ___ ___ r
4 b___ ___ ___ ___ n

5 c___ ___ t
6 T-___ ___ ___ t
7 d___ ___ s
8 p___ ___ ___ ___ t
9 j___ ___ s

10 t___ ___
11 sh___ ___ t
12 sk___ ___ t
13 sh___ ___ ___ s
14 sw___ ___ t___ r

2 **Look at the pictures on page 54 and answer the questions.** 根据P54的图片回答问题。

- Who's wearing jeans and a jumper? _Kim_____
1 Who's wearing a uniform? ....
2 Who's wearing shorts? ....
3 Who's wearing a suit? ....
4 Who's wearing a dress? ....
5 Who's wearing a skirt and top? ....
6 Who's taking off a jacket? ....
7 Who's putting a coat on? ....
8 Who's putting on a tie? ....

9 Who isn't wearing trousers? ....
10 Who's wearing a jumper? ....
11 Who's wearing a jacket with pockets? ....
12 Who's wearing an item of clothing with buttons? ....
13 Who's wearing three items of clothing? ....
14 Is anybody taking a coat off? ....

3 **Put the words in the correct column.** 将方框内的词填入相应表格栏。

jacket ✓   top   suit   trousers   skirt   shorts   dress   jeans   tie   T-shirt   coat   shirt   jumper   uniform

WHOLE BODY	ABOVE THE WAIST	BELOW THE WAIST
	jacket	

4 **Circle the correct word or words. Be careful: more than one answer may be correct.**
圈出正确答案，注意：答案可能不唯一。

- You wear (shorts) / a jacket / a jumper on a hot day.
1 Men don't usually wear *skirts* / *dresses* / *suits*.
2 When you go out, you *take your coat off* / *put your coat on*.
3 Women often wear *ties* / *trousers* / *jeans*.

4 You take your coat off when it's *cold* / *hot*.
5 Police officers usually wear *jeans* / *a uniform* at work.
6 A top is *an item of clothing* / *a dress* / *a uniform*.

5 **Is the pronunciation of the underlined letters the same or different? Write S or D.**
Practise saying the words. 划线部分的发音是否相同？相同填S，不同填D，并练习发音。

- cl<u>o</u>thes / t<u>o</u>p   D
1 w<u>ea</u>r / j<u>ea</u>ns   ....
2 sk<u>ir</u>t / sh<u>ir</u>t   ....
3 un<u>i</u>form / cl<u>o</u>thes   ....
4 t<u>ie</u> / <u>i</u>tem   ....

5 <u>j</u>umper / <u>u</u>niform   ....
6 <u>c</u>lothing / <u>c</u>oat   ....
7 <u>pu</u>mper / <u>pu</u>t on   ....
8 <u>s</u>uit / <u>u</u>niform   ....
9 <u>j</u>acket / <u>t</u>ake off   ....

6 ABOUT YOU **Write your answers, or ask another student.** 根据自身情况回答问题，也可以向同学提问。

1 What are you wearing today? ....
2 What did you wear yesterday? ....
3 Do you wear the same clothes at the weekend? If not, what is different? ....
4 What do you usually wear to parties? ....
5 Have you ever worn a uniform? If so, what was it for? ....

scarf (*pl* **scarves**)

hat

belt

handbag

umbrella

watch

a pair of shoes

a pair of boots

trainers

socks

tights

glasses

sunglasses

gloves

some jewellery

rings

necklace

GLOSSARY

accessory (usually *pl*) a thing you carry or wear with clothes, e.g. *a watch, a bag, a belt*

wear You **wear** items of clothing, glasses or jewellery, e.g. *a scarf, sunglasses, a ring.*

carry You **carry** a bag, a handbag or an umbrella.

gold The *rings* in the picture are made of **gold**.

silver The *necklace* is made of **silver**.

plastic The *umbrella* is made of **plastic**.

leather The *boots* are made of **leather**.

SPOTLIGHT plural nouns and *pairs*

Trousers, jeans, tights, clothes and **(sun)glasses** are always plural. They take a plural verb form.

- *These **tights are** very warm.* (NOT *The tights is …*)

We use **a pair of** in two ways:

1 two things of the same kind that we use together: ***a pair of*** *shoes/boots/trainers/socks/gloves*, etc.

2 a thing with two parts that are together: ***a pair of*** *glasses/sunglasses* ***a pair of*** *tights*

1 **True or false? Write *T* or *F*.** 判断正误，正确填T，错误填F。

▶ You can wear a watch.   T

1 Jewellery is often made of gold or silver.   ....

2 Glasses are made of leather.   ....

3 You can wear a belt.   ....

4 You can wear an umbrella on your shoulder.   ....

5 You can carry a handbag on your arm or shoulder.   ....

6 A necklace can be made of plastic.   ....

7 A pair of tights has two parts called *legs*.   ....

8 Most people wear a pair of scarves.   ....

2 **Complete the sentences with words from the box.** 将方框内的词填在横线上。

watch   hat   scarf   socks   belt ✓   glasses   umbrella   handbag   ring   boots   tights

▶ You wear it round your waist.   belt

1 You wear them inside your shoes.   ....

2 You wear it on your head.   ....

3 You wear it on your finger.   ....

4 You wear them on your feet.   ....

5 You wear them over your legs and feet.   ....

6 You wear them on your nose.   ....

7 You wear it round your neck.   ....

8 You wear it on your wrist.   ....

9 You carry it when it's raining.   ....

10 You carry things in it.   ....

3 **Is the pronunciation of the <u>underlined</u> letters the same or different? Write *S* or *D*.**
Practise saying the words. 划线部分的发音是否相同？相同填S，不同填D，并练习发音。

▶ h<u>a</u>t / neckl<u>a</u>ce   D

1 w<u>a</u>tch / s<u>o</u>cks   ....

2 t<u>igh</u>ts / r<u>i</u>ng   ....

3 b<u>oo</u>ts / <u>j</u>ewellery   ....

4 g<u>l</u>oves / g<u>o</u>ld   ....

▶ h<u>a</u>t / h<u>a</u>ndbag   S

5 sc<u>a</u>rf / sungl<u>a</u>sses   ....

6 l<u>ea</u>ther / b<u>e</u>lt   ....

7 p<u>ai</u>r / tr<u>ai</u>ners   ....

8 c<u>a</u>rry / pl<u>a</u>stic   ....

4 **Make the sentences singular if possible.** 用名词的单数形式改写句子。

▶ Are these your boots?   Is this your boot?

1 Give me the socks.   ....

2 Where are my tights?   ....

3 I've got two pairs of trainers.   ....

4 Where are my gloves?   ....

5 She's got my scarves.   ....

6 Where are my shoes?   ....

7 The jeans cost €30.   ....

8 I don't like these sunglasses.   ....

▶ Her glasses are nice.   Not possible.

5 **Label the pictures. Use *a pair of* where possible.** 填写图片中的物品名称，必要时使用a pair of。

▶ a pair of leather shoes	....	....
....	....	....
....	....	....

6 ABOUT YOU **Write your answers, or ask another student.** 根据自身情况回答问题，也可以向同学提问。

1 Which accessories do you always wear? ....

2 Which accessories do you never wear? ....

3 Do you wear trainers a lot? If you don't, what do you wear? ....

4 Do you wear glasses or sunglasses? Why? ....

5 When do you wear: jewellery? a watch? a hat? a scarf? ....

A Colours and adjectives 色彩及相关形容词

1 long
2 short
3 large/big
4 small/little
5 cheap
6 expensive
7 comfortable
8 uncomfortable

Colours

white   cream   yellow   green   blue   dark blue   light blue

black   grey   red   orange   brown   purple   pink

> **SPOTLIGHT** order of adjectives
>
> Adjectives describing size or opinion go before colour adjectives.
> - We say *a big blue umbrella* (NOT *a blue big umbrella*)
> - *large brown eyes* ▪ *a cheap black suit*

1 Find the end of each word. 找出单词。

red/greenpinkpurpleorangegreydarkbluecreambrownlightblueblackyellowwhite

2 Write your answers. 填写相应色彩。

▶ Red and yellow together make ..orange........ .
1 Red and blue together make ....
2 White and blue together make ....
....
3 Blue and yellow together make ....
4 Red and white together make ....

5 Black and white together make ....
6 Black and blue together make ....
....
7 Red and green together make ....
8 Yellow and white together make ....
9 Blue, yellow and purple are all ....

3 Circle the correct word. 圈出正确答案。

▶ My handbag's very *large* / *small*, so I can put lots in it.
1 I like these trainers, but they're very *comfortable / uncomfortable*.
2 I haven't got much money, so I don't wear *cheap / expensive* clothes.
3 He's only seven years old, so just buy him a *small / large* T-shirt.
4 You need your *long / short* coat today – it's really cold.
5 The good thing about the school café is that it's *cheap / expensive*.
6 You need *comfortable / uncomfortable* clothes when you are travelling.

4 Look at the pictures at the top of the page and describe the clothes and accessories.
描述上图中的服装和配饰。

▶ a c..heap........ grey........ tie
1 a s................. skirt
2 c................. shoes
3 a l................. handbag

4 a l................. skirt
5 u................. shoes
6 an e................. tie
7 a s................. handbag

B Size and appearance
尺码与外观

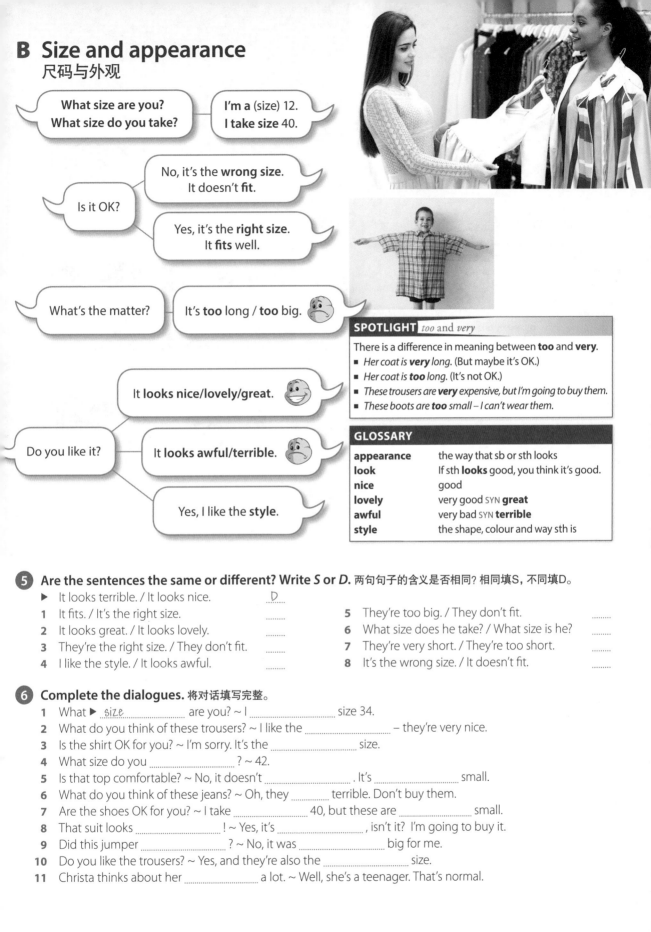

What size are you?
What size do you take?

I'm a (size) 12.
I take size 40.

Is it OK?

No, it's the **wrong size**.
It doesn't **fit**.

Yes, it's the **right size**.
It **fits** well.

What's the matter?

It's **too** long / **too** big.

It **looks** nice/lovely/great.

Do you like it?

It **looks** awful/terrible.

Yes, I like the **style**.

SPOTLIGHT *too* and *very*

There is a difference in meaning between **too** and **very**.

- *Her coat is **very** long. (But maybe it's OK.)*
- *Her coat is **too** long. (It's not OK.)*
- *These trousers are **very** expensive, but I'm going to buy them.*
- *These boots are **too** small – I can't wear them.*

GLOSSARY

appearance	the way that sb or sth looks
look	If sth **looks** good, you think it's good.
nice	good
lovely	very good SYN **great**
awful	very bad SYN **terrible**
style	the shape, colour and way sth is

5 **Are the sentences the same or different? Write *S* or *D*.** 两句句子的含义是否相同? 相同填S, 不同填D。

▶ It looks terrible. / It looks nice.   D
1 It fits. / It's the right size.   ....
2 It looks great. / It looks lovely.   ....
3 They're the right size. / They don't fit.   ....
4 I like the style. / It looks awful.   ....

5 They're too big. / They don't fit.   ....
6 What size does he take? / What size is he?   ....
7 They're very short. / They're too short.   ....
8 It's the wrong size. / It doesn't fit.   ....

6 **Complete the dialogues.** 将对话填写完整。

1 What ▶ _size_ are you? ~ I _____ size 34.
2 What do you think of these trousers? ~ I like the _____ – they're very nice.
3 Is the shirt OK for you? ~ I'm sorry. It's the _____ size.
4 What size do you _____? ~ 42.
5 Is that top comfortable? ~ No, it doesn't _____. It's _____ small.
6 What do you think of these jeans? ~ Oh, they _____ terrible. Don't buy them.
7 Are the shoes OK for you? ~ I take _____ 40, but these are _____ small.
8 That suit looks _____! ~ Yes, it's _____, isn't it? I'm going to buy it.
9 Did this jumper _____? ~ No, it was _____ big for me.
10 Do you like the trousers? ~ Yes, and they're also the _____ size.
11 Christa thinks about her _____ a lot. ~ Well, she's a teenager. That's normal.

A Money in shops 商店内与钱相关的词汇

You go into a shop to **buy** three books. They **cost** £9.50 **each**, so a **total** of £28.50. You think you have some **cash** (**notes** and **coins**) in your **wallet**, but when you look, you haven't got **enough** money with you to **pay in cash**, so you **pay by card**.

cash

notes

GLOSSARY	
buy *pt* **bought**	give money to get sth
cost *pt* **cost**	How much does it **cost**? = How much is it?
(£9.50) each	(£9.50) for one
total	the number you have when you add everything together
enough	(sounds like *stuff*) as much or as many as you need
pay *pt* **paid**	give sb money for sth. You **pay** in *cash*, but **pay by** *debit/credit card*.
debit card	If you use a **debit card**, the money comes out of your **bank account** (where you put money in and take it out).
credit card	A **credit card** is a bank card you use to buy sth and pay for it later.

coins

debit card

SPOTLIGHT	amounts of money
£10.99	*ten* **pounds** *ninety-nine (pence) / ten ninety-nine*
€5.30	*five* **euros** *thirty (cents) / five thirty*
■ *a one-***pound** *coin*	■ *a ten-***dollar** *note* (NOT ~~a ten-dollars note~~)

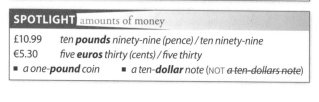
wallet

purses

1 True or false? Write *T* or *F*. 判断正误，正确填T，错误填F。

▶ You can pay for things in cash or by credit or debit card. T

1 If you pay in cash, you use coins and notes. ....
2 If you buy two things for £30 each, the total is £30. ....
3 If a cake costs $5 and you have a ten-dollar note, you haven't got enough. ....

4 You can put a debit card in a wallet. ....
5 Things cost more if you pay in cash. ....
6 When you pay by debit card, the money comes from your bank account. ....
7 The past tense of *cost* is *cost*. ....

2 Complete the sentences using a word from the box. 用方框内的词填空。

cost coins cash enough -dollar purse total dollars credit card bought ✓ each

▶ She ..bought.......... a new car yesterday.

1 I paid in ....
2 I put the notes in my ....
3 I paid by ....
4 I've got a few notes and ....
5 The ticket .... €50.

6 I need a ten .... note.
7 It cost five .... twenty.
8 That's a .... of £100.
9 Have you got .... money?
10 The peaches cost 50c ....

3 ABOUT YOU Write your answers, or ask another student. 根据自身情况回答问题，也可以向同学提问。

1 Do you always have a lot of cash with you? Why? / Why not? ....
2 Where do you keep your money when you go out? ....
3 Do you have enough money with you today to buy a coffee? A book? Some jewellery? ....
4 Do you pay at the supermarket in cash or by debit/credit card? ....

B Money in adverts 广告中与钱相关的词汇

 **Sell** your car for a great **price** on eSellers.com!

 **Spend £50** on food and get a **FREE** drink.

 Pay your gas **bill online** and **save** £40.

Earn $30 an hour in your own home.

☎ RING 0990 557731

Win cash and **prizes**! CALL US TODAY.

 SALE all **products** 50% **off**

GLOSSARY	
sell *pt* **sold**	give sth to sb who pays you money for it OPP **buy** *pt* **bought**
price	the money you have to pay for sth
spend money (on sth) *pt* **spent**	pay money for sth
free	If sth is **free**, you don't pay for it.
bill	a piece of paper which shows how much you must pay
online	on the internet
save	If you **save** £40 on a bill, you pay £40 less.
earn	get money by working
win *pt* **won**	get money or a prize, often because you are better than others or lucky
prize	sth that you give to a person who wins a game, race, etc.
sale	a time when a shop sells sth for less money than usual
product	sth that people make or grow to sell
(50%) off	50% (= 50 **per cent**) taken off the normal price

4 Circle the correct answer. 圈出正确答案。

▶ They're going to sell a new (product) / price.

1 What's the *price* / *bill* of these shoes?
2 I don't *spend* / *buy* a lot on food.
3 I bought ten boxes and *earned* / *saved* £3.
4 I *won* / *earned* £100 in a card game.
5 The *prize* / *price* of the classes was $400.

6 I bought this table *online* / *free*.
7 Doctors can *win* / *earn* a lot of money.
8 I *bought* / *sold* my old car and got a new one.
9 She paid the restaurant *bill* / *price*.
10 The shoes are 15% *out* / *off*.

5 Cover the glossary and write the past simple forms. 遮住单词表，写出动词的一般过去式。

▶ pay   paid
1 buy   ....
2 spend   ....
3 sell   ....
4 earn   ....
5 win   ....
6 save   ....

6 Complete the questions with a word from the glossary.
用单词表中的单词填空。

▶ How much do you spend on food every week?
1 Do you ever shop ....?
2 Do you pay restaurant .... in cash?
3 Is water .... in restaurants?
4 What's the .... of a litre of milk?
5 Do you often buy things cheaper in a ....?
6 Do women .... more than men?
7 What kind of .... do men buy a lot?
8 Have you ever won a ....?

ABOUT YOU AND YOUR COUNTRY

....
....
....
....
....
....
....
....

7 ABOUT YOU AND YOUR COUNTRY Write your answers to the questions in Exercise 6, or ask another student. 根据自身情况回答练习6中的问题，也可以向同学提问。

A Places 地点

PLACES	WHAT THEY SELL
shopping centre	everything
department store	everything (e.g. clothes, furniture, books, etc.) except food
supermarket	food, drinks, soap, cleaning products, etc.
chemist's/pharmacy	**medicine**, soap
baker's	bread and cakes
electrical store	TVs, computers, coffee machines, etc.
toy shop	dolls, model aeroplanes, building blocks
gift shop	T-shirts, toys, cups, etc.

toys

GLOSSARY

everything	all things
except	but not; not including
medicine	special liquids and pills to make you get better when you are ill
gift	sth that you give to or get from sb SYN **present**
toy	a thing for a child to play with

SPOTLIGHT *noun + shop*

For many shops, we often use a *noun + shop*, e.g. a shop where you buy books is a **bookshop**. ALSO **shoe shop, clothes shop, furniture shop, music shop** (for CDs, etc.), **fruit and vegetable shop**, etc.

1 Correct any spelling mistakes. 改正拼写错误。

▶ furnishure shop ___furniture___
1 cemist's _____
2 farmacy _____
3 department store _____
4 shoping centre _____
5 medecine _____
6 cloths shop _____
7 pressent _____
8 elektrical store _____

2 Underline the stressed part of the word. Practise saying the words. 在单词的重读音节下划线，并练习发音。

▶ <u>shop</u>ping <u>cen</u>tre   bookshop   department store   clothes shop   pharmacy
supermarket   electrical store   furniture shop   everything   medicine   except

3 Cross out the one wrong answer. 划掉错误答案。

▶ I got the vegetables from the …
  a) supermarket
  b) ~~baker's~~
  c) fruit and vegetable shop
1 I got the medicine from the …
  a) chemist's
  b) toy shop
  c) pharmacy
2 I got these jeans from the …
  a) department store
  b) gift shop
  c) clothes shop

3 I got these boots from the …
  a) shoe shop
  b) department store
  c) furniture shop
4 I got Gemma's present from the …
  a) bookshop
  b) fruit and vegetable shop
  c) gift shop

5 I got this coffee machine from the …
  a) shopping centre
  b) electrical store
  c) music shop
6 I got the bread from the …
  a) baker's
  b) shopping centre
  c) chemist's

4 Where can you buy the following things? More than one answer is possible.
以下物品在哪里能买到? 注意: 答案可能不唯一。
A shop where you can buy …

▶ sugar, rice and soap: ___a supermarket___
1 cakes and bread: _____
2 something for a child to play with: _____
3 something for somebody's birthday: _____
4 a CD: _____
5 medicine: _____
6 new shoes: _____
7 a chair and a bed: _____
8 trousers and a shirt: _____
9 a TV and a fridge: _____

B Why go shopping? 为什么要去商店购物?

Why go shopping?

A lot of people **shop online**, but sometimes they **prefer to** go shopping. Here's why:

• In the shops, you can **touch** and feel things, like clothes, and **try** them **on**.
• You can **choose particular** items, like fresh fruit or fish.
• You can see and **compare** the **quality** of items.
• You get a more **personal service** from a shop assistant than you do online.
• Often shops **reduce** the prices of items in the **sales**, which is very popular.

GLOSSARY	
online	using a computer or the internet **shop online**
prefer	like one thing or person better than another: *Would you **prefer** juice or water?* *I **prefer to** buy fruit in a shop.*
touch	(sounds like *much*) put your hand or finger on sth or sb
try sth on	put sth on to see if you like it and it is the right size: *I **tried** the shoes **on**, but they were too small.*
choose	decide which thing you want **choice** n
particular	one only, and not any other: *She eats a **particular** kind of bread.*
compare	think about or look at things together so that you can see how they are different
quality	how good or bad sth is
service	the work that sb does for customers in a shop, restaurant, etc. **serve** v; **personal service** service for one person
reduce	make sth smaller or less
sale(s)	a time when a shop sells things for less money than usual

5 **Underline** the correct word or phrase. 在正确的单词或短语下划线。

▶ *good* / *big* quality

1 compare *two things* / *a choice*
2 prefer *to* / *or* go home
3 try *the shoes* / *the shoes on*
4 a choice *of two things* / *shop online*

5 *person* / *personal* service
6 shop *the sales* / *online*
7 a particular *shop* / *sales*
8 reduce *the sales* / *the price*
9 touch *the sky* / *somebody's face*

6 Match 1–8 with a–h. 配对题。

▶ They gave more choice	..f..	a so I was very happy.
1 He tried the coat on	....	b and it felt very nice.
2 She reduced the price for me	....	c when I can't find what I want in the shops.
3 We compared the prices	....	d but it was too small.
4 The shop assistant had to	....	e so I didn't buy anything.
5 The quality of clothes was terrible	....	f to their customers. ✓
6 I touched the jacket	....	g serve three customers at the same time.
7 I shop online	....	h and bought the cheapest chair.

7 ABOUT YOU Complete the words in the questions. 将问句中的单词填写完整。

1 Do you p_____ supermarkets or small shops? _____
2 Is it easy for you to c_____ clothes in shops? _____
3 Is good s_____ in shops very important to you? _____
4 Is there a p_____ kind of shoe that you wear? _____
5 When you buy new clothes, do you always t_____ them _____? _____
6 Do you prefer to go to the shops, or shop o_____? _____
7 What time of year are the s_____ in your country? _____
8 Do you like to t_____ and feel things before you buy them? _____

8 Write your answers to the questions in Exercise 7, or ask another student.
根据自身情况回答练习7中的问题, 也可以向同学提问。

29 Possessions 物品

A Family possessions 家庭物品

One of my favourite **possessions** is a **diary**[1] that **belonged to** my aunt.

A **recording**[5] of my grandmother's **voice**. She was quite a famous singer. It has very happy **memories** for me.

My grandfather's old **camera**[2]. I've also got some of his old **tools**[3]. I had his **gun**, but I haven**'t** got it **any more** – I gave it to a museum.

A book of my mother's **recipes**[4]. I use it a lot.

GLOSSARY	
possessions	the things that you have or own
belong to sb	That book **belongs to** me. = It is my book.
gun	a weapon that shoots out pieces of metal to kill or hurt people or animals
(not) any more	used at the end of negative sentences and questions to mean 'any longer'
recording	sounds on CD, video or film
voice	the sounds that you make when you speak or sing
memory	sth that you remember

1 These words all have the same weak sound in them, as in *import**a**nt*, *rememb**e**r* and *comfort**a**ble*. <u>Underline</u> the sound in these words. Practise saying the words.
在单词的弱读音节下划线，如import**a**nt、rememb**e**r、comfort**a**ble，并练习发音。

▶ fam**i**ly   **1** recipe   **2** memory   **3** diary   **4** camera   **5** possession

2 Write the name of the possession that matches the definition. 根据定义写出物品。
▶ You use this when you do a special job with your hands. _a tool_

1 You take photos with this. ....
2 You read these when you're cooking. ....
3 things that belong to you ....
4 This can kill people or animals. ....

5 You use this when you're singing or talking. ....
6 You write what you're going to do in this. ....
7 sounds on a computer file, CD, etc. ....
8 something that you remember ....

3 Complete the dialogues. 将对话填写完整。
▶ Do you know the date of the party?   ~ Yes, I wrote it in my _diary_.
1 Do you still sing?   ~ I did a few years ago, but I don't ....
2 How are you going to cut that wood?   ~ I have a special .... for it.
3 How did you make that pasta dish?   ~ I used a .... from my Italian cookbook.
4 Have you still got that photo of grandfather?   ~ Yes, it brings back happy ....
5 That man looks very dangerous.   ~ Yes! He's got a .... !
6 I can't hear what she's saying.   ~ No, she's got a very quiet ....
7 Whose car is that?   ~ It .... to my brother.
8 You love that old diary of grandmother's.   ~ I do. It's one of my favourite ....

4 ABOUT YOU Write your answers, or ask another student. 根据自身情况回答问题，也可以向同学提问。
1 Have you got any important family possessions? If so, what are they? ....
2 Have you got happy memories of school? What did you like? ....
3 Do you use a camera, or do you use the camera on your phone? Why? ....
4 Have you got a recording of a family member's voice? If so, who and why? ....

B Describing possessions 描述物品

fan

electric fan

phone (ALSO **telephone**)

phone / mobile (phone)

A **fan** is an **unusual shape** and is used to make you cooler. It's made of **wood** and **material** or paper. There are also **electric fans**.

A **mobile phone** is a **device** made of **metal** and **plastic**. Modern phones are **flat** and thin. It has a lot of different **purposes** – a phone, an **alarm clock**, a **digital** camera, or a device for playing games.

GLOSSARY			
unusual	If sth is **unusual**, you do not see it often or it does not happen often.	**plastic**	an artificial substance that is used for making many different things, e.g. *plastic* flowers, *plastic* cups
shape	A circle ◯ and a square ☐ are two different **shapes**.	**flat**	thin and wide and with no parts higher than the rest
wood	**Wood** comes from trees.	**purpose**	the intention, aim or function of sth
material	cloth you use for making clothes, curtains, etc.	**alarm clock**	a clock that makes a noise to wake you up
device	a piece of equipment you use for doing a special job	**digital**	this is a **digital** clock ⸻
metal	Gold, silver and iron are types of **metal**.		ALSO *digital camera/TV*

5 **True or false? Write *T* or *F*.** 判断正误，正确填T，错误填F。

▸ Chairs are often made of wood.   T

1 Clothes are often made of plastic.   ....
2 Trousers are made of material.   ....
3 A digital television is flat.   ....
4 An alarm clock is often made of material.   ....
5 A circle and a square are different shapes.   ....

6 The purpose tells you why you are doing something.   ....
7 If something is unusual, it's normal.   ....
8 An electric fan is useful if it's very cold.   ....
9 Mobile phones and digital cameras are devices.   ....

6 **One word is missing in each sentence. What is it, and where does it go?** 在句中相应位置补上遗漏的单词。

▸ The / of that big electric fan is to make the room cooler.   _purpose_

1 I use my mobile as an clock in the mornings.   ....
2 My desk is made of and is very old.   ....
3 What is the table? ~ I think it's round.   ....
4 He's got a very alarm clock – it's made of wood.   ....
5 The garden chairs are made of white and they're very hard.   ....
6 A computer is made of and plastic.   ....
7 What do you call the that turns the TV on and off?   ....

7 **ABOUT YOU** **Write your answers, or ask another student.** 根据自身情况回答问题，也可以向同学提问。

1 What shape is the table in your living room / dining room? ....
2 Do you use the alarm clock on your mobile phone? ....
3 What can you see in front of you that is made of wood? Plastic? Metal? ....
4 Have you got a digital TV? ....
5 Do you ever use a fan or an electric fan? ....

30) Crime 罪行

A TV report 电视报道

Police have **found** the **body** of a 19-year-old man in a park in East London. The **dead** body was **discovered** by a woman walking her dog early this morning. The police have not **named** the man, but there has been a **series** of **crimes** in the **area** in **recent** weeks. They think the man was **killed** and the **attack** was **planned**.

1 **Same or different? Write *S* or *D*.** 两者的含义是否相同? 相同填S, 不同填D。

▶ The girl was alive. / The girl was a criminal. D
1 They found the body. / They discovered the body. ....
2 The dog was dead. / The dog was alive. ....
3 They named him. / They said who he was. ....
4 He attacked someone. / He killed someone. ....

5 It's a recent problem. / It's an old problem. ....
6 This is a nice area of town. / This is a nice part of town. ....
7 a series of crimes / a number of crimes ....
8 They planned the crime. / They discovered the crime. ....

2 **Answer *Yes* or *No*.** 填写Yes或No。

▶ Does a person have a *body*? Yes
1 If someone is *dead*, can they speak? ....
2 Can a *body* be a dead person? ....
3 If a person is *kill*, are they dead? ....
4 Do the police look for *criminals*? ....

5 If a crime was *recent*, was it a long time ago? ....
6 Is a *series* more than one? ....
7 If you *attack* somebody, are they happy? ....
8 If you *discover* something, have you lost it? ....

3 **Complete the sentences.** 将句子填写完整。

▶ There were purple marks on the body .
1 The police have .... a body in the woods outside town.
2 I never go there because it's a dangerous .... of town at night.
3 The woman was .... by the police as Josephine Smith.
4 Two men .... an old man in a bar, and he had to go to hospital.
5 The man died later in hospital but the police don't know who .... him.
6 The police are worried about the number of serious .... in the town.
7 There has been a .... of car accidents on that road.
8 The old man was still .... when they found him, and he was taken to hospital.

B Police statement 警方通报

… We think the crime **happened late** last night, so a **major search** of the area is now **taking place** and we would like to speak to any **members** of **the public** who were in that area last night or early this morning. I would also like to **stress** that we do not **believe** there is any **danger** to the public.

GLOSSARY

statement	sth you say or write, which is often formal
late	near the end of a period of time: *He's in his **late** 20s* (= 27-29).
major	large or important
search	when you try to find sb or sth **search** *v*
member	sb who is part of a group or team
the public	people in general; everybody
stress	say sth strongly to show that it is important
believe	think that sth is true or possible
danger	the possibility that sth bad may happen: *You may be in **danger** if you are alone.* **dangerous** *adj* OPP **safe**

SPOTLIGHT *happen* and *take place*

These words have the same basic meaning, but **happen** usually describes something that is not planned:
- *How did the accident **happen**?*

Take place usually describes something that is planned:
- *The meeting **took place** yesterday evening.*

4 Same or different? Write *S* or *D*. 两者的含义是否相同? 相同填S, 不同填D。
- ▶ a member of the team / one person in the team — S
- 1 a major problem / a small problem — ....
- 2 They believe it's true. / They think it's true. — ....
- 3 The place is dangerous. / The place is safe. — ....
- 4 It was late last night. / It was early last night. — ....
- 5 members of the public / members of the police — ....
- 6 They're searching for him. / They're trying to find him. — ....
- 7 They made a statement. / They made a decision. — ....
- 8 It happens every year. / It takes place every year. — ....

5 Complete the definitions. 将定义填写完整。
- ▶ A statement is something you say or _write_.
- 1 If you search an area, you try to .... somebody or something.
- 2 A member is somebody who is part of a ....
- 3 If you stress something, you are saying it is ....
- 4 If you believe something is true, then you .... it is true.
- 5 The public are .... in general.
- 6 If something takes place, it ....

6 Complete the dialogues. 将对话填写完整。
- ▶ Have the police spoken to anyone? ~ Yes, they're talking to the _public_ now.
- 1 He's about 28, isn't he? ~ Yeah, he's in his .... 20s.
- 2 Have the police said anything? ~ Yes, they've made a formal ....
- 3 Is he safe? ~ No, he could be in ....
- 4 Have the police found anything? ~ No, but they're .... the area now.
- 5 Is it important? ~ Yes, it's a .... problem.
- 6 Do you think they'll find the boy? ~ Yes, I .... they will.
- 7 How did the fire .... ? ~ I think it was a cigarette that started it.
- 8 Are the police talking to people? ~ Yes, they're interviewing members of the ....

A Common health problems 常见健康问题

> What's the matter?

> I don't feel well.

> I've got …

a headache

toothache

stomach ache

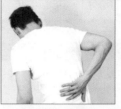
backache

a cold

a cough

(the) flu

a temperature

I feel sick.

GLOSSARY	
common	If sth is **common**, it happens often.
health	If you are in good **health**, you are well, not often ill. **healthy** *adj* OPP **unhealthy**
a cold	a common illness of the nose and throat
(the) flu [U]	an illness like a very bad cold, and often with a temperature

SPOTLIGHT *be ill* and *be sick*

Ill means not well. An **illness** is a period of feeling ill.
- *Rafa's not here today: he's **ill**. He didn't go to school because of **illness**.*

To **be sick** usually means to bring up food from your stomach (ALSO **vomit**). If you **feel sick**, you think you are going to **be sick**.
- *I felt **sick**, so I ran to the bathroom. I **was sick** on the floor.*

1 **Circle the correct answer.** 圈出正确答案。

▶ *I'm* / *I've got* a temperature.

1 *What* / *What's* the matter?
2 She *feels* / *'s got* a cold.
3 He doesn't *feel* / *be* well.
4 I *feel* / *'ve got* toothache.
5 I've got *headache* / *a headache*.
6 *Is* / *Has* she got a temperature?
7 She's a *healthy* / *health* person.

8 I don't *feel* / *be* ill.
9 Do you *feel* / *be* sick?
10 A cold is *a common* / *an often* illness.
11 She *is* / *'s* got backache.
12 He's got *flu* / *a flu*.
13 I *don't feel* / *haven't got* a cough.
14 *Does he feel* / *Has he got* stomach ache?

2 **Complete the sentences.** 将句子填写完整。

▶ I had to stand up for ten hours. Now I've got <u>backache</u> .

1 She smokes a lot, and now she's got a bad ....
~ Yes, and she doesn't do any exercise. She's very ....
2 He's got a .... Look, it's 39 degrees.
3 What's the .... ? You look terrible.
~ I don't feel .... and I've got .... : I need to see a dentist.

4 I ate too much at lunch, and now I've got ....
5 My little boy had four ice creams and now he feels ....
6 I've got a temperature and a terrible headache. I think I've got ....
7 She's often ill. She's not in good ....
8 Flu is a horrible .... , and it's very .... in winter.
9 I don't think he's got flu. It's probably just a bad ....

B What should I do? 我应该做些什么？

I feel **weak**. I think I **caught** a **virus** at work.

tablets SYN **pills**

If you need **medical advice**, you **should** go to the **chemist's**.

Take some of those **tablets** to help you **rest** and sleep well.

You should **stay in bed** for **a couple of** days. You'll soon **get better**.

Have soup and hot drinks to **keep** you warm.

SPOTLIGHT *should + verb*

You use **should** when you tell people what you think is the best thing for them to do. **Should** is used for giving advice.

■ *I feel terrible.* ~ *You **should** go to bed.*
  ~ *You **shouldn't** go to work today.*

GLOSSARY

weak	If you don't eat for a few days, you feel **weak**. OPP **strong**	**advice**	words you say that help sb decide what to do
catch an illness *pt* **caught**	get an illness, e.g. *a cold*, *a virus*	**chemist's**	a shop where you get medicine ALSO **pharmacy**
virus	a living thing that is too small to see but can make you ill. Flu is caused by a **virus**.	**rest**	relax, sleep or do nothing
		stay in bed	go to bed and not get up
		a couple	two or a small number: *a couple of days/weeks*, etc.
medical	connected to doctors, hospitals and medicine	**get better**	feel less ill SYN **improve**
		keep (warm)	stay (warm)

---

3 Are the <u>underlined</u> sounds the same or different? Write *S* or *D*. Practise saying the words.
划线部分的发音是否相同? 相同填S，不同填D，并练习发音。

▶ ill<u>ne</u>ss / m<u>e</u>dical   D

1 v<u>i</u>rus / adv<u>i</u>ce   ....
2 sh<u>ou</u>ld / c<u>ou</u>ple   ....
3 w<u>ea</u>k / k<u>ee</u>p   ....
4 c<u>ou</u>ple / impr<u>o</u>ve   ....
5 cat<u>ch</u> / <u>ch</u>emist's   ....
6 adv<u>i</u>ce / c<u>au</u>ght   ....

4 True or false? Write *T* or *F*. 判断正误，正确填T，错误填F。

▶ If you stay in bed, you can rest.   T

1 If you get better, you feel weaker.   ....
2 A couple of weeks is about four weeks.   ....
3 You can get tablets at the chemist's.   ....
4 If you don't sleep for a week, you feel strong.   ....
5 A chemist's is the same as a pharmacy.   ....
6 A doctor can give you medical advice.   ....
7 You shouldn't keep warm if you have flu.   ....
8 If you stay in bed, you get up.   ....
9 You shouldn't go to work if you have a virus.   ....
10 If you start to improve, you get better.   ....

5 Complete the text. 将短文填写完整。

Last week, I got home from travelling around Europe and I felt really ill. I probably ▶ _caught_ a virus on the plane. I **(1)** _____ in bed for a **(2)** _____ of days, but I didn't **(3)** _____ . I was worried, so I phoned my doctor to get some medical **(4)** _____ . She gave me the name of some **(5)** _____ and told me I **(6)** _____ go to the **(7)** _____ and get some. She also said I had to stay in bed and **(8)** _____ as much as possible. I had hot drinks to **(9)** _____ me warm. I think I'm **(10)** _____ better now, but I still feel quite **(11)** _____ .

Send

---

32) Injuries 伤痛

I **cut** my finger and there was a lot of blood!

I fell over and now I've got a terrible **pain in my** leg.

My arm really **hurts**. I **hit** it **on** the table.

I **burnt** my hand when I picked up the pan.

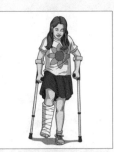

We were in a car **accident** and I **broke** my leg – my friend also had **serious injuries**. We've been put on **drugs** for the pain.

GLOSSARY

cut *pt* **cut**	(*see picture*) **cut** *n*	**accident**	sth bad that happens, but not because you planned it
pain (**in your** back, leg, etc.)	the feeling that you have in your body when you are hurt or ill	**break** *pt* **broke**	(*see picture*) **broken** *adj*: *a broken arm, leg,* etc.
hurt *pt* **hurt**	feel pain	**serious**	very bad
hit *pt* **hit**	touch sth very hard SYN **knock**	**injury**	A cut finger, a broken arm, etc. are **injuries** to your body.
burn *pt* **burnt/ burned**	(*see picture*)	**drug**	medicine you take to make you feel well again

SPOTLIGHT injuries

We say:
- *I **cut** my finger.* (NOT *I cut the finger.*)
- *She **hurt** her knee.* (NOT *She hurt the knee.*)
- *I **burnt** my arm.* (NOT *I burnt the arm.*)

1 **Complete the sentences.** 将句子填写完整。

▶ Did he _break_ his leg in the accident?

1 I hit my shoulder on the door, and it really ....

2 She fell off her bike and has a small .... on her knee.

3 Dad was driving at night in the rain and had a bad ....

4 I fell and hurt my ankle and the pain is terrible. I think it's probably ....

5 She's in hospital and they're giving her a lot of .... for the pain.

6 Joe was in a terrible accident and had a really bad .... to his back.

7 He went to the doctor because he had a terrible .... in his stomach.

8 He had to go to hospital because he .... his hand with a bread knife.

9 She had a car accident, but she's OK and it's not ....

2 **Correct one mistake in each sentence.** 改正句中的一处错误。

▶ He's got a ~~break~~ arm. _broken_

1 She had a pain on her arm. ....

2 He had a serious injure. ....

3 I hit my head at the door. ....

4 I knocked in my head on the wall. ....

5 I burnt the mouth on the hot soup. ....

6 She cutted her foot on the broken glass. ....

7 My arm is hurt a lot. ....

8 The doctor gave me some drogs for the pain. ....

9 I broken a bone in my ankle. ....

3 **Complete the questions.** 将问句填写完整。

1 Have you ever had a .... arm or leg?

2 Have you ever taken .... for pain?

3 Do you ever have bad .... in your back?

4 When did you last cut .... finger or hand?

5 Have you ever .... your hand when you were cooking?

ABOUT YOU

....
....
....
....
....

4 ABOUT YOU **Write your answers to Exercise 3, or ask another student.**
根据自身情况回答练习3中的问题，也可以向同学提问。

33) Geography 地理

ARE YOU GOOD
at geography?

rocks[1]

1 How many **islands** are there in the **world**?
1,000 / 2,000 / 3,000

2 Which is the largest **desert**?
the Gobi Desert / the Arabian Desert / the Sahara Desert

3 How old are the **rocks**[1] at the bottom of the Grand Canyon?
half a billion / a billion / two billion years old

4 Which is the **deepest** ocean?
the Atlantic Ocean / the Pacific Ocean / the Indian Ocean

5 Which **region** of the Earth has the largest area of **forest**?
Siberia in Russia / the Amazon in Brazil / Quebec in Canada

6 Is there **anywhere** on Earth where **humans** have never walked?
Yes, a few places. / No, **nowhere**.

GLOSSARY

island	a piece of land with water all around it
world	the Earth with all its countries and people
desert	a large, dry area of land, e.g. the Sahara
deep	Sth that is **deep** goes down a long way.
region	a part of a country or the world
forest	a large area of land covered by trees
human	a person **human** adj

SPOTLIGHT *somewhere, anywhere, nowhere, everywhere*

Somewhere means 'in or to a place', but you do not say or know where.
■ *They are **somewhere** in the Sahara Desert.*
Anywhere is used in questions and negative sentences.
■ *Is there a house **anywhere** on the island? I can't see a house **anywhere**.*
Nowhere means 'in no place'.
■ *There is **nowhere** to stay in this region.*
Everywhere means 'in every place'.
■ *There are rocks **everywhere** on the beach.*

1 **Is the pronunciation of the underlined letters the same or different? Write *S* or *D*.**
Practise saying the words. 划线部分的发音是否相同? 相同填S, 不同填D, 并练习发音。

▶ ro<u>ck</u> / every<u>wh</u>ere   D

1 d<u>e</u>sert / <u>a</u>nywhere   ....
2 <u>i</u>sland / <u>s</u>omewhere   ....

3 w<u>or</u>ld / f<u>or</u>est   ....
4 de<u>s</u>ert / re<u>g</u>ion   ....
5 de<u>s</u>ert / fore<u>s</u>t   ....

6 <u>s</u>omewhere / <u>n</u>owhere   ....
7 island / hum<u>a</u>n   ....
8 human / now<u>h</u>ere   ....

2 **Write *Yes* or *No*.** 填写Yes或No。

▶ Is the **world** bigger than the **sun**?   No

1 Is Sicily an **island**?   ....
2 Does it rain a lot in the **desert**?   ....
3 Are there trees in a **forest**?   ....
4 Is a **region** the same as a **country**?   ....

5 Are trees **human**?   ....
6 Do you find **rocks** in the sea?   ....
7 Is a river as **deep** as the middle of the sea?   ....
8 Is **everywhere** the same as **somewhere**?   ....

3 **Complete the sentences with *anywhere/somewhere/nowhere/everywhere*.**
用anywhere、somewhere、nowhere或everywhere填空。

▶ <u>Everywhere</u> in the world, there are good people and bad people.

1 Is there .... in the forest where we can buy a coffee?

2 Are there any seas in the desert?
~ No, ...

3 Are there any humans on the island?
~ Yes, they live .... in the north.

4 The rocks are .... under the water. I can see hundreds of them.

5 There was .... quiet in the forest; there were noises everywhere.

6 Ali is .... in the forest, but I'm not sure where exactly.

7 There isn't .... in the region where humans live.

8 The deepest river in the world is .... in Africa, I think.

4 ABOUT YOU **Write your answers to the quiz at the top of the page, or talk to another student.**
完成上文的知识测验, 也可以向同学提问。

34) The environment 环境

A Environmental problems 环境问题

Every year, we are **destroying** more and more forests.

15 billion trees are **disappearing** every year.

As the world population **increases**, the **land** is being used to **build** cities, grow food and make furniture.

This will be a **disaster** for **the environment** and will bring more **extreme** weather.

Governments around the world need to work together to stop this disaster.

GLOSSARY	
destroy	break sth completely so that you can't use it again or it is gone
disappear	If sth **disappears**, it goes away so that people can't see it.
increase	become bigger or more **increase** n
land	the part of the Earth that is not the sea
build pt/pp **built**	make sth by putting parts together: **build** houses
disaster	sth very bad that happens, and may hurt a lot of people
the environment	the air, water, land, animals, and plants around us **environmental** adj
extreme	very great or strong
government	**The government** is the group of people who control a country and decide what laws it will have.

1 **Underline** the stressed syllable. Practise saying the words. 在单词的重读音节下划线，并练习发音。

▶ to in<u>crease</u>

2 disaster

4 disappear

1 government

3 environment

5 destroy

2 Circle the correct word. 圈出正确答案。

▶ Extreme weather is a (disaster) / land for growing food.

1 The number of people in the world is *destroying / increasing*.

2 Forests around the world are *building / disappearing*.

3 The *government / environment* has to do something quickly.

4 We need to *build / destroy* more cities for people to live in.

5 Unfortunately, we are *increasing / destroying* more forests every year.

6 People need *land / the environment* to build houses on.

3 Cover the glossary and complete the sentences. 遮住单词表，将句子填写完整。

▶ If you make something like a house or factory, you _build_ it.

1 If something gets bigger, it _____ .

2 The people who are in control of a country are the _____ .

3 Something very bad that happens and hurts people is a _____ .

4 The place where people build homes or grow food is the _____ .

5 The water, air, land, animals and plants are all the _____ .

6 If something goes away and you can't see it any more, it _____ .

7 If you break something and can't use it again, you _____ it.

8 In the desert, you can have _____ heat and cold.

B Talking about the environment 谈论环境

coal

petrol

electricity

gas

Word	Example	Meaning
source	*The forests are a **source** of wood.*	a place, person or thing that you get sth from
energy	*Coal, petrol, gas and electricity are all sources of **energy**.*	**Energy** comes from *gas, electricity, coal, petrol*, etc. and is used to make machines work and to make heat and light.
develop	*Scientists are **developing** cleaner ways to use coal.*	think of or produce a new idea or product, etc.
pollution	*There is a lot of **pollution** in rivers and oceans.*	the act of making the air, rivers, etc. dirty and dangerous
cause	*What is the **cause** of the oceans getting warmer?*	the thing or person that makes sth happen **cause** *v*
recycle	*If we **recycle** more, we help the environment because we don't make so many products from new materials.*	do sth to paper, glass, etc. so that they can be used again

4 **Correct the spelling mistakes.** 改正拼写错误。

▶ polution   ..pollution..
1 recicle   ....
2 energie   ....

3 gaz   ....
4 cole   ....
5 petrole   ....

6 elektricity   ....
7 develope   ....
8 cuase   ....

5 **True or false? Write *T* or *F*.** 判断正误，正确填T，错误填F。

▶ You can't see electricity.   T
1 Pollution is a good thing.   ....
2 Smoking cigarettes causes illness.   ....
3 If you recycle something, you use it again.   ....
4 Coal is black and hard.   ....
5 You can see gas.   ....

6 You put petrol in cars.   ....
7 If you develop something, you destroy it.   ....
8 We use coal to get energy.   ....
9 Pollution is good for fish and animals.   ....
10 Humans are one cause of pollution.   ....

6 **Match 1–6 with a–g.** 配对题。

▶ We should recycle   e
1 Gas is a   ....
2 We need to develop   ....
3 We use electricity   ....
4 Pollution is the cause   ....
5 Coal is used to   ....
6 Petrol in cars causes   ....

a of serious illness.
b a lot of pollution.
c make a fire.
d new types of energy.
e more bottles. ✓
f source of energy.
g to keep our houses warm.

7 ABOUT YOU **Write your answers, or ask another student.** 根据自身情况回答问题，也可以向同学提问。

1 In your home, what type of energy do you use? ....
2 In your country, which is more expensive: gas, electricity or coal? ....
3 Is there a lot of air pollution where you live? ....
4 What causes pollution in your home town? ....
5 Do you recycle a lot? If so, what do you recycle? ....

Where are you from?

Where do you come from?

Continents and areas in the world	Country *I'm from / I come from …*	Nationality (and language) *I'm …*
Europe	the Czech Republic	Czech
	France	French
	Germany	German
	Greece	Greek
	Hungary	Hungarian
	Italy	Italian
	Poland	Polish
	Portugal	Portuguese
	Russia	Russian
	Spain	Spanish
	Switzerland	Swiss (German, French, Italian)
	Turkey	Turkish
Asia	India	Indian (Hindi)
	China	Chinese
	Japan	Japanese
	South Korea	Korean
	Thailand	Thai
North America	Canada	Canadian (English, French)
	Mexico	Mexican (Spanish)
	the United States (of America)	American (English)
South America ALSO **Latin America**	Argentina	Argentinian (Spanish)
	Brazil	Brazilian (Portuguese)
Africa and the Middle East	Egypt	Egyptian (Arabic)
	Saudi Arabia	Saudi (Arabic)
Australia	Australia	Australian (English)

The word for the language and the word for the nationality are usually the same word, e.g. *Czech*.
Jana is **Czech**. *Do you speak* **Czech?**
Sometimes they are different, e.g. people from **Mexico** are **Mexican**, but the language they speak is **Spanish**. Countries, nationalities and languages begin with capital letters: *Japan* (NOT *japan*).

GLOSSARY

country	e.g. *France, China, Brazil*
nationality	e.g. *American, Swiss, French*
language	e.g. *German, Japanese, Arabic*
continent	e.g. *Asia, Europe, Africa*
(Great) Britain	= *England, Wales* and *Scotland*
the United Kingdom / **the UK**	= *England, Wales, Scotland* and *Northern Ireland*

SPOTLIGHT people from a country

To talk about people from a country, we often add *s* to the nationality.

- *Italians, Brazilians, Thais, Greeks*

Some plural forms are irregular.

- *The British, the French, the English, the Spanish, the Chinese, the Japanese, the Swiss*

1 <u>Underline</u> the stressed syllable for the nationalities. Practise saying the words.
在单词的重读音节下划线，并练习发音。

▶ <u>Po</u>land / <u>Po</u>lish
1 <u>Chi</u>na / Chi<u>nese</u>
2 <u>Hun</u>gary / Hun<u>ga</u>rian
3 <u>Ger</u>many / <u>Ger</u>man
4 <u>I</u>taly / I<u>ta</u>lian

▶ <u>Por</u>tugal / Portu<u>guese</u>
5 Ja<u>pan</u> / Japa<u>nese</u>
6 <u>Ca</u>nada / Ca<u>na</u>dian
7 Ko<u>rea</u>/ Ko<u>rean</u>
8 <u>E</u>gypt / E<u>gyp</u>tian

2 True or false? Write *T* or *F*. 判断正误，正确填T，错误填F。

▶ Argentinians speak Spanish   T
1 Saudis speak Arabic. ....
2 Mexicans speak Spanish. ....
3 Thais speak Japanese. ....
4 Hungarians speak Hungarian. ....

5 Australians speak Australian. ....
6 Brazilians speak Portuguese. ....
7 Americans speak English. ....
8 The Swiss speak French, Spanish or German. ....

3 Complete the sentences. 将句子填写完整。

▶ Northern Ireland is in <u>the UK</u> .
1 Scotland is in Great ....
2 Hungary is in ....
3 Mexico is in .... America.
4 Africa is a ....
5 Argentina is in .... America.

6 Egypt is in ....
7 Saudi Arabia is in ....
8 India is in ....
9 Asia is a ....

4 Write the first letter of each word. Remember, countries and nationalities begin with CAPITAL LETTERS. Then write *C* (*country*) or *N* (*nationality*) next to each one.
填写单词的首字母，并标明该词表示国家（C）还是国籍（N）。注意：表示国家与国籍的单词首字母应大写。

▶ S audi   N
1 ___taly ___
2 ___ungary ___
3 ___exico ___
4 ___wiss ___
5 ___hina ___

▶ B ritain   C
6 ___zech ___
7 ___gypt ___
8 ___panish ___
9 ___razil ___
10 ___urkey ___

11 ___reek ___
12 ___rench ___
13 ___ermany ___
14 ___ussia ___
15 ___rgentinian ___
16 ___ortugal ___

5 Complete the text. 将短文填写完整。

My name's Magda, and I'm studying ▶ En glish .... in London at the moment. I'm from
(1) Po.................... , and I live with two students: Silvia, who's (2) Br.................... , and Irina who's
from (3) Ru.................... . Irina speaks (4) Ru.................... and (5) Po.................... . We go to a
language school in the centre. Our class has many nationalities: there are two (6) Ja.................... students,
a (7) Ko.................... man, three (8) Tu.................... women, a young (9) It.................... girl,
a (10) Ch.................... boy and four students from (11) Sp.................... . Our teacher is Dennis, and
he's (12) Au.................... .

6 Complete the boxes with nationalities ending in these letters. 根据表格中的后缀，填写相应国籍。

-ian		-ish	-an	-ese
▶Italian				
....	....	....	....	....
....	....	....	....	....
....	....	....	....	....
....	....	....	....	....

7 ABOUT YOU Do you know people from any of these countries? Put a (✓) next to the country if you do. If possible, tell another student. 你是否认识这些国家的人？如果认识，在国名后打钩（√）。如有条件，可告诉其他同学。

36 My country 我的国家

A Geography 地理情况

Brazil is **enormous**. The Atlantic **Ocean**[1] is in the **east**. The **coast**[2] is 3,000 **kilometres long**. In the **north, south** and **west,** there are **borders**[3] with ten different countries. The longest **river**[4] is the Amazon, and Pico da Neblina is about 3,000 metres **high**: it's the **highest mountain**[5] in Brazil. Many of the **major** cities are **on the coast**, but not the **capital,** Brasilia. The most **famous** city is Rio de Janeiro, which has Sugarloaf Mountain and Corcovada, plus some great **beaches**, like Copacabana. It is very **popular** with tourists.

GLOSSARY

enormous	very big SYN huge	capital	a city where a country has its government
3,000 kilometres (km) long	3,000 km from one end to the other	famous	If sth is famous, many people know about it: Rio is famous for Carnival.
3,000 metres (m) high	3,000 m from top to bottom (A mountain is high. NOT tall)	beach	an area of sand next to the sea, e.g. Copacabana
major	large and important	popular	If sth is popular, many people like it.

1 **Study the map of Brazil and the text, then complete the sentences.** 根据巴西地图及以上短文填空。

▶ Brasilia is the _capital_ .

1 The Amazon is the longest ....
2 Pico de Neblina is the highest ....
3 Porto Alegre is on the ....
4 Pico de Neblina is 3,000 m ....
5 The Amazon is nearly 7,000 km ....
6 There's a .... between Brazil and Argentina.

7 The Atlantic .... is on the .... coast.
8 Sao Paolo is a .... city.
9 The Amazon is in the .... of Brazil.
10 Brazil is an .... country.
11 Rio's beaches are .... with tourists.

2 **Complete the dialogues.** 将对话填写完整。

▶ Is Porto Alegre a small place? ~ No, it's a _major_ city.

1 Is Iguape .... ? ~ No, most people don't know about it.
2 China's enormous. ~ Yes, it's .... , isn't it?
3 Is California on the east coast? ~ No, it's on the .... coast.
4 Is New York in the south? ~ No, it's in the .... of the USA.
5 Is the Pacific a sea? ~ No, it's an ....
6 How .... is the Nile? ~ It's 6,853 kilometres ....
7 Is Copacabana the capital? ~ No, it's a famous ....
8 Do people go there a lot? ~ Yes, it's very ....

3 ABOUT YOUR COUNTRY **Write your answers, or ask another student.**
根据自身情况回答问题，也可以向同学提问。

1 What's the capital, and where is it? ....
2 What are some of the other major cities? ....
3 Does it have borders with any other countries? If so, what are they? ....
4 What's the longest river? ....
5 What's the highest mountain? ....
6 Which are the most famous places in your country? ....

B Facts about places 地点概况

I live in …	
a big **city**	**in** the **north-west of** Poland
a **town**	**on** the coast
a small **village**	**on** the River Dee

It has a **population** of **over** / **just under** a million/100,000.

Interesting **facts**:
It's famous for …
- its **ancient** buildings
- its **industry** (computers, cars, etc.)
- its **culture**
- its fantastic **climate**

north
north-west   north-east
west   east
south-west   south-east
south

GLOSSARY

city	a very large town, e.g. 2 million people
town	smaller than a city, e.g. 30,000 people
village	smaller than a *town*, and in the countryside
population	the number of people who live in a place
over (a thousand)	more than (a thousand) OPP **under**
just under	a little under ALSO **just over**
fact	a piece of true information
ancient	very old OPP **modern**
industry	the work of making things, e.g. *cars*, *electronics*
culture	activities like art, music, theatre, literature, etc.
climate	the normal weather in a place

4 **Is the pronunciation of the <u>underlined</u> letters the same or different? Write *S* or *D*. Practise the words.** 划线部分的发音是否相同? 相同填S, 不同填D, 并练习发音。

▶ <u>c</u>ulture / <u>i</u>ndustry   D

1	t<u>ow</u>n / s<u>ou</u>th	....	3	f<u>a</u>mous / <u>a</u>ncient	....	5	<u>c</u>ity / <u>c</u>ulture	....
2	<u>a</u>ncient / <u>c</u>limate	....	4	popula<u>ti</u>on / cul<u>t</u>ure	....	6	villa<u>g</u>e / <u>j</u>ust	....

5 **Write the phrases in the correct columns.** 将方框内的短语填入表格对应栏。

in the north-east ✓   on the coast   famous for its modern buildings   over two million
mobile phone industry   just under 50,000   on the River Duero   a small village   south-west of the capital
about 3,000   a large city   a warm climate   a small town   a city full of culture

SIZE	WHERE?	POPULATION	INTERESTING FACTS
....	in the north-east	....	....
....	....	....	....
....	....	....	....
....	....	....	....

6 **Complete the text about Turin.** 将短文填写完整。

Turin is a large ▶ <u>city</u> , 140 km south-west **(1)** _____ Milan, **(2)** _____ the north-west **(3)** _____ Italy. It is **(4)** _____ the River Po and three other rivers. It has a **(5)** _____ of about one million (in fact, it is 908,000). It is famous for one very important **(6)** _____ : car-making. It also has many **(7)** _____ buildings, including palaces and castles. The **(8)** _____ is cold in winter and hot in summer.

7   ABOUT YOU   **Write a similar text about your city/town/village.**
根据你住的地方(城市/城镇/村庄),仿写一段话。

....
....
....

A What's the weather like? 天气怎么样?

What's the weather like?

It's **sunny**. The **sun's shining**. It's a **bright** day.

It's **cloudy**. There are **a lot of** grey **clouds**.

It's **raining**. The roads are **wet**. There's a lot of **rain**.

It's **windy**. The **wind** is **blowing**. *pt* **blew**

There's **snow** on the mountains and **ice** on the river. **icy** *adj*

SPOTLIGHT *a lot (of)* and *a bit (of)*

a lot of / **a bit of** + noun	verb + **a lot** / **a bit**	**a bit** + adjective
■ *We had **a lot of** rain.*	■ *It snowed **a lot**.*	■ *It's **a bit** cold today.*
■ *There's **a bit of** snow.*	■ *It's raining **a bit**.*	■ *It was **a bit** windy.*

We don't usually use **a bit** with positive adjectives: NOT *a bit sunny/good*.

① **Match 1–9 with a–j.** 配对题。

▶ It's ___d___   a   clouds in the sky today.
1 It ....   b   it bright and sunny outside?
2 The wind   c   isn't raining.
3 It isn't ....   d   cold this morning. ✓
4 The sun ....   e   of snow on the roads.
5 Is ....   f   rain a lot here.
6 There's a bit ....   g   the weather like?
7 There are lots of ....   h   very windy.
8 It doesn't   i   blew my hat off.
9 What's ....   j   is shining.

② **Rewrite the sentences keeping the same meaning.** 改写句子, 保持句意不变。

▶ There was a lot of rain. It rained _a lot_.
1 It isn't wet outside. It isn't ....
2 Is the sun shining? Is it .... ?
3 We often have snow. It often ....
4 She doesn't like wind. She doesn't like .... weather.
5 Is it hot or cold today? What's the .... like?
6 There are a few clouds. It's a bit ....
7 Is there any ice on the roads? Is it .... ?
8 It's windy today. The wind is .... today.

③ **Write *a lot, a lot of, a bit* or *a bit of*.** 用a lot、a lot of、a bit或a bit of填空。

▶ We had _a lot of_ rain this morning, but it's good for the garden.
1 It's .... wet today.
2 There was .... wind this morning. I couldn't use my umbrella.
3 It snows .... in the mountains – sometimes over twenty centimetres a day.
4 There's .... rain, but not much. You don't need your umbrella.
5 It snowed .... last night – only two centimetres.
6 It rained .... yesterday – I couldn't go out.
7 It's not a bad day. It's .... cloudy but with some sun.
8 Don't go out in your car. There's .... ice on the roads.

B Weather in the seasons 四季天气

storm

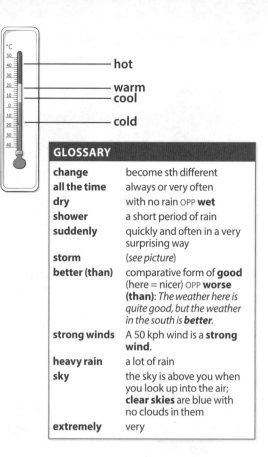

— hot
— warm
— cool
— cold

GLOSSARY

change	become sth different
all the time	always or very often
dry	with no rain OPP **wet**
shower	a short period of rain
suddenly	quickly and often in a very surprising way
storm	(*see picture*)
better (than)	comparative form of **good** (here = nicer) OPP **worse (than)**: *The weather here is quite good, but the weather in the south is better.*
strong winds	A 50 kph wind is a **strong wind**.
heavy rain	a lot of rain
sky	the sky is above you when you look up into the air; **clear skies** are blue with no clouds in them
extremely	very

In my country, the weather in spring **changes all the time**. It can be **dry** and **warm**, but we often have **showers**. It can get very hot in the cities in summer and then **suddenly** we have a **storm**. It's a lot **better** on the coast, where it's cooler. In autumn, we have **strong winds** and **heavy rain**. Winter brings clear **skies** and sunny days, but it's **extremely** cold.

4 **Circle the correct word.** 圈出正确答案。

▶ Warm weather is very (nice) / *uncomfortable*.

1 It was very sunny between the *showers / storm*.
2 *Suddenly / Extremely*, it started raining.
3 The sky is very *warm / clear* this morning.

4 Showers usually last a few *hours / minutes*.
5 We had some very *big / strong* winds last night.
6 The weather *changes / rains* all the time.

5 **Rewrite the sentences using the words on the right and the word IN CAPITALS.** 用所给单词改写句子。

▶	It's wet outside.	RAIN	It's _raining outside._	.
1	It rained a lot last night.	HEAVY	There was	.
2	The weather here isn't as good as Spain.	BETTER	The weather in Spain	.
3	There was a bit of rain in the afternoon.	SHOWER	There	.
4	The weather's different every day.	CHANGE	The weather	.
5	It isn't wet today.	DRY	It	.
6	We had heavy rain and strong winds.	STORM	We had	.
7	There are no clouds in the sky.	CLEAR	There are	.
8	There's snow every day in winter.	ALL THE TIME	It	.

6 ABOUT YOUR COUNTRY **Does your country have …** 根据自身情况回答问题：你的国家有没有……

▶ storms in summer? _We often have storms in summer._
1 a lot of showers in spring?
2 much snow?
3 good weather in summer?
4 dry winters?
5 heavy rain in spring?
6 strong winds?

lion

tiger

elephant

bear

monkey

snake

whale

bird

horse

cow

sheep (*pl* sheep)

pig

dog

cat

mouse (*pl* mice)

spider

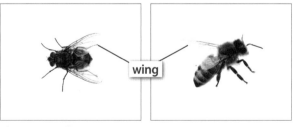
wing

fly

bee

SPOTLIGHT *both*

Both means 'each of two'.
- *Dogs and cats are **both** common in England.* (= Dogs are common and cats are also common in England.)
- *Do lions swim? Yes, and tigers. They can **both** swim.*
- *Do you like cows and sheep? Yes, I like **both of them**.*

GLOSSARY

animal	any living thing that can move or feel. **Animal** is sometimes used to talk only about *cats, dogs, cows,* etc. and not about *people, birds, fish* or *insects.*
wild animal	A **wild animal** lives in nature, not with people, e.g. *a lion* or *an elephant.*
pet	an animal or bird that lives with people in their home. *Dogs* and *cats* are common **pets** in Britain.
insect	a small animal with six legs and usually wings, e.g. *a bee, a fly*
zoo	(sounds like *you*) a place, often in or near a town, where people can go and look at wild animals
farm	land and buildings where people keep animals and grow things. The person who does this is a **farmer**. *Pigs* and *cows* are **farm** animals.

1 **Write the names of these animals and insects in order from big to small.** 将动物和昆虫按体型大小排序。

bear   cat   fly   whale ✓   monkey   sheep   elephant   lion   mouse

big _whale_ .... small

2 **Put the animals in the correct column.** 将方框内的动物填入表格对应栏。

sheep ✓   elephant   tiger   cow   cat   fly   dog   horse   pig   bee   lion   bear

PETS	FARM ANIMALS	INSECTS	WILD ANIMALS
....	► sheep	....	....
....	....	....	....
....	....	....	....
....	....	....	....

3 **Think about the pronunciation of the underlined letters, then answer the questions. Practise saying the words.** 根据单词划线部分的发音回答问题，并练习发音。

► Is c<u>ow</u> the same as n<u>ow</u> or kn<u>ow</u>? _now_

1 Is b<u>o</u>th the same as m<u>o</u>st or d<u>o</u>g? ....

2 Is t<u>i</u>ger the same as s<u>i</u>t or l<u>i</u>on? ....

3 Is sn<u>a</u>ke the same as b<u>a</u>ck or wh<u>a</u>le? ....

4 Is m<u>o</u>nkey the same as s<u>o</u>n or g<u>o</u>ne? ....

5 Is b<u>ear</u> the same as h<u>air</u> or h<u>ear</u>? ....

6 Is <u>e</u>lephant the same as c<u>a</u>t or t<u>i</u>ger? ....

7 Is sp<u>i</u>der the same as w<u>i</u>ld or m<u>i</u>ss? ....

4 **Complete each sentence with one word.** 将句子填写完整，每空格只填一词。

► Lions and tigers can both _swim_ .

1 Dogs usually live with ....

2 People often sit on ....

3 Whales live in the ....

4 Birds often eat ....

5 Birds and bees can both ....

6 Cats sometimes catch and eat ....

7 Pigs live on ....

8 People often see wild animals in a ....

9 Flies have two ....

5 **Complete the sentences.** 将句子填写完整。

► Elephants are one of the biggest _animals_ in the world.

1 Are dogs and cats common .... in your country?

2 My uncle is a .... He has a .... with over 500 sheep and cows.

3 You can see lots of .... animals in parts of Africa.

4 Did you see a lion or tiger at the zoo? Yes, I saw .... of them.

5 A spider is not an .... because it has eight legs.

6 I've seen wild animals in the .... near where I live.

7 The bird had a problem with one of its .... and it couldn't fly.

8 I often go to the zoo with my brother: we .... like wild animals.

6 **Which animal(s) or insect(s) has/have:** 哪种动物或昆虫有：

► eight legs? _spider_

1 four legs? ....

2 two legs? ....

3 six legs? ....

4 no legs? ....

7 ABOUT YOU AND YOUR COUNTRY **Write your answers, or ask another student.**

根据自身情况回答问题，也可以向同学提问。

1 Do you have any pets? If so, what? ....

2 Have you ever seen wild animals (not on TV)? If so, where? ....

3 Are you afraid of any animals or insects? ....

4 What animals are usually used as farm animals in your country? ....

5 Do people often go to zoos in your country? What do you think about zoos? ....

6 Is there an animal or insect on the opposite page that you especially like or dislike? ....

Here are some common irregular verbs in English, which follow similar patterns. They are all taught in different parts of the book, so use the Word List to help you if necessary. A more complete list is on page 198.

fight

ring

build

hold

hurt

ride

pt/pp -a/-u	pt/pp – one vowel change	pt/pp -o/-en
sing/sang/sung	get/got/got	write/wrote/written
swim/swam/swum	forget/forgot/forgotten	drive/drove/driven
ring/rang/rung	sit/sat/sat	ride/rode/ridden
drink/drank/drunk	come/came/come	break/broke/broken
begin/began/begun	hold/held/held	speak/spoke/spoken
run/ran/run	fall/fell/fallen	wake (up)/woke/woken
	win/won/won	

pt/pp -ought/-ought	pt/pp -t	pt/pp – no change
bring/brought/brought	lend/lent/lent	put/put/put
think/thought/thought	send/sent/sent	cut/cut/cut
buy/bought/bought	spend/spent/spent	hurt/hurt/hurt
fight/fought/fought	build/built/built	cost/cost/cost
pt/pp -aught/-aught	spell/spelt/spelt ALSO spelled	shut/shut/shut
catch/caught/caught	lose/lost/lost	let/let/let
teach/taught/taught	burn/burnt/burnt ALSO burned	hit/hit/hit

SPOTLIGHT *ever*

We often use **ever** (= any time before now) in questions in the present perfect (*has/have* + past participle).

- *Have you **ever** bought a car?* ~ *No, I haven't.* OR *No, I've never bought one.*
- *Has your sister **ever** written a blog?* ~ *Yes, she has.* (NOT *Yes, she ever has.*)

1 Cover the left-hand page, then write the past tense of the verbs. 遮住左页，写出动词的过去式。

- sit   sat
1 teach   ....
2 put   ....
3 let   ....
4 bring   ....

5 buy   ....
6 sing   ....
7 spend   ....
8 drive   ....
9 speak   ....

10 hold   ....
11 spell   ....
12 ring   ....
13 sit   ....
14 burn   ....

2 For each question, which two verbs ... 下列问题中，哪两个动词……

- don't change in the past tense?   (hurt) / fight / (shut)
1 change *i* to *a* in the past tense?   swim / begin / hit
2 change *i* to *o* in the past tense?   write / sit / drive
3 change to *-ought* in the past tense?   buy / catch / think
4 change from *d* to *t* in the past tense?   hold / send / build
5 don't change in the past tense?   put / forget / cut
6 have one vowel change in the past tense?   get / fall / cost

3 Answer the questions using the same verb in the past tense. 用动词的过去式回答问题。

- What did Olivia sing?   ~ She sang a pop song   .
1 How far did you swim?   ~ I ....
2 What did the teacher forget?   ~ He ....
3 What did Ava send?   ~ She ....
4 What did Mason lend you?   ~ He ....
5 Where did your sister put the books? ~ She ....
6 Where did Liam fall?   ~ He ....
7 How much money did Isabella lose?   ~ She ....
8 How far did the children run?   ~ They ....

4 Complete the sentences with verbs in the past tense from page 82. 用P82所列动词的过去式填空。

- My sister taught   in a school for five years.
1 I .... across the river.
2 My dad .... a fish in the lake last week.
3 I .... the horse, and Ben .... his bike.
4 When Esther .... her finger, she said it really ....
5 My grandmother .... a car until she was 90.
6 I .... an email to my aunt last week to thank her for my birthday present.

7 This book only .... £3.99.
8 The children .... home at 10.00 and went to bed.
9 Darius .... me early this morning to tell me the good news.
10 I went shopping and .... a pair of shoes.
11 Martina .... her new Italian course yesterday and really enjoyed it.
12 I .... at 6 a.m. because I had to get up early.

5 ABOUT YOU Complete the questions with the past participle of verbs from page 82.
Then answer the questions about you. 用P82所列动词的过去分词填空，并根据自身情况回答问题。

Have you ever ...

- got   ill from eating eggs?   No, I haven't.
1 .... a very fast car?   ....
2 .... a horse?   ....
3 .... your own hair?   ....
4 .... a large amount of money?   ....
5 .... to a famous person? What did you say? ....
6 .... somebody because you were very angry? ....
7 .... a bone in your body?   ....
8 .... from a tree?   ....

40) *have got* and *have* have got与have

A *have got* and *have* have got与have

My brother —[**has got** / **has**] a small car.

His wife —[**has got** / **has**] a large motorbike.

They —[**'ve got** / **have**] two daughters.

The girls —[**haven't got** / **don't have**] boyfriends yet.

> **SPOTLIGHT** *have got* and *have*
>
> You can use **have got** or **have** to talk about something that is yours (= belongs to you). You can also use **have (got)** to describe illness, relationships and appearance. **Have got** is the usual form in spoken British English.
>
> - **Have** you **got** a car? ~ Yes, I **have**. (NOT ~~Yes, I have got.~~)
>   OR
> - *Do* you **have** a car? ~ Yes, I **do**.

1 **Change *have* to the correct form of *have got* in each sentence.** 将各句的have改为have got的正确形式。

▶ I have an old car. — I've got an old car.
1 She has blue eyes. ....
2 They have a small dog. ....
3 I don't have a smartphone. ....
4 He doesn't have any money. ....
5 Do you have any sisters? ....
6 Does she have a flat in town? ....
7 They don't have a shop now. ....
8 Do they have a big office? ....

2 **Correct the mistakes.** 改错题。

▶ He have a car. — He's got a car. OR He has a car.
1 She got any children? ....
2 They has got a lovely garden. ....
3 Have she got long hair? ....
4 My sister no have a boyfriend. ....
5 Have you a computer? ....
6 We don't got any friends here. ....

3 **Complete the questions.** 将问题填写完整。   ABOUT YOU

▶ Have .... you got a car? If so, what kind?   Yes, I have. It's a Ford.
1 Have you .... a bike? If so, when do you use it?   ....
2 .... you have a computer? If so, what kind?   ....
3 .... your parents got a dog? If so, what's its name?   ....
4 .... your parents have a house in the country? If so, where? ....
5 .... you got an English dictionary? If so, what's it called? ....
6 .... you have any English-speaking friends? If so, who are they? ....

4 **ABOUT YOU** **Write your answers to Exercise 3, or ask another student.**
根据自身情况回答练习3中的问题，也可以向同学提问。

B *have* + noun have+名词

We use **have** + *noun* (NOT ~~have got~~) in a number of common expressions in English.

have a wash/shower/bath (NOT ~~have got a wash~~, etc.)		*I **had a** quick **shower** before I left.*
have breakfast/lunch/dinner (NOT ~~the breakfast~~, etc.)		*We **had lunch** in a pizzeria.*
have a drink/sth to eat		*I **had a drink** with Leo last night.* *Let's **have something to eat.***
have a swim/walk/run (activities you do because you enjoy them)		*I didn't **have a run** this morning.* *We **had a** nice **walk** yesterday.*
have a (great/nice/terrible) time/day		*We **had a great time** in Kyoto.*
have a (good/nice) weekend/holiday/journey		***Have a nice weekend!*** ***Have a good journey.***
have a look (at sth)	look at sth to see it closely or read it	*Can I **have a look at** your camera?*
have a break	stop working for a short period and relax	*OK, let's **have a break** for 10 minutes.*
have a rest	relax and do nothing	*I **had a rest** in the afternoon.*

5 **Cover the table above. Make four more groups of phrases with *have* from the words below.**
遮住以上表格，将方框内可与have组成词组的单词分类。

swim	breakfast	holiday	bath	journey	rest ✓	lunch
shower	weekend	break ✓	dinner	walk	wash	run

GROUP 1	GROUP 2	GROUP 3	GROUP 4	GROUP 5
rest				
break				

6 **Complete the email.** 将电子邮件填写完整。

Dear Carla,

We're having a great ▶ _time_ here in Parati. The hotel's nice, and we've got a lovely view of an old church from our room. Yesterday we had a **(1)** _____ round the town and bought a few things. In the evening, we had a **(2)** _____ in the bar you recommended. Afterwards, we had **(3)** _____ in a very nice fish restaurant. We're going to spend this morning on the beach so I can have a **(4)** _____ in the sea, then maybe do some more shopping this afternoon. I think we'll have a **(5)** _____ after that. I hope you're enjoying yourself in Rio, and have a good **(6)** _____ back to Buenos Aires on Saturday. See you in two weeks' time.

Love, Nicky

Send

7 **Complete the sentences.** 将句子填写完整。

▶ I got up late and didn't have any _breakfast_ .
1 Would you like to have something to _____ ? We've got lots of food.
2 We often have a _____ after lunch – along the river or in the park.
3 We have a twenty-minute _____ between the lessons.
4 I want to have a _____ round town this afternoon, maybe buy a few things.
5 Did you have a good _____ in London yesterday?
6 Have a nice _____ . See you on Monday.
7 They had a fantastic _____ in Mallorca. They were there for three weeks.
8 I always have a shower in the summer, but in winter I prefer to have a _____ .

A *make* and *do*: general differences make和do的一般区别

Here are two common meanings of **make**:

1 produce or create sth:	
*The factory **makes** cars.* *I'm **making** a cake for Tom's birthday.* *This shirt is **made of** cotton.*	

2 produce a change in sb or sth:	
*Chocolate **makes you** fat.* *Romantic films sometimes **make me** cry.* *The book **made them** laugh.*	

Here are two common meanings of **do** as an ordinary verb (not an auxiliary verb):

1 used about activities:	
*What are you **doing** this evening?* *I didn't **do** much at the weekend.*	

2 have a job, or study sth:	
*What do you **do**?* *~ I'm a doctor.* *I want to **do** medicine at university.*	

1 Put the words in the correct order to make sentences. 连词成句。

▶ did / what / do / yesterday / you <u>What did you do yesterday</u> ?
1 does / his / wife / do / what _____ ?
2 makes / his / software / company / programs _____ .
3 make / does / you / why / English / tired _____ ?
4 school / Spanish / to / I / next / want / year / do / at _____ .
5 is / jumper / of / made / this / wool _____ ?
6 you / night / did / do / what / last _____ ?

2 Complete the sentences with the correct form of *do* or *make*. 用do或make的正确形式填空。

▶ The long walk <u>made</u> the children tired.
1 These shoes are _____ of leather.
2 She doesn't work at the bank any more. ~ Oh. What does she _____ now?
3 Matthew wants to _____ law when he goes to university.
4 Flying _____ me nervous.
5 I've just _____ sandwiches for lunch. Is that OK?
6 Cheese is _____ from milk.
7 What are you going to _____ next year?
8 My nephew wants to _____ a film about his school.

3 ABOUT YOU Write your answers, or ask another student. 根据自身情况回答问题，也可以向同学提问。

1 What kinds of things are made in your country? _____
2 Do you ever make things for other people, e.g. clothes? _____
3 Do films or music ever make you cry? _____
4 What subjects did you do at school? (or are you doing at school?) _____
5 What are you doing this evening? _____
6 What did you do last weekend? _____

4 Look at the example sentences at the top of the page. How would you translate *make* and *do* in each sentence? If possible, talk to somebody who speaks your own language.
上文例句中的make和do如何翻译？如有条件，可以和同学用母语交流讨论。

B *Do or make?* do还是make?

Both **do** and **make** are used with a number of nouns with the meaning 'perform an action'.

do + action:	make + action:
your best	the bed
exercise [U] (in the gym)	a decision
exercises (in class)	a mistake
the housework [U]	money
your homework [U]	a noise
the shopping	sense

do exercise

do the housework

GLOSSARY	
do your best	do all that you can: *I may not finish the work today, but I'll **do my best**.*
make a decision	choose what you want to do
make money	get money, often from work: *She **made** a lot of **money** when she worked in America.*
make a noise	make a sound, especially one that is loud and not nice
make sense	be possible to understand: *This sentence doesn't **make sense**.*

do your homework

5 <u>Underline</u> **the correct verb.** 在正确答案下划线。

▶ I always try to <u>*do*</u> / *make* my best.

1 Have you ***done*** / ***made*** the shopping?

2 I ***make*** / ***do*** most of the housework at the weekend.

3 Don't become a teacher if you want to ***do*** / ***make*** a lot of money.

4 The children ***did*** / ***made*** a lot of noise last night.

5 We ***did*** / ***made*** a couple of grammar exercises in class.

6 Mia ***did*** / ***made*** a terrible mistake in her essay.

7 This exercise doesn't ***do*** / ***make*** sense.

8 I have to ***do*** / ***make*** a decision soon about the flat.

6 Match 1–5 with a–f. 配对题。

▶ do exercise   d

1 make sense   ....

2 make a mistake   ....

3 do the shopping   ....

4 do your best   ....

5 make a decision   ....

a try as much as you can

b buy food

c choose what you want to do

d move your body to keep it strong ✓

e be possible to understand

f do something wrong

7 ABOUT YOU **Complete the questions.** 将问题填写完整。

▶ Do you _do_ many written exercises in class?   No, we usually do written exercises for homework.

1 Do you .... your own bed?

2 Do you often .... mistakes with English?

3 Do your neighbours often .... a lot of noise?

4 Do you .... much housework?

5 Do you often .... the shopping?

6 Is it important for you to .... a lot of money?

7 Do you always try to .... your best?

8 ABOUT YOU **Write answers to the questions in Exercise 7, or ask another student. If possible, also explain why / why not in your answers.**
根据自身情况回答练习7中的问题，也可以向同学提问。如有条件，对答案稍作解释。

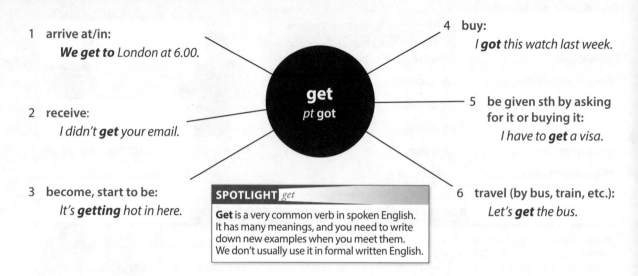

1 **arrive at/in:**
We get to London at 6.00.

2 **receive:**
I didn't get your email.

3 **become, start to be:**
It's getting hot in here.

get
pt **got**

4 **buy:**
I got this watch last week.

5 **be given sth by asking for it or buying it:**
I have to get a visa.

6 **travel (by bus, train, etc.):**
Let's get the bus.

SPOTLIGHT *get*

Get is a very common verb in spoken English. It has many meanings, and you need to write down new examples when you meet them. We don't usually use it in formal written English.

1 **In column 2, rewrite each sentence with the correct form of *get*.** 用get的正确形式改写左栏的句子，填入中栏。

▶	I must buy some new clothes.	I must get some new clothes.	buy
1	Did you receive my message?		
2	He becomes angry if you're late.		
3	We arrived home late last night.		
4	It's becoming cold.		
5	I received three letters today.		
6	Where did you buy that bag?		
7	He needs to be given a job.		
8	Do you want to travel by train?		

2 **Cover sentences 1–8 in Exercise 1. Look at the sentences you wrote. What does *get* mean in each one? Write your answer in column 3.** 遮住练习1表格左栏各句，将中栏内get的含义填入右栏。

▶   I must get some new clothes.   buy

3 **Complete the sentences in a logical way using *get*.** 用get填空，使句意通顺。

▶ There weren't any buses, so we ..got the train.. .
1 Could you close the window? It's ....
2 What time did you .... ?
3 Those shoes are lovely. Where did you .... ?
4 Do you want to walk or .... ?
5 I need a map of the town. Where can I .... ?

6 She sent me an email but I didn't ....
7 I must go now, it's ....
8 I have to be at the cinema in ten minutes, so I'm going to ....
9 Tom worked hard for his maths and he ....
10 How many text messages do you .... ?

4 **ABOUT YOU** **Write your answers, or ask another student.** 根据自身情况回答问题，也可以向同学提问。

▶ What time do you get home from work/college/school? *I get home from school at 5 o'clock each day.*
1 How often do you get the bus? ....
2 How cold does it get in your country? ....
3 How many texts do you get every day? ....
4 What was the last new item of clothing you got? ....
5 Where can you get information about your town/city? ....

1 know or notice sth with your eyes:

*Can you **see** that church over there?*

2 find out about sth by looking, asking, etc:

*I'll **see** what time the train leaves.*

3 visit or spend time with sb:

*I went to **see** my parents at the weekend.*

see
pt saw *pp* seen

4 watch a film / TV programme / game:

*I **saw** a film at the cinema.*

5 understand sth:

*Do you **see** what I mean?*

SPOTLIGHT *see* and *watch*

When you **see** something, you know about it with your eyes.
■ *Can you **see** that bird in the tree?* (NOT ~~watch~~)
When you **watch** something, you look at it for a long time.
■ *We **watched** a spider for about 15 minutes.* (NOT ~~saw~~)
You can **see** or **watch** a film, TV programme or game.
■ *I **saw**/**watched** a football match in the park yesterday.*

1 Write down the meaning (1–5) of *see* in each of the sentences. 根据上文，用1-5表示下列各句see的含义。

▶ I saw them at the show last night. ....1....
1 I can't see the road from here. ....
2 Martin wants to see if he can buy tickets for the concert. ....
3 I want to see the new Spielberg film. ....
4 We're going to see friends this evening. ....
5 I may go, but it depends on the weather. ~ OK. I see. ....
6 It was so dark I couldn't see. ....
7 Did you see the news on TV? ....
8 I can't see why he wants to leave his job. ....

2 Underline the correct verb. Be careful: both verbs are correct in two of the sentences.
在正确答案下划线，注意：其中两句有两个正确答案。

▶ Come and *see* / *watch* us for coffee next week.
1 I looked for Will, but I couldn't *see* / *watch* him.
2 The police know where the criminal lives, so they're going to *see* / *watch* his house.
3 Did you *see* / *watch* that new detective series on TV?
4 I must *see* / *watch* how much the tickets cost.
5 I have to *see* / *watch* the children carefully when they're in the street.
6 When are you going to *see* / *watch* the doctor?
7 I *saw* / *watched* in the paper that they're building a new theatre.
8 We *saw* / *watched* a great basketball game on Saturday.

3 Complete the questions with the correct form of *see* or *watch* or either. 用see或watch的正确形式填空，注意：两者可能通用。

ABOUT YOU

▶ Can you ..see.. any trees from where you live?
Yes, I can see lots. We're opposite a park.
1 Can you .... very well without glasses? Why? / Why not?
2 Do you ever .... your father when he's working?
3 Are there some programmes on TV that you always .... ? If so, what?
4 What was the last TV programme you .... ?
5 How often do you .... your best friend?
6 How often do you .... your parents?
7 Can you .... why *get* is a difficult verb for students learning English?

4 ABOUT YOU Write answers to the questions in Exercise 3, or ask another student.
根据自身情况回答练习3中的问题，也可以向同学提问。

- Many verbs in English can be used as nouns, with the same form and a similar meaning.

  *Did you **promise** to help him?*   *Did you **make** a promise to help him?*

- When the verbs are used as nouns, you need to learn which verb to use with the noun.

  *She **surprised** me.*   *She **gave** me a surprise.*

  *Could I **look** at your paper?*   *Could I **have a look** at your paper?*

  *What **caused** the accident?*   *What **was the cause** of the accident?*

The boys were **fighting**.
The boys were **having a fight**.

I **called** Jim.
I **gave** Jim **a call**.

I **slept** well.
I **had a** good **sleep**.

Does it **smell nice**?
Does it **have a nice smell**?

I **dream** about Ava.
I **have dreams** about Ava.

She **smiled at** me.
She **gave** me **a smile**.

Here are some more examples.

*Did you **reply**?*	*Did you **write/send** Jana **a reply**?*
*Did they **comment on** your work?*	*Did they **make a comment on** your work?*
*He can't **control** that dog.*	*He **has no control over** that dog.*
*I **emailed** you yesterday.*	*I **sent** you **an email** yesterday.*
*We often **chat**.*	*We often **have a chat**.*
*How much did the hotel **cost**?*	*What **was the cost** of the hotel?*
*Can you **copy** this?*	*Can you **make a copy** of this?*

GLOSSARY

promise	say you will certainly do or not do sth **promise** n	**control**	make sb/sth do what you want **control** n
surprise	do sth that sb does not think you are going to do **surprise** n	**chat (to sb)**	talk in a friendly informal way to sb **chat** n
cause	be the reason why sth happens **cause** n	**copy**	write, draw or make sth exactly the same as sth else: *We **copied** a list of words into our notebooks.* **copy** n
comment (on sth)	say or write what you think about sth **comment** n		

1 **Circle the sound that is different. Practise saying the words.**
圈出划线部分发音与其他两个不同的单词发音，并练习发音。

▶ prom(ise)   surpr<u>i</u>se   c<u>au</u>se   **3** <u>o</u>ver   c<u>o</u>mment   c<u>o</u>st
1 c<u>o</u>mment   c<u>o</u>ntrol   prom<u>i</u>se   **4** surpr<u>i</u>se   sm<u>e</u>ll   c<u>au</u>se
2 prom<u>i</u>se   surpr<u>i</u>se   wr<u>i</u>te   **5** c<u>o</u>py   surpr<u>i</u>se   c<u>o</u>ntrol

2 **Do you need your hands and/or your mouth? Write *H*, or *M*, or *H and M*.**
做以下事情需要动手（H）还是动口（M）？或者都要？

▶ make a promise ..... M .....   ▶ send an email ..... H .....
1 make a copy ....   **4** give someone a call ....
2 give someone a smile .... **5** send a reply ....
3 have a fight ....   **6** have a chat ....

3 **Complete the sentences using the correct form of the verbs in the box.** 用方框内动词的正确形式填空。

control	dream	fight	sleep	surprise	cost
cause	promise	smell	comment ✓	chat	

▶ The boss __commented__ on your work – he was very pleased with it.
1 The hotel was expensive, but I don't know exactly how much it ....
2 The police caught the young men – they were .... outside a night club.
3 It's a very big dog, and I'm afraid my wife can't .... it.
4 I can't come tomorrow because I .... to take my children to the zoo.
5 I stopped to .... with a couple of friends. We talked about the game last Saturday.
6 Molly expected me at 8.00, so I arrived at 7.30 to .... her.
7 I could .... something wonderful coming from the kitchen: roast beef.
8 I was .... about our holiday when I woke up.
9 There was something wrong with the computer, but I don't know what .... the problem.
10 I went to bed early but I couldn't ....

4 **Rewrite the sentences using the verb as a noun.** 改写句子，将相关动词转换为名词。

▶ She emailed me.   She _sent me an email_ .
1 I dreamt about you.   I ....
2 Did he comment on the report? Did he .... ?
3 She promised to help me.   She ....
4 Does this soap smell nice?   Does this soap .... ?
5 They surprised him.   They ....
6 I must reply to Jilly's letter. I must ....
7 Did you call Mo?   Did you .... ?
8 I looked at her newspaper.   I ....
9 Could you copy this?   Could you .... ?
10 He smiled at me this morning   He ....

5 ABOUT YOU **Write down something that ...** 根据实际情况写下答案。
▶ you promised to do _I promised to help my father at the weekend._
  you sometimes dream about ....

  costs a lot of money in your country ....

  has a strong smell ....

  is the main cause of problems in your country ....

  surprises you about people in your country ....

  the world cannot control ....

45) Shopping for food 采购食物

A Food 食物

milk [U]

bread [U]

butter [U]

a piece of cheese

cheese [U]

eggs

sugar [U]

a piece of cake
cake [U]

a cake

jam [U]

biscuits

olives

olive oil [U]

rice [U]

pasta [U]

SPOTLIGHT uncountable nouns

The nouns with a [U] are usually uncountable.

- **butter** OR **some butter**   (NOT ~~a butter/butters~~)
- *This bread* **is** *nice.*   (NOT ~~These breads are nice.~~)

We can use phrases to count or talk about an amount of an uncountable noun.

- *a piece of* cheese   • *two bars of* chocolate

Some nouns can be countable or uncountable. Uncountable is for the food, etc. generally. Countable is for a small unit of it.

- *I like* **chocolate**. [U]   • *Would you like* **a chocolate**? [C]

chocolate [U]
a bar of chocolate

a box of chocolates

---

1 Tick (✓) the answers that are right, and correct the answers that are wrong. Practise saying the words.
在正确的表述后打钩 (√)，改正错误的表述，并练习发音。

▶ a butter   butter / some butter
1 biscuits   ....
2 a piece of cheese ....
3 two butters   ....
4 a piece of chocolate ....
5 a bread   ....

6 some sugar   ....
7 an olive oil   ....
8 rices   ....
9 a jam   ....
10 olives   ....
11 a cheese   ....

2 Circle the correct word. 圈出正确答案。

▶ There (is) / are sugar in jam.
1 You make *cheese / pasta* with eggs.
2 You can put *cheese / cake* on bread.
3 There's a lot of sugar in *cake / bread*.
4 You can eat *rice / biscuits* with meat.

5 There's no sugar in *chocolate / pasta*.
6 I've got a box of *milk / chocolates*.
7 *Butter / Pasta* comes from milk.
8 We have *olives / biscuits* with coffee.

3 ABOUT YOU Look at the pictures. Which things do you: often buy? sometimes buy? never buy?
Write your answers, or tell another student.
根据图片，结合自身情况回答问题: 哪些东西经常买/有时买/从来不买? 也可以告诉其他同学。

▶ I often buy eggs.

B Buying food 购买食物

shop assistant   customer

Customer	Could I have a **kilo** of onions, **please**?
Shop assistant	OK. Do you **need** a **bag**?
Customer	No, I've got one, thanks. And **have you got any** peaches?
Shop assistant	Yes. **How many** do you want?
Customer	Four, please. Are they **ready** to eat?
Shop assistant	Yes, they're lovely.
Customer	Great. **That's all, thanks.**

Customer	I need some cheese, please.
Shop assistant	Sure. **How much**?
Customer	Oh, **half a kilo**. And some of those olives, please. About 200 **grams**.
Shop assistant	**Right**. This is **just over**.
Customer	**That's fine**, thanks.

GLOSSARY

Could I have …, please?	This is a polite way of saying 'I want'.
kilogram	= 1,000 **grams**. **Kilo** is short for **kilogram**. **Half a kilo** = 500 **grams**.
bag	(see picture)
Have you got any …?	= Do you have any …? (**Any** is usually used in questions.)
ready	If sth is **ready to eat**, you can eat it now.
That's all, thanks.	= I don't want any more things.
need	If you **need** sth, you must have it.
right	OK. This means 'Yes, I understand you'.
just over (a kilo)	a little more than (a kilo) OPP **just under**
That's fine.	= That's OK.

SPOTLIGHT *how much?* and *how many?*

We use **how much** with uncountable nouns and **how many** with countable nouns:
- *How much butter do you want?*
- *How many apples do we need?*

---

4 Match 1–6 with a–g. 配对题。

▶ Right. .... d
1 shop assistant ....
2 customer ....
3 that's all ....
4 ready to eat ....
5 need something ....
6 just under ....

a a person who works in a shop
b I don't want to buy any other things.
c OK to have it now
d I understand what you mean. ✓
e must have something
f a little less than
g a person who buys things in a shop or on the internet

5 Put the words in the correct order to make sentences. 连词成句。

▶ all / that's / thanks That's all, thanks. / Thanks. That's all.
1 twelve / have / could / please / eggs / I ....?
2 need / you / a / do / bag ....?
3 got / French / you / cheese / any / have ....?
4 much / do / pasta / how / need / you ....?
5 kilo / just / half / a / over / that's ....
6 oranges / many / need / do / how / you ....?

6 Complete the dialogues. 将对话填写完整。

▶ A Yes? B I'd ___like___ six lemons, please.
1 A Have you .... any apples?
  B Yes. How .... would you like?
2 A Could I .... some cheese, please.
  B Sure, how ....?
  A Oh, about 100 .... And that's ...., thank you.

3 A .... I have a kilo of potatoes, please?
  B Sure. That's .... under a kilo.
  A .... fine.
4 A These bananas don't look .... to eat.
  B No, they .... two or three more days.

A Fruit 水果

banana

orange

peach

apple

pear

lemon

strawberry

grapes

pineapple

nuts

GLOSSARY	
fruit [U]	*Oranges, pears* and *nuts* are types of fruit: *I buy my **fruit** at the supermarket.*
taste	If sth **tastes** of lemon, it's like lemon when you eat or drink it: *This ice cream **tastes** of orange. It **tastes** sweet.*
sweet	tasting of sugar: *These strawberries are very **sweet**.*

1 **Find the end of each word.** 找出单词。

banana/grapeslemonnutsstrawberriespineapplepearorangepeachapple

2 **Circle the correct answer.** 圈出正确答案。
- ▶ Which fruit is green: strawberries or (apples)?
- **1** Which taste sweet: oranges or nuts?
- **2** Which are yellow: grapes or lemons?
- **3** Which are round: peaches or pears?
- **4** Which are big: pineapples or grapes?
- **5** Which are long: bananas or apples?
- **6** Which are hard: strawberries or nuts?

3 **Complete the definitions.** 将定义填写完整。
- ▶ _Apples_ can be green, red or yellow, and are round.
- **1** .... are long and yellow.
- **2** .... are like lemons but are sweet and round.
- **3** .... are yellow inside and have green leaves on top.
- **4** .... are small and dry, and hard on the outside.
- **5** .... things taste of sugar.
- **6** .... are green or red/purple, and we use them to make wine.
- **7** .... are small, soft and red.
- **8** .... are soft and round, with a big stone in the centre.
- **9** Pears and lemons are types of ....

4 ABOUT YOU **Write your answers, or tell another student.**
根据自身情况回答问题, 也可以将答案告诉其他同学。
Which fruit do you ...
eat every week? .... eat every month? ....
often eat in summer? .... never eat? ....

B Vegetables 蔬菜

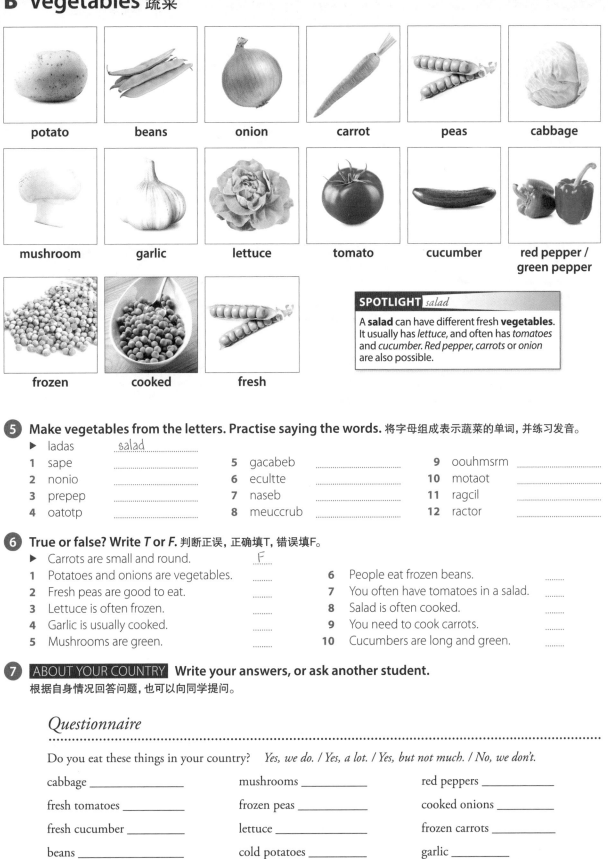

potato   beans   onion   carrot   peas   cabbage

mushroom   garlic   lettuce   tomato   cucumber   red pepper / green pepper

frozen   cooked   fresh

SPOTLIGHT *salad*

A **salad** can have different fresh **vegetables**. It usually has *lettuce*, and often has *tomatoes* and *cucumber*. *Red pepper*, *carrots* or *onion* are also possible.

5 **Make vegetables from the letters. Practise saying the words.** 将字母组成表示蔬菜的单词，并练习发音。

▶ ladas   salad

1	sape	....	5	gacabeb	....	9	oouhmsrm	....
2	nonio	....	6	ecultte	....	10	motaot	....
3	prepep	....	7	naseb	....	11	ragcil	....
4	oatotp	....	8	meuccrub	....	12	ractor	....

6 **True or false? Write *T* or *F*.** 判断正误，正确填T，错误填F。

▶ Carrots are small and round.   F

1	Potatoes and onions are vegetables.	....	6	People eat frozen beans.	....
2	Fresh peas are good to eat.	....	7	You often have tomatoes in a salad.	....
3	Lettuce is often frozen.	....	8	Salad is often cooked.	....
4	Garlic is usually cooked.	....	9	You need to cook carrots.	....
5	Mushrooms are green.	....	10	Cucumbers are long and green.	....

7 **ABOUT YOUR COUNTRY** **Write your answers, or ask another student.**
根据自身情况回答问题，也可以向同学提问。

Questionnaire
....

Do you eat these things in your country?   *Yes, we do. / Yes, a lot. / Yes, but not much. / No, we don't.*

cabbage _____   mushrooms _____   red peppers _____

fresh tomatoes _____   frozen peas _____   cooked onions _____

fresh cucumber _____   lettuce _____   frozen carrots _____

beans _____   cold potatoes _____   garlic _____

47) Meat and fish 肉与鱼

animal						
	cow	sheep	lamb	chicken	duck	pig

types of meat
(part of the animal or bird that you eat)

beef	lamb	chicken	duck	pork	ham

fish

salmon	tuna		bacon	sausages

seafood

squid	prawns	crab

SPOTLIGHT saying what you eat
- I eat **meat**. = **Meat** is OK for me.
- I **don't eat pork**. = **Pork** is no good for me.
- I'm **(a) vegetarian**. = I don't eat **meat** or **fish**.

1 **True or false? Write *T* or *F*.** 判断正误，正确填T，错误填F。

▶ Tuna is a kind of meat. ....F....

1 Vegetarians eat salmon. ....
2 Lamb is an animal and a type of meat. ....
3 Duck is a type of fish. ....
4 You get bacon from cows. ....
5 You can make sausages from pork. ....

6 Prawns are smaller than crab. ....
7 Salmon and squid are both fish. ....
8 Pig is a type of meat. ....
9 Chicken is a type of bird. ....
10 You get ham from sheep. ....

2 **Complete the names of *meat*, *fish* or *seafood*.** 填写肉类、鱼类或海鲜的名称。

▶ lam b

1 ....ee...... 2 ....a...... 3 ....un...... 4 ....uc...... 5 ....ra......
6 ....qui...... 7 ....aco...... 8 ....ausa...... 9 ....or...... 10 ....raw......

3 **Which one is different? Why?** 找出与其他三个不同的单词，并解释原因。

▶ cow sheep salmon pig   Salmon , because it's a type of fish, not an animal .
1 cow pig pork sheep   .... , because ....
2 ham lamb sausages bacon   .... , because ....
3 lamb pork beef tuna   .... , because ....
4 vegetarian squid chicken tuna   .... , because ....
5 sausage beef pork cow   .... , because ....
6 crab salmon prawns squid   .... , because ....

4 ABOUT YOU **Write your answers, or ask another student.** 根据自身情况回答问题，也可以向同学提问。

Do you eat these things? Why? / Why not?

▶ bacon Yes, I like bacon. / No, I'm vegetarian. / No, I don't eat bacon because I don't eat meat from pigs.

1 beef .... 4 crab .... 7 duck ....
2 squid .... 5 tuna .... 8 lamb ....
3 salmon .... 6 prawns ....

48) A restaurant table 饭店餐桌

1	**fork**	8	**(black) pepper**
2	**plate**	9	**bowl**
3	**knife**	10	**glass of red wine**
4	**spoon**	11	**bottle of fizzy water**
5	**bottle of beer**	12	**vinegar**
6	**dish** (of pasta)	13	**oil**
7	**salt**	14	**glass of white wine**

> **SPOTLIGHT** plural forms of nouns
>
> For nouns ending in *-sh*, *-ch*, *-s* and *-x*, add *-es* in the plural.
> - *dish/dishes*   - *church/churches*
> - *glass/glasses*   - *box/boxes*
>
> For nouns ending in *-f* or *-fe*, change to *-ves* in the plural.
> - *wife/wives*   - *knife/knives*

1 Look at the picture. Write the numbers. 根据图片, 填写数字。

▶ How many glasses are there?   9

1 How many knives are there?   ....

2 How many bowls?   ....

3 How many spoons?   ....

4 How many wine glasses?   ....

5 How many plates?   ....

6 How many bottles?   ....

7 How many large dishes?   ....

8 How many forks?   ....

2 Look at the picture and complete the text. 根据图片, 将短文填写完整。

On the table, each person has a ▶ knife, **(1)** f_____k, and **(2)** s_____n.
They each have a white **(3)** p_____e and a **(4)** b_____l. To drink, there's a **(5)** b_____e
of **(6)** f_____y w_____r, and two **(7)** g_____s of **(8)** w_____e: one **(9)** r___d
and the other **(10)** w_____e, plus a **(11)** b_____e of **(12)** b_____r. There is also some
(13) s_____t and **(14)** b_____k p_____r, and little **(15)** b_____s of **(16)** o___l
and **(17)** v_____r.

4 ▊ABOUT YOUR COUNTRY▊   Think about the things on the table, in the picture and complete the
sentences. 对照图中餐桌上的物品, 根据自身情况填空。

On restaurant tables in my country, we usually or sometimes have _____

We don't usually have _____

We never have _____

Food and drink 食物与饮料   97

A The menu 菜单

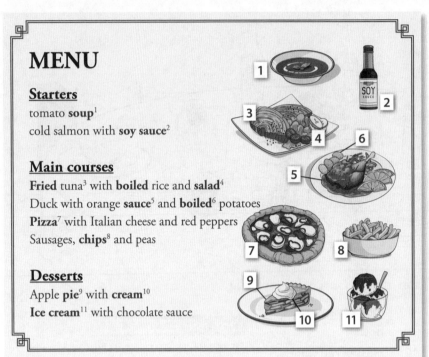

MENU

Starters
tomato **soup**[1]
cold salmon with **soy sauce**[2]

Main courses
Fried tuna[3] with **boiled** rice and **salad**[4]
Duck with orange **sauce**[5] and **boiled**[6] potatoes
Pizza[7] with Italian cheese and red peppers
Sausages, **chips**[8] and peas

Desserts
Apple **pie**[9] with **cream**[10]
Ice cream[11] with chocolate sauce

GLOSSARY

fried	cooked in hot oil **fry** v
boiled	cooked in hot water **boil** v

SPOTLIGHT *menus*

A **menu** is a list of food you can have in a restaurant.
The **starter** (or **first course**) is usually small. The **main course** is the most important part of the meal.
Desserts are sweet and come at the end of the meal.

1 Correct the mistakes. 改错题。

▶ Chips aren't a ~~start~~.   *starter*

1 It's boil rice. ....
2 The potatoes are fry. ....
3 A cheese sorce. ....
4 The first course was salade. ....

5 Did you have ice creme? ....
6 There was fruit for desert. ....
7 I had tomato soap. ....
8 How was the apple pea? ....

2 True or false? Write *T* or *F*. 判断正误，正确填T，错误填F。

▶ You eat the starter after the main course.   F

1 You eat ice cream with a knife and fork. ....
2 You eat the main course before dessert. ....
3 You can have eggs fried or boiled. ....
4 You eat chips in a bowl of soup. ....
5 The list of food to eat is called a menu. ....

6 The starter is the first thing you eat. ....
7 People often have cream on pizza. ....
8 Chips are fried. ....
9 Pasta usually has a sauce on it. ....
10 Apple pie is a starter. ....

3 Complete the sentences. 将句子填写完整。

▶ I'd like fried *fish* .

1 Do you like cheese s................... on pasta?
2 Could I have the apple p..................., please?
3 I don't like f................... chicken.

4 My starter was fish s................... .
5 What's your main c...................?
6 I love ice c................... .
7 I had chicken with b................... rice.

4 ABOUT YOU Look at the menu. Write your answers, or ask another student.
对照菜单，根据自身情况回答问题，也可以向同学提问。

Which starter would you like? ....
Which main course would you like? ....
Which dessert would you like? ....

B Ordering the meal 点单

waiter

customer

Waiter	**Are you ready to order**?
Customer	Yes, **I'll have** the duck, please, but **without** the potatoes.
Waiter	**Sure**. Would you like rice **instead**?
Customer	Yes, please. And a glass of red wine, and some water.
Waiter	**Fizzy** or **still**?
Customer	Oh, still is fine.
	(Later …)
Customer	Could I have **another** bottle of water, please? Oh, and **some more** bread.
Waiter	Yes, **of course**.
	(Later …)
Waiter	Was everything **all right** with your **meal**?
Customer	Yes – the duck was **delicious**. Could I have **the bill**, please?
Waiter	**Certainly**.

SPOTLIGHT *another and some more*

Say **another** (= one more) with countable nouns.
- *another glass/biscuit/apple*

Say **some more** with nouns in the plural and uncountable nouns.
- *some more biscuits/glasses*
- *some more water/wine/bread*

GLOSSARY

Are you ready to order?	= Do you know what you want to eat?	**instead**	in the place of sth or sb
order	ask for food or drinks in a restaurant, bar, etc.	**still water**	water without gas (**fizzy water** = water with gas)
I'll have tuna.	= I'd like/I want tuna.	**all right**	OK
without	*without sugar* = with no sugar	**meal**	Breakfast, lunch and dinner are **meals**.
sure / of course / certainly	These phrases all mean 'Yes, no problem'.	**delicious**	very good to eat
		the bill	a piece of paper that shows how much money you must pay for sth

---

5 **Circle the correct word.** 圈出正确答案。

▶ I *like* / *(d like)* a coffee, please.

1 Could I have *some more* / *another* potatoes?
2 Are you ready *order* / *to order*?
3 Do you want *another* / *some more* bottle?
4 We had a delicious *meal* / *food* last night.
5 Is everything *right* / *all right* with your meal?
6 There's no salmon. Would you like *some more* / *tuna instead*?

7 Yes, *course* / *of course*.
8 Could I have *a* / *the* bill, please?
9 *I* / *I'll* have the prawns, please.
10 Yes, *certainly* / *certain*.
11 You order from the *customer* / *waiter*.
12 Black coffee is *with* / *without* milk.

---

6 **Complete the conversations.** 将会话填写完整。

Conversation 1

w Are you ▶ _ready_ to order?
c Yes, I'll **(1)** _____ the chicken, please.
w And is that with or **(2)** _____ cream sauce?
c With, please. And a bottle of water.
w Yes, of **(3)** _____ . Fizzy **(4)** _____ ?
c Fizzy, please.

Conversation 2

c Could I have **(5)** _____ more water, please?
w **(6)** _____ . And would you like a dessert?
c Er, yes, I **(7)** _____ have the ice cream. Then could I have the **(8)** _____ ?
w Yes, **(9)** _____ .

A Food and drinks 食物与饮料

DRINKS

1	**(white) coffee**
2	**black coffee**
3	**tea (with milk or lemon)**
4	**hot chocolate**
5	**orange juice (with ice)**
6	**a fizzy drink**

SNACKS

7	**a sandwich (white bread)**
8	**a sandwich (brown bread)**
9	**a toasted sandwich**
10	**a roll**
11	**crisps**
12	**cakes**

> **SPOTLIGHT** *café, bar, pub*
>
> In a **café**, you can have a *drink* or a *snack*. In a **bar** or **pub**, you can have *drinks*, e.g. *juice*, but also *alcoholic drinks*, e.g. *beer* or *wine*. People go to pubs in Britain to have a drink, meet people and often eat food.

1 **Find the end of each drink or snack.** 找出表示饮料或点心的单词或短语。

You can have a ▶ roll/crispssnackcheesesandwichcaketoastedsandwich

You can have a ▶ hotchocolate/teawithlemondrinkblackcoffeefizzydrinkorangejuice

2 **True or false? Write *T* or *F*.** 判断正误，正确填T，错误填F。

▶ White coffee has milk in it.   T

1	Ice is a drink.		6	You can eat in a café or some pubs. ....
2	Crisps and rolls are snacks.		7	You can have wine in a café. ....
3	Beer is an alcoholic drink.		8	You can have a fizzy drink in a bar. ....
4	Hot chocolate is a snack.		9	Crisps are sweet. ....
5	Cakes and orange juice are sweet.		10	A toasted sandwich is hot. ....

3 **Complete the phrases.** 将短语填写完整。

▶ a ham <u>sandwich</u>

1	brown	5	black	9	brown or .... bread?
2	a toasted	6	alcoholic	10	.... or white coffee?
3	hot	7	.... drinks	11	apple ....
4	juice with	8	bar, café or .... ?	12	.... with milk

4   ABOUT YOU   **Look at the drinks and snacks. Which do you like most? Which don't you like? Write a list, or tell another student.** 以上饮料与点心，你最喜欢/不喜欢什么? 列一张清单，也可以告诉其他同学。

B Buying food and drinks 购买食物与饮料

A Hi, **what can I get you**?

B **I'd like** a ham sandwich on brown bread and two cheese rolls, **please**.

A Is that to **have** here or **take away**?

B To have here, please.

A **Fine. Anything else**?

B Yes, **can I have two coffees** and an apple juice?

A **Would you like** ice in the juice?

B **No, thanks.**

A **Is that everything?**

B Yes, **that's all, thanks.**

A OK, the **food** will be **a couple of** minutes. Take a seat.

SPOTLIGHT *please* and *thanks*

You use **please** when you ask for something politely.
- *Can I have a coffee, **please**?*

Yes, please is a polite way of saying 'yes'.

No, thanks/thank you is a polite way of saying 'no'.
- *Would you like a drink? **Yes, please.** / **No, thanks.***

That's all, thanks. = I don't want anything else.

GLOSSARY

What can I get you?	a polite way to ask 'What do you want?' ALSO **What would you like?**
I'd like	= I would like; a polite way to say 'I want'
have	You **have** (= eat) a sandwich. You **have** (= drink) a coffee.
take away	eat in another place, not the café
fine	= OK
anything else?	= Do you want any more things? ALSO **Is that everything?**
Can I have …?	a polite way to say 'I want' ALSO **Can I get …?**
two coffees	two cups of coffee ALSO **three teas**, etc.
food	things that people or animals eat
a couple of	two or three (e.g. minutes)
take a seat	sit down ALSO **have a seat**

---

5 **The same or different? Write *S* or *D*.** 两者的含义是否相同? 相同填S, 不同填D。

▶ Would you like a drink? / Do you want a drink? `S`

1 a couple of minutes / two or three minutes ....

2 Please sit down. / Please have a seat. ....

3 Do you want some food? / Do you want something to drink? ....

4 No, thanks. / No, thank you. ....

5 What can I get you? / What would you like? ....

6 That's fine. / No, thanks. ....

7 Two teas, please. / Two cups of tea, please. ....

8 I'd like a beer, please. / I like beer. ....

9 Can I get a coffee, please? / Would you like a coffee? ....

10 Anything else? / Is that everything? ....

---

6 **Put the words in the correct order to complete the conversation.** 连词成句, 使会话完整。

▶ A please / yes `Yes, please` .

B two / sandwiches / ham / please / toasted / like / I'd ....

A that / have / is / here/ to / away / take / or .... ?

B have / please / to / here ....

A everything / that / is .... ?

B teas / get / can / two / I / please ....

A be / will / a / minutes / of / it / couple ....

  please / seat / a / take ....

---

7 **One word is missing in each line of the conversation. What is it and where does it go?**
在句中相应位置补上遗漏的单词。

▶ A Hi, What / I get you?

B Can I a tea with lemon, please.

A To drink here or away?

B To here. And a chicken sandwich, please.

A Would you brown bread?

B Yes.

A OK, anything?

B Thanks.

A Fine. It will be a couple minutes.

  a seat, please.

Hi, what `can` I get you?

1 ....

2 ....

3 ....

4 ....

5 ....

6 ....

7 ....

8 ....

9 ....

A Vehicles and public transport 车辆与公共交通

car

bus

coach

van

lorry/truck

bicycle/bike

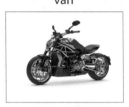

motorbike/
motorcycle

taxi

the underground

GLOSSARY	
vehicle	A car, a bus, a lorry, etc. are all types of **vehicles**.
public transport	buses, trains, etc. that everybody can use
coach	in Britain, a comfortable bus that takes people on long journeys
truck	is more common than **lorry** in American English.
motorcycle	is more common than **motorbike** in American English.
the underground	is called **the subway** in America.

SPOTLIGHT verbs used with vehicles

We **drive** a car, bus or taxi, but **ride** a bike or motorbike.
We often use **go** and **take** when we say how we travel.

- *I* **go to** *work* **by** *bus or* **by** *car.* (BUT *I* **go to** *work* **on foot.** = walk)
- *My children* **take** *the bus or the underground to school.*

1 Underline the correct answer(s). Sometimes both answers are correct.
在正确答案下划线，注意：可能两个答案都正确。

▶ You don't see much if you take *the bus / the underground*.

1 I go *for / to* work by bus.
2 She often drives her brother's *car / bike*.
3 He's just bought a new *motorcycle / motorbike*.
4 Do you often go *by / on* foot?
5 Can you *ride / drive* a motorcycle?
6 We often use *public transport / the underground*.
7 My uncle drives a *lorry / truck*.
8 I went from London to Scotland by *bus / coach*.

2 Complete the sentences. 将句子填写完整。

▶ When it's late, I take a _taxi_ but they can be very expensive.

1 He never .... his bike in the winter: it's too cold.
2 I can take the train from Paris to Amsterdam but the .... is cheaper.
3 You often see very large .... on the motorways and other big roads.
4 I like taking the bus in big cities but the .... is usually quicker.
5 I'm too afraid to ride a big ....
6 I could drive, but I prefer to go on .... – and it's good exercise.
7 All .... can be dangerous, but especially large lorries.
8 Workmen often have .... so they can carry everything they need for their work.

3 ABOUT YOU Complete the sentences. If possible, ask someone else the questions.
根据自身情况回答问题。如有条件，可以向同学提问。

1 Can you drive? If so, when did you learn? ....
2 When did you learn to ride a bike? ....
3 How do you get to school, college or work? Are there different ways you can go? ....
4 Can you ride a motorbike? If not, would you like to ride one? ....
5 Is public transport good in your country? Is it expensive? ....
6 Do you go anywhere by coach? Why? / Why not? ....

B On the road 旅途中

Beth and Marco, who is from Italy, are talking about a **journey**.

Marco	Beth, **how far is it** from London to Bath?
Beth	Oh, about 110 miles. That's about 180 kilometres, Marco.
Marco	And what's the best way to **get there**?
Beth	I think the best way is the M4 **motorway** from London. Then, at **exit** 18, keep on the **main road**, the A46 – and that goes all the way to Bath. It's about ten miles.
Marco	Right. And are the motorways very **busy**?
Beth	Yes, **unfortunately** they are – there's a lot of **traffic**, especially in the **rush hour**, or if there is an accident.
Marco	OK. And how fast can you go on motorways here?
Beth	Well, the **speed limit** is 70 **miles per hour**, but lots of people go faster.

GLOSSARY	
journey	an act of travelling from one place to another
How far is it?	= How many kilometres/miles is it?
get there / to a place	arrive at a place
motorway	a large and wide fast road between towns
exit	the place where you leave, e.g. a motorway, a cinema, etc.
main road	a large, important road
busy	A **busy** road has a lot of cars on it. OPP **quiet**
unfortunately	a word that shows you are not happy about sth
traffic [U]	all the cars and vehicles that are on a road
rush hour	the busy time when people are going to and from work
speed limit	the fastest that you are allowed to travel on a road
miles per hour (mph)	how fast sb is travelling (ALSO **kilometres per hour** OR **kph**)

4 **Cover the glossary, then write your answers.** 遮住单词表，并填写答案。

▶ the place where you leave somewhere such as a motorway   _exit_
1 all the cars and vehicles that are on a road   ....
2 a busy time when people go to and from work   ....
3 an important road in or around a town   ....
4 What does *mph* mean?   ....
5 the fastest you can travel on a road   ....
6 the opposite of *a busy road*   ....
7 a very large fast road between big towns and cities   ....

5 **Complete the sentences.** 将句子填写完整。

▶ You can take a country road, but the _motorway_ is quicker.
1 It's a very .... road in the rush ....
2 I saw an accident this morning on the .... road into town.
3 How .... is it from Paris to Marseille? ~ It's 740 kms.
4 Does it take long to .... there? ~ Yes, ... it does. It's very tiring.
5 It's a long .... and takes about five hours.

6 ABOUT YOUR COUNTRY **Write your answers, or ask another student.**
根据自身情况回答问题，也可以向同学提问。

1 Is there a lot of traffic on motorways? If so, why? ....

2 How fast can cars travel on motorways? ....

3 Do you use motorways a lot? Why? / Why not? ....

4 Do you drive on the left in your country? ....

5 What time is the rush hour in the morning and evening? ....

6 What was the last long journey you went on? ....

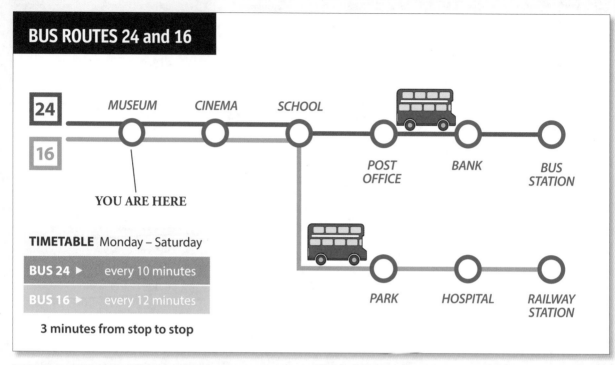

BUS ROUTES 24 and 16

24

16

MUSEUM   CINEMA   SCHOOL

POST OFFICE   BANK   BUS STATION

YOU ARE HERE

PARK   HOSPITAL   RAILWAY STATION

TIMETABLE Monday – Saturday

| BUS 24 ▶ | every 10 minutes |
| BUS 16 ▶ | every 12 minutes |

3 minutes from stop to stop

Questions	Answers
Excuse me, which bus do I **get** to the park?	The 16.
Does the 24 **go** to the railway station?	No, it doesn't.
Does the 24 stop **near** the bank?	Yes, it does.
Does the 16 stop **outside** the park?	Yes, it does.
How often does the 16 **run**?	**Every** 12 minutes.
How many **stops** is it to the park?	Three.
Which is the **last stop** for the 24?	The bus station.
Where do I **get off** for the cinema?	At the **next stop**.
How long does it take to the bus station?	**It takes** about 15 minutes.

GLOSSARY

route	the way you take to go somewhere. A **bus route** is the way a bus usually takes.
timetable	a list of times when sth happens: *a bus/train timetable*
excuse me	We say **excuse me** when we start talking to sb we don't know, especially in the street to ask a question.
get a train, bus, etc.	travel on a bus, train, etc. ALSO **take a train**, **bus**, etc.
go	travel to a place
near the bank	outside the bank
run	take passengers on a bus, train, etc.
every (12 minutes)	e.g. 9.00, 9.12, 9.24, etc.
(bus) stop	the place where you get on or off a bus
last stop	the bus stop at the end of the route
get off	leave the bus OPP **get on**
next stop	the first stop after now

SPOTLIGHT *How long does it take?*

How long? = how much time? (NOT *how long time*?)
- *How long does it take (to get) to the station?*
  - ~ *It takes about 10 minutes.*
  - ~ *It takes a long time.*
  - ~ *It doesn't take long.* = It takes a short time.

1 Match a word or phrase from group A to a word or phrase from group B to make a new phrase or sentence. 从A、B两组各选一个单词或短语，组成新的短语或句子。

A	▶ bus ✓	get off	How long	the next	It doesn't	Excuse
B	the bus	stop	me	take long	route ✓	does it take?

▶ bus route ....

....

....

2 Write the words in the correct order to make questions. 连词成问句。

▶ near / bank / stop / does / the 24 / the _Does the 24 stop near the bank_ ?

1 post office / the 24 / does / outside / stop / the .... ?

2 off / do / get / I / where / cinema / for / the .... ?

3 park / the 24 / does / to / go / the .... ?

4 often / run / does / the 24 / how .... ?

5 which / stop / last / the / is / for / the 16 .... ?

6 stops / many / to / how / it / railway station / is / the .... ?

7 school / me / bus / which / excuse / get / I / to / do / the .... ?

8 take / the / long / how / does / to / railway station / it .... ?

3 Answer the questions in Exercise 2, using the bus information on page 104. Remember, you are at the museum. 根据P104的公共汽车信息，回答练习2中的问题。注意：你所在的位置是博物馆。

▶ _Yes, it does._ ....

1 ....

2 ....

3 ....

4 .... minutes.

5 ....

6 ....

7 ....

8 .... minutes.

4 Complete the text, using the bus map information on page 104.
根据P104的公交线路图填空。

If you ▶ ..get.......... a bus from the museum, there are two bus **(1)** .... you can take: the 24 and the 16. For the 24, the first **(2)** .... is the museum, and the **(3)** .... stop is the cinema. The **(4)** .... stop is the bus station, where everybody has to **(5)** .... the bus. The 16 starts at the museum too, but it **(6)** .... to the railway station. The **(7)** .... tells you how often the buses **(8)** .... The 24 route is very frequent: it runs **(9)** .... ten minutes. It only **(10)** .... two or three minutes to get from the school to the park, and it stops **(11)** .... the park. After that, it goes to the hospital. And it doesn't take **(12)** .... – only another three or four minutes.

5 ABOUT YOU Write your answers, or ask another student. 根据自身情况回答问题，也可以向同学提问。

1 Is there a bus stop near your house? If so, where is it? ....

2 Which bus routes stop there? ....

3 Where do they go? ....

4 How often do they run? ....

5 Do you often get the bus? If so, where to? ....

6 How many stops is it? ....

7 How long does it take? ....

53 / Trains 列车

A At the station 在车站

GLOSSARY

get/take a train	travel by train
the 12 o'clock train	= the train that leaves at 12.00
journey	an act of travelling from one place to another
fare	money that you pay to travel by train, and also by bus, taxi, etc.
a fast train	a train that goes very quickly OPP **a slow train**
railway/train station	a place where trains stop and people get on and off. People meet **at a station**.

SPOTLIGHT *last*

Last has different meanings:
1 final: The **last** train leaves at 11.30 p.m. (= there are no trains after 11.30 p.m.) *Marseille is the **last** stop.*
2 most recent, the one before now: *My **last** train journey was two weeks ago.*

1 Answer the questions. 回答问题。

▶ What's another verb for *get a train*? .... take a train ....
1 What's the opposite of *a slow train*? ....
2 What's the opposite of *get on the train*? ....
3 What do you call the money you pay to travel by train? ....
4 What's another way of saying *the train that leaves at 7*? ....
5 What do you sit on in a train? ....
6 Where do you get a train? ....
7 Where do you look for the train times? ....
8 What's another word for a *coach* on a train? ....

2 Complete the sentences. 将句子填写完整。

▶ We can get the 7.45 ...train......
1 How much was the train .... ?
2 Our seats are in the second ....
3 I'm sorry I'm late. I .... the train.
4 We can .... a train from Zug to Bern.
5 The .... train is just after midnight.
6 Quickly, ... the train before it goes.
7 We .... for the train in the café.
8 Look at the .... for a later train.
9 They had to wait .... the last train.
10 Don't take the 7.15 – that's a .... train.
11 It's long train .... from Rome to Paris.

B Buying a ticket 购票

over there

It's now 9.30. A **passenger** is talking to someone at the **ticket office** in the station.

Passenger	A **return** to Cardiff, please.
Ticket office	That's £21.40.
	*(The passenger takes the **ticket**.)*
Passenger	Thank you … when's the **next** train?
Ticket office	There's one that **leaves** at 10.07.
Passenger	OK. Do I have to **change**?
Ticket office	No, it's **direct**.
Passenger	That's good. And when does it **get to** Cardiff?
Ticket office	10.56.
Passenger	Right. And which **platform** is it?
Ticket office	Platform 6, **over there**.
Passenger	OK. Thanks a lot.

GLOSSARY

passenger	a person travelling or going to travel in a train, bus, etc.
ticket office	the place where you buy tickets at a station
return (ticket)	a ticket to travel from a place and back again OPP **single** one way only
next	The **next** train is the first one after now.
leave	go away from a place or person OPP **get to / arrive at** (Oxford, the station, etc.)
change (trains)	get off one train and get on another
direct	A journey is **direct** if you don't need to change trains.
platform	the part of the station where you get on and off the train
over there	*(see picture)* OPP **over here** a place or position near you

SPOTLIGHT *book/reserve something*

If you **book/reserve a seat**, you buy a train ticket days or weeks before you travel, with a seat number on the ticket. For a hotel, you can **book/reserve a room**, and in a restaurant you can **book/reserve a table**.

---

3 **Complete the sentences using words from the box.** 用方框内的词填空。

direct   London   office   change   train   is it ✓   there   return   passengers   seat

▶ Which platform _is it?_

1 Can I book a _____?
2 Do I have to _____?
3 Do you want a single or _____?
4 Is the train _____?
5 Were there many _____?
6 When do we get to _____?
7 Where's the ticket _____?
8 When's the next _____?
9 The ticket office is over _____.

---

4 **Look at the timetable and complete the text.** 根据时刻表填空。

Platform	Cheltenham	Kemble	London Paddington
2	dep 8.35	9.08	
		9.22	arr 10.45

I'm going from Cheltenham to London Paddington next month. There isn't a ▶ _direct_ train around 8.30, so I have to **(1)** _____ at Kemble. The train **(2)** _____ Cheltenham at 8.35 from **(3)** _____ 2, and it **(4)** _____ to Kemble at 9.08. Then I have to **(5)** _____ the 9.22, which gets **(6)** _____ London Paddington at 10.45. A **(7)** _____ costs £22, but if I want to come back the same day, I'll get a **(8)** _____. I'll probably **(9)** _____ my seat because it will be very busy at that time in the morning.

---

5 ABOUT YOU **Write your answers, or ask another student.** 根据自身情况回答问题，也可以向同学提问。

1 When was your last train journey? _____
2 Was it a single or a return? _____
3 Where did you go, and why? _____
4 Can you remember the train fare? _____
5 Did you book a seat before you travelled? _____
6 Was it direct, or did you have to change trains? _____

GLOSSARY

directions	words that tell you how to get to a place
excuse me	When you want to talk to sb you don't know, especially in the street, it is polite to say **Excuse me**.
near	not far away, close to sb or sth
nearest	the first one from where you are
way	a road that you must take to get to a place

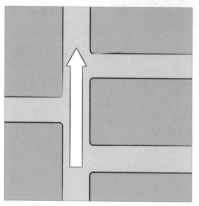

Go straight on. OR **Keep going.** It's about ten minutes.

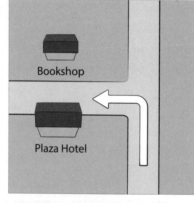

Go along here and **turn left**. The bookshop is **opposite** the Plaza Hotel.

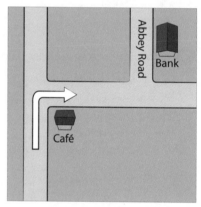

Turn right at the café, then **left into** Abbey Road, and the bank is **on your right**.

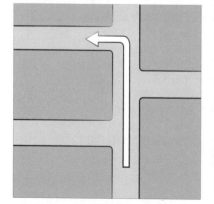

Go along here and **take the second turning on the left**.

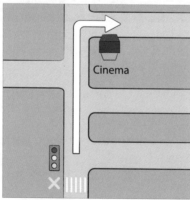

OK. **Cross** the road at the **traffic lights**, then go straight on and it's the **third turning on the right**. There's a cinema **on the corner**.

1 **Cross out one word in each sentence.** 划掉各句中多余的一个单词。

▶ Turn right into ~~the~~ Duke Street.

1 The bookshop is opposite of the hotel.

2 Go straight on and keep to going.

3 Is there a cinema near from here?

4 It's on your left side.

5 Turn to left and go straight on.

6 It's the third road turning on the right.

7 Where's the most nearest post office?

2 **Is the pronunciation of the <u>underlined</u> letters the same or different? Write *S* or *D*.**
Practise saying the words. 划线部分的发音是否相同? 相同填S, 不同填D, 并练习发音。

▶ h<u>ere</u> / th<u>ere</u>   D

1 c<u>ro</u>ss / c<u>o</u>rner   ....

2 th<u>ir</u>d / t<u>ur</u>ning   ....

3 sec<u>o</u>nd / <u>o</u>pp<u>o</u>site   ....

▶ h<u>ere</u> / n<u>ear</u>   S

4 stra<u>igh</u>t / w<u>ay</u>   ....

5 r<u>igh</u>t / <u>o</u>pp<u>o</u>site   ....

6 <u>th</u>ere / <u>th</u>anks   ....

3 **Make sentences from the words.** 连词成句。

▶ turn / and / go / right / here / along *Go along here and turn right.*

1 excuse / I / get / do / museum / the / me / how / to _____?

2 here / left / along / and / turn / go _____.

3 post office / me / near / there / is / a / excuse / here _____?

4 the / turning / it's / right / on / the / third _____.

5 way / the / excuse / to / know / me / do / station / the / you _____?

6 traffic / the / lights / road / at / the / cross _____.

4 **Complete the phrases with a single word.** 填入一个单词将短语补充完整。

▶ turn *left* (OR *right*)

1 Take the second _____ .

2 Thanks very _____ .

3 It's on the _____ .

4 Excuse _____ .

5 Cross the _____ .

6 Keep _____ .

7 Go straight _____ .

8 Go along _____ .

9 I want to go to the bank. Do you know the _____?

10 Turn left at the traffic _____ .

5 **Complete the dialogues. Use the maps to help you.** 根据右侧地图填空。

1 A Excuse ▶ *me* _____ . How do I **(1)** _____ to the cinema from here?

B OK. Go **(2)** _____ on, and it's the second ... no, the third **(3)** _____ on the **(4)** _____ .

A Thanks very **(5)** _____ .

B That's OK, no **(6)** _____ .

2 A **(1)** _____ me. Is there a post office **(2)** _____ here?

B Yes. Go **(3)** _____ here and **(4)** _____ the second **(5)** _____ on the **(6)** _____ . The post office is **(7)** _____ the bank.

A **(8)** _____ very much.

B **(9)** _____ OK. No problem.

6 **Look at the map. Give directions.** 根据右侧地图为A指路。

1 A Excuse me. Do you know the way to the Bonham Hotel?

YOU Yes. Go straight on, then _____

2 A Excuse me. How do I get to the museum?

YOU _____ .

3 A Excuse me. Is there a post office near here?

YOU _____ .

GLOSSARY

sign	a small piece of writing or a picture that tells you sth
notice	a piece of writing that tells you sth, usually information
closed	not open SYN **shut**
toilet	(*see picture*)
exit	a way to go out of a building SYN **way out**
sale	a time when a shop sells things for less money than usual
keep left	stay on the left ALSO **keep right**
out of order	broken; not working correctly
no parking	= do not leave your car here
danger	the possibility that sth bad may happen
entrance	a way to go into a building **enter** v
feed	give food to sb or sth
no vacancies	In a hotel window, **no vacancies** means that the hotel is full.
queue	wait in a line of people
mind	be careful of sb or sth: ***mind** the step; **mind** your head* (above a low door)
gap	the space between two things (here, the space between a train and the platform)
keep off (the grass)	do no go on (the grass)

SPOTLIGHT *allow* and *let*

If you **allow** somebody to do something, you say that they can do something SYN **let**.
- *My parents **allow me to go** on holiday with friends.*
- *My parents **let me go** on holiday with friends.*

Allow is often used in the negative.
- *Smoking **is not allowed** = no smoking.*

In spoken English, you can say.
- *You **aren't allowed to** smoke in cinemas.* (NOT ~~It's not allowed to smoke in cinemas.~~)

1 Match 1–9 with a–j. 配对题。

▶	NO SMOKING	..g...	**a**	The hotel is full.
1	No parking	....	**b**	It's broken.
2	Exit	....	**c**	It's not safe here.
3	Please queue here	....	**d**	You can go in here.
4	OUT OF ORDER	....	**e**	Everything is cheaper at the moment.
5	Mind the gap	....	**f**	You can't leave your car here.
6	SALE	....	**g**	Do not smoke here. ✓
7	Entrance	....	**h**	This is the way out.
8	No vacancies	....	**i**	Be careful when you get off the train.
9	DANGER	....	**j**	Wait in a line here.

2 Where can you see these signs? Circle the correct answer. 圈出标识适用的场景。

▶ Keep left: *in the underground* / *in a supermarket*

1 No Parking: *in a road* / *in a shop*
2 Toilets: *in a restaurant* / *in a kitchen*
3 Entrance: *in a school* / *in a house*
4 SALE: *in a shop window* / *in a restaurant*

5 OUT OF ORDER: *on a menu* / *on a drinks machine*
6 No vacancies: *on a bridge* / *in a hotel window*
7 DANGER: *near the sea* / *near a shopping centre*
8 Please queue this side: *in a bank* / *on a telephone*

3 Complete the sentences. 将句子填写完整。

▶ It clearly says no ..parking.......... in front of the garage doors.

1 There are NO SMOKING .... everywhere on the underground.
2 Did you read that .... ? It said, dogs are not allowed on the beach.
3 There was a big sign for a .... in the window of that clothes shop.
4 The notice says that you aren't .... to walk on the grass.
5 It said CLOSED on the door, but the sales assistant .... me go in and buy something.
6 You have to mind the .... when you get off the train.
7 I'm afraid the shop is .... for lunch at the moment. It doesn't .... again until 2.30.
8 The sign says: 'Don't .... the ducks'. Bread is bad for them.
9 .... the step when you go out of the door.
10 We found the .... for women, but we couldn't find one for men.

4 Complete the dialogues. 将对话填写完整。

▶ Can we go up on the right side? ~ No, the sign says ..keep left..

1 Can I leave my car here? ~ No, it says ....
2 Can we go out here? ~ No, it says ....
3 Can I have a cigarette? ~ No, the sign says ....
4 Can we walk across the park here? ~ No, look, the sign says ....
5 Can we use the machine over there? ~ No, it says ....
6 Can we give this bread to the monkeys? ~ No, the sign says ....
7 Can we take the dog in the park? ~ No, it says that dogs aren't ....
8 Can we stand and wait over there? ~ No, it says, please ....
9 Is it safe to swim here? ~ No, it says ....
10 Can we walk up the left side? ~ No, it says ....

5 Complete these notices. 将告示填写完整。

NO PARKING	NO	PLEASE	MIND	MIND	KEEP

56 My town 我住的小城镇

A Buildings and places in a town 小城镇的建筑与场所

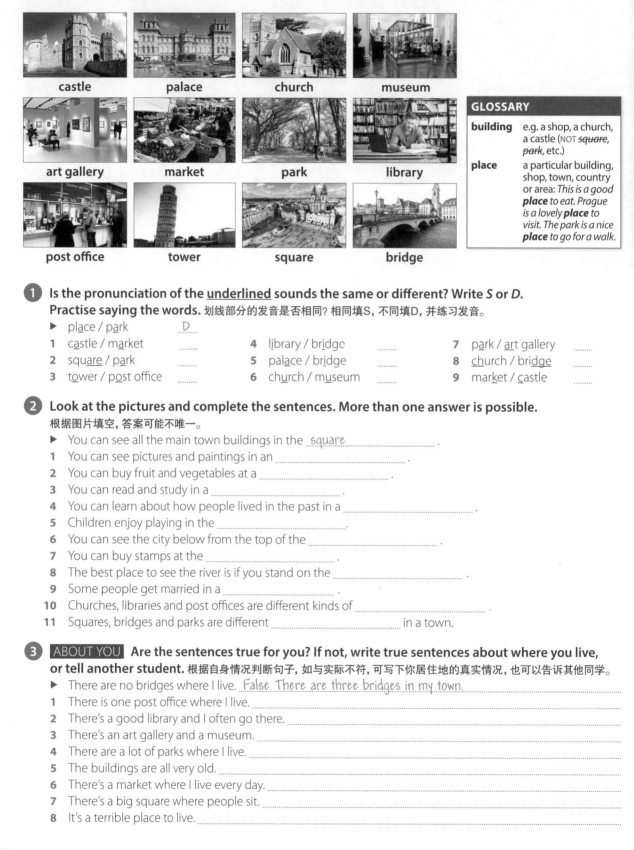

castle   palace   church   museum

art gallery   market   park   library

post office   tower   square   bridge

GLOSSARY

| building | e.g. a shop, a church, a castle (NOT *square*, *park*, etc.) |
| place | a particular building, shop, town, country or area: *This is a good **place** to eat. Prague is a lovely **place** to visit. The park is a nice **place** to go for a walk.* |

1 **Is the pronunciation of the <u>underlined</u> sounds the same or different? Write *S* or *D*. Practise saying the words.** 划线部分的发音是否相同? 相同填S, 不同填D, 并练习发音。

▶ pl<u>a</u>ce / p<u>a</u>rk   D

1 c<u>a</u>stle / m<u>a</u>rket   ....
2 squ<u>a</u>re / p<u>a</u>rk   ....
3 t<u>o</u>wer / p<u>o</u>st office   ....
4 l<u>i</u>brary / br<u>i</u>dge   ....
5 pal<u>a</u>ce / br<u>i</u>dge   ....
6 ch<u>u</u>rch / m<u>u</u>seum   ....
7 p<u>a</u>rk / <u>a</u>rt gallery   ....
8 ch<u>u</u>rch / br<u>i</u>dge   ....
9 mar<u>k</u>et / <u>c</u>astle   ....

2 **Look at the pictures and complete the sentences. More than one answer is possible.** 根据图片填空, 答案可能不唯一。

▶ You can see all the main town buildings in the <u>square</u>   .
1 You can see pictures and paintings in an ....
2 You can buy fruit and vegetables at a ....
3 You can read and study in a ....
4 You can learn about how people lived in the past in a ....
5 Children enjoy playing in the ....
6 You can see the city below from the top of the ....
7 You can buy stamps at the ....
8 The best place to see the river is if you stand on the ....
9 Some people get married in a ....
10 Churches, libraries and post offices are different kinds of ....
11 Squares, bridges and parks are different .... in a town.

3 **ABOUT YOU** **Are the sentences true for you? If not, write true sentences about where you live, or tell another student.** 根据自身情况判断句子, 如与实际不符, 可写下你居住地的真实情况, 也可以告诉其他同学。

▶ There are no bridges where I live. <u>False. There are three bridges in my town.</u>
1 There is one post office where I live. ....
2 There's a good library and I often go there. ....
3 There's an art gallery and a museum. ....
4 There are a lot of parks where I live. ....
5 The buildings are all very old. ....
6 There's a market where I live every day. ....
7 There's a big square where people sit. ....
8 It's a terrible place to live. ....

B Describing a town 描述小城镇

Word	Example	Meaning
opinion	What's your **opinion of** the new bridge? ~ I think it's wonderful. **In my opinion**, it's too big.	Your **opinion** is what you think about something. SYN **view**
busy	It's **busy** in the summer when the tourists arrive.	If a place is **busy**, it is full of people, cars, activity, etc. OPP **quiet**
crowded	The bars get very **crowded** at night.	full of people or too full of people **crowd (of people)** n
safe	It's **safe** during the day, but can be **dangerous** at night.	If a town is **safe**, there is not much crime there. OPP **dangerous**
dirty	Some of the old buildings are very **dirty**.	OPP **clean**
pollution	There's a lot of **pollution** because of all the industry.	dirty and dangerous air, gas, water, etc.
there's a lot to do there's lots to do	**There's a lot to do** in the evening – clubs, cinemas, and so on.	= there are many activities and places to visit OPP **there's nothing to do**
noise	There's too much **noise** at night. It's impossible to sleep.	something that you can hear that is often loud and not nice **noisy** adj OPP **quiet**

4 <u>Underline</u> **the correct word.** 在正确的答案下划线。

▶ The trains are usually <u>crowded</u> / crowd when people are going to work.

1 It's *noise / noisy* down by the station.

2 There's *lots / lot* to do in the city.

3 What's your *view / think* of the town?

4 In my *opinion / idea*, it's quite safe.

5 Is your town a *dangerous / safe* place to live? ~ Yes, there isn't much crime.

6 It's a *dirty / busy* place – there's so much paper on the streets.

7 *It's / There's* nothing to do in the village.

8 What do you think about the *noise / pollution* in the river?

5 **Do the speakers like the places they're talking about? Tick (✓) *yes* or *no*.**
说话者是否喜欢这个地方? 在yes或no下打钩 (√)。

		YES	NO
▶	'The streets are very dirty.'	☐	✓
1	'I think there's a lot of pollution, don't you?'	☐	☐
2	'There's lots to do during the day.'	☐	☐
3	'I always feel safe at night.'	☐	☐

		YES	NO
4	'It's always very crowded at the weekends.'	☐	☐
5	'There's nothing to do at night.'	☐	☐
6	'It's so clean on the coast.'	☐	☐
7	'There's very little noise at night.'	☐	☐
8	'It's a really dangerous city.'	☐	☐

6 **Complete the dialogue.** 将对话填写完整。

A What's your ▶ <u>view</u> of Walton?

B Well, in my **(1)** ...., it's a great place to live and work.

A Yes, but is it safe?

B Well, every town or city is a bit **(2)** .... at night, but there's a lot to **(3)** .... here.

A And is it very **(4)** .... in the centre?

B There aren't so many people on weekdays, but there are big **(5)** .... of people at the weekends, mainly local people and tourists. One thing I don't like is that there is so much traffic. The air isn't very **(6)** .... because there's a lot of **(7)** .... from the cars.

A How about outside the centre?

B Well, there are some beautiful parks, and nice, **(8)** .... places to sit in the sun and do nothing.

57 The countryside 乡村

A On a farm 在农场

1	wood
2	valley
3	hill
4	lake
5	farmer
6	farm (the house and the fields)
7	tree
8	field
9	gate
10	grass

Jack Robson's family have been in **farming** for over a hundred years, and Jack now **owns** Eatwell **Farm**. He keeps cows and **produces** about a million litres of milk a year. He also **grows** fruit: pears and apples.

GLOSSARY

farming	managing a **farm**, or working on it
own	If you **own** sth, it is yours. The person who **owns** sth is the **owner**.
produce	make or grow sth, e.g. milk, cheese, cars
grow	Farmers **grow** potatoes, rice, fruit, etc. to sell.

1 **Circle the verbs.** 圈出动词。

woodhavevalleyowngategrassfieldproducetreefarmerlakegrowhill

2 **Look at the picture. Are the sentences true or false? Write *T* or *F*.** 根据图片判断正误，正确填T，错误填F。

▶ There's a lake near the trees.   T

1 There is nothing in the field.   ....
2 The dog's next to the gate.   ....
3 The farmer owns fruit trees.   ....
4 The wood is on the hill.   ....
5 A dog lives on the farm.   ....

6 Some of the cows are eating grass.   ....
7 The owner of the farm produces milk.   ....
8 There are a lot of trees near the farmer.   ....
9 The farmer grows vegetables.   ....
10 The lake's in the valley.   ....

3 ABOUT YOU **Complete the words.** 将单词填写完整。

▶ Do you live near a w_o__o_d?   Yes, I do. There's one up the hill.
1 Do you live in a v____ll____y or on a h____ll?   ....
2 Is there a l____k____ near your home?   ....
3 Can you see any gra........ .... where you are now?   ....
4 Can you see a g........e where you are now?   ....
5 Are there any f............ds near your home?   ....
6 Do you ____wn a dog?   ....
7 Is fa............g very important in your area?   ....
8 What do farmers gr____w or pr____d........e in your country?   ....

4 ABOUT YOU **Answer the questions in Exercise 3, or ask another student.**
根据自身情况回答练习3中的问题，也可以向同学提问。

B In a garden 在花园

WHY I LOVE **my garden** (Joel, 38)

My **garden** is so important to me because it's the place where I can be **creative**. I love being out there in the **fresh air**, enjoying the beauty of **nature**. In one **area** of my garden, I grow fruit and vegetables. My children love to get their fingers dirty in the **earth** when they **plant** our strawberries. They **water** the strawberry plants and **pick** the strawberries in summer. Another area is full of **flowers**, but I leave another part **wild** and **natural** to help birds and insects.

garden

plant v plant n

water v

pick v

GLOSSARY	
creative	Someone who is **creative** has a lot of ideas or is good at making new things. **create** v
fresh air	clean and cool air
nature	all the plants, animals, etc. in the world, and all the things that happen in it that are not made or caused by people **natural** adj
area	part of a place that you use for a particular activity
wild	Plants or animals that live and grow in nature are **wild**.

5 Match 1–6 with a–g. 配对题。

▶ Plants grow in _e_
1 Don't pick the ....
2 I need fresh ....
3 Please water ....
4 I've planted ....
5 She created ....
6 I've got a wild ....

a flowers.
b some beans.
c a beautiful garden.
d area in my garden.
e earth. ✓
f air.
g the plants.

6 Complete the sentences with words from the box. 用方框内的词填空。

water   nature   creative   pick   earth   garden ✓   natural   area   fresh

▶ Do you grow fruit and vegetables in your _garden_ ?
1 You have to .... plants in the summer if it doesn't rain.
2 .... air is good for you; get as much as possible.
3 Some people like to have an .... where they can grow vegetables.
4 You grow plants in the .... ; then they just need water.
5 Nowadays, people like gardens which are ....
6 Freida's garden is full of interesting ideas – she's very ....
7 The strawberries in dad's garden are ready to eat. Let's go and .... them.
8 My sister is very interested in .... : trees, plants, animals, etc.

7 ABOUT YOU Write your answers, or ask another student. 根据自身情况回答问题，也可以向同学提问。
1 Do you ever pick flowers from a garden? ....
2 Do you ever pick fruit? ....
3 Do you grow any plants – inside or outside your home? If so, what? ....
4 How important are these things to you?
   fresh air ....   the beauty of nature ....
   wild flowers ....   areas in towns with plants and grasses ....

A Flats 公寓

1　roof
2　flat/apartment
3　(on) the top floor
4　(on) the second floor
5　(on) the first floor
6　(on) the ground floor
7　steps *pl*
8　front door
9　stairs *pl*
10　lift
11　lock
12　key (Put the **key** in the **lock** to open the door.)
13　neighbour (Miki and Ferdy are **neighbour**s.)

1 **Look at the picture. Write your answers.** 根据图片回答问题。

▶　Who lives on the second floor?　　Hannah and Simon
1　Who lives on the ground floor?　　..............................
2　Where does Miki live?　　..............................
3　Who is Josh's neighbour on the first floor?　　..............................
4　Which floor does Ferdy live on?　　..............................
5　What is above the top floor?　　..............................
6　How many flats are there?　　..............................
7　Where are the steps?　　At the ....
8　What's below the top floor?　　..............................
9　Where does Lucy live?　　..............................
10　How does Ferdy get up to his flat?　　He uses .... or ....
11　How do you get in the front door?　　..............................

2 **Complete the words.** 将单词填写完整。

▶　k e y
1　l___ ___t
2　ap___ ___ ___ ___ ___nt
3　g___ ___ ___ ___d f___ ___ ___r
4　f___ ___ ___t d___ ___r
5　s___ ___ ___s
6　ne___ ___ ___ ___ ___ ___r
7　r___ ___f
8　s___ ___ ___ ___s
9　t___p f___ ___ ___r

3 **Complete the words.** 首字母填空。　　ABOUT YOU
1　Do you live in a flat/apartment............? If so, which f.................. do you live on?　..............................
2　What's on the g.................. floor?　..............................
3　Who are your n..................?　..............................
4　Has the building got a l.................., or just s..................?　..............................
5　Are there s.................. to the front door?　..............................
6　Do you need a k.................. to open the front door?　..............................

4　ABOUT YOU　**Write your answers to the questions in Exercise 3, or ask another student.**
根据自身情况回答练习3中的问题，也可以向同学提问。

B Houses 房屋

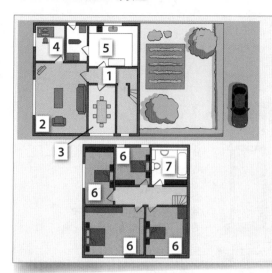

BATHFORD

Modern family **home** in this quiet village with lovely **views** of the countryside. Through the **hall**[1], you come to the **living room**[2], **dining room**[3], **study**[4] and a **kitchen**[5]. **Upstairs** there are four good-sized **bedrooms**[6] and a family **bathroom**[7]. **Outside** there is a large garden and **parking** for two cars.

GLOSSARY	
modern	of the present time OPP **old**
view	what you can see from a place
upstairs	to or on a higher level in a building OPP **downstairs**
outside	not in a house or other building OPP **inside**
parking [U]	a place where you can **park** (= leave) your car

SPOTLIGHT *flat, house, home*
A **flat** is a number of rooms on one floor of a building. SYN **apartment**
A **house** is a building that is made for people to live in. It can have more than one floor.
Home is where you live (in a flat or a house).

5 **Find the end of each word.** 找出单词或短语。

study / viewmodernlivingroomhallkitchenhomediningroomupstairsbedroomparkingbathroom

6 **Complete the texts.** 将短文填写完整。

I live in a small ▶ _modern_ house – it's only four years old. It's got a **(1)** .... room, dining room, kitchen, two bedrooms and a **(2)** .... It's in the town centre, and from the living room I've only got a **(3)** .... of the railway station, which is not very nice. To the left of the house, I've got a space to **(4)** .... my car, and there's a beautiful, small garden, so I can eat **(5)** .... when the weather is nice.

My brother's got a big house in a village near me, and from the house you can see fantastic **(6)** .... of the countryside. Through the front door, you come into the **(7)** .... , and from there you can see the living room, dining room, large **(8)** .... and a **(9)** .... , where my brother works. **(10)** .... , there are four **(11)** .... and two **(12)** .... , so there's lots of space when I visit with friends. There's also enough **(13)** .... for two cars, and a large garden. In the summer, they eat **(14)** .... all the time, and I think that's better than being **(15)** ....

7 ABOUT YOUR COUNTRY **Write your answers, or ask another student.**
根据自身情况回答问题，也可以向同学提问。

1 Where you live, do most houses have two floors, or more? ....
2 Do houses have the same rooms as the picture, or something different? ....
3 Do they have parking? If so, inside or outside? ....
4 Are there more houses in towns or the countryside? ....
5 Are houses more expensive if they have a good view or a garden? ....

A In the kitchen 在厨房

1 **cupboard**

2 **(kitchen) equipment** [U]

3 **tap**

4 **sink**

5 **fridge**

6 **cooker**

7 **oven**

8 **washing machine**

9 **dishwasher**

10 **rubbish**

11 **bin**
(The bin is **full**. OPP **empty**
You need to **empty** the bin.
OPP **fill**)

SPOTLIGHT *turn something on/off*

You can **turn on/off** something electrical.
- *Turn the light on. Turn the dishwasher off.*
- *Turn on/off the washing machine.*

You can also **turn on/off** water and gas.
- *Turn the tap on. Turn the gas cooker off.*
  (NOT *Open/close the tap/gas.*)

---

1 Is the pronunciation of the underlined sounds the same or different? Write *S* or *D*.
Practise saying the words. 划线部分的发音是否相同? 相同填S, 不同填D, 并练习发音。

▶ ki<u>tch</u>en / fri<u>dg</u>e   D

1 <u>o</u>ven / c<u>u</u>pboard   ....

2 t<u>ur</u>n on / r<u>u</u>bbish   ....

3 cook<u>er</u> / cupb<u>oar</u>d   ....

4 t<u>a</u>p / m<u>a</u>chine   ....

5 equipm<u>e</u>nt / <u>e</u>mpty   ....

6 di<u>sh</u>washer / ma<u>ch</u>ine   ....

7 c<u>oo</u>ker / f<u>u</u>ll   ....

2 Complete the sentences using vocabulary from the picture. 用图片中的单词填空。

▶ Put the milk in the fridge_____ .

1 Put those dirty clothes in the w_____
_____ .

2 Put the dirty plates in the d_____ or
the s_____ .

3 Put the cups and bowls in the c_____ .

4 Put the empty boxes in the b_____ .

5 Put the meat in the o_____ .

6 Put the dessert in the f_____ .

7 Is the dishwasher f_____ ?

8 Can you t_____ the oven _____,
please?

9 Is the r_____ bin full?

10 Can you e_____ the bin, please?

11 Could you turn the hot water t_____ off?

12 Have you got a lot of kitchen e_____ ?

13 The oven is part of the c_____ .

3 ABOUT YOU Write down anything in the picture you have got or haven't got in your kitchen.
对照图片, 根据自家情况填写厨房里有或没有的物品。

▶ We've got a dishwasher.
We haven't got a washing machine in the kitchen. It's in another room.

B Jobs in the kitchen 厨房里的家务

Everyday tasks: I have to ...

- **do the housework** [U]
- **do the washing-up**[1] [U]
  SYN **wash the dishes** [*pl*]
- **do the washing**[2] [U]
- **do the ironing**[3] [U]
- **clean**[4] the cooker and cupboards
- **prepare** and **cook**[5] meals for the family
- **look after** the children when they come home from school
- **feed**[6] the cats

GLOSSARY			
everyday	normal, not special	**do the**	do work in the house, e.g. cleaning and washing.
task	a piece of work that you must do, often difficult and not nice	**housework** [U]	Be careful: **housework** = cleaning the house; **homework** = work teachers give students to do after class.
have to (do sth)	used for saying that sb must do sth, or that sth must happen: *I **have to** cook the meals / clean the house.*	**prepare**	make something ready: ***prepare** the lunch/dinner*
		look after sb	do the things for sb that they need: *I **look after** my grandmother because she can't see very well.*

4 **Circle the correct word.** 圈出正确答案。

▶ a daily (task)/ ironing

1 I *feed / prepare* the breakfast.
2 I do my *housework / homework* on the bus.
3 I *make / do* the washing up.
4 I *clean / feed* the kitchen.
5 I *look after / cook* the dog.
6 I *have to / have* cook the dinner.

5 **Complete the sentences using different words** 用不同的单词将句子填写完整。

▶ Do you do it daily? ～ Yes, it's an ___everyday___ task.
1 Do you give the cats their food? ～ No, I never _____ them. My mother does.
2 Do you wash the clothes? ～ No, I don't _____ the _____ . My cousin does it.
3 Is it an easy job? ～ No, actually it's quite a difficult _____ .
4 Do you wash the dishes? ～ Yes, my mum says I have to do the _____ _____ .
5 Do you clean the house? ～ Yes, I always _____ the _____ . Nobody else does it!
6 Do you do the tasks your teacher gives you? ～ Yes, I _____ my _____ .
7 Do you spend a lot of time with the children? ～ Yes, I _____ them all day.
8 Is it necessary for you to do all these tasks? ～ Yes, I _____ do them.

6 ABOUT YOU **Write your answers, or ask another student.** 根据自身情况回答问题，也可以向同学提问。

WHO DOES THE MOST WORK IN YOUR HOME?

Who does the housework? _____
Who cooks the dinner? _____

Who does the washing-up? _____
Who cleans the kitchen? _____

Who does the washing? _____
Who does the ironing? _____

Who does most of the everyday tasks? Why? _____

A Bedroom 卧室

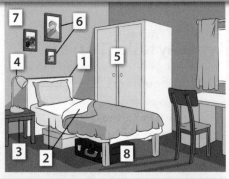

Hi! I'm Kimiko and I'm living in an **international** student house where I have all I need. There's a **bed**[1] with **sheets**[2], and a small **table**[3] and **lamp**[4] next to the bed. There's a large **wardrobe**[5] for my clothes, and a desk and chair, which I use all the time when I'm studying. I've put **a few pictures**[6] on the **wall**[7] to make it feel like home. There's **space** under the bed for my **suitcase**[8] and boxes. The **furniture** is all **wooden** and quite nice.

GLOSSARY			
international	**International** student accommodation has people from many different countries. **National** is about one country: *national newspapers/holidays*	space [U]	a place that is big enough for sth or sb to go into SYN **room** [U]: *There's **space/room** for you to sit here. There's **space/room** for three chairs here.*
a few	some, but not many	furniture [U]	tables, chairs, beds, etc. A bed is a **piece of furniture**.
		wooden	made of **wood** (*see picture*)

1 Put the words below into the correct group, according to the pronunciation of the <u>underlined</u> sound. Practise saying the words. 根据划线部分的发音，将方框内的单词分组，并练习发音。

ca̱t ✓   tu̱na ✓   na̱tional ✓   picture   sea̱t   Portuguese   ma̱tch

interna̱tional   sui̱tcase   ta̱ble   na̱ture   dictionary   shee̱t   furniture

GROUP A ▶ cat ....

GROUP B ▶ tuna ....

GROUP C ▶ national ....

2 Look at the picture. Match 1–9 with a–i. 配对题。

▶	The table's	d	**a**	made of wood.
1	The lamp's	....	**b**	pictures above the bed.
2	The sheets are	....	**c**	under the bed.
3	The pictures are	....	**d**	next to the bed. ✓
4	The furniture's all	....	**e**	the furniture she needs.
5	The wardrobe's	....	**f**	on the table, by the bed.
6	There are a few	....	**g**	next to the desk.
7	The suitcase is	....	**h**	on the wall.
8	Kimiko's room has all	....	**i**	on the bed.

3 Write the answers. 填写答案。

▶ You sleep on it: a bed ....

1 A place where you keep clothes: ....

2 You put these on a bed: ....

3 You put pictures on this in a room: ....

4 You put clothes in this when you travel: ....

5 You need it to read at night: ....

6 It means 'room to put something'. ....

7 A bed, a desk and a chair are all ....

8 If something is made of wood, it's ....

9 You put books or a clock by the bed on this: ....

10 It means 'connected to just one country'. ....

11 It means 'from many different countries'. ....

12 If you don't have many books, you only have ....

4 ABOUT YOU Look at Kimiko's text about her bedroom. Write a similar text about your bedroom at home. 参照上文内容，根据自身情况，仿写一段对自己卧室的描述。

B Bathroom 浴室

- You **have a wash** with **soap** [U].
- You **brush/clean** your teeth with a **toothbrush**.
- You **brush/do** your hair with a **brush/hairbrush**.
- You **have a shave** with a **razor** or an **electric razor**.
- You **put on make-up**.

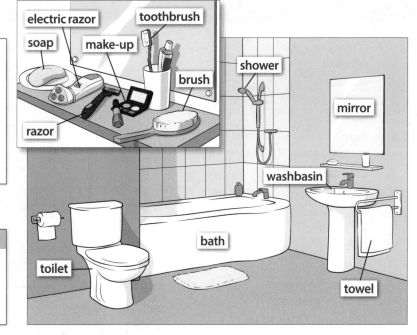

SPOTLIGHT *have* + noun

Notice these phrases with **have**:
- *I **have a shower** every day.*
- *I don't **have a bath** very often.*
- *Do you **have a shave** every morning?*
- *I **have a wash** after work.*

---

5 **Circle the correct word.** 圈出正确答案。

▶ I *wash* / (*clean*) my teeth after eating.
1 I *do* / *put on* my hair with *soap* / *a brush*.
2 Do you *have* / *do* a bath every day?
3 She *puts on* / *has* make-up when she goes out.
4 Do you often have a *shave* / *wash* with an electric razor?

5 I brush my teeth at the *toilet* / *washbasin*.
6 I use a *towel* / *soap* after I *have* / *make* a shower.
7 I lie down in the *shower* / *bath* for fifteen minutes after work.
8 I *brush* / *make* my hair in front of the *mirror* / *brush*.

6 **Complete the text.** 将短文填写完整。

AMELIA: When I get up in the morning, I usually have a quick ▶ ___shower___ , but in winter, if I have time, I like to have a **(1)** _____ . I dry myself with a **(2)** _____ , and quickly get dressed. Then I look in the **(3)** _____ and do my **(4)** _____ . I **(5)** _____ my teeth standing in front of the **(6)** _____ , and after that, I **(7)** _____ some make-up. I'm ready to go to work.

HARRY: I look terrible in the morning when I wake up. The first thing I do is to clean my **(8)** _____ , and that makes me feel better. If I don't have time for a shower, I have a quick **(9)** _____ with soap and hot water. My hair is very short so I don't have to **(10)** _____ it, but I always have a **(11)** _____ with an electric **(12)** _____ .

7 **Complete the questions.** 将问句填写完整。

▶ How many times a week do you have a bath or ___shower___ ?
1 Do you brush your t_____ before or after breakfast?
2 How many times a day do you do your h_____ ?
3 How many times a day do you look in the m_____ ?
4 Do you carry a b_____ in your bag?
5 If you wear m_____ - _____ , do you p_____ it _____ every day or only sometimes?
6 If you shave, how often do you h_____ a shave? Do you use a r_____ or an e_____ r_____ ?

I have a shower every day.

8 **ABOUT YOU** **Write your answers to the questions in Exercise 7, or ask another student.**
根据自身情况回答练习7中的问题，也可以向同学提问。

1   window
2   curtain
3   clock
4   fan
5   light
6   TV/television
7   DVD player
8   fire
9   sofa
10 armchair
11 carpet
12 floor
13 telephone/phone
14 shelf (*pl* **shelves**)
15 the **corner** of the room

1 **Complete the words.** 将单词填写完整。

▶ co_r_ _n_ _e_ r

1 arm___ ___ ___ ___r
2 car___ ___t
3 f___ ___ ___r
4 li___ ___t

5 wi___ ___ ___w
6 f___ ___e
7 s___ ___a
8 sh___ ___f

9 te___ ___ ___ ___ ___ ___n
10 cur___ ___ ___n
11 c___ ___ ___k
12 te___ ___ ___ ___ ___ ___e

2 **Look at the picture. True or false? Write *T* or *F*.** 根据图片判断正误，正确填T，错误填F。

In the living room, there is only one …

▶ DVD player   T
1 window   ....
2 TV   ....
3 sofa   ....

4 clock   ....
5 armchair   ....
6 telephone   ....
7 fan   ....

8 corner   ....
9 light   ....
10 curtain   ....
11 floor   ....

12 carpet   ....
13 shelf   ....
14 fire   ....

3 **Complete the answers.** 填写答案。

▶ You watch this in the evening: TV/television
1 You talk to somebody on this: ....
2 You sit on this: .... / ....
3 You close these at night: ....
4 You check the time with this: ....
5 You need this when it's hot: ....
6 You need this when it's cold: ....

7 You need this when it's dark: ....
8 You can put a clock on this: ....
9 This goes over the floor: ....
10 This is where two walls meet: ....
11 You look through this: ....

4 ABOUT YOUR HOME **Write your answers, or ask another student.**
根据自身情况回答问题，也可以向同学提问。

1 What furniture have you got in your living room? ....
2 Which electrical things have you got in your living room? ....
3 Have you got these in your living room: a clock? a telephone? a carpet? If so, where are they? ....
....

62) Adjectives with prefixes 带前缀的形容词

Are you sure you have the correct answers?	~ No, I'm **uncertain** about two of them.
Are you a **lucky** person?	~ I'm **lucky** with money, but **unlucky** in love.
How's your brother these days?	~ Well, he smokes a lot – I think he's very **unhealthy**.
Did you need to buy a new car?	~ No, it was completely **unnecessary**.
Did you think the manager was being **rude**?	~ Yes, I thought he was very **impolite**.
Can you get home before six o'clock?	~ No, that's completely **impossible**.
Did you enjoy the meeting?	~ Yes, thanks. It was quite **informal** and fun.
Is 'fall' a **regular** verb?	~ No, it's **irregular**: fall, fell, fallen.

GLOSSARY

uncertain	not sure OPP **certain** SYNS **unsure/sure**
lucky	If you are **lucky**, good things happen to you that you cannot control. OPP **unlucky**
unhealthy	not well, often ill OPP **healthy**
unnecessary	If sth is **unnecessary**, you don't need to do it, or you don't need it. OPP **necessary**
rude	not speaking or behaving in a way that is correct for the social situation SYN **impolite** OPP **polite**: *In Britain, it is **rude/impolite** to eat with your mouth open.*

SPOTLIGHT *-in, -im, -ir, -un*

Some adjectives form opposites with prefixes *in-, im-, ir-*.
formal OPP **informal**
possible OPP **impossible** (*im-* before **p**)
regular OPP **irregular** (*ir-* before **r**)
Some other adjectives form opposites with the prefix *un-*.
certain OPP **uncertain**   **healthy** OPP **unhealthy**

1 **Correct the mistakes. Be careful: two answers are correct.** 改错题。注意: 有两个单词是正确的。

▶ imformal _informal_
1 incertain ....
2 inlucky ....
3 inregular ....
4 impossible ....
5 innecessary ....
6 inhealthy ....
7 unsure ....
8 unpolite ....

2 **Circle the correct word.** 圈出正确答案。

▶ Can you help me? I'm *sure /* (*unsure*) what to do next.
1 People who open the door for you in a shop are very *polite / rude*.
2 Words like *hi* and *yeah* are *formal / informal*.
3 *Remember* is *a regular / an irregular* verb.
4 We had two weeks of sunny weather for our holiday, which was very *lucky / unlucky*.
5 It was *necessary / unnecessary* to take a taxi because the hotel was very near the station.
6 If you don't say *thank you* for a present, people may think you are *polite / impolite*.
7 He has to decide where to go, but at the moment he is very *certain / uncertain*.
8 My sister watches TV all day and eats lots of cakes. She's very *healthy / unhealthy*.

3 **Complete the sentences with a suitable word.** 首字母填空。   ABOUT YOU

▶ I think spelling in English is i_mpossible_ .
1 Where I live, the neighbours are all very p........ .
2 I........ verbs are difficult to remember in English.
3 My English lessons are i........ and fun.
4 I'm very u........ on holiday. The weather is always terrible.
5 I'm u........ where to go for my holidays next summer. I just can't decide.
6 I think it's u........ to eat your food too quickly.
7 I think it's r........ to look at your phone when you're having a meal with people.
8 I think it's important to be clean, but it's u........ to have a shower every day.

4 ABOUT YOU **Are the sentences in Exercise 3 true for you? If not, write them so that they are true.**
你是否符合练习3中各句描述的情况? 如果不符, 写下你的实际情况。
▶ I think spelling in English is _impossible_ . _I think it's difficult, but not impossible!_

63 Adjective opposites 形容词的反义词

A Common opposites 1 常见反义词1

1 She's **asleep**.
OPP **awake**

2 The river is **wide**.
OPP **narrow**

3 The man is **weak**.
OPP **strong**

4 This is **heavy**.
OPP **light**

5 It feels **soft**.
OPP **hard**

6 It's a **low** wall.
OPP **high**

7 The woman is **rich**.
OPP **poor**

8 The bird is **dead**.
OPP **alive**

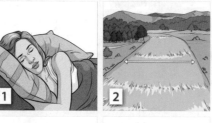

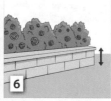

> **SPOTLIGHT** position of adjectives
>
> Adjectives usually go before a noun. They can also go after *be*.
> - *It's a **quiet** village. The village is **quiet**.*
>
> You can't use **alive**, **awake** or **asleep** before a noun.
> - *The man is **alive**.* (NOT ~~an alive man~~)

1 Write *Yes* or *No*. 填写yes或no。

▶ Is a 120 kg person heavy?   Yes

1 Is the River Nile narrow?   ....
2 Does wood feel hard?   ....
3 Is Nelson Mandela still alive?   ....
4 Are mobile phones light?   ....
5 Are elephants very strong?   ....

6 Are you asleep at the moment?   ....
7 Is America a rich country?   ....
8 If you are walking, are you awake?   ....
9 Are all the buildings in Dubai low?   ....
10 Is rice soft before you cook it?   ....

2 Write the opposite. 写出反义词。

▶ The bed is *hard*.   soft

1 His legs are *weak*.   ....
2 The dog's *asleep*.   ....
3 They're very *rich*.   ....

4 The roof is *high*.   ....
5 The road is *narrow*.   ....
6 The cat is *dead*.   ....
7 The bag was *heavy*.   ....

3 Complete the dialogues. 将对话填写完整。

▶ Is it safe to walk on this bridge?   ~ Yes, it's very strong.

1 Did you sleep well?   ~ No, the bed was too .... It was like sleeping on the floor.
2 Can Rowena walk very far?   ~ No, she's still .... after her illness.
3 Has Eric got a lot of money?   ~ Yes, he's very ....
4 Has Kelly still got a dog?   ~ No, it's ...., I'm afraid.
5 Can you see over the wall?   ~ No, it's too .... I can't see a thing.
6 Can we carry that table to the garden?   ~ Yes, it's quite ....
7 Can you swim across the river here?   ~ Yes, it's quite .... – that will be easy.
8 Dan's eyes are closed.   ~ Yes, I think he's .... He said he was very tired.
9 That family lives in one room.   ~ Yes, they're very ....
10 What a lovely little baby!   ~ Yes, his skin is so lovely and ....

B Common opposites 2 常见反义词2

OPPOSITES QUESTIONNAIRE

- Is it **common** or **unusual** for you to get a cold or flu?
- Do you prefer **traditional** houses or **modern** houses?
- Do you prefer to sleep in a **dark** room or a **light** room?
- Do you and your best friend enjoy **similar** things or **different** things?
- For you, is **social media** a **positive** thing or a **negative** thing?
- On holiday, do you prefer to have **general** plans or more **specific** plans?
- Is knowing about history **useful** or **useless** in your daily life?
- Do other people think you are **lazy** or **hardworking**?

GLOSSARY	
common	If sth is **common**, it happens often, or you find it in many places: *a common name* OPP **unusual**
traditional	If sth is **traditional**, it is typical of things that people have done for a long time. **tradition** *n* OPP **modern**
dark	with no light, or not much light OPP **light**
similar	the same in many ways, but not completely the same OPP **different**
social media	websites, e.g. WhatsApp, Instagram, where you can communicate with people who have similar interests
positive	thinking or talking about the good parts of a situation OPP **negative**
general	not in detail, giving only the main parts of sth OPP **specific**
useful	good and helpful for doing sth OPP **useless**
lazy	A **lazy** person doesn't like working hard. OPP **hardworking**

4 Tick (✓) the words with the main stress on the first syllable, like <u>narrow</u> and <u>tiny</u>. Put a cross (✗) for the others. Practise saying the words.
在重音在第一个音节上的单词后打钩（√），如<u>narrow</u>和<u>tiny</u>，其他情况则打叉（×），并练习发音。

▶ modern ✓   prefer ✗

1 useless ☐   3 different ☐   5 general ☐   7 unusual ☐   9 tradition ☐
2 common ☐   4 specific ☐   6 media ☐   8 useful ☐   10 similar ☐

5 True or false? Write *T* or *F*. 判断正误，正确填T，错误填F。

▶ A useful book is one that helps you to do something.   T

1 Two similar things are almost the same. ....   6 A useless thing will help you. ....
2 You can read easily in a light room. ....   7 If a type of car is common, you see it a lot. ....
3 The style of a traditional building is modern. ....   8 A lazy person works very hard. ....
4 An unusual event happens a lot. ....   9 In the middle of the day, it's usually dark. ....
5 Specific instructions are clear and with a lot of detail. ....   10 If somebody is on social media, they are online. ....

6 Complete the dialogues. 将对话填写完整。

▶ Do the two brothers look different?   ~ No, they look very similar .
1 Did you talk about anything specific?   ~ No, it was a very .... conversation.
2 Did you go to class yesterday?   ~ Yes, we had a very .... lesson on prepositions.
3 Is Paco's flat dark?   ~ No, it's very .... with lovely views of the sea.
4 Is Bythesea a common name?   ~ No, it's very .... I've never heard it.
5 Do you like modern architecture?   ~ No, I prefer .... styles.
6 Mariella seems a bit lazy to me.   ~ No, that's not true. She's very ....
7 Was the weather information helpful?   ~ No, it was .... , and we got very wet.

7 ABOUT YOU   **Write your answers to the questions in the questionnaire, or talk to another student.**
根据自身情况填写问卷，也可以向同学提问。

64 Common adverbs 常见副词

A Showing that something is important 表示强调的副词

Adverb	Example	Meaning
only	*She was **only** 17 when she got married.* (It's unusual to get married at 17.) *We can walk to the station – it's **only** five minutes.* (NOT 15 or 20.)	We use **only** to say 'no more than'.
even	*It's cold here, **even** in summer.* (In most places, it's warm in the summer.) *My older brother is 1.90 m, and my younger brother is **even** taller.*	We often use **even** before a fact that is surprising or difficult to believe, or to make (a comparative) another word stronger.
still	*After 25 years, I **still** love my job.* (I continue to love my job.) *Do they live in Paris now? ~ No, they're **still** in London.*	We use **still** to say that a fact or situation continues to be true.
especially	*We liked the towns in the south, **especially** Seville.* (Seville was the best.) *It's very hot here, **especially** in July and August.* (July and August are the hottest.)	We use **especially** to say 'more than others'.

1 <u>Underline</u> the correct answer. 在正确答案下划线。

▶ The food is good there, *only* / *especially* the fish.

1 He was *only* / *even* 15 when he left school.

2 I've seen the film five times and I *even* / *still* enjoy it.

3 The students are very nice, *still* / *especially* Marcel.

4 There are *even* / *only* three bridges like this in the world.

5 It was cold yesterday, but it's *even* / *only* colder today.

6 I study hard, but my English is *still* / *only* terrible.

2 Put the word in brackets in the correct place in the sentence. 将括号内单词置于句中正确位置。

▶ It's six kilometres to the next town. (only) It's only six kilometres to the next town.

1 He's 75 and he plays tennis. (still) ....

2 It's nice there, in the morning. (especially) ....

3 There are three students in the class. (only) ....

4 He works on Sundays. (even) ....

5 She's at university. (still) ....

6 Rio is big, but Sao Paolo is bigger. (even) ....

3 Complete the sentences. 将句子填写完整。

▶ He's ninety, but he .....still..... drives a car.

1 .... four people came to the party. It was a bit sad.

2 They have been in Singapore for ten years and they .... like living there.

3 I love fish, ... salmon.

4 He can't drive – he's .... 15.

5 This question isn't difficult. .... a child could answer it.

6 She enjoyed the book, ... the first part.

7 He lives in Italy now, but he .... speaks English most of the time.

8 The sign was difficult to read, ... with my glasses.

B Degree 表示程度的副词

0% ——— 100%

a bit / a little   quite/pretty/rather   very   extremely
                                              └─── really ───┘

a bit / a little	Use **a bit** or **a little** before an adjective or comparative adjective, but not before a positive adjective. (NOT ~~a bit good~~) *The lesson was **a bit** boring.* *It's **a little** warmer than yesterday.*
quite pretty *inf*	= more than *a bit*, but less than *very* *The film was **quite/pretty** interesting.* *The town is **quite/pretty** big.*
rather	= *quite* *The test was **rather** difficult.* *She was **rather** tired after the journey.* If you use **rather** with a positive adjective, you are often surprised and pleased. *The restaurant was **rather** nice.*
extremely	= a bit stronger than *very*. You can use **extremely** with adjectives, but not with verbs. *I was **extremely** tired by 6 o'clock.* *We were **extremely** busy on Saturday.*
really	= *very, extremely* You can use **really** with adjectives and verbs. *The restaurant was **really** good.* *The weather was **really** terrible.* *We were **really** tired.* *I **really** liked the film.*

4 **Circle the correct answers. Sometimes both answers are correct.** 圈出正确答案，注意：可能两个答案都正确。

▶ It was (quite) / *a bit* interesting.

1 She's *pretty / quite* untidy.
2 Her new shoes are *really / a bit* wonderful.
3 My sister is *a bit / a little* untidy.
4 I *really / extremely* enjoyed the meal.

5 She was *really / extremely* friendly.
6 Tina's flat is *a bit / quite* nice.
7 The restaurant was *rather / really* good.
8 The hotel's *a bit / really* comfortable.

5 **Rewrite the sentences using an adverb with a similar meaning to the underlined words.**
用与划线部分意思相近的副词改写句子。

▶ The film was <u>a bit</u> boring. The film was a little boring.
1 He was <u>very</u> good. ....
2 The holiday was <u>quite</u> interesting. ....
3 She's <u>a little</u> unfriendly. ....
4 The kitchen was <u>extremely</u> clean. ....
5 The room was <u>a bit</u> small. ....
6 Her new boyfriend is <u>rather</u> unfriendly. ....
7 They're <u>really</u> nice people. ....
8 The exam results were <u>quite</u> surprising. ....

6 **Complete the sentences in a suitable way.** 用恰当的单词将句子填写完整。

▶ I went to bed because I was extremely tired .

1 The food was excellent, but the service was rather ....
2 I like Maria's new boyfriend. He's extremely ....
3 I went to see a concert last night and I really ....
4 Nobody talked to me at the party, so I felt pretty ....

5 I thought the lesson might be boring, but in fact it was rather ....
6 We waited thirty minutes for the bus, so we arrived a bit ....
7 The dog looked horrible, but in fact it was quite ....
8 People think he's hardworking, but I know he's really ....

CLASS 9   Monday 3.30 – 5.30

Cora always does her homework very **carefully**. ☑

Juno is clever and answers most questions **correctly**. ☑

Eliane speaks very **clearly**. ☑

Rocco speaks too **fast**; he needs to speak more **slowly**. ☑

Lucas speaks too **loudly**, but Ines speaks too **quietly**. ☑

Jan speaks English very **well**, but he writes **badly**. ☑

Ewa always arrives **late** but just smiles **happily**. ☑

Mahmud tries very **hard**, but he thinks the lessons are **difficult**. ☑

Layla passes all her exams very **easily**. ☑

SPOTLIGHT adverbs of manner

Adverbs of **manner** are used with verbs to tell you more about the way you do something, or the way that something happens. They often end in -ly.
sad adj / **sadly** adv; **quiet** adj / **quietly** adv;
careful adj / **carefully** adv

■ He opened the door **quietly**. ■ Shona looked at me **sadly**.
A few adverbs are irregular.
fast adj / **fast** adv; **late** adj / **late** adv; **hard** adj / **hard** adv;
good adj / **well** adv

Adjectives ending in -y have adverbs ending in -ily.
happy / **happily**; **easy** / **easily**; **angry** / **angrily**

GLOSSARY

manner	the way you do sth or the way that sth happens: *Jacques has a friendly **manner**.* = He acts in a friendly way.
clearly	in a way that is easy to hear, understand or see
fast adv	quickly: *He drives **fast**.* **fast** adj: *She has a **fast** car.*
late adv	after the correct time **late** adj OPP **early**
hard adv	a lot: *work/try **hard*** **hard** adj difficult: *The test was **hard**.*

1 **Write the adverb form.** 写出相应副词。

▶ careful   *carefully*

1	slow	....	**5**	clear	....	**9**	easy	....
2	bad	....	**6**	happy	....	**10**	quiet	....
3	angry	....	**7**	good	....	**11**	correct	....
4	late	....	**8**	hard	....	**12**	fast	....

2 **Rewrite the sentence using the verb in CAPITALS and an adverb.** 用所给动词和相关副词改写句子。

▶ Jesse is bad at playing football. PLAY Jesse *plays football badly.*
1 I have very clear writing. WRITE I ....
2 My cousin is a good singer. SING My ....
3 My boss is a hard worker. WORK My ....
4 Lola is a careful driver. DRIVE Lola ....
5 Robina's answers to the questions were correct. ANSWER Robina ....
6 Julio's pronunciation of words isn't clear. PRONOUNCE Julio ....
7 The exercise was easy for Miriam. DO Miriam ....
8 Amina is very fast at doing the work. WORK Amina ....
9 My little boy is a slow reader. READ My ....
10 She was angry when she spoke to Sam. SPEAK She ....

3 **Complete the questions.** 将问题填写完整。 ABOUT YOU

▶ Do you speak English slowly or *fast* ?
1 Do you arrive for work/classes at the right time or .... ?
2 Do people in your family speak quietly or .... ?
3 Does your teacher speak .... so that you can understand?
4 Do you drive well or .... ?
5 Do you think .... about what you want to say in English?
6 Do you relax in class, or do you work .... ?

4 ABOUT YOU **Write your answers to the questions in Exercise 3, or ask another student.**
根据自身情况回答练习3中的问题，也可以向同学提问。

66) School subjects 学科

SCIENCE SUBJECTS

  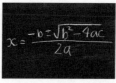 

| chemistry | physics | biology | maths | computer science |

ARTS SUBJECTS

| geography | history | literature | languages | art |

| PE | design and technology |

GLOSSARY

subject	*Physics*, *history*, etc. are school **subjects**.
maths	short for **mathematics**
PE	sport and exercise as a school subject, short for **physical education**
design	(sounds like *fine*) pictures or plans that show how to make sth
technology	the science or information about how things work

SPOTLIGHT *be good at something*

If you are **good at something**, you do it well. If you are **bad at** it, you do it very badly. SYN **terrible at sth**

- *I'm (quite) good at* languages. - *I'm terrible at* maths.

---

1 Is the pronunciation of the <u>underlined</u> letters the same or different? Write *S* or *D*. Practise saying the words. 划线部分的发音是否相同? 相同填S, 不同填D, 并练习发音。

▶ <u>a</u>rt / m<u>a</u>ths ... D ...
1 de<u>s</u>ign / phy<u>s</u>ics ....
2 bio<u>l</u>ogy / <u>sc</u>ience ....
3 biol<u>o</u>gy / ge<u>o</u>graphy ....

4 hi<u>s</u>tory / <u>s</u>tory ....
5 <u>ch</u>emistry / te<u>ch</u>nology ....
6 comp<u>u</u>ter / lang<u>u</u>age ....
7 literat<u>u</u>re / pict<u>u</u>re ....

2 Write the name of a school subject or subjects. 填写学科名称或学科大类。

▶ algebra, geometry ... maths ...
1 exercises in the gym ....
2 Shakespeare, Tolstoy ....
3 wars in the past ....
4 rivers in Africa ....
5 Picasso, Da Vinci ....
6 Japanese, Arabic ....

7 CO_2, H_2O ....
8 Apple and Google ....
9 parts of a flower or animal ....
10 create a new product ....
11 What is light? ....
12 History and geography are ....
13 Maths and chemistry are ....

3 ABOUT YOU Complete the sentences about yourself using the right verb form. If possible, tell another student. 根据自身情况, 选择正确的动词形式将句子填写完整。如有条件, 可以告诉其他同学。

1 At school, *I'm* / *I was* good at ....
2 *I'm* / *I was* also quite good at ....
3 *I'm* / *I was* terrible at ....

4 *I don't* / *didn't* study ....
5 The subject I *like* / *liked* most *is* / *was* ....
6 And the subject I *hate* / *hated* most *is* / *was* ....

67) The education system 教育体系

A The education system 教育体系

uniform

In the **education system** in England and Wales, you **start school at the age of** four or five and **continue up to** the age of 16. At 16, you can **leave school**, and then you must **either get a job** with **training**, **or** do some training in a **college** for a particular job, e.g. working in the hotel business. The other **option** is to **stay at school** for two more years. After that, you can get a job or go to university.

SPOTLIGHT *either ... or ...*

We use **or** to show there are two things/people you can choose, and we use **either ... or ...** to make this contrast stronger.
- *After 16, you can **either** do arts subjects **or** science subjects.*
- ***Either** you go to university, **or** you get a job.*

1 **Put the story in order.** 将句子排序。
- a He then went to a local college
- b He carried on up to the age of 16,
- c When Tom was five, ▶ 1
- d and finally he got a job in a local hairdresser's.
- e when he decided to leave school.
- f where he trained to become a hairdresser,
- g he started school.

2 **Complete the text with words from the glossary.** 用单词表中的单词填空。
▶ <u>At</u> the age of 16, French students can **(1)** _____ school and **(2)** _____ a job, but around 65% **(3)** _____ at school for another two years. They then have two **(4)** _____ : they can **(5)** _____ go to a *lycée général* **(6)** _____ go to a *lycée technique* or *lycée professionnel*. At the *lycée général*, many students go on to university. At the other types of school, students do some **(7)** _____ in order to prepare for a particular job.

3 ABOUT YOUR COUNTRY **Complete the questions, but don't write answers.** ABOUT YOU
将问题填写完整。
▶ At what age do children <u>start</u> school? ....
1 Do they usually wear a _____ ? ....
2 At what age can they _____ school? ....
3 At this age, do they _____ a job or do more _____ ? ....
4 Do many students _____ at school after 16? ....
5 What can they do when they leave school _____ 18? ....
6 What did you do? OR What are you going to do? ....

4 ABOUT YOU AND YOUR COUNTRY **Write your answers to the questions in Exercise 3, or ask another student.** 根据自身情况回答练习3中的问题，也可以向同学提问。

B Exams 考试

When I was at school, I went to all the **lessons** and **did** my **homework**, but I didn't **work** very hard. So, when I **took exams** at 16, my **results** weren't fantastic. I **passed** six, which was good, but I **failed** physics. It was my **worst** result – I got a **grade** F, which was terrible. After that, I went to a college where I worked hard and **did well**. I passed all my exams at 18 and went to university. That's where I am now.

Seth

GLOSSARY

lesson	a period of time (e.g. 45 minutes) in school when you learn/teach
do homework [U]	do work the teacher has given you at home (NOT ~~homeworks~~)
work hard	work a lot
result	the grade or mark you get in an exam, e.g. A or 9/10
(the) worst	superlative of **bad** OPP **(the) best** superlative of **good**
grade	You **get a grade**, e.g. A or B, or a **mark**, e.g. 15/20, in a test or an exam.
do well	be good at sth and get better at it OPP **do badly**

SPOTLIGHT *exams*

Exam is short for **examination**. It's an important test at the end of a period of study. We say:

take/do an exam sit down and write your answers in the exam

pass an exam take an exam and do well, e.g. grade A / a mark of 85%

fail an exam take an exam and do badly, e.g. grade D / a mark of 35%

---

5 **Look at Rafael's exam results on the right and answer the questions.** 根据拉斐尔的考试成绩回答问题。

▶ How many exams did he take? _7_
1 Did he take an exam in chemistry? ....
2 How many did he pass? ....
3 How many did he fail? ....
4 What was his best grade? ....
5 What was his worst grade? ....
6 What did he get in English? ....

EXAM	GRADE A, B, C = pass / D, E = fail
French	B
IT	C
Geography	D
Biology	A
English	C
History	B
Maths	E

6 **Complete the sentences.** 将句子填写完整。

▶ Six out of ten isn't a very good _mark_ .
1 I have to .... an English exam tomorrow.
2 Did you .... your homework last night?
3 Paula did very .... in her German exam; she got a good ....
4 I got my exam .... yesterday. I passed all of them.
5 Andre is very unhappy at the moment. He's doing .... at school, and last week he ....
   an important maths exam.
6 Maths is my .... subject. I'm terrible at it.

7 **ABOUT YOU** **Complete the sentences about yourself using the right verb form, then write answers to the questions, or ask another student.**
选择正确的动词形式，根据自身情况回答问题，也可以向同学提问。

1 How long *are / were* your lessons at school? ....
2 *Do / Did* you work hard at school most of the time? ....
3 At what age *do / did* you take important exams? ....
4 How many *did / will* you take? ....
5 *Did / Will* you pass all of them? ....
6 What's your best subject? ....

68) University 大学

A A university degree 大学学位

I started university two years ago when I was nineteen, and I'm **doing a degree in** Spanish and French. The **course lasts** four years, and there are three **terms** a year. I work in the **library** a lot because I have to **write** lots of **essays**. I also have to take exams, and last term I failed one and had to take it **again**. I got the result two weeks ago – **fortunately** I passed this time. When I've got my degree, I want to **do research**.

Seth

GLOSSARY	
do a degree (in sth)	study a subject or subjects at university. You **do a degree in** a subject.
course	a number of classes on a subject, e.g. an English **course**
term	a period of study, usually about ten weeks
library	a place where you can read and borrow books (Be careful: a **bookshop** is a place where you buy books.)
write an essay	do a piece of writing on a subject
again	one more time
fortunately	We say **fortunately** when we start talking about sth good. OPP **unfortunately**
do research	study a subject for a long time (usually after a first degree) to learn new information about it

SPOTLIGHT *How long does it last? | How long does it take?*

Last means 'continue for a period of time'.
- *A university term **lasts** ten weeks.*
- *My French course **lasts** a year.*

We use **take** (often with *it*) to talk about how long we need to do something.
- *It **took me** three years to do my research.*
- *He **took** two days to write the essay. It **took him** two days to write the essay.*

1 **Circle the correct word.** 圈出正确答案。

▶ She did an English (course) / term.

1 I want to *do / make* a degree in maths.
2 A *term / degree* lasts about ten weeks.
3 I have to *learn / write* essays.
4 Most lessons *take / last* an hour.

5 I study a lot in the *library / bookshop*.
6 I want to *do / make* some research.
7 *Fortunately / Unfortunately*, I failed the exam.
8 *Before / After* a degree, some people do research.
9 It *takes / lasts* a long time to do a degree.

2 **Complete the dialogues.** 将对话填写完整。

▶ How long does the term _last_ ? ~ About twelve weeks.

1 Are you doing a .... ? ~ Yes, ... Medicine.
2 Are you planning to do .... ? ~ Yes, when I've got my first degree.
3 Did he get his exam results? ~ Yes, ... he passed.
4 Can he take the exam .... if he fails the first time? ~ Yes, in September.
5 Did she have to write an .... ? ~ Yes, and it .... her a long time.
6 How long does the course .... ? ~ It's only one term.
7 Did you buy that new dictionary? ~ Yes, I got it in the college ....
8 Did Miriam pass all her exams? ~ No, ... she failed two subjects.

3 ABOUT YOUR COUNTRY **Write your answers, or ask another student.**
根据自身情况回答问题，也可以向同学提问。

1 How long do you need to study for a degree in Medicine? ....
2 What percentage of young people do a degree? ....
3 Do many students go on and do research? ....
4 How long does a university term last? ....
5 If you fail your exams, can you always take them again? ....

B University subjects and people
大学学科与专业人士

	Degree Subject	Person
1	medicine	a doctor
2	architecture	an architect
3	engineering	an engineer
4	law	a lawyer
5	business studies	a businessman/woman
6	journalism	a journalist OR a reporter
7	computer science	e.g. software designer, IT manager

SPOTLIGHT *teacher, lecturer, professor*

A **teacher** is a person who teaches for a job, usually in a school (NOT *a professor*). In the UK, a person who teaches in a university is a **lecturer**, and they give **lectures** (NOT *lessons*). A **professor** in a university is a lecturer of the highest level.

4 Is the pronunciation of the <u>underlined</u> letters the same or different? Write *S* or *D*. Practise saying the words. 划线部分的发音是否相同? 相同填S, 不同填D, 并练习发音。

▶ des<u>ig</u>n / med<u>ic</u>ine   D

1 l<u>aw</u> / f<u>ou</u>r   ....
2 <u>c</u>omputer / do<u>c</u>tor   ....
3 bu<u>s</u>iness / journali<u>s</u>t   ....

4 comp<u>u</u>ter / w<u>o</u>man   ....
5 law<u>y</u>er / bo<u>y</u>   ....
6 s<u>c</u>ience / de<u>s</u>ign   ....
7 tea<u>ch</u>er / ar<u>ch</u>itect   ....

5 Complete the sentences. Use the word on the right to help you. 用所给单词的相关词汇填空。

▶ He always wanted to be a _teacher_ .   TEACHING
1 She wants to be a _____ .   MEDICINE
2 When did Tom become an _____ ?   ENGINEERING
3 Emily is studying to become an _____ .   ARCHITECTURE
4 My sister is a _____ .   LAW
5 Edward now works as a _____ .   LECTURE
6 After his degree he became a software _____ .   DESIGN
7 Is it difficult to become a _____ ?   JOURNALISM
8 I knew he'd become a _____ .   BUSINESS STUDIES

6 Complete the words in the sentences. 首字母填空。

▶ He wants to be a hospital d_octor_ .
1 My uncle is a university p_____ .
2 It's not easy to get a place to study l_____ .
3 My friend got a job as an IT m_____ .
4 He's a j_____ for a national paper.
5 I don't go to all my university l_____ .

6 My degree was in b_____ studies.
7 I studied journalism to be a r_____ .
8 I enjoyed my e_____ degree.
9 She wants to do computer s_____ .
10 She's a b_____ now. She works for a large company.

7 ABOUT YOU Take six jobs from this unit and put them in order from 1) a job I would like, to 6) a job I would not like. If possible, talk to another student.
选择本单元涉及的六种职业, 按个人好恶从1至6排序。如有条件, 可以和同学交流讨论。

69) Jobs 职业

What do you do?　　What's your job?　　I'm …

a police officer/
policeman/policewoman

a businessman/
businesswoman

a secretary
in a company

a dentist

a model

a shop assistant/
sales assistant

a nurse

a fashion designer

a soldier

a pilot

a builder

a teacher

a chef

a cleaner

a lorry driver
(ALSO a train/bus/taxi driver)

a hairdresser

GLOSSARY

job　the work that you do for money:
I've got a **job** as a waiter (NOT as waiter.)

work [U]　the job that you do: I need **work**.
(NOT a work OR works) **work** v

boss　a person who tells people what to do in their job

career　the work you do for many years: I want a **career**
in teaching. His **career** is very important to him.

SPOTLIGHT employ

If you **employ somebody**, you pay somebody to work for you.
- The factory **employs** 800 people.

A **company** is a group of people who work together and make or sell things. A person or company who does this is the **employer**, and the person who works for somebody is the **employee**.
- We have 800 **employees** in the company.

If you are able to work but don't have a job, you are **unemployed**.

1 **Circle the correct answer.** 圈出正确答案。

▶ A *lorry driver* / (*chef*) works in a kitchen.
1 I'm looking for a *work* / *job*.
2 A *shop assistant* / *bus driver* sells things.
3 A *model* / *nurse* works in a hospital.
4 A career is work that you do for a *short* / *long* time.
5 A fashion designer designs *clothes* / *furniture*.
6 An unemployed person *has* / *hasn't* got a job.

7 If you are an *employer* / *employee*, you work for other people.
8 A *boss* / *hairdresser* tells people what to do.
9 A *pilot* / *dentist* looks after people's teeth.
10 *Models* / *Secretaries* are usually very tall.
11 A *builder* / *cleaner* works outside a lot.
12 You can have a career *in the police* / *when you stop work*.

2 **Is the pronunciation of the <u>underlined</u> letters the same or different? Write *S* or *D*.**
Practise saying the words. 划线部分的发音是否相同? 相同填S, 不同填D, 并练习发音。

▶ f<u>a</u>shion / <u>a</u>ssistant ....D....
1 p<u>i</u>lot / dent<u>i</u>st ....
2 p<u>i</u>lot / dr<u>i</u>ver ....
3 b<u>u</u>siness / b<u>u</u>ilder ....

4 p<u>o</u>lice / m<u>o</u>del ....
5 tea<u>ch</u>er / <u>ch</u>ef ....
6 w<u>or</u>k / n<u>ur</u>se ....
7 <u>de</u>signer / <u>dri</u>ver ....

3 **Complete the sentences with jobs from page 134.** 用P134的职业填空。

▶ You have to walk a lot if you are _a nurse, a police officer or a soldier._
1 You probably have to go to university to be _____.
2 You need to work with your hands to be _____.
3 You may need to be good at maths if you are _____.
4 You have a lot of free time if you are _____.
5 You usually have to wear a uniform if you are _____.
6 You work in an office a lot of the time if you are _____.

4 **Complete the dialogues.** 将对话填写完整。

▶ Does he work in a shop?   ~ Yes, he's _a sales assistant._
1 Do you work for the boss?   ~ Yes, I'm her _____.
2 Does he work for British Airways? ~ Yes, he's _____.
3 Does Lisa cut people's hair?   ~ Yes, she's _____.
4 Does he tell people what to do?   ~ Yes, he's _____.
5 Do you see her clothes in magazines? ~ Yes, she's _____.
6 Is her picture in fashion magazines? ~ Yes, she's _____.
7 Does your brother work in a school? ~ Yes, he's _____.
8 Does Fergus work in that restaurant? ~ Yes, he's _____.
9 Hashem sells computers, doesn't he? ~ Yes, he works for a very big _____.

5 ABOUT YOU **Think about your family and people you know. Do you know anybody who does these jobs? Write your answers, or talk to another student.**
你的家人和熟人中, 是否有人从事这些职业? 写下你的答案, 也可以和同学交流讨论。

▶ a nurse _My neighbour, Mrs Petrova, is a nurse._
  a soldier _I don't know anyone who's a soldier._
1 a secretary _____
2 a chef _____
3 a hairdresser _____
4 a teacher _____
5 a taxi driver _____
6 a dentist _____
7 a businessman or businesswoman _____
8 a boss _____

70 Describing jobs 描述职业

A Basic information 基本信息

Where does he work?

He **works in an office**[1] / **a factory**[2] / **a hospital**[3].

What does she do?

She's a **manager**.   She **manages** a company.
She works **as** a secretary.   She's **in advertising / in the army**.

Who does he work for?

He **works for** ─┌ a car **company**. (e.g. Toyota, Mercedes)
                  └ an **airline**. (e.g. Emirates, KLM)

What hours does she work?

She works ─┌ **from** nine **to** five.
           │ **long** hours.
           └ 12 hours **a day**.

How much does he earn?

He **earns** a lot. His **salary** is $100,000 **a year**.

GLOSSARY	
manager	a person who controls an organization, e.g. a company or shop **manage** v
advertising	the business of telling people about things to buy
army	a large group of soldiers who fight on land
earn	get money for the work that you do
salary	money you get every month/year for the work that you do

1 Complete the sentences with words and phrases from the box. 用方框内的词或短语填空。

| an office | an American airline | work for | she work ✓ | hours a day |
| long hours | earn much | a year | ten to six | advertising | does he earn |

▶ Where does _she work_ ?
1 She works _____ .
2 I work in _____ .
3 He's in _____ .
4 Who do you _____ ?
5 How much _____ ?
6 I work eight _____
7 She works for _____
8 She doesn't _____
9 He earns €50,000 _____
10 I work from _____ .

2 Complete the sentences. 将句子填写完整。

▶ Who does he work _for_ ?
1 She's a doctor in the local _____ . Her husband works _____ a factory.
2 I work for a computer _____ , and my _____ is now €60,000 _____ year.
3 He doesn't work _____ hours: he only works _____ 9.00 _____ 3.00.
4 She's a nurse, so she doesn't _____ much money.
5 My brother is a soldier _____ the _____ .
6 Who do you work _____ ? ~ I'm a pilot. I work for a Spanish _____ called Air Europa.
7 TV gets a lot of money from _____ .
8 He _____ a large company in France. He has worked there for 15 years and he has been the _____ for the last five.

3 ABOUT YOU **If you have a job, write your answers. If not, ask someone with a job, or write about somebody in your family.** 根据自身情况回答问题，如果你没有工作，可以咨询有工作的人或填写家人相关情况。
1 What do you do? _____
2 Who do you work for? _____
3 Where do you work? _____
4 What hours do you work? _____
5 Do you think people in your job earn a lot of money? _____

B What does it involve? 工作内容

Daniela Alessi, architect

My job **involves** many things:

- I **design buildings**[1], mostly big **projects**.
- I **meet**[2] **clients** and **discuss** problems with them.
- I **organize meetings**[3] with **colleagues**.
- I **send** hundreds of emails.
- I write **reports**.
- I **spend a lot of time** talking to people.

GLOSSARY

involve	have sth as a part: *The job **involves** using a computer.*
project	a big plan to do sth, e.g. *a **project** to build a new airport*
client	a person who pays an architect, lawyer, etc. for their work
discuss	talk about sth seriously (NOT ~~discuss about~~)
organize	If you **organize** a meeting, you find a time and a place when everybody can go to it.
colleague	a person who works with you
send	You write a letter or email, then you **send** it to sb.
report	a piece of writing that gives information about your work
spend time doing sth	do sth for a period of time

SPOTLIGHT *meet* and *meeting*

Meet has different meanings:

1 see and speak to somebody for the first time: *I haven't **met** my boss's wife.*

2 come together, usually because you planned it: (*see picture 2*)

A **meeting** is a time when people come together, usually to talk about something (*see picture 3*).

---

4 Match 1–5 with a–f. 配对题。

▶ spend time	*c*	**a** problems
1 meet	....	**b** emails
2 organize	....	**c** making phone calls ✓
3 send	....	**d** bridges
4 discuss	....	**e** clients
5 design	....	**f** meetings

5 Correct the mistakes in the sentences. 改错题。

▶ I have ~~sended~~ the letters. _sent_

1 We discussed about our problems. _____

2 I have a meet this afternoon. _____

3 She spends a lot of time travel. _____

4 Could you organize the meeting? _____

5 My job involves to use a computer. _____

6 I knew her for the first time last week. _____

6 Complete the text. 将短文填写完整。

I work for Daniela's company as her secretary. I often ▶ _meet_ many of her **(1)** _____ when they come to her office to **(2)** _____ work. At the moment, we have a big **(3)** _____ : Daniela is **(4)** _____ a new department store for the town centre.

My job **(5)** _____ doing other things as well: I **(6)** _____ meetings with different people about the project; I receive and **(7)** _____ lots of emails, and sometimes I write **(8)** _____ about the project for Daniela. Fortunately, I am not alone. I have two other **(9)** _____ in the office with me. We work hard but we also **(10)** _____ time talking to each other.

71 Job interview 求职面试

Two months ago, I saw an **advertisement** online for a job working with young people in the **community**. You needed a university degree, but no **experience**, so I decided to **apply**. I **filled in** the **form** and **posted** it, and two weeks later I went for an **interview**. I was very nervous and the **interviewer** asked some difficult questions, but they **offered** me the job, by email. The money is not bad and I will get a lot of **training**, so I **accepted**. I'm starting next week.

GLOSSARY	
advertisement	a notice, picture or film telling people about a job, product or service ALSO **advert/ad**
community	all the people who live in a place; the place where they live
experience	knowing about sth because you have seen it or done it
apply (for sth)	write to ask for sth
form	a piece of paper or a document with questions and spaces for you to write answers **fill in a form** write answers on the form
post	send a letter
interview	a meeting when sb asks you questions to decide if you will get a job. The person who does this is the **interviewer**. **interview** v
offer	say you will give sth to sb, e.g. a job or help, if they want it **offer** n
training	the activity of learning how to do a job
accept	say yes to sth

1 **Put the story in order.** 将句子排序。

She offered me the job. ☐
I went for an interview. ☐
I posted it. ☐
I decided to apply. ☐
I saw an advertisement for a job. [1]
I accepted the job. ☐
I filled in the form. ☐
The interviewer asked me questions. ☐

2 **Complete the sentences.** 将句子填写完整。

▶ Life in a small fishing _community_ is different from life in a big city.
1 My boss was very busy, so I _____ to help her.
2 Don't _____ the form. You should email it instead.
3 My brother has an _____ for a job next week. I hope he gets it.
4 The company asked me to _____ in a form.
5 I have a friend who is doing a lot of _____ in his new job at the bank.
6 At the moment I'm _____ for a place at university. I want to go next year.
7 It's easy to get a job in a shop, but you need more _____ to become a manager.
8 The job they offered me wasn't very interesting, so I didn't _____ it.
9 I saw a funny _____ on TV last night for a new Italian car.
10 I was surprised at some of the questions the _____ asked me.

3 ABOUT YOU **Write your answers, or ask another student.** 根据自身情况回答问题，也可以向同学提问。

1 Have you applied for any jobs? If so, what are they? _____
2 Do you have experience of interviews? If so, what? _____
3 Have you had training for a job? If so, what? _____
4 What forms have you filled in this year? _____
5 Would you like a job working in the community with young people? Why? / Why not? _____
_____

My first day **at work** was **surprising**. I was nervous when I **entered** the building, but everyone was **so** friendly **that** I didn't need to **worry**. I was **part of** a small **unit** (six of us), and it was our job to **support** local **charities** in the community. Caroline, my boss, introduced me to the rest of the group, and I spent the **whole** day watching and listening. It was **such** an **amazing** day.

GLOSSARY

at work	This shows where you are. ALSO *at school/home*, etc.
surprising	If sth is **surprising**, it is different from what is normal or usual.
enter *formal*	come or go into a place
worry	think or feel that sth bad will happen **worry** *n*
part of sth	some but not all of sth
unit	one complete thing or group that may be part of sth larger
support	If you **support** sb, you are there to help them if they need it.
charity	an organization that collects money to help people who need it
whole	all of sth
amazing	If sth is **amazing**, it is difficult to believe, and usually very good. SYN **incredible**

SPOTLIGHT *so and such*

So and **such** are used before words to make them stronger. You use **so** before an adjective without a noun, and **such** before an adjective with a noun.

- *My job is **so** interesting.*
- *I'm **so** busy **that** I can't go.*
- *I've got **such** an interesting job.*
- *I've got **such** a busy day **that** I can't go.*

1 **Answer the questions. Write *Yes* or *No*.** 回答问题，填写Yes或No。

▶ If something is surprising, is it what you think it will be? No

1 Does a charity help people? ....

2 If you worry about something, are you happy? ....

3 Does the whole day mean all of the day? ....

4 If something is amazing, is that good? ....

5 If you enter a building, are you leaving? ....

6 Is a unit a complete thing? ....

7 If something is *so good*, is that more than good? ....

8 Does *amazing* mean the opposite of *incredible*? ....

2 **Rewrite the sentences using the words in CAPITALS. The meaning must stay the same.** 用所给单词改写句子，保持句意不变。

▶	He's got such a quiet voice.	SO	His voice is so quiet.
1	He's in the office today.	WORK	He ....
2	This book is so good.	SUCH	This is ....
3	Stand up when she comes into the room.	ENTER	Stand up ....
4	It was such a long film.	SO	The film ....
5	She's one person in a small group.	PART	She's ....
6	This job is so difficult.	SUCH	This is ....

3 **Complete the sentences.** 将句子填写完整。

▶ This book has 100 units .

1 She always .... that she won't have enough money.

2 Last month I spent the .... time working with Caroline.

3 I left the job because the money was .... bad.

4 You can .... the building at the front or the back.

5 It was .... an interesting job – I loved it.

6 There are a number of .... that help people in poor .... of the world.

7 It's important to .... people who are very young or new in a job.

8 It's difficult working with these children, and I think she does an .... job with them.

4 ABOUT YOU **Write your answers, or ask another student.** 根据自身情况回答问题，也可以向同学提问。

1 What was your first day at work like? ....

2 Did you worry about anything before starting? ....

3 Did your colleagues support you? ....

4 Were you part of a unit? ....

A Devices 设备

1 PC (personal computer)
2 printer
3 screen
4 mouse
5 keyboard
6 laptop
7 window
8 tablet
9 program
10 menu

SPOTLIGHT *keep*

Keep means to put something in a place so that you know where it is.
- I **keep** my laptop in a bag in my office.
- Where do you **keep** your tablet?
- I **keep** it in my handbag.

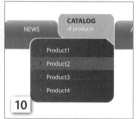

1 **Complete the words.** 将单词填写完整。
▶ k e e p
1 k___ ___b___ ___ ___d
2 w___ ___ ___ ___w
3 l___ ___ ___ ___p
4 m___ ___u
5 t___ ___ ___ ___t
6 m___ ___ ___e
7 sc___ ___ ___n
8 p___ ___ ___ ___ ___r
9 p___ ___g___ ___m

2 **Complete the sentences.** 将句子填写完整。
▶ You type information using the keyboard.
1 A small computer you can carry is called a ....
2 You read your e-mails on the ....
3 A list on the screen that shows what you can do is a ....
4 You can make a paper copy of something using a ....
5 A very small computer you use where you touch the screen is a ....
6 A set of instructions that we put into a computer is a ....
7 On a computer, you can open or close a ....
8 You can move things on the screen using the ....
9 You can .... pictures on a computer, tablet or laptop.

3 ABOUT YOU **Write your answers, or ask another student.** 根据自身情况回答问题，也可以向同学提问。
1 Have you got a PC? If so, what kind is it? ....
2 Have you got a printer? If so, how often do you use it? ....
3 Have you got a laptop or tablet? If so, where do you keep it? ....
4 Do you keep photos on your computer? If so, what kind of photos? ....
5 Which is better for you: a PC or a laptop? Why? ....

B Working on a computer
使用计算机

For homework, our teacher asked us to write a short **text** about our families. I **opened** a new **document** on my laptop, and **typed** ten **lines** about my husband and son. Then I **moved** a **photo** from my personal **files** into the document. It didn't look good, so I **cut** it and **replaced** it **with** a different photo. I read the text **carefully** to see if it was all correct. Then I **saved** it and **printed** a **copy** to give to my teacher.

GLOSSARY			
text	a piece of writing	**replace sth**	put a new or different thing in the place of another:
open	start sth: **open** a document/file OPP **close**	**(with sth)**	I **replaced** my old computer **with** a new laptop.
type	write sth using a keyboard	**carefully**	If you do sth **carefully**, you think about what you are
move	take sth and put it in another place		doing so that you don't make mistakes. **careful** adj
file	information that is stored on a computer with a particular name: I must save that **file** on my computer.	**save**	You must **save** a document before you close it, or you will lose it.
cut	take text or pictures away from a document	**copy**	a thing that is exactly the same as another thing: make/print a **copy**; **copy** v

4 Circle the verbs. 圈出动词。

opencarefulsavemovephototyperemovelinereplacefileclosetextdocument

5 Put the sentences in the correct order. 将句子排序。

- **a** I saved the text. ☐
- **b** I printed a copy. ☐
- **c** I didn't like it, so I removed it. ☐
- **d** I moved a photo into the document. ☐
- **e** I typed a text. ☐
- **f** I read the text carefully. ☐
- **g** I closed the document. ☐
- **h** I opened a document. ☐ 1

6 Complete the sentences. 将句子填写完整。

▶ I opened a new document and started typing.
1 The text has about 15 .... in it.
2 I have to be very .... when I'm typing in English.
3 I always make two .... of my work: one for me, and one to give to my teacher.
4 I keep my letters to the doctor in a medical .... on my PC.
5 Can you .... a copy of the letter for me, please?
6 Remember to .... your work before you close a document.
7 I'm going to .... my old laptop .... a new one.
8 I wasn't happy with the second paragraph in the text, so I .... it.
9 Her fingers are painful so she .... very slowly.
10 She opened the email, started reading it and quickly .... it when her father came in.

A Email and letters 电子邮件与信件

Have you **checked** your **messages** today?

No, I haven't got wifi or **the internet** where I'm staying.

What's your **email address**?

It's lucy@gmail.com

Can you **email** the documents to me, please?

Oh, but I've already **sent** them **by post**.

Oh no! The post is very slow here, and **letters** often **get lost**.

Have you **received** Donna's email?

Yes, I have. I'll **reply** this evening.

GLOSSARY

email	= **electronic mail** a message that is written on one computer and sent to another **email** v
check	look to see if sth is there
message	words that one person sends to another
the internet	the international computer system: I saw it **on the internet**.
send	make a letter or email go somewhere
post [U]	the system for sending and receiving letters, parcels, etc: send sth **by post**; **post** v
letter	a piece of writing on paper sb sends to another person
get lost	If sth **gets lost**, you don't know where it is.
receive formal	get sth that sb has sent to you SYN **get**
reply (to sb)	say or write sth as an answer to sb **reply** n

SPOTLIGHT saying email addresses

@ = **at**   . = **dot**
We say jo.xi@gmail.com like this:
'jo dot xi at gmail dot com'.

1 One word is not correct. Cross it out. 划掉错误的单词或短语。
- ▶ send a *letter* / ~~post~~ / *message*
- 1 *get* / *send* / *reply* a message
- 2 reply to *the internet* / *a letter* / *an email*
- 3 send something by *post* / *email* / *document*
- 4 check *your emails* / *a reply* / *your messages*
- 5 get *a letter* / *the internet* / *a message*

2 One word is missing. What is it, and where does it go? 在句中相应位置补上遗漏的单词。
- ▶ I got an / from Luisa this morning.   email
- 1 Did you the email I sent you yesterday?
- 2 The letter lost in the post – it never arrived.
- 3 Have you to Juan's letter yet?
- 4 I can't email you because I'm not the internet here.
- 5 My email address is 'jamie gmail dot com'.
- 6 Could you me the information, please?
- 7 I need to my emails before I go out.
- 8 Did you give Zach the letter, or send it by?
- 9 Email me at 'sue 1 at gmail com'.

3 Complete the dialogues. 将对话填写完整。
- A   A Hi, Arun. Have you ▶ _checked_ your messages this morning?
  - B Yes, I have. Malu **(1)** _____ me an email with some documents from our lawyer.
  - A Oh? I thought the lawyer sent you a **(2)** _____ with the documents, not an email.
  - B I didn't get them. I think they got **(3)** _____ in the post.
- B   A Did you **(4)** _____ the email I sent you last night?
  - B Yes, I'm sorry I haven't had time to **(5)** _____ yet.
- C   A I emailed the information to Jesse, but I haven't had a **(6)** _____ yet.
  - B He's camping this week, so he probably isn't **(7)** _____ the **(8)** _____ .

B The internet 互联网

STAY SAFE online

- When you **shop online**, only use **websites** which you know or **recognize**.

- If you get an email with a **link**[1] in it, don't **click on**[2] it if you don't know the person who sent it. It could **contain** a **virus**.

- Make sure your children are safe online. Only let them go online and **search for** information and look at **blogs** and **videos** when you are at home with them.

- Never tell anybody your **passwords**.

www.oup.com/elt — link

click on something

4 Circle the words which contain the same vowel sound as in *buy*, *right*, *wine*. Practise saying the words. 圈出与buy、right、wine元音发音相同的单词，并练习发音。

link　　(like)　　website　　contain　　video　　virus　　recognize　　click　　online

5 Is the meaning the same or different? Write *S* or *D*. 两者的含义是否相同？相同填S，不同填D。

▶ click on something / search for something　　D

1 a website / a site　　........

2 search for something / look for something　　........

3 a video / a blog　　........

4 recognize somebody / meet somebody　　........

5 contain something / click on something　　........

6 password / passport　　........

7 a link / a virus　　........

8 online / on the internet　　........

6 Complete the questions with words from the box. 用方框内的词填空。

websites　passwords　blog　virus　click
recognize　online ✓　videos　search　contains

▶ What kinds of things do you buy _online_ ?

1 Do you watch many .... on YouTube?

2 Do you ever tell people your .... ?

3 Have you ever written a .... ?

4 Which .... do you use a lot?

5 Has your computer or tablet ever had a .... ?

6 Do you use Google to .... for information on the internet?

7 Do you .... on a link if you don't .... the person who sent you the email?

8 What do you do if you think an email .... a virus?

Mostly books and things for the house.

7 ABOUT YOU　Write your answers to the questions in Exercise 6, or ask another student.
根据自身情况回答练习6中的问题，也可以向同学提问。

A Phone vocabulary 与电话相关的词汇

PHONE NUMBERS	What's your phone number?	~ It's 245731.
	What's your mobile number?	~ It's 07700 900154.
PHONE VERBS	call/phone/ring (*pt* **rang**) somebody	speak to sb by phone ALSO **make a (phone) call**
	answer the phone	pick up the phone when it rings and speak
	message somebody	send sb a **message / text (message)**
	take a message	take information during a call and give it to sb else
	leave a message	give information to sb on the phone, who then gives it to another person
PHONE PROBLEMS	The **line** is **busy**.	The person you phoned is speaking **on the phone** already.
	It's the **wrong number**.	You make a mistake with the number.

mobile phone
smartphone (= with internet)

landline

SPOTLIGHT saying phone numbers

Say each number.
- 245731 is: *two four five, seven three one*.
Say **double** when two numbers are the same.
- 33 = *double three*.
For '0', say **oh** or **zero**.
- 602448 is: *six oh/zero two, double four eight*.

1 Is the meaning the same or different? Write *S* or *D*. 两者的含义是否相同? 相同填S, 不同填D。

▶ What's your *landline* / *mobile* number?   D
1 He *phoned* / *rang* his sister.   ....
2 He's got *a smartphone*. / He's got *a landline*.   ....
3 six two *four four* / six two *double four*   ....
4 I *messaged him*. / I *sent him* a text.   ....
5 She *made a call* / *answered the phone*.   ....
6 Please *call* / *ring* me later.   ....
7 *four oh seven nine* / *four zero seven nine*   ....

2 Complete the words in the dialogues. 首字母填空。

1 Did you ▶ ring_____ Jo this morning? ~ Yes, but she was out, so I left a m_____ . I r_____ her mobile too, but she didn't a_____ the phone.
2 What's your phone n_____? ~ It's 345489.
3 Did you c_____ Sue last night? ~ Yes, but the line was b_____. I'll p_____ her later.
4 Hello, can I speak to Charlie, please? ~ Sorry, you've got the w_____ number.
5 Did you speak to Lisa? ~ I tried to call her but she was on the p_____, so I m_____ her and I'm waiting for a reply.
6 Can you come to the meeting? ~ Yes, but I just need to m_____ a call first.
7 Can I speak to Riccardo? ~ I'm sorry, he's busy. Can I take a m_____ ?
8 What's your m_____ number? ~ It's zero d_____ seven double oh, nine double oh, one six nine.

3 ABOUT YOU Write your answers, or ask another student. 根据自身情况回答问题, 也可以向同学提问。

1 What's your phone number and mobile number? (Write it in words.) _____
2 Who do you ring most often? _____
3 Do you send a lot of texts? If so, who to? _____
4 What do you say when you answer the phone? _____
5 Do you often get the wrong number? _____

B Phone conversations 电话交谈

A Hello?

B **Is that** Mia?

A Yes, **speaking**.

B Oh, hello. **This is** Laura, Laura Freebairn.

A Hi, Laura, how are you?

B I'm fine thanks. Is Jessica **in**, please?

A Yes, **just a moment** – I'll **get** her for you …

C Hello?

D Oh, hello, **can I speak to** Mr Ellis, please?

C I'm sorry, but he's out **at the moment**. **Who's calling**?

D **It's** Leo Jackson from Delta Electronics.

C Right. Do you want to leave a message for him?

D Yes, please. Can you tell him I'll **ring** him **back** after lunch.

C Of course, no problem.

D Thanks very much. **Goodbye.**

GLOSSARY			
Is that Isabella?	(NOT *Are you Isabella?*)	**get sb**	go and find sb and bring them to the phone
speaking	You say **speaking** when you are the person sb on the phone has asked to talk to.	**at the moment**	now
		Who's calling?	This is a polite way of asking 'Who are you?'.
This is Laura.	OR **It's** Laura. (NOT *I am. / Here is Laura.*)	**phone/call/ring sb back**	phone sb again
in	at home OPP **out**	**goodbye**	short form: **bye** *inf*
just a moment	wait a minute		

4 **Tick (✓) the correct answers.** 在正确答案后打钩 (√)。

▶ Can I speak to Martyn Ellis, please? ~ He's not in at the moment. ✓ / He's not in just a moment. ☐

1 Hello? ~ Speaking. ☐ / Oh, hello, is that Jackie? ☐

2 Can I speak to Lia Ponte, please? ~ Just a moment … ☐ / It's Natasha. ☐

3 Hello, is that Gosia? ~ Oh hello, this is Carla. ☐ / Speaking. ☐

4 Hello, this is Jamie Little. ~ Oh, hello, how are you? ☐ / Who's calling? ☐

5 Hello, can I speak to Alfonse, please? ~ I'm sorry, he's out. ☐ / I'm sorry, he's in. ☐

6 Mohammed's not here at the moment. ~ OK, I'll call back later. ☐ / OK, I'll get him. ☐

7 See you this evening, Dmitri. ~ Yes, bye. ☐ / Speaking. ☐

5 **Complete the conversations.** 将会话填写完整。

1 A Hello?

 B Hello. ▶ <u>Is that</u> Marisa?

 A Yes, **(1)** ....

 B Oh, hello. **(2)** .... Alice.

 A Oh, hello, Alice.

 B Is Mikki **(3)** ...., **(4)** .... ?

 A I'm sorry, he's out **(5)** .... Can I take a message?

 B Yes, please. Tell him I'll **(6)** .... him .... after lunch.

 A OK, **(7)** ....

2 A Hello?

 B Oh, can I **(8)** .... Ben, please?

 A Yes, **(9)** .... moment. I'll **(10)** .... him for you.

3 A Hello?

 B Oh, hello. **(11)** .... Joanna?

 A Yes, **(12)** ....

 B Hello, Joanna, **(13)** ....'s Luke.

 A Hi, Luke. How are you?

6 ABOUT YOU **Look at the conversations again. Think about the way people answer the phone in English, and the phrases they use. Is it very different in your language? If possible, talk to somebody who speaks your language.**

根据上文，思考英语的电话沟通方式和用词，是否和你的母语很不一样？如有条件，可以和同胞同学用母语交流讨论。

76 -er / -or / -r nouns 以-er/-or/-r结尾的名词

It is common in English to add *-er*, *-or* or *-r* to a verb to describe the person who does the action of the verb.

Teachers are people who teach as a job.

Visitors are people who visit a place, often as tourists.

Here are more examples.

A **driver** is a person who **drives**, often as a job: *a bus/taxi driver.*

Workers are people who **work**, especially in a particular kind of work: *office/farm/factory workers.*

The **listener** is the person who is **listening**, e.g. to the radio, the **speaker** is the person who is **speaking**, e.g. to an audience, and the **reader** is the person who is **reading**, e.g. a book.

An **owner** is a person who **owns** something:
I'm the owner of that car. I bought it last week.

An **actor** is a person who **acts** as a job: *a TV/film actor.*

The **winner** is the person who **wins** something,
e.g. a **competition** or a **race**.

Travellers are people who are **travelling**:
Rail travellers often have difficult journeys.

An **instructor** is a person who **instructs** people.

GLOSSARY	
winner	the person who is the best or the first in a game, competition or race
competition	a game or test that people want to win: *a painting competition*
race	In a **race**, people run, drive, ride, etc. in a competition to see who is fastest.
instructor	a person who teaches you how to do sth: *a driving instructor*

1 **Complete the sentences.** 将句子填写完整。

▶ A person who teaches is a _teacher_ .

1 A person who owns something is the ....

2 A person who visits somewhere is ....

3 A person who travels is a ....

4 A person who wins something is a ....

5 A person who instructs people is an ....

6 A person who drives is a ....

7 A person who acts on television is a ....

8 A person who works in a factory is a ....

2 **Make six phrases using a word from each box.** 从两个方框内各选一词，组成六个短语。

radio	film	bus	driving	travellers ✓	instructor	worker	driver
office	air ✓	English		listener	teacher	actor	

▶ _air travellers_ ....

   ....

3 **Complete the sentences.** 将句子填写完整。

▶ My cousin has been a film _actor_ for a few years.

1 The museum gets a lot of .... every year.

2 Mr Jacobs is the .... of that big house on the corner of the road.

3 He was the winner of the .... last year.

4 I have a neighbour who is a taxi ....

5 The farm employs about ten ....

6 The BBC Radio morning programme has about five million ....

7 Some .... always want books to have a happy ending.

8 I often have to ask the .... to repeat what they said.

9 My brother came second but I don't know who the .... was.

10 Our English .... explains things to our class very well.

77) -ing forms 以-ing形式结尾的单词

In English, we often add **-ing** to a verb to describe an activity in these situations:
1 As the subject of a sentence: *Reading English is easier than **writing**.*
2 After prepositions: *I'm not very good **at spelling**.*
3 After certain verbs: *I love **driving**.*
These words with **-ing** are also called gerunds.

Other common **-ing** forms include:

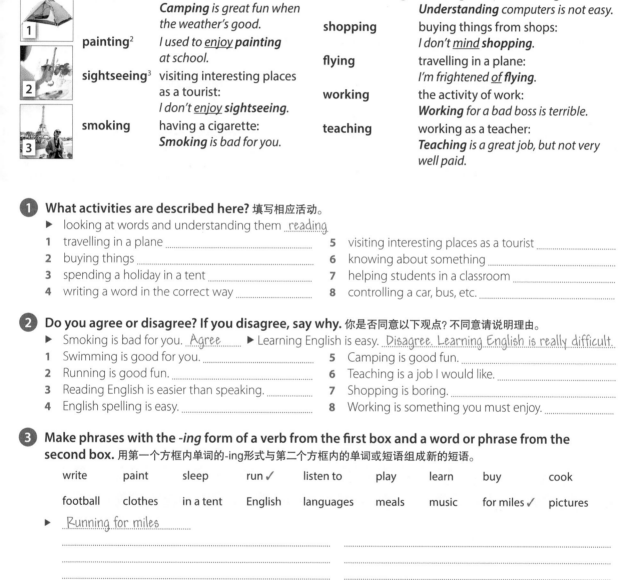

camping[1] spending a holiday in a tent:
Camping is great fun when the weather's good.

painting[2] *I used to enjoy painting at school.*

sightseeing[3] visiting interesting places as a tourist:
I don't enjoy sightseeing.

smoking having a cigarette:
Smoking is bad for you.

understanding knowing about something:
Understanding computers is not easy.

shopping buying things from shops:
I don't mind shopping.

flying travelling in a plane:
I'm frightened of flying.

working the activity of work:
Working for a bad boss is terrible.

teaching working as a teacher:
Teaching is a great job, but not very well paid.

1 **What activities are described here?** 填写相应活动。
▶ looking at words and understanding them _reading_
1 travelling in a plane ....
2 buying things ....
3 spending a holiday in a tent ....
4 writing a word in the correct way ....
5 visiting interesting places as a tourist ....
6 knowing about something ....
7 helping students in a classroom ....
8 controlling a car, bus, etc. ....

2 **Do you agree or disagree? If you disagree, say why.** 你是否同意以下观点? 不同意请说明理由。
▶ Smoking is bad for you. _Agree_ ▶ Learning English is easy. _Disagree. Learning English is really difficult._
1 Swimming is good for you. ....
2 Running is good fun. ....
3 Reading English is easier than speaking. ....
4 English spelling is easy. ....
5 Camping is good fun. ....
6 Teaching is a job I would like. ....
7 Shopping is boring. ....
8 Working is something you must enjoy. ....

3 **Make phrases with the -*ing* form of a verb from the first box and a word or phrase from the second box.** 用第一个方框内单词的-ing形式与第二个方框内的单词或短语组成新的短语。

write	paint	sleep	run ✓	listen to	play	learn	buy	cook
football	clothes	in a tent	English	languages	meals	music	for miles ✓	pictures

▶ _Running for miles_

4 [ABOUT YOU] **Write sentences that are true for you, using the phrases in Exercise 3. Compare with another student if possible.** 根据自身情况,用练习3中的短语造句。如有条件,可以与同学的句子作比较。
▶ _Running for miles is not something I do._

A Nouns ending in *-ion* 以-ion结尾的名词

Can you **predict** the result of a football match?

No, it's very hard to make a **prediction**.

Someone's **invented** a way to clean plastic from the oceans.

That's a great **invention**!

Do you always **celebrate** your birthday?

Yes, I often have a small **celebration** with friends.

I have to **organize** my son's wedding.

Well, that will need careful **organization**.

Can you **describe** the criminal?

Yes, I can give the police a good **description**.

How do we **solve** the population problem?

I've got no idea. There's no easy **solution**.

We have to **decide** where to live.

That's a very important **decision**.

GLOSSARY

predict	say what you think will happen **(make a) prediction** n
invent	make, design or think of sth for the first time **invention** n
celebrate	do sth to show that you are happy for a special reason, or because it is a special day **(have a) celebration** n
organize	plan or arrange sth **organization** n
describe	say what sb or sth is like, or what happened **(give a) description** n
solve	find the answer to a question or problem **solution** n
decide	choose sth after thinking about the possibilities **(make a) decision** n

SPOTLIGHT suffix *-ion*

Many verbs form nouns by adding a suffix, and *-ion/-tion/-sion/-ation* are very common.
predict/prediction   celebrate/celebration
Sometimes the ending of the noun changes.
solve/solution   decide/decision
Stress can also change. Use a dictionary to check the sounds and the stress.

1 <u>Underline</u> the main stress in each word. Practise saying the words. 在单词的重读音节下划线，并练习发音。

- ▶ in<u>vent</u>   ▶ so<u>lu</u>tion
- 1 celebrate   celebration
- 2 describe   description

3 predict   prediction
4 decide   decision
5 organize   organization

2 What words are being defined here? 根据定义填写单词。

- ▶ choosing something after thinking   *decision*
- 1 something somebody has made for the first time   ....
- 2 a time when you enjoy yourself for a special reason ....
- 3 words that tell what somebody or something is like   ....
- 4 an answer to a problem   ....
- 5 a statement about what you think will happen   ....
- 6 planning or arranging something so that it is successful ....

3 Complete the sentences with the correct form of a word from this unit. 用本单元单词的正确形式填空。

- ▶ Can you *describe* what happened when the car hit the tree?
- 1 It wasn't easy to make a .... , but in the end, we .... to sell the car.
- 2 We have to .... the traffic problems quickly. The .... is probably to have better trains and buses.
- 3 I didn't see the man, so I couldn't give a good .... of him.
- 4 After the exams, the students go out and .... all night.
- 5 I think it was Tim Berners Lee who .... the World Wide Web.
- 6 My boss is .... tomorrow's meeting. He's very bad at ....
- 7 The government has .... that business will get better next year.
- 8 The mobile phone is one of the most important .... of the last fifty years.

B Other noun endings 其他名词词尾

Verb / Noun	Example	Meaning (verb)
discover v discovery n	Herschel **discovered** the planet Uranus. Herschel **made an important discovery**.	find a place or thing that nobody knew about before
succeed v success n	They want the discussions to **succeed**. They want them to be a **success**.	do or get what you wanted to do or get
complain v complaint n	You need to **complain** to the manager. You should **make a complaint**.	say you do not like sth or are unhappy about sth
choose v choice n	I had to **choose** a gift for my sister. I **made a bad choice**.	decide which thing or person you want
think v thought(s) n	I was **thinking** about our next holiday. I **had a few thoughts** about our holiday.	have an opinion or idea about sth
arrange v arrangement n	I have **arranged** to see Jo tonight. I have **made an arrangement** with Jo.	make a plan for the future
argue v argument n	We mustn't **argue** about money. We mustn't **have an argument**.	talk angrily with sb because you do not agree
move v movement n	Something **moved** behind me. There was a **movement** behind me.	change place or position

> **SPOTLIGHT** suffix -ment
>
> The suffix **-ment** is also common in English: **advertise** v / **advertisement** n   **improve** v / **improvement** n

4 **Complete the table.** 将表格填写完整。

VERB	NOUN	VERB	NOUN
move	movement	discover	
	success		thought
arrange		argue	
choose		complain	

5 **Circle the correct answer.** 圈出正确答案。

▶ When you dance, you make (movements) / complaints with your body.

1 She had *an argument* / *a movement* with her boyfriend last night.

2 Did you make a *complaint* / *choice* to the waiter about the cold soup?

3 I had a *discovery* / *thought* about the business: I think we should sell it.

4 They thought the plan would fail, but in fact it was a great *success* / *arrangement*.

5 The *arrangements* / *successes* for the wedding were really good – it went very well.

6 They have made an important *discovery* / *thought* about the crime.

6 **Complete the questions.** 将问句填写完整。

▶ Have you ever complained about bad service on buses or trains?

ABOUT YOU

Yes, often!

1 Have you ever made a c_____ about noise to a neighbour?

2 In a restaurant, do you c_____ what to eat quickly?

3 At school, did you have a c_____ of different subjects?

4 Do you a_____ a lot in your family?

5 Have you ever had an a_____ with a shop assistant?

6 Would you like to s_____ in business?

7 Is s_____ the most important thing in life?

8 Do you often have t_____ about what to do in your future?

7 ABOUT YOU **Write your answers to the questions in Exercise 6, or ask another student.**
根据自身情况回答练习6中的问题，也可以向同学提问。

A What are compound nouns? 什么是复合名词？

This is common in English: word + word = new word. For example:

police + officer = **police officer**	phone + number = **phone number**
bath + room = **bathroom**	art + gallery = **art gallery**

- We write some compound nouns as one word, e.g. **bathroom**, but many are two words, e.g. **phone number**.
- Many compound nouns are easy to understand when you know the other words, e.g. **railway station**, **address book**, **first floor**, **dining room**, **bus stop**, **dishwasher**. Sometimes they are less easy to understand, e.g. a **disc jockey** (usually called a **DJ**) is a person who plays music on the radio and in clubs.
- You will meet many compound nouns as you learn English: **past tense**; **past participle**; **phrasal verb** (*see Unit 99*); **capital letter**, e.g. ABC; **full stop** (at the end of a sentence); **question mark** = ?
- With compound nouns, the main stress is usually on the first word, e.g. <u>phone</u> number, but sometimes it is on the second word, e.g. full <u>stop</u>.

1 <u>Underline</u> the main stress on these compound words. Practise saying the words.
在复合词的重读部分下划线，并练习发音。

▶ <u>art</u> gallery   ▶ full <u>stop</u>   bathroom   railway station   first floor   address book
bus stop   phone number   dishwasher   capital letter   police officer

2 What do we call these places or things? Use a compound noun to label each picture.
用复合名词填写图中的地点或物品。

1 _____ 2 _____ 3 _____ 4 _____

5 _____ 6 _____ 7 _____ 8 _____

3 Complete the sentences. 将句子填写完整。

▶ I'd like to visit that art _gallery_ .

1 My phone _____ is 07897 493321.
2 I found a police _____ and spoke to him.
3 My brother would like to be a disc _____ on the radio.
4 If it's a question, don't forget the question _____ .
5 What's the past _____ and past _____ of *forget*?
~ That's easy. *Forgot* and *forgotten*.

6 My parents live on the first _____ of the building.
7 I waited at the bus _____ for about twenty minutes.
8 *Get on* and *get off* are both _____ verbs.
9 You have to put a _____ stop at the end of the sentence.
10 A new sentence always begins with a _____ letter.

B In the town centre 在市中心

> … just after the **traffic lights**, we found a **car park**. Millie went to the **sports centre** to use the **swimming pool,** while Dan and I went to the **department store** in the new **shopping centre** to look at **washing machines**. We didn't buy one, but we had a very helpful **sales assistant**. After that, I did some shopping in the **high street**, and Dan went to the **ticket office** at the theatre. We came home after that, but Millie stayed and came back on **public transport**.

GLOSSARY

car park	an area or a building where you can leave your car
sports centre	a large building where you can play different sports
swimming pool	a place that is built for people to swim in
shopping centre	a large building or area with a lot of shops
sales assistant	a person who serves you in a shop ALSO **shop assistant**
high street	the main street in a town or city where the shops are
ticket office	a place in a railway station, cinema, etc. where you can buy tickets

SPOTLIGHT *centre* and *card*

One word often forms part of several compound words, e.g. **sports centre**, **shopping centre**, **town centre**. Another example is **card**: you give people a **birthday card** when it is their birthday; an **identity card** is a card with your name, photo, etc. on it; a **credit card** is a plastic card you use to buy things and pay for them later.

4 **Find eight compound words using a word from each box.** 从两个方框内各选一词，组成八个复合词。

car ✓	department	sports		office	transport	street
ticket	traffic	swimming		lights	park ✓	card
credit	public	high		pool	store	centre

car park ....
....
....

5 **Complete the sentences.** 将句子填写完整。

▶ Matt uses the gym in the sports _centre_ .
1 I don't travel much on .... transport these days.
2 Do you normally use your .... card to buy expensive things?
3 Did you remember to send Tia a .... card? She was 21 last week.
4 A police officer asked to see my .... card yesterday. I was very surprised.
5 There are lots of cafés now in the .... street. They're replacing shops.
6 The .... lights were red when that car went through.
7 By 10.30 there are very few spaces in the car ....
8 I need to buy a new washing ....
9 They had to go to the ticket .... to collect the tickets.
10 We had a terrible .... assistant in the .... store yesterday.

6 **Complete the sentences.** 将问句填写完整。

	ABOUT YOU
▶ How often do you use _public_ transport?	_Quite a lot. I use the buses every day._
1 Do you have an .... card? What information is on it?	....
2 Do you go to a sports .... ? If so, what do you do there?	....
3 Do you have a .... card? If so, what do you buy with it?	....
4 Do you use a local swimming .... ? If so, how often?	....
5 How many .... cards do you buy and send every year?	....
6 Do you often shop in a department .... ? If so, what do you buy there?	....

7 **ABOUT YOU** **Write answers to Exercise 6, or talk to another student.**
根据自身情况回答练习6中的问题，也可以向同学提问。

A Love it or hate it? 热爱还是痛恨?

1 I **love** football.

2 I **really like** it.

3 I **like** it.

4 I **quite like** it.

5 I don't **mind** it.

6 I **don't like** it **very much**.

7 I **don't like** it.

8 I **hate** it. I don't like it **at all**.

> **SPOTLIGHT** *love/like/hate + -ing*
>
> After **love**, **like**, **hate** and **don't mind**, use a noun, a pronoun, or an *-ing* form:
>
> ■ *I love / like / hate / don't mind* ⎡ *football.* ⎣ *it.*
>
> ■ *I love / like / hate / don't mind playing* football.
>
> **Like** and **dislike** can also be nouns: *We all have different **likes** and **dislikes**.*

1 Who is more positive (+)? Who is more negative (–)? Complete the answers with *A* or *B*.
A和B谁的好恶程度更高/低?

▶	**A** loves coffee.	**B** likes coffee.	A̱ is more positive.
1	**A** likes tea.	**B** quite likes tea.	.... is more positive.
2	**A** likes chocolate.	**B** loves chocolate.	.... is more positive.
3	**A** really likes sport.	**B** doesn't mind it.	.... is more positive.
4	**A** doesn't like sport.	**B** doesn't like it at all.	.... is more negative.
5	**A** hates pop music.	**B** doesn't like pop music very much.	.... is more negative.
6	**A** doesn't like studying.	**B** doesn't mind studying.	.... is more negative.

2 Correct the mistakes. 改错题。

▶ Do you like watch tennis? — *Do you like watching tennis?*

1 I hate it chocolate. ....

2 They don't like to doing homework very much. ....

3 He doesn't like very much speaking English. ....

4 I like quite shopping. ....

5 She doesn't like drive. ....

6 I'm not mind working at night. ....

3 Complete the sentences with one word. 将句子填写完整, 每空格只填一词。

▶ I don't like swimming very _much_ .

1 I .... going to the cinema – it's my favourite hobby.

2 I don't like classical music at ....

3 I don't .... shopping – it's OK.

4 I .... like driving. I find it exciting.

5 I .... writing emails – it's so boring.

6 I don't .... watching TV very much.

7 Most people hate housework, but I .... like it.

8 I don't like talking on the phone .... all.

4 ABOUT YOU Do you agree with the sentences in Exercise 3? Write your ideas, or ask another student.
你是否同意练习3中的表述? 根据自身情况回答问题, 也可以向同学提问。

▶ *I really like swimming, and I go swimming a lot in the summer.*

B My favourite things 我最喜欢的事物

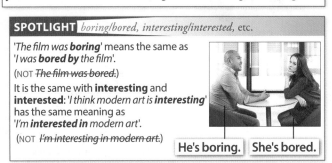

meetpeopleontheweb.com

NAME	Mirko Zitec
WORK	I work for a TV company. It's a **wonderful** job – I love it.
STUDY	I'm learning to play the guitar. It's good **fun** and my teacher's **incredible**.
SPORTS	My **favourite** sport is tennis, but I also **enjoy** playing football.
TV/CINEMA	I don't watch TV – it's very **boring**, but **I'm interested in old** films from the 1960s. In fact, I **prefer** old films **to modern** ones.
MUSIC	I think **jazz** is really **interesting** – I go to a jazz club every Friday.

GLOSSARY

wonderful	very good SYNS **incredible**, **amazing**
fun	If sth is **fun**, it makes you happy.
favourite	Your **favourite** thing or person is the one you like most.
enjoy doing sth	If you **enjoy doing sth**, you like it a lot and it makes you happy. **enjoyable** *adj*
boring	OPP **interesting**
old	made or bought a long time ago OPP **new** OR **modern**
prefer (X **to** Y)	like sb or sth more than another person or thing
jazz	a kind of music, e.g. Louis Armstrong, Duke Ellington

SPOTLIGHT *boring/bored, interesting/interested, etc.*

'*The film was **boring**'* means the same as '*I was **bored by** the film*'.
(NOT *The film was bored.*)

It is the same with **interesting** and **interested**: '*I think modern art is **interesting**'* has the same meaning as '*I'm **interested in** modern art*'.
(NOT *I'm interesting in modern art.*)

He's boring. | She's bored.

---

5 Write eight more sentences using words from 1, 2, and 3. 从三栏中各选一个单词或短语，组成八句句子。

	1	2	3	
▶	It's ✓	not interested	boss.	It's a wonderful city.
1	I	the party	city. ✓	
2	I'm	favourite	watching TV.	
3	My	enjoy	film is *Star Wars*.	
4	She	amazing	enjoyable.	
5	He's an	a wonderful ✓	in politics.	
6	Was	is	programme.	
7	It's	prefers reading	good fun?	
8	Singing	a boring	to writing.	

6 ABOUT YOU **Complete the questions, using the words in the box.** 用方框内的词填空。

interesting   fun   interested   modern   enjoy
prefer   favourite   incredible   enjoyable ✓

▶ Do you think flying is _enjoyable_ ? ....
1 Is learning English good .... ? ....
2 Do you .... meat to fish? ....
3 What's your .... city? ....
4 Are you .... in jazz? ....
5 Do you think history is .... ? ....
6 Do you .... walking in the countryside? ....
7 Do you know a restaurant where the food is .... ? ....
8 Do you like old houses, or do you prefer .... houses? ....

7 ABOUT YOU **Write answers to the questions in Exercise 6, or ask another student.**
根据自身情况回答练习6中的问题，也可以向同学提问。

81) Free time 闲暇

A Common activities 常见活动

> **What do you do in your free time?**

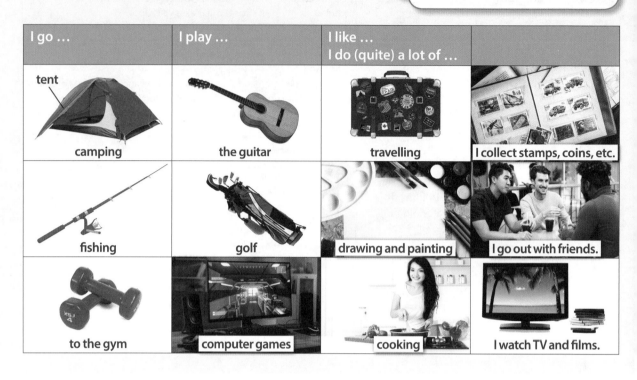

I go …	I play …	I like … I do (quite) a lot of …	
tent camping	the guitar	travelling	I collect stamps, coins, etc.
fishing	golf	drawing and painting	I go out with friends.
to the gym	computer games	cooking	I watch TV and films.

1 Can you do these things inside your home? Write *Yes* or *No*. 下列活动能否在家里做? 能的填Yes, 不能的填No。

> watch TV _Yes_

    go fishing _____

    play computer games _____

    do a lot of drawing _____

> go to the gym _No_

    do some travelling _____

    go out with friends _____

    go camping _____

    collect stamps _____

    play golf _____

2 Match 1–6 with a–g. 配对题。

> do   _e_
1. go _____
2. collect _____
3. do some _____
4. go out _____
5. play _____
6. watch _____

a painting
b football magazines
c the guitar
d television
e a lot of travelling ✓
f with my brothers
g camping

3 Complete the sentences with the correct form of *do, go, collect, watch, play* or *make*.

用do、go、collect、watch、play或make的正确形式填空。

> I often _go_ to the gym.
1. Jojo _____ a lot of cooking.
2. My brother _____ old clocks.
3. I'd like to _____ the guitar.
4. Do you often _____ camping?
5. I don't _____ much travelling now.
6. She _____ out every night to a club.
7. Do you _____ golf?
8. He _____ too much TV.
9. They _____ fishing every weekend.
10. She _____ quite a lot of painting.

4 ABOUT YOU Look at the table again. Make a list of the activities you do now, the activities you would like to do, and the ones you aren't interested in.

根据上文表格, 列出你正在参与的、想要参与的, 以及不感兴趣的活动。

B Hobbies 爱好

Favourite hobbies in Russia

Russian people have many **hobbies**. Older people enjoy **gardening**, fishing, and **repairing** cars. For younger people, there are **various clubs** in and outside school where children learn a lot of activities. **Popular** hobbies include sport, the arts, computers, listening to music, and collecting different things.

NATASHA: I like listening to **rock music**. I also like playing football with my friends, and I do a lot of drawing and reading. But my favourite hobby is **dancing**[1] (you can see me in the photo), and I'm quite **good at** it.

KOLYA: I play the guitar, and I can **sing** Russian and English **songs**. I often sing in the shower! I'm **good at** swimming and skiing. I also like travelling very much.

GLOSSARY			
hobby	an activity that you like doing in your free time	**popular**	If sth is **popular**, many people like it.
gardening	working in your garden	**rock music**	music by, for example, The Rolling Stones and Bruce Springsteen
repair	make sth work when there is a problem, e.g. cars, bikes	**good at sth**	able to do sth well (NOT ~~good in sth~~)
various	some that are different: *There are **various** places to go.*	**sing**	make music with your voice: *Ed Sheeran is a*
club	a group of people who do sth together, or the place where they meet		***singer**. He sings **songs**.*

5 Are the <u>underlined</u> sounds the same or different? Write *S* or *D*. Practise saying the words.
划线部分的发音是否相同? 相同填S, 不同填D, 并练习发音。

▶ <u>r</u>ock / <u>c</u>lub ......S....

1 rep<u>air</u> / v<u>ar</u>ious ....
2 g<u>oo</u>d at / sh<u>oo</u>ting ....
3 g<u>ar</u>dening / s<u>i</u>ng ....
4 var<u>iou</u>s / p<u>o</u>pular ....
5 h<u>o</u>bby / s<u>o</u>ng ....
6 rock m<u>u</u>sic / cl<u>u</u>b ....

6 Look at the text again. Tick (✓) the true sentences, and correct the false sentences.
根据上文, 在正确的句子后打钩 (✓), 并改正错误的句子。

▶ Natasha doesn't like rock music. *False. She likes rock music.*
1 Older people enjoy gardening. ....
2 Natasha is a good singer. ....
3 Kolya plays the piano. ....
4 There are no clubs in schools. ....
5 Kolya has various hobbies. ....
6 Natasha is very good at dancing. ....
7 Computers and collecting things are not popular hobbies. ....
8 Younger people like repairing cars. ....

7 Complete the sentences. 将句子填写完整。

ABOUT YOU

▶ Do you go to any sports c<u>lubs</u> ....? If so, what kind?
1 What's your favourite h..................... ?
2 What hobbies are p..................... with younger people?
3 Do you have v..................... hobbies, or only one or two?
4 Are you a good s..................... ?
5 Write the name of one s..................... you can sing.
6 Write down something you are good ....
7 Are you good at r..................... things, e.g. a broken cup?

8 ABOUT YOU **Write your answers to the questions, or ask another student.**
根据自身情况回答练习7中的问题, 也可以向同学提问。

82) Sport 运动

A Games and sports 比赛与运动

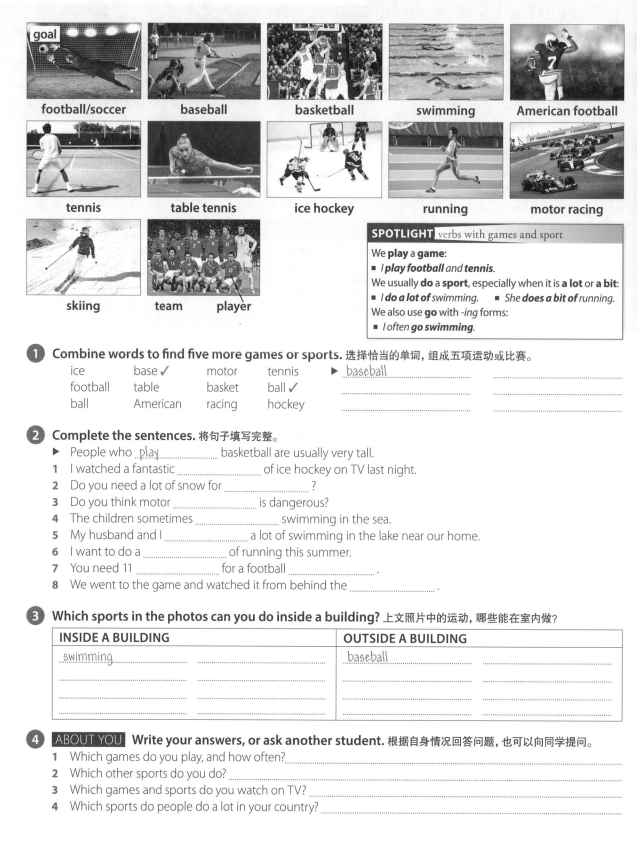

football/soccer baseball basketball swimming American football

tennis table tennis ice hockey running motor racing

skiing team player

SPOTLIGHT verbs with games and sport

We **play** a **game**:
- *I **play** football and **tennis**.*

We usually **do** a **sport**, especially when it is **a lot** or **a bit**:
- *I **do a lot of** swimming.*   *She **does a bit of** running.*

We also use **go** with *-ing* forms:
- *I often **go swimming**.*

1 **Combine words to find five more games or sports.** 选择恰当的单词, 组成五项运动或比赛。

ice	base ✓	motor	tennis	► baseball	....
football	table	basket	ball ✓	....	....
ball	American	racing	hockey	....	....

2 **Complete the sentences.** 将句子填写完整。

► People who ..play.................. basketball are usually very tall.
1 I watched a fantastic .... of ice hockey on TV last night.
2 Do you need a lot of snow for .... ?
3 Do you think motor .... is dangerous?
4 The children sometimes .... swimming in the sea.
5 My husband and I .... a lot of swimming in the lake near our home.
6 I want to do a .... of running this summer.
7 You need 11 .... for a football ....
8 We went to the game and watched it from behind the ....

3 **Which sports in the photos can you do inside a building?** 上文照片中的运动, 哪些能在室内做？

INSIDE A BUILDING		OUTSIDE A BUILDING	
swimming	....	baseball	....
....	....	....	....
....	....	....	....
....	....	....	....

4 ABOUT YOU **Write your answers, or ask another student.** 根据自身情况回答问题, 也可以向同学提问。

1 Which games do you play, and how often? ....
2 Which other sports do you do? ....
3 Which games and sports do you watch on TV? ....
4 Which sports do people do a lot in your country? ....

B Football 足球

ITALY	Played	Won	Drawn	Lost	Goals for	Goals against	Points
Juventus	34	24	9	1	63	22	81
Inter Milan	34	24	4	6	75	27	76
AS Roma	34	22	5	7	61	26	71

On Friday, Juventus **won** their important **match against** Inter Milan. Cuadrado **scored** the only **goal** in the 70th minute. This means they are still **top** and now **lead** Inter **by** five points. On Saturday, Sampdoria was only able to **draw** their match **with** Torino. At Napoli, Roma were leading two goals to **nil** at **half-time**, but then Napoli played much better in the second half to make the **final score** 2–2. Lazio **beat** Genoa 3–1, while Fiorentina **lost** 2–1 **to** Milan.

5 Correct the <u>underlined</u> mistakes. 改正划线部分的错误。

▶ Fiorentina <u>draw</u> with AS Roma. _drew_
1 Lazio have a <u>play</u> next Saturday. ....
2 Inter are playing <u>with</u> Parma. ....
3 Genoa lost 3–1 <u>with</u> Fiorentina. ....
4 Messi <u>did</u> two goals. ....

5 Parma won by two goals to <u>zero</u>. ....
6 Cagliari <u>beated</u> Sampdoria. ....
7 Milan <u>win</u> their game last week. ....
8 Did they <u>drew</u> the match? ....
9 Milan won 3–1 <u>with</u> Roma. ....

6 Complete the sentences. 将句子填写完整。

▶ They _scored_ in the first minute.
1 It's an important .... next week.
2 We are playing .... Valencia.
3 Seville .... 1–2 to Barcelona.
4 Bilbao .... 2–2 .... Villareal.
5 It was 0-0 at half– ....

6 They have 24 .... from 13 games.
7 On Sunday, Espanyol .... Real Betis 2–1.
8 Ronaldo .... the goal.
9 We .... our last match 4–1.
10 They were .... 1–0 at half-time.
11 What was the final .... ?

7 ABOUT YOU AND YOUR COUNTRY **Which football match impressed you the most last season? Write down the final scores in English, and the people who scored the goals.**
上赛季哪场足球赛给你印象最深刻? 写几句话，介绍比分和进球队员。

▶ _Boca Juniors beat River Plate one nil. Cristian Pavón scored the only goal._

83) Music 音乐

A Classical music 古典乐

concert
The **orchestra** is playing
a **piece of music by** Haydn.

violinist Vanessa Mae
She's playing a concerto
by Vivaldi.

pianist Lang Lang
He's playing music by
Gershwin.

opera singer
Jonas Kaufmann is **performing**.

GLOSSARY

concert	a public performance of music
classical music	Western **classical music** includes music by Bach, Beethoven and Stravinsky. **musical** *adj*
a piece	a single thing: *a piece of music*
(musical) instrument	A piano and a violin are **musical instruments**.
perform	do sth in front of an audience, e.g. act in a play, sing, etc. **performance** *n*

SPOTLIGHT *by*

We say *a book* **by** *Tolstoy, a song* **by** *Beyoncé, a painting* **by** *Picasso, a film* **by** *Martin Scorsese*, etc.

1 **Make music words from the letters.** 将字母重新排列，组成与音乐相关的单词或短语。

▶ lioniv _violin_

1 onctecr _____

2 choartser _____

3 tiaspni _____

4 deniacue _____

5 froeprm _____

6 rapoe grisne _____

7 refrancepom _____

2 **Complete the sentences.** 将句子填写完整。

▶ Last night we went to a _concert_ at the Royal Albert Hall.

1 Beethoven wrote _____ music.

2 A person who plays the piano is a _____ .

3 A person who plays the violin is a _____ .

4 A large group of people who play classical music together is called an _____ .

5 A piano and a violin are types of _____ _____ .

6 A concert is a public _____ of music.

7 The people who listen to a concert are the _____ .

8 The orchestra _____ some music by Mozart. It was wonderful!

9 Bach wrote some wonderful _____ of music.

10 *La Bohème* is an opera _____ Puccini.

3 ABOUT YOU **Write your answers, or ask another student.** 根据自身情况回答问题，也可以向同学提问。

1 Do you go to classical music concerts? If yes, when was the last time? _____

2 Can you think any of pieces of classical music that you like? _____

3 Did you ever learn the piano or the violin as a child? If yes, do you still play? _____

4 Do you play a different musical instrument? _____

5 What is your favourite musical instrument? _____

B Pop and rock 流行乐与摇滚乐

In the past, **bands recorded** an **album** onto a **CD**, people bought the album, and the **performers** made money. Now, most people **are able to download music** onto their computers and phones. This is good for listeners, but not so good for **musicians**, because most of them do not get much money from music streaming websites.

So, many performers are now going back **on tour**, travelling around the country (and the world), playing **live** concerts and at music **festivals** to earn more money. And audiences seem to love this opportunity to see their favourite singers and **groups** performing all their **hit records** live.

> **SPOTLIGHT** *record something* and *a record*
>
> If you **record** something, you put music or film on a CD. A **record** (note the different pronunciation) is a song, or sometimes an album.
> - *David Bowie made his last **record** only days before he died.*

GLOSSARY

band	(ALSO **group**), e.g. Coldplay, Guns N'Roses	**musician**	a person who plays a musical instrument
album	a number of songs, often about ten, on a CD or record	**on tour**	travelling to many different places to play live concerts
CD	(*see picture*)	**live**	(sounds like *five*) If sth is **live**, you see it or hear it at the same time as it happens.
performer	sb who performs music, or acts in the theatre	**festival**	a big event, e.g. concerts or shows, in one place
be able to	If you **are able to** do sth, you can do it; you have the knowledge you need. **ability** *n*	**hit**	a thing that a lot of people like: *The song was a **hit** in the US.* ***a hit record***
download music	copy music from the internet onto a computer, phone, etc.		

4 **What can you remember? Underline the correct answer.** 根据上文, 在正确答案下划线。

▶ Bands record albums onto a *hit* / *CD*.

1 In the past, performers *made* / *didn't make* money from albums.
2 Downloading music is *good* / *not good* for most performers.
3 Downloading music is *more expensive* / *cheaper* than buying CDs.
4 Bands *go* / *don't go* on tour to make more money.
5 Groups *are able to* / *aren't able to* perform at music festivals.
6 People *like* / *don't like* seeing groups live.

5 **Complete the sentences.** 将句子填写完整。

▶ Metallica are still a very famous ..band/group...

1 Coldplay are planning to go on .... again next year.
2 I once saw Beyoncé .... at Carnegie Hall in New York. She was amazing.
3 *Sergeant Pepper* is still the most famous .... by the Beatles.
4 *You Belong With Me* was a big .... for Taylor Swift.
5 I bought three .... last week.
6 Paul McCartney is a great .... He plays guitar and piano.
7 Adele was the first .... that I ever saw live.
8 I saw Radiohead and the Foo Fighters at a summer .... in 2017.
9 David Bowie .... his last album, *Blackstar*, shortly before he died.
10 With a computer or smartphone, you have the .... to download music.

6 **ABOUT YOU** **Write your answers, or ask another student.** 根据自身情况回答问题, 也可以向同学提问。

1 Who's your favourite group/band? ....
2 Do you buy their CDs or download their music? ....
3 Have you ever seen them live? ....
4 What's their best album? ....
5 Do they often go on tour? ....
6 Do they have many hit records? Why? / Why not? ....

A Describing films 描述电影

A **thriller** is often **exciting**.   A **comedy** is **funny**.   A **war film** is often **violent**.   A **love story** is **romantic**.

An **action film**
(ALSO an **adventure film**)
is exciting.

A **horror film** is **scary**.   A **cartoon** is often funny.   A **science fiction film**
(ALSO **sci-fi**) can be scary.

> **SPOTLIGHT** *What kind/type/sort of …?*
>
> - ***What kind of*** *film is it?*   ~ *It's a thriller.*
> - ***What type of*** *music do you like?*   ~ *Rock music.*
> - ***What sort of*** *films are exciting?* ~ *Action films.*

1 **Tick the words with the same pronunciation as the <u>underlined</u> letters in *buy, fly, like*.**
Practise saying the words. 在与buy、fly、like拥有相同元音发音的单词后打钩（√），并练习发音。

describe ✓	fiction	science	film
violent	exciting	scary	crime

2 **Complete the kinds of films.** 将电影类型填写完整。

▶ w_a_r f_i_ _l_m
1 th___ ___ ___le r
2 c___m___ ___ ___
3 ___ct___ ___n f___ ___ ___

4 sc___ ___n___ ___   f___ _t___ ___n
5 c___ ___t___ ___n
6 l___v___   st___ ___ ___
7 h___r___ ___ ___   f___ ___ ___

3 **Complete the sentences.** 首字母填空。

▶ Was the film a thriller?
   ~ Yes, and quite v<u>iolent</u>.
1 What s_____ of film is it?
2 I went to see an a_____ film.
3 What k_____ of films do you like?

4 Do you like r_____ films?
5 It was a very scary h_____ film.
6 Was it a good comedy?
   ~ Yes, it was f_____ .
7 The film was a t_____ of thriller.

4 **Write one adjective to describe each picture.** 用一个形容词分别描述下列各图。

▶ <u>exciting</u>   1 _____   2 _____   3 _____   4 _____

B What's on? 什么片子正在上映?

A **What's on** at the **cinema**?

B There's a film **on** called *Pacific Rim Uprising*.

A What kind of film is it?

B It's a sci-fi **movie**. **It's about** people from another **planet** who arrive on **Earth**. It's had **brilliant reviews**.

A OK. **Who's in it**?

B It **stars** John Boyega – he's the **hero**.

A Oh, I like John Boyega– he's a good **actor**. Who's the **director**?

B Stephen DeKnight. I've never heard of him, actually.

A And **where's it on**?

B The Odeon.

A OK. Well, **let's** go and see it.

GLOSSARY

What's on?	= What films can we see?	**star**	be one of the main actors in a film/programme. The person is a **star**.
cinema	a place where you see films		
movie	film	**hero**	the most important man in a book or film. A woman is a **heroine**.
It's about …	the subject is …		
planet Earth	where we live. Mars and Venus are also **planets**.	**actor**	e.g. Idris Elba or Meryl Streep. A female actor can also be called an **actress**.
brilliant	*inf* very good		
review	an article about a film in a newspaper or on the internet	**director**	a person who makes a film, e.g. Alfred Hitchcock
		Where's it on?	= Where can we see the film?
Who's in it?	= Which actors are in the film?	**let's**	used for making a suggestion for sth to do

5 **True or false? Write *T* or *F*.** 判断正误, 正确填T, 错误填F。

▶ A film is a movie. ..... T

1 Antonio Banderas is an actress. ....

2 The star is the main actor in a film. ....

3 A review is a kind of article. ....

4 Mars is a planet. ....

5 The heroine is a man. ....

6 The Earth is round. ....

7 Steven Spielberg is an actor. ....

6 **Complete the conversation.** 将会话填写完整。

▶ ...What...'s on at the cinema? ~ An old film called *Dark Star*.

Oh, what sort of film is it? ~ It's a sci-fi movie, but it's also funny.

What's it **(1)** ....? ~ I'm not sure, but it's had **(2)** .... reviews.

OK, and who's **(3)** .... it? ~ It **(4)** .... Dan O'Bannon, who plays the **(5)** ....

Oh, I like him. He's a good **(6)** ....

Who's the **(7)** .... ? ~ John Carpenter. He's great.

OK. And where's it **(8)** .... ? ~ At the ABC cinema.

OK. **(9)** .... go and see it tonight. ~ Fine.

7 **ABOUT YOU** **Write your answers, or ask another student.** 根据自身情况回答问题, 也可以向同学提问。

1 What kind of films do you like? ....

2 What was the last film you saw? ....

3 Where was it on? ....

4 Who are the stars of the film? ....

5 Who's the director? ....

6 What's it about? ....

A Media questionnaire 关于大众传媒的调查问卷

1 What do you **watch on TV / the internet**?
   a ☐ **the news**
   b ☐ **crime drama**
   c ☐ films
   d ☐ nothing

2 Why do people read a **newspaper** or look at the news online?
   a ☐ to **find out** what has **happened**
   b ☐ because it has interesting **articles**
   c ☐ for the sports results
   d ☐ for the business **news**

3 What do you **listen to on the radio**?
   a ☐ the news
   b ☐ music **programmes**
   c ☐ something else
   d ☐ nothing

4 Do you **believe** what you read or hear in the news?
   a ☐ yes, **all** of it
   b ☐ **most** of it
   c ☐ **some** of it
   d ☐ no, **none** of it

GLOSSARY

the news [U]	a TV or radio programme about important things happening in the world. **News** [U] is information about things that have just happened.
crime drama	a police story on TV
newspaper	e.g. *The Times, The Washington Post* ALSO **paper**
find out	get information or facts about sth
happen	take place: *We don't know what will **happen** tomorrow.*
article	a piece of writing in a newspaper or magazine, or on the internet
on TV / on the radio	(NOT *in TV / in the radio*) ALSO **in the (news)paper**
programme	a TV/radio show, e.g. the news, a comedy
believe	think that sth is true
all (of sth)	100%
most (of sth)	80%
some (of sth)	30–50%
none (of sth)	0%

SPOTLIGHT *watch, see, listen, hear*

We **watch TV**, but we **see** or **watch a programme, a film**, etc.
We **listen to the radio**, but we **hear a programme** or **listen to a programme**.

❶ Circle the correct answer. – means that no word is needed. 圈出正确答案，注意："–"表示无需填词。

▶ See ⊖/ *to* the film.
1 Read an article *on / in* the paper.
2 Let's listen to *the / a* news.
3 Watch a programme *in / on* TV.
4 Find *– / out* what has happened.
5 I heard it *in / on* the radio.
6 See the *programme / article* on TV.
7 Did you hear *– / to* the sports results?
8 I heard all *– / of* it.
9 I bought *a newspaper / the news*.
10 I watched most *– / of* it.
11 There's a new *crime / news* drama.

❷ Complete the dialogues. 将对话填写完整。

▶ I always _read_ a paper at the weekend. ~ But do you read _all_ of it?
1 Did you _____ TV last night? ~ Yes, I _____ a programme about dogs.
2 I read the story but I don't _____ it's true. ~ No, _____ of it is true. It's completely false.
3 Have you heard the _____? ~ No, what's _____?
4 Did you _____ to the radio this morning? ~ Yes, I _____ the 8 o'clock news.
5 What's in the _____ this morning? ~ I don't know – I never buy one.
6 What did you watch _____ TV? ~ A new crime _____. It was good.
7 What did you listen _____? ~ Oh, nothing interesting.
8 Did you see anything on Saturday? ~ Yeah, a _____ about climate change.

❸ ABOUT YOU **Read the questionnaire again. Tick (✓) your answers, or write a different answer. If possible, ask another student.**
根据自身情况填写问卷。在符合条件的选项前打钩（√），或写下你认为恰当的答案。如有条件，可以向同学提问。

B Media vocabulary 与大众传媒相关的词汇

Word	Example	Meaning
media	*The **media** often write about famous people.*	TV, radio, newspapers, magazines and the internet
magazine	*Do you read women's **magazines**?*	something you can buy every week or month, e.g. *Time, National Geographic*
opinion	*What's your **opinion** of this story?*	what you think about sth
report	*Journalists **report** the news from all over the world.*	give information on the news. The person is a **reporter/journalist**.
event	*The Olympic Games is a very big **event**.*	something important that happens. It can be good or bad.
die	*Nobody **died** in the accident.*	stop living
war	*The two countries were **at war** for ten years.*	fighting between countries or groups of people. When a **war** ends, there is **peace**.
disaster	*The tsunami was a terrible **disaster**.*	something very bad that happens, often when a lot of people die
celebrity (*pl* celebrities)	*There were a lot of **celebrities** at the first night of the film.*	a famous person, usually from TV, film or sport
advertisement (ALSO **advert/ad** *inf*)	*There are too many **adverts** on TV and in the papers.*	text, a picture or a short film which tries to sell you sth

4 Is the meaning of the sentences the same or different? Write *S* or *D*.
下列两句句子的含义是否相同？相同填S，不同填D。

▶ What do the media say about him? / What does the newspaper say about him?   D

1 There is peace between the two groups. / There is war between the two groups. ....
2 What's your opinion of the news? / What do you think of the news? ....
3 It was a great event. / It was a great advertisement. ....
4 I read a magazine article. / I read a newspaper article. ....
5 He is reporting from Seoul. / He is a journalist working in Seoul. ....
6 I saw it in an ad. / I saw it in an advertisement. ....
7 She's a TV celebrity. / She's on TV a lot. ....
8 Where did he live? / Where did he die? ....
9 She's a good reporter. / She's a good journalist. ....

5 Complete the text with words from the table in the correct form. 用表格内单词的正确形式填空。

The ▶ _media_ is TV, radio, newspapers, (1) _____ and the internet. The media (2) _____ important (3) _____ from around the world, for example, (4) _____ like the Asian Tsunami, or (5) _____ between different countries. As well as reporting the news, the media give their (6) _____ of events round the world. And, of course, (7) _____ also like to write about (8) _____ such as Taylor Swift and Usain Bolt, and so on.

6 ABOUT YOU AND YOUR COUNTRY **Write your answers, or ask another student.**
根据自身情况回答问题，也可以向同学提问。

1 What has happened in the news this week? _____
2 What has been an important event in the last five years? _____
3 Do you usually get news from TV, radio, newspapers or the internet? _____
4 Can you think of a popular TV advert now? _____
5 Can you name a famous TV news reporter? _____

A Fiction 虚构文学

J.K. Rowling is a famous British **author**. She has written a **series** of **novels** in which the **main character** is a young boy called Harry Potter, who is always **in trouble**. Rowling has also **created** a number of novels about a private **detective** called Cormoran Strike. He's also in trouble a lot because, like Harry Potter, he doesn't like **rules**. But in the end, like Harry, he **solves** the crime or the problem.

GLOSSARY	
fiction	stories that sb writes that are not about real events OPP **non-fiction**
author	a person who writes books or stories SYN **writer**
series	a number of things of the same kind that come one after another: *a TV series*
novel	a book of fiction
main character	the most important person in a book, film, etc.
create	make sth new happen or be
detective	a person who tries to find out who did a crime; usually a police officer
rule	sth that tells you what you must or must not do: *school rules*. If you **break a rule**, you do sth you mustn't do.
solve	find the answer to a question or problem **solution** *n*

SPOTLIGHT *trouble*

Trouble *(often singular)* means difficulty, problems or worry:
- *I had a lot of **trouble** finding a job.*

If you **are in trouble**, you are in a situation which is dangerous or where you have problems, often with parents, the police or a boss.

1 **True or false? Write *T* or *F*.** 判断正误，正确填T，错误填F。
- ▶ A series is more than one. ⎯T⎯
- **1** *Non-fiction* and *fiction* are the same thing. ....
- **2** An *author* is a *writer*. ....
- **3** A *detective* is often a policeman. ....
- **4** If you are *in trouble*, that's good. ....
- **5** The *main character* in a book is the most important person. ....
- **6** *Rules* are things that you must do and follow. ....
- **7** A *novel* is a book of real events. ....
- **8** If you *solve* something, you find an answer to a problem. ....
- **9** If you *create* something, you break it. ....
- **10** A *solution* to a problem is an answer. ....

2 **Complete the text.** 将短文填写完整。

Adrian McKinty is an Irish ▶ ⎯author⎯ who has written a **(1)** ⎯⎯⎯ of crime **(2)** ⎯⎯⎯. The main **(3)** ⎯⎯⎯ in these stories is a **(4)** ⎯⎯⎯ called Sean Duffy, but he isn't a typical policeman. McKinty has **(5)** ⎯⎯⎯ a character who often breaks **(6)** ⎯⎯⎯, and because of this, he's often in **(7)** ⎯⎯⎯ with his bosses. But in the end, of course, he always **(8)** ⎯⎯⎯ the crime.

3 ABOUT YOU AND YOUR COUNTRY **Write your answers, or talk to another student.**
根据自身情况填写答案，也可以和同学交流讨论。
- **1** A famous author from your country who writes novels. ⎯⎯⎯
- **2** A novel that this person has written. ⎯⎯⎯
- **3** A popular series on TV in your country. ⎯⎯⎯
- **4** One of the main characters in this TV series. ⎯⎯⎯
- **5** The name of a famous detective in fiction. ⎯⎯⎯
- **6** A rule that you sometimes break or have broken. ⎯⎯⎯

B Fact and fiction 事实与虚构

Mary Shelley is a famous English writer from the 19th century. **In the past**, she was **mostly** famous for the novel *Frankenstein*, but in **recent** years, people have **realized** that she **achieved** much more. **In fact**, she wrote a **variety** of books, **including** novels, short stories, travel books and biographies (stories about other people's lives). During her life, she also **tried** to **publish** work written by her husband, Percy Bysshe Shelley, who died when he was only 29.

GLOSSARY	
in the past	in the time before now
mostly	almost all: *My students are mostly Japanese.* SYN **mainly**
recent	that happened or began only a short time ago
realize	understand and know something: *I studied law, but I realize now that it was a mistake.*
achieve	do sth well after trying hard: *She achieved a lot in her life.*
in fact	often used for introducing more information
variety	a lot of different things
including	with: *There were 12, including me.* (= 11 plus me)
try	If you **try** to do sth, you work hard to do it: *I tried to call Clara yesterday, but she was busy all day.*
publish	prepare a book so you can sell it

4 **Circle the two words that have the same sound underlined. Practise saying the words.**
圈出划线部分发音相同的两个单词，并练习发音。

▶ (p<u>a</u>st) (<u>a</u>rm) / <u>a</u>t

1 m<u>i</u>ne / s<u>a</u>me / m<u>ai</u>nly
2 m<u>o</u>stly / h<u>o</u>t / h<u>o</u>me
3 f<u>i</u>t / r<u>ea</u>lize / f<u>i</u>ne
4 ach<u>ie</u>ve / ch<u>i</u>ld / rec<u>ei</u>ve

5 p<u>u</u>ll / b<u>u</u>tter / p<u>u</u>blish
6 m<u>a</u>n / v<u>a</u>riety / <u>a</u>nother
7 bl<u>ue</u> / r<u>u</u>n / incl<u>u</u>ding
8 r<u>e</u>cent / r<u>e</u>d / s<u>ee</u>

5 **Circle the correct answer.** 圈出正确答案。

▶ *In the past* is **around** / (**before**) now.

1 *Including you* is **with you** / **without you**.
2 If you *realize* something, you **know it** / **don't know it**.
3 If you *achieve* something, that's **bad** / **good**.
4 A *variety* is **one thing** / **lots of different things**.
5 If you *publish* a book, it **is** / **isn't** ready to sell.
6 If something is *recent*, it happened a **long** / **short** time ago.
7 I *mostly* work means the same as I **possibly** / **mainly** work.
8 You use *in fact* to give **more information** / **an example of something**.

6 **Complete the sentences.** 首字母填空。

▶ The book isn't difficult. In f<u>act</u>, it's a very easy book to read, and also quite short.

1 In the p_____, bookshops were closed on Sundays, but now they are m_____ open.
2 I've got ten books in English, i_____ this one.
3 I wanted to buy a dictionary, but I r_____ I didn't have enough money.
4 The company p_____ Maria's first book last year, and it is selling very well.
5 You will find a wide v_____ of books on cooking in this shop.
6 He t_____ many times to write a novel. Finally at the age of 36, he a_____ it. Now he's a famous author.

A Things you need to do 待办事项

Things you **might** do or **arrange** before you **go on holiday**:

* **book** the **flight**

* **book** the **accommodation**

* **check** your **passport** [1]

* **get foreign** money

* **pack** your **suitcase**

GLOSSARY

arrange	plan and organize sth
holiday	a period of rest from work or school
(go) on holiday	If you **go on holiday** or **are on holiday**, you are not at work and you are usually away from home.
book	arrange to do or have sth, e.g. a table at a restaurant
flight	a journey by plane **fly** *v pt* **flew** *pp* **flown**
accommodation [U]	a place to stay, e.g. a hotel
check	look at sth to see it is right, good or safe
foreign	of another country
pack	put clothes in a suitcase
suitcase	a large bag you put your clothes in when you travel

SPOTLIGHT *might + verb*

Might means 'it is possible that / perhaps'. **Might** is the same in all forms.

- *You **might** be ill on holiday.* = It's possible that you will be ill.
- *He **might** forget his passport.*   - *He **might** be on holiday now.*

---

1 **Match 1–6 with a–g.** 配对题。

▶ fly ......e......   a   on holiday
1 book ....   b   the accommodation
2 get foreign   c   your passport
3 pack ....   d   money
4 arrange ....   e   to Rome airport ✓
5 go ....   f   your suitcase
6 check ....   g   a flight

2 **Complete the text.** 将短文填写完整。

I'm going on ▶ ..holiday............... for two weeks this Saturday. I finally decided to go to Turkey, so I booked the **(1)** .... with Turkish Airlines. I needed **(2)** .... too, so I looked on the internet for hotels in Izmir. I found a nice one and **(3)** .... to stay there for the first week. After that, we're not sure but we **(4)** .... go and stay near the beach. I also got some **(5)** .... money. I'm very organized, so I have already **(6)** .... that my passport is OK, and I have also **(7)** .... my suitcase. I'm ready to go. Unfortunately, my husband is not so organized. He never looks at his passport and won't pack his **(8)** .... until the night before we travel.

3 **ABOUT YOU** **Write answers to the questions, or ask another student.**
根据自身情况回答问题，也可以向同学提问。

When you go on holiday …
▶ do you arrange it yourself, or does somebody else do it? I don't do it. My wife does. She usually arranges everything.
1 do you usually book a flight a long time before you travel? Why? / Why not? ....
2 do you usually need to book accommodation? Why? / Why not? ....
3 do you usually get foreign money before you travel? ....
4 do you always pack your suitcase yourself? ....
5 do you often check your passport? ....

B Booking accommodation
预订住宿

double room

single room

A Hotel Metropole. How can I help you?

B Oh, good morning. I'd like to book a room for next Friday please, that's the 24th.

A OK. Yes, we have rooms **available**. **Single** or **double**?

B A double room, please.

A OK. A double room is £90 **a night**, and all our rooms are **en suite**.

B Good. And is breakfast **extra**?

A No, breakfast is **included**.

B OK, great. How about **parking**?

A **I'm afraid** we don't have parking at the hotel.

B **Oh dear**!

A But there's a car park very near.

B OK, well **it doesn't matter.** Yes, I'll take the room.

A Fine. Could I just take a few **details** then ...

GLOSSARY	
available	ready for you to use, have or see
(£90) **a night**	= (£90) for one night ALSO (£90) **a week/a month**
en suite	a bedroom with a bathroom
extra	more than is usual: *You pay an* **extra** *£20 for a large room.*
include	have sth or sb as part of sth else: *The meal will be about £30, but that* **includes** *service.*
parking	a place to leave a car
I'm afraid	= I'm sorry (NOT *I'm afraid but*) **I'm afraid not** = I'm sorry but no.
Oh dear!	used for showing that you are surprised or unhappy about sth
it doesn't matter	= it isn't important
details	information, e.g. your name, address, phone number

4 **Is this good news? Write *Yes* or *No*.** 下列情况是好消息吗? 是的填Yes, 不是填No。

▶ There is parking. <u>Yes</u>
1 I'm afraid ... .
2 The room's en suite. ....
3 Breakfast is extra. ....
4 There are rooms available. ....
5 Oh dear! ....
6 Breakfast is included. ....
7 I'm afraid not. ....

5 **Match 1–5 with a–f.** 配对题。

▶ Breakfast <u>c</u>
1 book ....
2 I'm afraid ....
3 It doesn't ....
4 Oh ....
5 £100 ....

a matter.
b dear!
c is included. ✓
d a room
e a week
f not.

6 **Complete the dialogue. Write one word in each space.** 将对话填写完整, 每空格只填一词。

A Regent Hotel, can I ▶ <u>help</u> you?

B Oh, hello. Do you have any rooms **(1)** .... for this weekend?

A Would you like a **(2)** .... room or a **(3)** .... ?

B A double, please.

A OK. All our rooms are **(4)** ....

B Good. Is that with a bath and shower?

A Just a shower.

B Oh **(5)** .... – I prefer baths. Oh well, it doesn't **(6)** .... A shower's OK.

A And a double room is €75 **(7)** .... night.

B That's fine. And does that **(8)** .... breakfast?

A No, I'm **(9)** .... not. Breakfast is **(10)** ....

B Right. And what about **(11)** .... ?

A Yes, there is a car park at the hotel. Is there anything else?

B No, that's great. I'd like to book the room.

A Fine. Could you just give me a few **(12)** .... , please?

88 〉Hotels 酒店

A Describe a hotel 描述酒店

travel blog

Atlanta Hotel (VILNIUS Lithuania)

When we **went on a trip** to Lithuania, we **stayed** at this hotel near the Old Town. The bedrooms were good, and the **service** was **excellent**: everyone was friendly and very **helpful** with all the information that **tourists** need. There was also a café bar where we could meet and **chat** to other **guests**. I would **definitely recommend** both Vilnius and the Atlanta for a short **stay**.

GLOSSARY			
trip	a journey to a place and back again: *go on a trip*	**tourist**	sb who goes to a place on holiday **tourism** *n*
stay (at a hotel)	live for a short time (in a hotel) **stay** *n*	**chat**	talk in a friendly informal way to sb **chat** *n*
service [U]	the work that sb does for guests in a hotel, customers in a shop or restaurant, etc.	**guest**	a person staying in a hotel or your home
		definitely	for sure; 100% SYN **certainly**
excellent	very good: *an **excellent** student/musician*	**recommend**	tell sb that a thing or a person is good
helpful	wanting to help		

1 **Circle the correct answer.** 圈出正确答案。

▶ We *lived* / (*stayed*) at a hotel for our holiday.
1 We *went on* / *made* a trip to India last month.
2 It was lovely – I *recommend* / *don't recommend* it.
3 The dinner was *excellent* / *helpful*.
4 A lot of *tourists* / *guests* visit our city.
5 It was great, so I *definitely* / *possibly* want to go again.
6 We had a short *service* / *stay* in Budapest last year.
7 I think *service* / *tourism* is important to Lithuania.
8 We often *stay* / *chat* to other guests in the hotel in the evening.

2 **Complete the text.** 将短文填写完整。

Last month we had a short ▶ _stay_ in Amsterdam. We were at quite a small hotel, but all the people who worked there spoke **(1)** _____ English, and they were very **(2)** _____ . They told us about the best places for **(3)** _____ to visit such as the Van Gogh Museum, and they also introduced us to other **(4)** _____ who were **(5)** _____ at the hotel. If you are thinking of going to Amsterdam, I would **(6)** _____ this hotel, and you should **(7)** _____ go to the Van Gogh Museum while you are there.

3 ABOUT YOU **Complete the questions.** 将问句填写完整。

▶ What was the last hotel you stayed _at_ ? _I stayed in the Hotel Victoria in Turin._
1 How long did you _____ there? _____
2 Was the _____ good? _____
3 Did you _____ to other guests in the hotel? _____
4 Would you _____ this hotel to other people? _____
5 Was the place popular with _____ ? _____

4 ABOUT YOU **Write your answers to the questions in Exercise 3, or ask another student.**
根据自身情况回答练习3中的问题，也可以向同学提问。

B In a hotel 在酒店

A hotel guest might ask these questions:

Could I have my **key**, please?
   It's room 402.
When do you **serve** breakfast?
Could I **pay my bill**, please?
Can I **change** money here?
Can I **leave** my luggage here?
Could you **call** a taxi, please?
Do I **have to** pay now?

The hotel receptionist might say or ask:

Could you just **sign** here, please?
You can **collect** your passport later.
You **have to check out of** your room by 10 o'clock.
Breakfast is served **until** 9.30.

GLOSSARY		
key		
serve	give food or drink to sb	
pay	give sb money for work or services	
bill	a piece of paper that shows how much money you must pay, e.g. in a hotel or restaurant	
change (money)	If you give sb pounds (£), and they **change** them **into** dollars, they give you dollars for the pounds.	
leave sth somewhere	let sth or sb stay in the same place *leave the door open*	
call	phone sb (**make**) **a call** n	
sign	write your name on a form or letter	
collect	go and get sth from a place	
check out	pay the bill and leave a hotel OPP **check in**	
until	up to a certain time SYN **till**	

SPOTLIGHT *have to* + verb

Have to is used for saying that somebody must do something or that something must happen.
- *You **have to** pay the hotel bill when you leave.*
- ***Do I have to** pay for breakfast? ~ No, breakfast is included.*
- *You **don't have to** work on Sunday, but you can if you want.*

5 **Match 1–6 with a–g.** 配对题。

▶	change	_c_	**a**	the bill	
1	call	....	**b**	food	
2	pay	....	**c**	money ✓	
3	sign	....	**d**	a bag in the hotel	
4	leave	....	**e**	a ticket from the station	
5	serve	....	**f**	a form	
6	collect	....	**g**	a taxi	

6 **Complete the sentences.** 将句子填写完整。

▶ If you want to get in your room, you need a _key_ .
1 If you write your name on a form, you .... it.
2 If your room is hot at night, you can .... the window open.
3 If you want to get somewhere quickly, you can .... a taxi.
4 If you're leaving a hotel or restaurant, you have to .... the bill.
5 If you give food and drink to people, you .... them.
6 If you have pounds (£) and want euros (€), you need to .... some money.
7 If you go to a place to get a key, you .... it.
8 When you arrive at the hotel, you .... in at reception.

7 **Complete the dialogues.** 将对话填写完整。

▶ I'm leaving now, so could I _pay_ the bill? ~ Yes, of course.
1 Can I have my ...., please? ~ Of course. What's your room number?
2 Do the shops close at 5.30? ~ No, they're open .... 7.30.
3 Excuse me, what time do you .... lunch? ~ From 12.00 to 2.00.
4 Will I .... to get a taxi to the airport? ~ No, you don't .... to. There is a bus from the hotel that will take you to the airport.
5 When do I have to leave my room and pay? ~ You have to check .... by 10 a.m.
6 I'd like to go to the train station. Could you .... a taxi for me? ~ Yes, of course.

A Check-in 办理登机手续

ticket machine

passenger

check-in desk

luggage

Some **passengers** buy a ticket online and **print** a **boarding pass** 24 hours before they fly. Some passengers print a **boarding pass** at a **ticket machine** when they **reach** the airport. Some get one at the **check-in desk**. You need to **check in** if you have a lot of **luggage** (e.g. suitcases and bags), but you can take some **hand luggage** on the plane with you. After check-in, you can go through **security**, then look for the **gate** number where your flight leaves from and wait to **board** the plane.

GLOSSARY	
print	put words or pictures onto paper using a machine
boarding pass	a card that you must show when you get on a plane or ship SYN **boarding card**
reach	arrive somewhere
check-in *n*	(*see picture*) **check in** *v*: You **check in** at the **check-in desk**.
hand luggage	a bag you can take on the plane with you
security	the place in an airport where people check you and your hand luggage
gate	in an airport, the place near your plane where you wait to get on
board	walk onto a plane, ship or bus

SPOTLIGHT *airports*

An **airport** is a place where people get on and off **planes/aeroplanes**. An **airline** is a company that takes people by plane to different places.

1 Complete the words. 将单词填写完整。

▶ p a s s enger   3 b___ ___ ___d___ ___g c___ ___d   6 h___nd l___gg___ge
1 b___ ___rd   4 ac___ ___pl___ ___ ___   7 a___ ___l___ ___e
2 ch___ ___ ___-i___   5 a___ ___p___ ___t   8 s___c___ ___it___

2 Make five more phrases from the words in the box. 用方框内的词组成五个短语。

airline ✓	boarding	desk	board	check-in	pass
ticket	company ✓	luggage	machine	the plane	hand

▶ airline company   ....

    ....

3 Complete the sentences. 将句子填写完整。

▶ We flew in a large ___aeroplane___ .
1 There were a lot of _____ waiting at the _____ desk.
2 If we hurry, we'll _____ the airport by 3.30.
3 I printed my _____ card at home, and I only had hand _____ , so I didn't need to _____ in when I got to the airport.
4 I went to _____ 7, but I sat there for half an hour before we could _____ the plane.
5 Heathrow and Charles de Gaulle are very busy _____ .
6 If you don't have a boarding pass, you can _____ one at the ticket _____ .
7 I had a lot of _____ : a large suitcase and a heavy bag as well.

4 ABOUT YOU Are these sentences true for you? 以下情况与你是否相符?

▶ I travel by plane a lot. _No, I don't travel by plane very much._
1 I usually use the same airline when I fly. _____
2 I usually print my boarding pass at home. _____
3 When I reach the airport, the first thing I do is have a coffee. _____
4 I want to go through security very quickly. _____
5 I like to be one of the first people to board the plane. _____
6 I like to sit at the front of the plane. _____

B Departure and arrival 出发与抵达

You **get on / board** the plane.

You **fasten your seat belt**.

The plane **takes off**.

Flight attendants provide food and drinks.

The plane **lands** and passengers get off.

GLOSSARY	
departure	leaving a place
arrival	coming to a place: *There's always someone to meet me **on arrival**.* **arrive** v
provide	give sth to sb who needs it
check	look at sth to see if it is correct or good: *check your ticket* (NOT ~~control your ticket~~)
collect	go and take sth from a place

Somebody **checks** your passport.

You **collect** your luggage and **leave** the airport.

5 Cover the pictures and put the phrases in order. Write numbers in the boxes.
遮住图片，将句子排序，在方框内填写序号。

You collect your luggage. ☐
You get on the plane. ☐ 1
You get off the plane. ☐
You fasten your seat belt. ☐
Someone checks your passport. ☐

The plane lands. ☐
You leave the airport. ☐
The plane takes off. ☐
Flight attendants provide drinks. ☐

6 Complete the text. 将短文填写完整。

I don't like sitting in airports, and now you often have to ▶ <u>arrive</u> at the airport two hours before
(1) .... , which is terrible. When I **(2)** .... the plane, the first thing I do is
(3) .... my seat belt. I then sit nervously until the plane **(4)** .... Fortunately, the
(5) .... attendants are usually very kind, and always **(6)** .... food and drinks, but I'm so
nervous I can't eat anything. I only feel safe when the plane has **(7)** .... On **(8)** .... ,
I'm very happy when someone has **(9)** .... my passport, so that I can **(10)** .... my
luggage and **(11)** .... the airport with my brother, who usually meets me.

7 ABOUT YOU Write answers to the questions, or ask another student.
根据自身情况回答问题，也可以向同学提问。

▶ What's the first thing you do when you get on a plane? <u>I fasten my seatbelt.</u>
1 How do you feel when the plane takes off? ....
2 Do you always eat the food the airlines provide? ....
3 How do you feel when the plane lands? ....
4 Do you usually need to collect luggage, or do you travel with hand luggage? ....

A A beach holiday 海滩度假

For many years, we **used to** go to Hyères – a **typical** little town by the sea in the south of France. We used to **fly** to Nice, then get a bus to Hyères, where we stayed in an apartment. In the mornings, I was happy to sit on the **beach**[1] near the **rocks**[2] and read and write **postcards**, **while** my husband used to go out on a **boat**[3] or go swimming – the **sea**[4] was lovely and warm. We usually had lunch in the apartment, then **relaxed** for **a couple of** hours. In the evening, there were nice restaurants near the beach where we could have dinner.

GLOSSARY	
typical	Something that is **typical** is a good example of its kind.
fly *pt* **flew** *pp* **flown**	travel by plane
postcard	a card with a picture on one side. You write on the other side and then send it by post.
while	at the same time as: *Max watched TV **while** I cooked dinner.*
relax	do nothing and enjoy yourself
a couple of (**hours/days**, etc.)	two or maybe three (hours/days, etc.)

SPOTLIGHT *used to* + verb

We use **used to** + **verb** to talk about something that happened often or was true in the past, but not now.

- *I **used to live** in New York, but now I live in London.*
- *My father **used to be** a police officer; now he works in a bank.*

1 Write five more things that the wife, the husband, or both of them used to do on their holiday.
上文中的夫妻在度假时会分别或一起做哪些事? 请再写出五件。

▶ They used to fly to Nice.   3 ....

1 ....   4 ....

2 ....   5 ....

2 Complete the sentences. 将句子填写完整。

▶ Bournemouth is a _typical_ place for a beach holiday in England.

1 We stayed there for a .... of weeks.

2 We just sat on the .... and looked at the sea.

3 I would like to go on a .... on the river.

4 We sat on the .... at the back of the beach. You could see more from there.

5 My idea of a perfect holiday is to .... and do nothing.

6 We .... from London to Rome, then took a train for the rest of the journey.

7 My cousin didn't like beach holidays. He .... to go to the mountains every year.

3 One word is missing in each line of the text. What is it and where does it go?
在句中相应位置补上遗漏的单词。

▶ We had lovely / in France when   _holidays_
I was a child. We to stay in Cassis   1 ....
usually for a couple weeks. Every   2 ....
morning I to swim a lot, but I also   3 ....
played with my dad, my mum   4 ....
wrote lots of to family and friends.   5 ....
That was a day.   6 ....

4 ABOUT YOU Write your answers, or ask another student. 根据自身情况回答问题, 也可以向同学提问。

▶ Where did you go for holidays as a child? _We used to have beach holidays in England or Spain._

1 Did you go to several places or the same place? ....

2 How long did you usually go for? ....

3 Did you ever go on a boat? ....

4 Do you enjoy relaxing on holiday, or do you do many things? ....

B A sightseeing holiday 观光度假

Tourist questionnaire

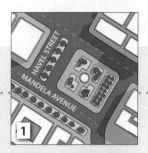

When you **go sightseeing** on holiday do you:

* buy a **map**[1] of the town?   Yes / No
* buy a **guidebook**?   Yes / No
* **go on a guided tour** with a **guide**?   Yes / No
* **prefer to** go sightseeing on your own?   Yes / No
* **visit** museums and art galleries?   Yes / No
* like to **look round**?   Yes / No
* **take** lots of **photos**[2]?   Yes / No
* often **get lost**?   Yes / No

What is your **ideal** place for a sightseeing holiday? _____

GLOSSARY			
go sightseeing	go as a tourist to look at interesting buildings and places	**prefer to do sth**	like to do one thing more than another
guidebook	a book that describes a place for tourists	**visit**	go to see a person or place for a short time **visit** n
tour	a short visit around a town or building; **go on a guided tour** visit a place with a person who tells you about it	**look round**	visit a place
		get lost	If you **get lost** or **are lost**, you don't know where you are.
guide	a person who gives a guided tour and tells tourists about places	**ideal**	the best or exactly right SYN **perfect**

5 **Circle the correct word.** 圈出正确答案。

▶ prefer (to go) / go

1 go / *have* sightseeing
2 a *guide map* / *guidebook*
3 *go on* / *make* a tour
4 *visit* / *go* a museum

5 *guide* / *guided* tour
6 *make* / *take* photos
7 look *round* / *about* a place
8 *a guide* / *an ideal* holiday

6 **Complete the sentences with one word.** 将句子填写完整，每空格只填一词。

▶ We went on a ...*guided*... tour.

1 She took a lot of _____ of old buildings in the town centre.
2 We _____ on a tour of the town, and the _____ was interesting and very funny.
3 I _____ lost because I didn't have a _____ .
4 We went _____ the day after we arrived. It was quite tiring.
5 I don't like _____ tours of places – I _____ to visit places on my own.
6 You get a lot of useful information in a _____ .
7 Do you want to go on a guided _____ ?
8 I want to _____ the Science Museum when I'm in London.
9 My sister can never find her way – she often _____ lost.
10 I like to look _____ a place and _____ lots of photos.
11 A beach holiday is _____ for families with young children.
12 When you're on holiday, do you prefer to _____ round on your own?

7 **ABOUT YOU** **Write your answers to the tourist questionnaire, or ask another student.**
根据自身情况填写游客问卷，也可以向同学提问。

A Introductions 介绍朋友相识

Liam and Sienna meet for the first time …   … and two hours later …

> Liam, let me **introduce** you **to** Sienna. Sienna, **this is** Liam.

> Hello.

> Hi. Nice to meet you. And **welcome to** Oxford!

> shake hands

> OK, **bye** Liam. **Good to meet you.**

> Yes. **Hope to see you again.** Goodbye.

GLOSSARY

greet	say hello when you meet a new person or a friend **greeting** n
introduce sb (to sb)	bring people together for the first time and say their names **introduction** n
This is …	When we introduce people, we say **this is** Liam, etc. (NOT ~~he/she is~~ OR ~~here is~~)
hi	inf hello
welcome	If sb is **welcome**, you are happy to see them: **Welcome to** our home! **welcome** v, n: He **welcomed** us. They gave us a warm **welcome**.
bye	a short form of goodbye
hope to (see you again)	used for saying that you want sth to happen

SPOTLIGHT introductions

You often use **Nice to meet you** or **Good to meet you** when you meet people for the first time, and when you say goodbye after the first time you meet them.

How do you do? was common in the past, but is now very formal and not used very much.

1 **Make correct sentences from the words.** 连词成句。

▶ do / how / do / you   How do you do   ?
1 meet / nice / hello / you / to   ....
2 this / Max / Emma / is   ....
3 again / hope / you / bye / to / see   ....
4 you / goodbye / to / nice / meet   ....

2 **Complete the sentences.** 将句子填写完整。

▶ Bye .... is just a short form of goodbye.
1 When we .... somebody to another person, we say: 'This is (Sophy)'.
2 We often .... hands when we meet people for the first time.
3 When we .... friends, we usually say *hello* or *hi*.
4 .... and greetings are often different in other countries and languages.
5 When we visit my aunt and uncle, they always give us a warm ....
6 *Hello* and *Hi* are common .... in English.

3 **Complete the dialogues.** 将对话填写完整。

1 LUCY   Emma, ▶ this .... is Alex.
   EMMA   ....
   ALEX   Hi. .... to .... you.

2 EMMA   Goodbye, Alex. Hope to see you ....
   ALEX   Yes. ....

3 MAX   Lucy, ... is Dan.
   LUCY   Hi, Dan. Good to ....
          .... And .... to Cambridge.
   DAN   Thank you.

4 LUCY   Bye, Dan. .... to see you again. Have a good journey.
   DAN   Thanks. ....

B Meeting a friend 与朋友见面

Matt meets his friend Tess in a café.

Matt Hi, Tess. **How are you?**
Tess **Fine, thanks.** And you?
Matt Yeah, **very well.**
Tess Good. And how's Sarah?
Matt She's in bed, actually.
Tess Oh! What's the matter?
Matt Flu, I think.
Tess Oh dear!

An hour later they say 'goodbye'.

Tess **Anyway**, Matt, **I've got to** go now. **See you later.**
Matt Yeah. About 7.00?
Tess Yes, that's fine.
Matt Good. **See you then.**
Tess Sure. And **give my love to** Sarah. Hope she gets better soon.
Matt Yes, I **will.**

GLOSSARY	
How are you?	You say this to a friend when you meet. ALSO **How are things?**
fine	OR **very well** OR **good** OR **not bad** are common replies to 'How are you?'. (NOT ~~very fine~~)
oh!	used for showing a strong feeling, e.g. when you're surprised or afraid
What's the matter?	= What's the problem?
Oh dear!	sth you say if you are surprised or sad
anyway	a word you can use when you start to talk about sth different
have got to do sth	have to do/must do **Have got to** is more informal than **have to**. It is usually contracted, e.g. *I've got to go.*
give my love to sb	say a big, warm hello to sb
will	You use **will** when you agree or promise to do sth

SPOTLIGHT *see you …*

We say this when we know we will meet someone again.
See you later is usually the same day. Other common expressions are: **see you soon**, **see you** (next Saturday, etc.), **see you then**, etc.

4 Complete the phrases. 将短语填写完整。

▶ H o w a r e y o u ?
1 S___ ___ you tomorrow.
2 He's v___ __y w___ ___l.
3 Wh___ ___' ___ the m___ ___ ___ ___ ___?
4 S___ ___ you l__t___ ___.
5 S___ ___ you s___ ___ ___.
6 H___w ___r___ th___ ___ ___s?
7 G___ ___ ___ my l___ ___ ___ to Suki.
8 I'v___ g___t t___ go n___w.
9 Th___ ___'s f___n___.

5 Replace the <u>underlined</u> words with another word or words that have the same meaning.
用其他单词或短语替换划线部分，保持句意不变。

ROB <u>Hello</u>. ▶ Hi .... How are <u>you</u>? ....
FINN <u>Good</u>. And you? ....
ROB Hmm, not great.
FINN What's the <u>problem</u>? ....
ROB I <u>have to</u> work all weekend. ....
FINN Oh <u>no</u>. ....
ROB Yes, so I can't come on Sunday. But <u>say hello</u> to Elle. ....
FINN Yes, I <u>promise</u>. ....

6 Cover the conversations above and complete the dialogues. Don't use the same word more than once.
遮住以上会话并填空，每词限用一次。

1 JIM Hi, How ▶ are you ....?
   SAM I'm very .... And you?
   JIM Yeah, ...
     And .... your wife?
   SAM She's ....

2 JIM ...., Sam, I ....
     .... go now.
   SAM OK. See you ....
   JIM Sure. What time?
   SAM 6.30.
   JIM Yeah, ... fine. See you ....

A About people 关于人的信息

Who do you live with, Tracey?	~ My parents, and my younger brother.
And **what's** your brother **like**?	~ He's OK – he's quite funny.
And your boyfriend – **what does** he **do**?	~ He works for an airline company.
How long have you known him?	~ About two years.
And you're learning Spanish. **How often** do you study?	~ **Twice** a week.
And **why** Spanish?	~ Because we want to live in Spain.
Whose idea was it to live in Spain?	~ My boyfriend's.
OK. But what do <u>you</u> think?	~ **Yeah**, I think it's a good idea.
What kind of work can you do in Spain?	~ I can probably get a job in a restaurant.

GLOSSARY

twice (**a week**/ **month**, etc.)	two times every week/month, etc.
idea	a plan or a new thought: *It was a good **idea** to arrive early.*
yeah *inf*	yes
kind (of sth)	a group of things or people that are the same in some way SYNS **sort**/ **type**: *What **kind/sort/type** of books do you read?*

SPOTLIGHT *whose and belong to someone*

Whose money **is that**?	~ *It's **mine**.* = It's my money.
Who does that money **belong to**?	~ *It **belongs to** my brother.*
Whose is this bag?	~ *It's Ben's.* = The bag **belongs to** Ben.
Who does this bag **belong to**?	~ *It's Ben's.*

1 **Make correct questions from the words.** 连词成问句。

▶ for / do / work / who / you — Who do you work for ?
1 you / often / there / go / how / do — ?
2 like / what / music / do / sort of / you — ?
3 he / does / what / do — ?
4 have / lived / how long / there / you — ?
5 type of / do / watch / what / films / you — ?
6 this / to / belong / does / who — ?
7 his / like / what's / flat — ?
8 like / you / why / her / do — ?

2 **Find the right question in Exercise 1 for these answers.** 根据下列回答，从练习1中找出相应问题。

▶ Because she's very kind. *8*
a Ten years. ....
b I like romantic movies. ....
c It's small but very nice. ....
d Twice a year. ....
e It's mine. ....
f He's a doctor. ....
g Rock and pop. ....

3 **Complete the dialogues with one word in each space.** 将对话填写完整，每空格只填一词。

▶ _Why_ did you leave your job? ~ Because I didn't like it.
1 How _____ do you go to Italy? ~ _____ a year.
2 _____ jacket is this? ~ It's _____ . I bought it yesterday.
3 _____'s Alicia like? ~ She's very nice.
4 Do you speak German? ~ _____ , a bit.
5 Who does this _____ to? ~ I think it's Mark's.
6 What _____ of animal is it? ~ I think it's a horse.
7 Do you want to go out this evening? ~ Yeah, that's a good _____ .
8 How _____ have you worked there? ~ Six months.

B About places 关于地点的信息

How long is it open?
(= how many hours?)

What do you **recommend**?
(= What do you think is good?)

What time / When does the palace **close/shut**?
(OPP **open**)

How far is it to the river?
(= how many metres?)

Where's the nearest bank?
(= Where's the first bank from here?)

How many places can we visit with this ticket?
(= what number?)

Is the castle **worth** seeing?
(= Do you recommend the castle?)

How much are the tickets?
(= How much money?)

Which restaurant do you recommend?

SPOTLIGHT *which* or *what*?

Use **which** when there is a small number of possibilities.
- *We have a double room or a single.* **Which** *would you like?* (There are only two possibilities.)
In other situations with more possibilities, use **what**.
- **What's** *the address of the hotel?* (NOT ~~Which is the address?~~)

---

4 Circle the correct answer. 圈出正确答案。

▶ *When time* / *What time* does it close?

1 *Which / What* is your address?
2 How *long / long time* do you need?
3 What *hour / time* does it open?
4 How *many / much* places did you visit?

5 Where's the *next / nearest* café?
6 Is the museum worth *to see / seeing*?
7 There are two films. *What / Which* do you prefer?
8 How *far / long* is it to the museum?

5 Complete the questions. 将问句填写完整。

▶ When does the post office open?
1 How .... is it to the station?
2 It opens at 8.00, but when does it .... ?
3 How .... places did you go to?
4 Is it .... going to see Angkor Wat?

5 We've got two or three types of pen.
.... one do you want?
6 Where's the .... underground station?
7 .... 's the phone number of the bank?
8 There's a lot to see. What do you .... ?

6 ABOUT YOUR TOWN **Write your answers, or ask another student.**
根据自身情况回答问题，也可以向同学提问。

1 Where do you live? ....
2 How long have you lived there? ....
3 Which places are worth visiting? ....
4 How far are they from your home? ....
5 Can you recommend any restaurants? ....
6 Where's the nearest restaurant? ....

A Requests and responses 请求与回答

Requests (in the classroom)	Responses
Can you bring[1] the dictionaries here, **please?**	✓ Yes, **of course.** Sure. Yeah, **no problem.**
Could you finish this exercise for homework, **please?**	
Yuri, **could you take**[2] these books to the library?	
Elena, can you **change places** with Gabi, **please?**	✗ (No), **I'm afraid I can't.**
Could you **lend** me a pen, Oleg?	
Please make sure you **put** the books **back.**	

GLOSSARY

1 **bring**   2 **take**

request	asking for sth in a polite way
response	an answer to sb or sth **respond** v
finish	do/complete the last part of sth
change places	e.g. Elena sits in Gabi's seat, and Gabi sits in Elena's seat
lend	give sth to sb to use for a short time
make sure (you do sth)	be certain (that you do sth)
put sth back	return sth to its place
I'm afraid I can't	= I'm sorry, but I can't. (NOT *I'm afraid but I can't.*)

SPOTLIGHT being polite

In English, it is **polite** to say **please** when you ask a person for something, and to say **thank you** if the person says *yes*.
I'm afraid is a polite way to say *no*, and to say you are sorry about something.
- *I'm afraid I can't come this evening.*
- *Can you come this evening? ~ I'm afraid not.*
Can and **could** are both used for requests. **Could** is a bit more polite.

1 Complete the dialogues with one word in each space. 将对话填写完整，每空格只填一词。
- ▶ _Can_ you clean the board, _please_ ?
- **1** Can .... lend .... a pen, please? ~ Yes, of ....
- **2** Could you .... the books here, ... ? ~ Yeah, no ....
- **3** .... you lend me some money? ~ No, I'm .... not. I don't have any.
- **4** Is it .... to say *please* and *thank you* in English? ~ Yes, it is.
- **5** Do you often use *sure* and *no problem*? ~ Yes, they're common .... to requests in English.
- **6** Can I .... this book home tonight? ~ Yes, but please .... it back tomorrow.
- **7** I must .... sure I remember Katya's book next week.
- **8** Do you use *can* and *could* for .... in English? ~ Yes. *Could* is a bit more ....
- **9** We have to .... all the books back on the shelf when we finish the lesson.

2 Write requests and responses using *can* and *could*, and different responses.
用can或could提出请求，并作相应回答。
- ▶ put / books / over there
  - A _Could you put these books over there, please?_
  - B _Yes, sure._
- **1** finish / exercise / homework
  - A ....
  - B ....
- **2** Luca / change places / Maria
  - A ....
  - B ....
- **3** bring / notebook / tomorrow
  - A ....
  - B ....
- **4** lend / pencil
  - A ....
  - B ....
- **5** take / books / library
  - A ....
  - B ....
- **6** finish / essay / Monday
  - A ....
  - B ....

B Asking for and giving permission 请求和给予许可

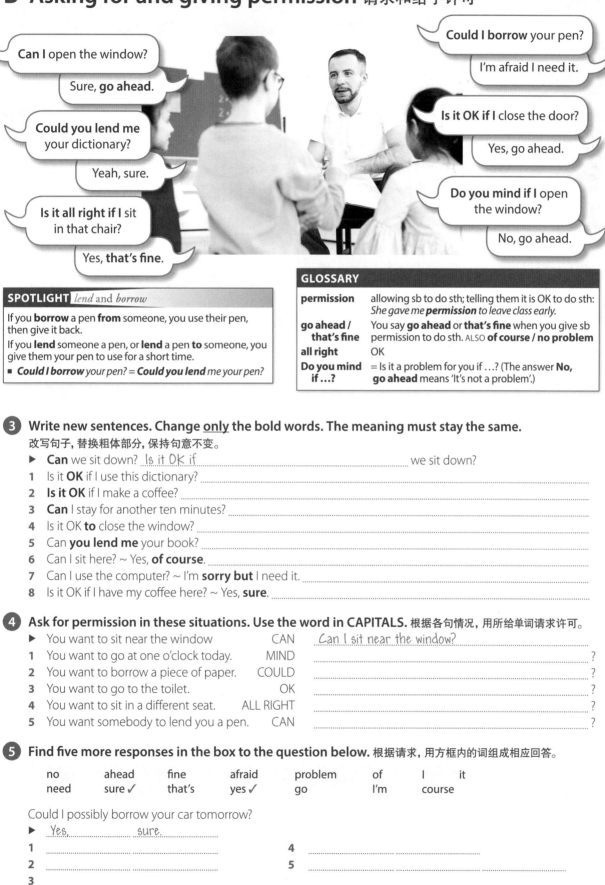

Can I open the window?

Sure, **go ahead.**

Could you lend me your dictionary?

Yeah, sure.

Is it all right if I sit in that chair?

Yes, **that's fine.**

Could I borrow your pen?

I'm afraid I need it.

Is it OK if I close the door?

Yes, go ahead.

Do you mind if I open the window?

No, go ahead.

SPOTLIGHT *lend* and *borrow*

If you **borrow** a pen **from** someone, you use their pen, then give it back.

If you **lend** someone a pen, or **lend** a pen **to** someone, you give them your pen to use for a short time.

- *Could I borrow your pen?* = *Could you lend me your pen?*

GLOSSARY	
permission	allowing sb to do sth; telling them it is OK to do sth: *She gave me **permission** to leave class early.*
go ahead / that's fine	You say **go ahead** or **that's fine** when you give sb permission to do sth. ALSO **of course / no problem**
all right	OK
Do you mind if …?	= Is it a problem for you if …? (The answer **No, go ahead** means 'It's not a problem'.)

3 Write new sentences. Change <u>only</u> the bold words. The meaning must stay the same.
改写句子，替换粗体部分，保持句意不变。

▶ **Can** we sit down? Is it OK if .... we sit down?

1 Is it **OK** if I use this dictionary? ....

2 **Is it OK** if I make a coffee? ....

3 **Can** I stay for another ten minutes? ....

4 Is it OK **to** close the window? ....

5 Can **you lend me** your book? ....

6 Can I sit here? ~ Yes, **of course**. ....

7 Can I use the computer? ~ I'm **sorry but** I need it. ....

8 Is it OK if I have my coffee here? ~ Yes, **sure**. ....

4 Ask for permission in these situations. Use the word in CAPITALS. 根据各句情况，用所给单词请求许可。

▶ You want to sit near the window   CAN   Can I sit near the window?

1 You want to go at one o'clock today.   MIND   .... ?

2 You want to borrow a piece of paper.   COULD   .... ?

3 You want to go to the toilet.   OK   .... ?

4 You want to sit in a different seat.   ALL RIGHT   .... ?

5 You want somebody to lend you a pen.   CAN   .... ?

5 Find five more responses in the box to the question below. 根据请求，用方框内的词组成相应回答。

no	ahead	fine	afraid	problem	of	I	it
need	sure ✓	that's	yes ✓	go	I'm	course	

Could I possibly borrow your car tomorrow?

▶ Yes, ... sure. ....

1 ....   4 ....

2 ....   5 ....

3 ....

A Inviting people 提出邀请

Inviting	Saying yes

Would you like to …
 Do you want to …
  go out for a meal / a drink?
  come round for a coffee?
  come to a **party**?
	Yes, great!
	 Yeah, I'd love to!
	 That sounds lovely/fun/good.
	 That would be lovely/nice.

	Saying no
	I'd love to, but I'm going to the cinema. **I'm sorry, but** I'm busy. **I'm afraid I can't.**

GLOSSARY	
invite	ask sb to come to a party, your house, etc. **invitation** n
Would you like to …?	= **Do you want to …?** (**Would you like to** is a bit more polite.)
go out for (a meal/drink)	go to a restaurant or a café/ bar
come round	visit a person at their house, often near your house
party	a time when friends meet to eat, drink, dance, etc.
great	very good SYNS **lovely/wonderful**
I'd love to	= I want to very much; **I'd** = I would ALSO **That would be lovely. / That sounds lovely.**
busy	If you're **busy**, you have a lot of things to do.
I'm afraid I can't	= I'm sorry, (but) I can't (NOT ~~I'm afraid but I can't.~~)

1 Are the <u>underlined</u> sounds the same or different? Write *S* or *D*. Practise saying the words.
划线部分的发音是否相同? 相同填S, 不同填D, 并练习发音。

▶ m<u>ea</u>l / gr<u>ea</u>t   D

1 l<u>o</u>ve / w<u>o</u>nderful ....
2 w<u>ou</u>ld / s<u>ou</u>nd ....

3 s<u>o</u>rry / c<u>o</u>me ....
4 afr<u>ai</u>d / gr<u>ea</u>t ....

5 <u>yea</u>h / th<u>ere</u> ....
6 b<u>u</u>sy / b<u>u</u>t ....

2 One word is missing in each sentence. What is it, and where does it go? 在句中相应位置补上遗漏的单词。

▶ Do you / to go out later?   want

1 Would you to come round later? ....
2 Yes, I'd love. ....
3 Do you want to out for dinner? ....
4 That lovely. ....
5 I've just got an to a party. ....

6 I'm afraid can't. ....
7 That be nice. ....
8 Do you want come to a party? ....
9 I'm, but I'm busy tonight. ....
10 Ben me to lunch on Saturday. ....

3 Complete the questions and answers. 将问题和回答填写完整。

▶ Invite someone for a drink in a bar.
Say yes.
Do you want to go out for a drink?
That would be lovely.

1 Invite a friend for a meal in a restaurant.
Say yes.
Would _____?
Yes, g _____!

2 Invite a friend to your home for a coffee.
Say no politely.
Do _____?
I'm a _____.

3 Invite someone to a party tomorrow.
Say yes.
Would _____?
Yes, that s _____.

4 Invite someone for a coffee in a café.
Say no politely.
Do _____?
I'd _____, but _____ gym.

B Making suggestions 提出建议

ask for a suggestion	What **shall we** do / Where **shall we** go ⎱ **this weekend?**	
make a suggestion	**Shall we** go to the beach? **Maybe we could** go out for a meal.	**What about** going to an art gallery? **Let's** go out for a drink.

say 'yes'	Yes, (that's a) **good/great idea!** Yeah, **let's do that.** **OK, fine.**	say 'no', or make another suggestion	**I'm not sure** (about that). I think **I'd prefer to** stay at home. Yeah, or **perhaps we could** go to the mountains.

> **GLOSSARY**
>
> **suggestion**   an idea that sb gives you to think about **suggest** v
> **maybe**   possibly SYN **perhaps**
> **that's a great idea** = that's a very good plan
> **prefer to do sth**   like to do one thing more than another

4 **Put the dialogues in order. Write the numbers in the boxes.** 将句子排序，在方框内填写序号。

dialogue 1
- [ ] I'd prefer to get them at the station.
- [ ] The weather's nice, so
- [ ] Yes, that's a good idea.
- [1] What shall we do this weekend?
- [ ] And maybe we could take the train.
- [ ] Fine. Shall we get the tickets online?
- [ ] what about going to the beach?

dialogue 2
- [ ] But it's going to rain.
- [ ] I think I'd prefer to go out.
- [ ] OK, fine.
- [ ] What about a nice meal at home?
- [ ] OK, then let's order a pizza.
- [ ] Where shall we go tomorrow?

5 **Correct the mistakes.** 改错题。

▶ We could to have a party this weekend.   We could have a party this weekend.

1 What do we do this evening?   ....

2 Do you have a suggest?   ....

3 What about go to see a film?   ....

4 I'd prefer go by train.   ....

5 Yes, is a good idea.   ....

6 Where we shall go tomorrow?   ....

6 **Write in a word where there is a /.** 在/处补上遗漏的单词。

1 ▶ A What / we do / evening?   What shall we do this evening?

  B What / going / the theatre?   ....

  A I'm / sure / that.   ....

2 A What / we / on Saturday?   ....

  B Perhaps we / go out for a meal.   ....

  A OK, let's / that.   ....

3 A Where / we go / afternoon?   ....

  B / go to a museum.   ....

  A Yeah, / 's a good / .   ...

A Offers 主动提供

Offering food/drink

Would you like a drink?

Do you want something to eat?

Offering help

Do you **need** some **help**?

Let me help you.

Accept	Refuse
Yes, please. Thanks. Thanks. Could I have …?	No, thanks.

Accept	Refuse
Yes, please. Thanks a lot. Thank you (very much).	No, I'm fine, thanks. No, don't worry.

GLOSSARY

offer	say or show that you will give sth if another person wants it **offer** *n*	accept	say 'yes' OPP **refuse**
need	If you **need** sth, you must have it.	thanks a lot *inf*	= thanks very much
help	the act of doing sth good for sb **help** *v*	don't worry	used to tell sb that sth is not important **worry** *n*
let me …	used for asking permission to help another person		

1 **Correct the mistakes.** 改错题。

▶ ~~Could~~ you like a drink?   Would

1 You want something to eat? ....

2 Thanks, no. ....

3 I fine, thanks. ....

4 Do you like something to eat? ....

5 Let me to help you. ....

6 I thank you very much. ....

7 Thanks. Could I take a coffee? ....

2 **Complete the sentences with one word.** 将句子填写完整，每空格只填一词。

▶ Would .... you like something to eat? ~ Oh, thank you very much ....

1 Do you need some .... with your luggage? ~ Oh, yes, ...

2 Did you .... her a drink when she arrived? ~ Yes, of course.

3 Do you .... some help with those books? ~ Yes I do. .... a lot.

4 Here, ... me help you. ~ No, don't .... I'm OK, thanks.

5 I offered to help but she .... She said she didn't need help.

6 When people offer me a drink, I usually say 'yes'. I think it's polite to ....

3 **Complete the questions and answers.** 将问题和回答填写完整。

▶ Offer someone food.   Do you want something to eat?

1 Offer someone a drink.
   Accept, and ask for some water.
   A Would .... drink?
   B Yes, ... water?

2 Offer someone help.
   Say no politely.
   A Do .... help?
   B No, ... , thanks.

3 Offer someone food.
   Accept, and ask for an apple.
   A Would .... eat?
   B .... an apple?

4 Offer someone help.
   Say no politely.
   A Let ....
   B No, ... worry.

B Saying sorry 表达歉意

He pushed me but didn't **say sorry**.

Really! That's so **rude**.

SPOTLIGHT *(I'm) sorry*

You use **(very/really/so) sorry** when you:

1 feel bad about something you've done:
I'm sorry, I've broken your cup.

2 feel sad about something:
I'm sorry you can't come to the party.

3 want somebody to repeat something:
Sorry, could you repeat that, please?

Saying sorry	Responses
Sorry, I don't speak English very well.	**That's all right**. I'll speak slowly.
Oh no! I've broken a cup. I'm **so sorry**.	That's OK. **Don't worry.**
I'm very sorry – **I've lost** your pen.	**It doesn't matter.** I've got lots of pens.
I forgot to post your letter – **I'm really sorry.**	**Never mind.** I can post it later.
Sorry I'm late – the traffic was terrible.	Oh, don't worry about it.

GLOSSARY

rude	not speaking or behaving in a way that is correct for the social situation OPP **polite**	**break** *pt* **broke** *pp* **broken**	make sth go into smaller pieces, e.g. by dropping it
that's all right / don't worry / it doesn't matter / never mind	These phrases all mean 'it's not important'/ 'it's OK'.	**lose** *pt/pp* **lost** **forget** *pt* **forgot** *pp* **forgotten**	If you **lose** sth, you can't find it. = not remember
		(I'm) sorry I'm late	(NOT ~~Sorry for be late.~~)

4 **Match 1–8 with a–i.** 配对题。

▶	That's	c	a	bring your book.
1	It doesn't	....	b	my car keys.
2	I forgot to	....	c	all right. ✓
3	Never	....	d	I'm late.
4	Don't	....	e	sorry.
5	Sorry	....	f	matter.
6	I'm really	....	g	your pencil.
7	I've broken	....	h	worry.
8	I've lost	....	i	mind.

5 **Complete the dialogues with a word or a contraction (e.g. *don't*).** 用单词或缩约形式 (如don't) 填空。

▶ I'm very _sorry_ ~ That's OK.

1 I'm really sorry. ~ _____ all right.

2 I'm sorry _____ late. The traffic was terrible. ~ That's OK.

3 I'm afraid I've _____ my homework. ~ That's all _____. Bring it tomorrow.

4 I'm _____ sorry. ~ It doesn't _____.

5 Sorry I'm late. ~ Oh, never _____. It's not important.

6 Did he say _____ to you? ~ Yes, he did. He's always very _____.

7 I think I've _____ your chair. I'm very sorry. ~ Don't _____. It's very old.

8 Did he say sorry? ~ No, he's very _____.

6 **Write down:** 根据要求写出答案。

1 three words you can use before sorry ▶ _very_ _____

2 four phrases you can use to say 'it's OK' or 'it's not important':

_____

3 three different meanings of 'sorry':

_____

…?

Sonja

Noah   Ava

GLOSSARY

wedding	a time when a man and woman get married
attend *formal*	go to or be present at a place where sth is happening
certain	sure about sth **certainly** adv SYN **definitely**
probably	If sth will **probably** happen, you think it will happen but you are not sure. **probable** adj
likely (to)	If sth is **likely to** happen, it will probably happen.
chance	a possibility that sth may happen. **A good chance** means it is more probable.
possible	If sth is **possible**, it can happen. OPP **impossible**; **possibility** n
maybe	a word that shows that sth is possible SYN **perhaps**
may	a word that shows that sth is possible, and will perhaps happen. SYN **might**: *He may/ might come with us.* (NOT *He may/might to come with us.*)

Noah and Ava are getting married. Sonja is an old girlfriend of Noah's, and Noah has invited her to the **wedding**. Ava doesn't like Sonja very much. Do you think Sonja will **attend** the wedding?

100%	CERTAIN	Yes, She'll **definitely** go.
	PROBABLE	Yeah, **I think so.**
		Yeah, she's **likely to** go.
		Yeah, she'**ll probably** go.
		I think there's **a (good) chance** that she'll go.
	POSSIBLE	I think she { **may** / **might** } go.
		Yeah, **maybe/perhaps.**
	UNLIKELY	No, **I don't think so.**
		No, I don't think she'll go.
0%	IMPOSSIBLE	No, she definitely won't go.

SPOTLIGHT *I think so / I hope so*

You can use these expressions if you think or hope something is going to happen. Notice the difference in the negative.

- *Are you going? ~ Yes,* **I think so.** (= it is likely that this will happen)
- *Is the exam difficult? ~ No,* **I don't think so.**
- *Will you get more money? ~* **I hope so.** (= I would like this to happen)
- *Is it going to rain? ~* **I hope not.**

1 **Underline** the main stress in these words. Practise saying the words. 在单词的重读音节下划线，并练习发音。

▶ <u>pos</u>sible
1 certainly
2 impossible
3 possibility

4 definitely
5 likely
6 probably
7 perhaps

2 Are the sentences similar in meaning or different? Write *S* or *D*. 两句句子的含义是否相近？ 相近填S，不同填D。

▶ It's certainly true. / It's definitely true. .... S
1 The team will probably win. / The team will definitely win. ....
2 I may stay in tonight. / I might stay in tonight. ....
3 John and Shar are likely to come. / John and Shar will definitely come. ....
4 Will Jo come? ~ Maybe. / Will Jo come? ~ Perhaps. ....
5 Is it sunny outside? ~ I think so. / ~ I hope so. ....
6 I'm probably going to change jobs. / I'm likely to change jobs. ....
7 I think it's likely. / I think it's impossible. ....
8 There's a chance it will happen. / There's a possibility it will happen. ....

3 One word is missing in each sentence. What is it, and where does it go?

在句中相应位置补上遗漏的单词。

▶ Is Marta coming with you? ~ It's not / but I think she will.   certain

1 I probably work this evening.   ....

2 My parents are not likely come this afternoon.   ....

3 Are you going tonight? ~ Yes, I think.   ....

4 Have you lost your money? ~ No, I hope.   ....

5 I think there's chance that he'll be here.   ....

6 Are you seeing Jacob this evening? ~ I'm not sure. I see him.   ....

4 Complete the conversations. 首字母填空。

▶ A Are you going tonight?
  B I don't know yet. _Perhaps_ .

1 A What are you doing this evening?
  B I'll p.................... stay at home, and I m.................... finish reading my book.

2 A Who's coming to the cinema this evening?
  B Well, Elle will d.................... come, and Briony will p.................... come with her. And I think three or four more are l.................... to come. So, about seven or eight, including us.

3 A What are you doing this weekend?
  B I'm going to a w.................... . My cousin is getting married.
  A Well, enjoy yourself.
  B Thanks. It will c.................... be interesting – I don't think the two families like each other very much.

4 A Is the team going to win this weekend?
  B Yes, there's a good c.................... we will – we're playing quite well.

5 A What are you doing next week?
  B I have to a.................... an important meeting for my company in Manchester.
  A Are you going to drive?
  B I don't think that's l.................... : it's a long way. I m.................... take the train. Then I can work.

6 A Will everyone come to the meeting this afternoon?
  B There's a p.................... they will all be here, but I don't think s.................... .

7 A Are you leaving at the end of the year?
  B Well, m.................... , but nothing's c.................... yet. I'll p.................... decide at the end of this month.

8 A Will you finish the exercise by the end of the lesson?
  B No, that's i.................... . It's really difficult.

5 ABOUT YOU   Answer the questions using words and phrases from page 184.

根据自身情况，用P184的单词或短语回答问题。

▶ Are you going to do anything this evening? _I might do some work. I'm not sure._

1 Are you going to have a good weekend? ....

2 Are you going to go out with friends? ....

3 Are you going to stay at home on Sunday? ....

4 Are you going to do any work? ....

5 Are you going to watch much TV? ....

6 Are you going to spend a lot of money? ....

7 Are you going to visit other members of your family? ....

8 Are you going to go shopping? ....

A Giving more information 提供更多信息

These words give more information.

Word	Example	Meaning
and	*The city centre is dirty **and** very expensive.*	links two ideas in one sentence, sometimes with a comma (,)
also	*The centre is dirty.* { *It's **also** very expensive.* / *It **also** costs a lot to live there.*	goes after auxiliary verbs, e.g. *be, can*, but before the main verb
too and **as well**	*The centre is dirty.* { *It's very expensive* **too.** / *It costs a lot to live there* **as well.**	go at the end of the sentence **Too** and **as well** are used more in spoken English.

1 Are *also, too* and *as well* in the correct position? Put a tick (✓) or a cross (X). Then correct the mistakes. 下列句子中, also、too、as well的位置是否正确? 正确的打钩 (√), 错误的打叉 (×) 并改正。

▶ You need a dictionary, and as well a grammar book is useful. <u>X   and a grammar book is useful as well.</u>

1 The house is beautiful, and it's near the park also. ....

2 He speaks German, and he understands too Greek. ....

3 We went out for dinner and Lucy came as well. ....

4 I cleaned the house and washed also the car. ....

5 She worked in Rome, and I think she worked in Ravenna too. ....

6 We've got a big garden, and there's as well a park near the house. ....

2 Put the words in the correct order to make sentences. 连词成句。

▶ too / and it's good / the weather's / in autumn / nice / in winter
The weather's <u>nice in autumn and it's good in winter too.</u>

1 I often eat / ice cream / cake / also / like / and I
I often eat ....

2 I enjoy / and I go / too / watching tv / to the cinema a lot
I enjoy ....

3 I can speak / German / as well / understand / English / I can / and
I can speak ....

4 I read a lot / also / and I / music / of books / listen to
I read a lot ....

5 and / on TV / I play / I watch it / as well / football
I play ....

6 I drive / too / a lot / and / I / walk
I drive ....

3 ABOUT YOU Are the sentences in Exercise 2 true for you or your country? Write your answers, or talk to another student. 练习2中描述的情况与你或你的国家是否相符? 回答问题, 也可以和同学交流讨论。

The weather's <u>nice in autumn and it's good in winter too.</u>
<u>That's not true. The weather in winter is very cold and it rains a lot as well.</u>

1 ....

2 ....

3 ....

4 ....

5 ....

6 ....

B Introducing a surprising idea 表示转折

These words link two ideas when the second idea is surprising after the first idea.

Word	Example	Meaning
but	*We had sunny weather, **but** it was quite cold.* *He worked hard, **but** he didn't pass the exam.*	links two ideas, usually in one sentence. Sometimes there is a comma (,) with a longer sentence.
however	*We had sunny weather. **However**, it was quite cold.* *He worked hard. **However**, he didn't pass the exam.*	links two ideas, usually in two different sentences. There is a comma after **however**. **However** is more formal than **but**.
although/ though	***Although** we had sunny weather, it was quite cold, especially in the morning.* *He worked hard, **although** he didn't pass the exam.* *I went to the party. I was quite tired, **though**.*	(the second part sounds like *go*) links two ideas in one sentence. **Although** often goes at the beginning of the sentence, but can go in the middle, after a comma. In spoken English, you often use **though**.

> **SPOTLIGHT** *still*
>
> You can use **still** to make the second idea a bigger surprise:
> - *We had sunny weather, **but** it was **still** quite cold in the evenings.*
> - *He worked hard. **However**, he **still** didn't pass the exam.*

4 **Rewrite the sentences using the link word in CAPITALS.** 用所给连接词改写句子。

- ▶ The exam was easy. I didn't pass.   HOWEVER   The exam was easy. However, I didn't pass.
- 1   He went to bed late. He couldn't sleep.   BUT
- 2   People don't like her very much. She's very kind.   HOWEVER
- 3   The food was terrible. The service was good.   ALTHOUGH
- 4   It was snowing. We decided to go out.   BUT/STILL
- 5   We lost our dog. We found it after an hour.   HOWEVER
- 6   I wore a coat. I was cold.   ALTHOUGH/STILL
- 7   I watched the whole programme. I didn't enjoy it.   THOUGH
- 8   We had a big lunch. Jason was hungry.   HOWEVER/STILL

5 **Make six sentences or pairs of sentences from the table using *but* or *however*.**
用but或however连接左右两栏的句子。

▶ I didn't feel well. ✓		I only had to wait five minutes.
I was really hungry,		I stayed at work to finish the job.
I was last in the queue.		someone lent me a jacket.
I was very cold.	**but** **However,**	I had to wait until 10.00 for dinner.
I was very frightened,		someone held my hand.
I was late for the party.		I was fine the next day. ✓
I was really tired.		everybody was still there.

- ▶ I didn't feel well. However, I was fine the next day.

6 **Complete the sentences in a way that makes sense.** 将句子填写完整, 使句意通顺。

- ▶ I took my umbrella but it didn't rain.
- 1   Everyone says it's a great film, though   .
- 2   Although it was raining,   .
- 3   The dog looked dangerous but   .
- 4   Although she was ill,   .
- 5   She's very intelligent. However,   .
- 6   I thought the shop was open. However,   .

98 Link words (2) 连接词（2）

A Reason and result 表示原因与结果

Why did you go into the café?

Link word before the **reason**:

because + clause because of + noun	*I went into the café **because** it was raining.* *I went into the café **because of** the rain.*
(in order) to + verb **In order to** is more formal than **to**.	*I went into the café **(in order) to** get out of the rain.*

Link word before the **result**:

so + clause = because of this	*It was raining, **so** I went into the café.* = 'I went in the café' is the result of the rain.
as a result + clause = because of this **As a result** can also start a new sentence.	*I went to bed very late, and **as a result** I was tired the next morning.* *The others had a map but I didn't. **As a result**, I was the last person to arrive.*

GLOSSARY

reason	an explanation for why you do sth
result	sth that happens because of sth else

1 **Circle the correct word(s).** 圈出正确答案。

▶ I took my umbrella *because* / *so* it was raining.
1 I stayed at home *because* / *because of* the weather.
2 We went to Paris *so* / *to* see a friend.
3 I couldn't go out *because* / *because of* I had to study.
4 I got lost and *in order to* / *as a result* I was late for the meeting.
5 It was my birthday, *so* / *because* we had a party.
6 She went to the market *in order to* / *as a result* get some meat.
7 She lost her passport, *so* / *because* she couldn't go to China.

2 **Write *because, because of, so, (in order) to* or *as a result*.**
在句中填写because、because of、so、(in order) to或as a result。

▶ They were late _because of_ the traffic.
1 I'm going to the chemist's _____ get some medicine.
2 It was a nice day, _____ we went out.
3 I bought the house _____ the beautiful view.
4 I didn't take a coat. _____, I was cold most of the time.
5 I don't go to the theatre very often _____ it's too expensive.
6 I'm going out now, _____ I will phone you later.
7 She went to the town centre _____ meet her friend.
8 Our two best players were ill, and _____ we lost the game.

3 **Complete the sentences with your own reasons and results.** 根据自身情况填写原因和结果。

I stayed at home last night ...
▶ because _I had to do some work._
1 because of _____
2 in order to _____

I had to wait half an hour for a train, ...
3 so _____
4 and as a result _____

I went to bed very late ...
5 because _____
6 so _____

B A series of actions or events 表示顺序

Luke is a waiter now. **Before that**, he worked in a factory.

... and we had a really nice time. **Firstly**, we spent a couple of days in Budapest. **After that**, we went to Vienna, where we spent the rest of the week. It was very easy to ...

First of all, you fry the meat. **Secondly**, you fry some onions and add them to the meat. **After that**, you add the red wine and water and cook it slowly for three hours. **Finally**, you add the mushrooms and cook it for another fifteen minutes.

GLOSSARY	
before that	earlier than sth
firstly	You say **firstly** when you are talking about the first thing in a list. ALSO **first / first of all**
after that	You say **after that** when you are talking about the next thing in a list. ALSO **(and) then**
secondly	You say **secondly** to talk about the second thing in a list.
finally	You use **finally** when you are talking about the last thing in a list, usually a long list of four or more things.

4 **Complete the link words in the texts.** 在短文中填写连接词。
For this job, ▶ ‿firstly‿‿‿‿ , you have to fill in a form. **(1)** S‿‿‿‿‿‿‿‿ , you have to go and talk to the boss. **(2)** A‿‿‿‿‿‿‿‿‿‿‿‿‿ , you meet other people who work in the company.
(3) F‿‿‿‿‿‿‿ , you have to do a written test.

(4) F‿‿‿‿‿‿‿‿‿‿‿‿‿‿ , I checked the train times on the internet, and
(5) t‿‿‿‿‿‿ I looked at flights to see if they were cheaper.

James got his first job last year. **(6)** B‿‿‿‿‿‿‿‿‿‿‿ , he was a student.

5 **Put the sentences in the correct order. Then add link words.** 将句子排序，并补充连接词。
▶ I checked the answers. / I did the grammar exercises.
   ‿First of all, I did the grammar exercises. Then I checked the answers.‿
1 You make the pasta sauce. / You boil the pasta. / You add the sauce to the pasta.

2 I trained to be a teacher. / I did a degree in History. / I got a teaching job in Liverpool.

3 We flew back to Rome. / We stayed in Munich for a week. / We spent the second week in Heidelberg. / We left our home in Rome.

4 I came home and had a cup of tea. / I cooked the dinner. / I went to the market. / I made a shopping list.

5 I rang for a taxi and left home. / I had a shower. / I got dressed. / I had breakfast.

6 ABOUT YOU **Write three or four things you did last weekend. Use link words.**
写下三到四件你在上周末做过的事，需使用连接词。
▶ ‿First of all, I ...‿

99) Phrasal verbs 短语动词

A Meaning 含义

Most phrasal verbs are very common in spoken English. They have a verb (*sit, stand, get,* etc.) and a particle (*up, on, off,* etc.). Sometimes, the meaning of the two parts is easy to understand.

sit down   **stand up**   **lie down**   **fall over**

Sometimes the two parts form a new meaning.

Phrasal verb	Example	Meaning
give sth **up**	*He had to **give up** football.*	stop doing something
look sth **up**	*I had to **look up** the meaning.*	try to find information in a book or on the internet
take off	*The plane couldn't **take off**.*	leave the ground and start flying
grow up	*When Ben **grows up**, he wants to be a doctor.*	slowly change from a child to an adult
find sth **out**	*I must **find out** the times of the trains to Southampton.*	find a fact or piece of information you need or want
go out	*Let's **go out** this evening.*	leave your home to do a social activity, e.g. go to a cinema, a club, etc.

1 **Underline** the correct particle. 在正确的小品词下划线。

▶ I'd like to lie *up* / *down* for a minute.
1 Can we find *out* / *over* how much it costs?
2 Where did she grow *out* / *up*?
3 He fell *over* / *off* when he left the house.
4 Do you want to go *out* / *off* tonight?
5 Pepe wants to give *on* / *up* his job.
6 Look it *out* / *up* in your dictionary.
7 The plane couldn't take *off* / *up*.

2 **Complete the sentences with the correct particle.** 用正确的小品词填空。

▶ Paola doesn't want to go _out_ this evening. She's tired.
1 I don't know the name of the hotel, but I can find ....
2 Everyone stood .... when he came into the room.
3 Susana lives in England now, but she grew .... in Spain.
4 She sat .... at the table and started eating.
5 The doctor told me to lie .... on the bed.
6 I told my brother to give .... smoking.
7 The plane took .... half an hour late because of the bad weather.
8 She fell .... in the street, but several people helped her.
9 I asked James to look .... the meaning of a word for me.

3 [ABOUT YOU] **Write your answers, or talk to another student.**
根据自身情况回答问题，也可以和同学交流讨论。

▶ Do you often look up English words in a dictionary? _Yes, quite often._
1 Is there anything you would like to give up? ....
2 Where did you grow up? ....
3 When you fly, how do you feel when the plane takes off? ....
4 How often do you go out in the evenings? What do you do? ....

B Grammar 语法

Some phrasal verbs never have an object.

Phrasal verb	Example	Meaning
go up	*The price of petrol will **go up** soon.*	⬆ increase, become more OPP **go down** ⬇
carry on (with sth)	*Can we **carry on** with the exercise?*	continue with something
go back	*She wants to **go back** to London.*	return to a place
wake up	*I always **wake up** at 7.00 a.m.*	stop sleeping
go away	***Go away**! I'm working.*	leave a person or a place

Other phrasal verbs need an object. In the following verbs, the object can go before or after the particle.

Take off <u>your jacket</u>.

Take <u>your jacket</u> **off**.

Could you **turn on** <u>the light</u>?

Could you **turn** <u>the light</u> **on**?

Put on <u>your shoes</u>.

Put <u>your shoes</u> **on**.

When the object is a pronoun (*it*, *them*, etc.) it must go before the particle.

Take <u>it</u> **off**. (NOT ~~Take off it.~~)   **Put** <u>them</u> **on**. (NOT ~~Put on them.~~)

4 **Change the <u>underlined</u> noun to *it* or *them*, and put it in the correct place.**
将划线部分的名词替换成it或them，必要时可调整语序。

- ▶ Look up <u>the word</u>.   *Look it up.*
- ▶ Look up <u>both words</u>.   *Look them up.*
- 1 Take off <u>your jacket</u>. ....
- 2 Put on <u>this tie</u>. ....
- 3 Turn on <u>the TV</u>. ....
- 4 Put <u>those socks</u> on. ....
- 5 Take off <u>your shoes</u>. ....
- 6 Give up <u>chocolate</u>. ....
- 7 Turn on <u>the lights</u>. ....
- 8 Put <u>your coat</u> on. ....

5 **Are the sentences correct, or do they need the pronoun *it*? Where? Look at the examples.**
下列句子是否正确？正确的填Correct，错误的在相应位置添加it。

- ▶ Look up in the dictionary. *Look it up in the dictionary.*   ▶ Please sit down. *Correct*
- 1 The price will soon go down. ....
- 2 Do you want to go back? ....
- 3 Could you turn on, please? ....
- 4 You can take off if you're hot. ....
- 5 His salary will go up soon. ....
- 6 Do they want to stop or carry on? ....
- 7 Did you put on? ....
- 8 What time do you usually wake up? ....

6 **Replace the <u>underlined</u> word(s) with a phrasal verb that has the same meaning.**
用短语动词替换划线部分，保持句意不变。

- ▶ The price will <u>decrease</u> soon.   *go down*
- 1 I loved Tokyo, and I want to <u>return</u> next year. ....
- 2 When we finish Exercise 1, we can <u>continue</u> with Exercise 2. ....
- 3 I was busy so I told them to <u>leave me on my own</u>. ....
- 4 Can I <u>remove</u> my coat? ....
- 5 I think my salary will <u>increase</u> next year. ....
- 6 I was so tired, I didn't <u>stop sleeping</u> until 9 o'clock this morning. ....

100 Common expressions 常见表达

A Expressions with *get* 含get的表达

Expression	Example	Meaning
get ready	We need to **get ready** now – the film starts at 6.30.	be prepared and able to do sth
get dressed	I **got dressed**, had breakfast, then went to work.	put on clothes
get to know sb	I **got to know** Charlie when we were at university.	meet sb and become friends
get changed (into sth different)	I've been for a long walk, so I'm going to **get changed**.	take your clothes off and put on different clothes
get in	What time does our train **get in**?	arrive at a place
get to sleep	Do you have problems **getting to sleep**?	start to sleep
go and get sth	Could you **go and get** a clean towel from the bathroom?	go to a place and return with sth SYN **fetch**
get back	I want to **get back** by 7.00, if possible.	return from a place
get better	I feel my English is **getting better** now.	reach a higher level, improve
get out of sth	Be careful when you **get out of** the car.	leave a vehicle such as a car or taxi
we/you get	**We get** a lot of tourists where I live.	= there are / you can see

1 **Match 1–6 with a–g.** 配对题。

▶ get better ..g..
1 get in ....
2 get back ....
3 get to know somebody ....
4 go and get ....
5 get dressed ....
6 get changed ....

a put on clothes
b meet and become friends
c return
d arrive
e put on different clothes
f fetch
g reach a higher level ✓

2 **Complete the sentences.** 将句子填写完整。

▶ I started learning the guitar last year, and I'm definitely getting _better_ now.
1 Ed, could you .... and get my laptop from the bedroom?
2 We all got .... of the car and pushed it to the side of the road.
3 I'm meeting Sophia at the station. Her bus gets .... at 3.15.
4 I left Amelia's flat at 10.00, but I didn't get .... until 11.30.
5 We're going out in ten minutes, so we need to get ....
6 You .... a lot of people sleeping on the streets in big cities.

3 **Complete the sentences.** 将问句填写完整。

▶ Do you get to _know_ people easily?
1 Do you usually get .... before or after you have breakfast?
2 When you go out, does it take you a long time to get .... ?
3 When you get home from school/college/work, do you usually get .... into different clothes?
4 Do you ever have problems getting to .... at night?
5 Do you think your English is getting .... ?
6 Do you .... a lot of tourists in your town?

4 ABOUT YOU **Write your own answers to Exercise 3, or talk to another student.**
根据自身情况回答练习3中的问题，也可以和同学交流讨论。

▶ Do you get to know people easily? _Yes, I think so._

B In conversation 会话中的常用表达

These expressions are common in informal spoken English.

Guess what! I passed the exam. I heard this morning.

Wow! Well done! That's great.

Yes, I can now relax for **the rest** of the week.

I don't **feel like** going to the beach.

But **everyone else** will be there.

I know, but I'm going to stay here and **take care of** the dog.

Are you going to the meeting on Friday?

I guess so.

Well, can you **let me know** by tomorrow?

Come on! We have to go.

What, now?

Yes, **right now.**

SPOTLIGHT *else*

You can use **else** to mean 'different' after words like **everyone**, **somewhere** and **nothing**.

- *I didn't like it, but **everyone else** did.* (= all the other people)
- *The restaurant was full so we went **somewhere else**.* (= to another place)
- *We had bread because there was **nothing else** to eat.* (= no other thing)

GLOSSARY

Guess what!	used for introducing surprising news
Wow!	a word that shows you are surprised and happy
Well done!	You say this to sb when you are happy because they have done sth well. SYN **Congratulations!**
the rest	the part that is left or remains: *the rest of the* day/time
feel like (doing) sth	want (to do) sth: *I **feel like** a nice cold drink.*
take care of sth/sb	do everything to make sth/sb safe: *I can **take care of** the children while you go shopping.* SYN **look after sth/sb**
I guess so	= I think so SYN **I suppose so**
let sb know	tell sb
Come on!	used for telling sb to hurry, be quick SYN **hurry up!**
right now	at this minute; immediately SYN **right away**

5 **Find eight more expressions using words from each box.**
从两个方框内各选一个单词或短语，组成八种表达。

somewhere ✓	let	come	hurry	on!	up	so	done
the rest	I guess	well	right	me know	now	of the time	else ✓

▶   <u>somewhere else</u> ....

....

6 **Complete the dialogues.** 将对话填写完整。

▶   We need to go right __away__ or we'll be late. ~ Yes, let's go.
1   You had all the biscuits. ~ Sorry, there was _____ else to eat.
2   Do you feel _____ a drink? ~ Yes, let's go out.
3   Do we need to get ready now? ~ Yes, right _____ , so _____ up!
4   _____ what? I came first in the English exam.   ~ _____ ! Well _____ !
5   Are you staying? ~ Yes, I'm going to look _____ the two girls.
6   Are you staying at Jon's? ~ Yes, I _____ so. I'll _____ you know at the weekend.
7   Why are you going back to the flat? ~ Because there's nowhere _____ to go.

7 **Rewrite the sentences using the word in CAPITALS. The meaning must stay the same.**
用所给单词改写句子，保持句意不变。

▶ We need to go right now.	AWAY	<u>We need to go right away.</u>
1 The bar was busy, so we went to another place.	ELSE	....
2 Could you tell me later?	LET	....
3 Who is going to look after the children?	TAKE	....
4 Come on, Sacha!	HURRY	....
5 Do you want to go out?	FEEL	....
6 Penny is here. All the others went out.	EVERYONE	....

粗体单词本书均已收录。

蓝色单词表示相应人物。

遮住其中一栏，说出另一栏的对应单词。

1 Verbs and nouns 动词与名词

Verb	Noun(s)
act	actor, actress
advertise	advert/advertisement, advertising
agree	agreement
appear	appearance
argue	argument
arrange	arrangement
arrive	arrival
begin	beginning
build	building, builder
choose	choice
clean	cleaner
climb	climbing
collect	collection
complain	complaint
cook	cooker
dance	dance, dancing, dancer
decide	decision
depart	departure
describe	description
design	designer
disagree	disagreement
discover	discovery
discuss	discussion
draw	drawing
drive	driving, driver
educate	education
employ	employer, employee
enter	entrance
examine	exam/examination
explain	explanation
fail	failure
farm	farming, farmer
feel	feeling
fly	flight, flying
greet	greeting
grow	growth
hear	hearing
improve	improvement
instruct	instruction, instructor
invent	invention
invite	invitation
listen	listening, listener
manage	manager

mean	meaning
meet	meeting
move	movement
organize	organization
own	owner
park	parking
pay	payment
perform	performance, performer
play	player
prefer	preference
print	printer
pronounce	pronunciation
read	reading, reader
recommend	recommendation
record	record, recording
report	report, reporter
reserve	reservation
respond	response
ride	riding, rider
run	run, running, runner
serve	service
sign	signature
sing	song, singer
smoke	smoke, smoking
solve	solution
speak	speaking, speaker
spell	spelling
study	study, student
succeed	success
suggest	suggestion
swim	swim, swimming
teach	teaching, teacher
think	thinking, thought
travel	travelling, travel, traveller
visit	visiting, visitor
walk	walk, walking
wash	wash, washing
weigh	weight
win	winner
work	working, worker

2　Adjectives and nouns 形容词与名词

Adjective	Noun(s)
attractive	attraction
beautiful	beauty
cloudy	cloud
cold	cold
crowded	crowd
dangerous	danger
different	difference
direct	direction
electric, electrical	electricity

excited, exciting	excitement
friendly, unfriendly	friend
happy, unhappy	happiness
healthy, unhealthy	health
icy	ice
ill	illness
industrial	industry
intelligent	intelligence
long	length
lucky, unlucky	luck
medical	medicine
musical	music
national	nationality
natural	nature
noisy	noise
painful	pain
peaceful	peace
personal	person
possible, impossible	possibility
scientific	science, scientist
strong	strength
sunny	sun
surprised, surprising	surprise
true	truth
various	variety
wide	width
windy	wind
wooden	wood
young	youth

3 Verbs and nouns with the same form 同形的动词与名词

粗体单词的动词和名词形式本书均已收录。

answer	help	reply	work
brush	hope	request	worry
call	increase	research	
cause	interview	rest	
change	jump	ride	
chat	land	ring	
circle	laugh	score	
comment	look	search	
control	love	share	
cook	matter	shave	
copy	name	smell	
cost	need	smile	
cough	offer	snow	
cut	phone	star	
dance	plan	start	
download	plant	stay	
dream	post	taste	
drink	promise	text	
email	queue	tour	
fall	rain	use	
guess	record	visit	
guide	repair	wash	

4 Nouns, verbs and adjectives 名词、动词、形容词

Noun	Verb	Adjective(s)
death	**die**	**dead**
employment	**employ**	employed, **unemployed**
enjoyment	**enjoy**	**enjoyable**
excitement	excite	**exciting, excited**
help	**help**	**helpful**
interest	interest	**interested, interesting**
marriage	marry/**get married**	**married**
organization	**organize**	organized
pollution	pollute	polluted
sleep	**sleep**	asleep
speaking, speaker	**speak**	spoken
surprise	surprise	**surprised, surprising**
writing, writer	write	written
worry	**worry**	**worried**, worrying
reading, reader	read	reading

5 Verbs and adjectives 动词与形容词

Verb	Adjective(s)
boil	**boiled**, boiling
bore	**bored, boring**
break	**broken**
clean	**clean**
close	**closed**
complete	complete
correct	**correct**
empty	**empty**
include	**included, including**
lose	**lost**
open	open
relax	**relaxed**, relaxing
shut	**shut**
sleep	**asleep**
speak	spoken
tidy	**tidy**
tire	**tired**, tiring
wake up	**awake**

Common irregular verbs 常见不规则动词

be	was/were	been
beat	beat	beaten
become	became	become
begin	began	begun
blow	blew	blown
break	broke	broken
bring	brought	brought
build	built	built
burn	burnt/burned	burnt/burned
buy	bought	bought
catch	caught	caught
choose	chose	chosen
come	came	come
cost	cost	cost
cut	cut	cut
do	did	done
draw	drew	drawn
dream	dreamt/dreamed	dreamt/dreamed
drink	drank	drunk
drive	drove	driven
eat	ate	eaten
fall	fell	fallen
feel	felt	felt
fight	fought	fought
find	found	found
fly	flew	flown
forget	forgot	forgotten
get	got	got
give	gave	given
go	went	gone/been
grow	grew	grown
have	had	had
hear	heard	heard
hit	hit	hit
hold	held	held
hurt	hurt	hurt
keep	kept	kept
know	knew	known
learn	learnt/learned	learnt/learned
leave	left	left

lend	lent	lent
let	let	let
lie	lay	lain
lose	lost	lost
make	made	made
mean	meant	meant
meet	met	met
pay	paid	paid
put	put	put
read	read	read
ride	rode	ridden
ring	rang	rung
run	ran	run
say	said	said
see	saw	seen
sell	sold	sold
send	sent	sent
shake	shook	shaken
shine	shone	shone
show	showed	shown
shut	shut	shut
sing	sang	sung
sit	sat	sat
sleep	slept	slept
speak	spoke	spoken
spell	spelt/spelled	spelt/spelled
spend	spent	spent
stand	stood	stood
swim	swam	swum
take	took	taken
teach	taught	taught
tell	told	told
think	thought	thought
throw	threw	thrown
understand	understood	understood
wake (up)	woke (up)	woken (up)
wear	wore	worn
win	won	won
write	wrote	written

Answer key 参考答案

Unit 1

1 You can put these things in a bag: pencil, notice, CD player, coursebook, dictionary, piece of paper. You can't put these in a bag: desk, table, chair, noticeboard.

2
1. board pen
2. coursebook
3. noticeboard
4. exercise book
5. piece of paper
6. CD player

3
1. a whiteboard/board
2. a dictionary
3. a desk/table
4. a notebook / an exercise book
5. a noticeboard
6. a CD
7. a bag
8. a coursebook

4 *possible answers*:
I've got a dictionary, a CD player, a desk and a pen. I haven't got a noticeboard, a board, a board pen or a notice.

Unit 2

1
1. indefinite
2. noun
3. preposition
4. an irregular
5. pronouns
6. verbs
7. adverbs
8. past participle

2
1. I
2. an
3. lesson
4. young
5. from/in
6. a
7. quietly
8. spoke
9. asked
10. This morning
11. class
12. think/'s
13. wrong
14. I/he
15. I think he's in the wrong class.

3
1. preposition
2. definite article
3. noun
4. verb (past tense)
5. preposition
6. indefinite article
7. adjective
8. noun
9. pronoun
10. verb (past tense)

Unit 3

1
1. third
2. Circle
3. ~~sentence~~
4. small/little
5. *possible answers*: wonderful/marvellous/great
6. mistake
7. thanks
8. false
9. is
10. yes
11. wrong
12. do

2
1. d
2. a
3. e
4. b

3
1. for example
2. yes/correct/right
3. informal
4. synonym
5. equals / is the same as
6. etcetera / and so on

4
1. etc.
2. missing
3. order
4. wrong
5. symbol; the same as
6. mistakes; corrects
7. test; cover
8. short form
9. match
10. informal
11. false
12. Error
13. columns
14. underline
15. circle

Unit 4

1
1. helped
2. loud
3. record
4. down
5. pronounce
6. situation
7. use
8. things

2
1. out loud
2. notebook; keep
3. meaning
4. use
5. situations

3
1. To practise the pronunciation. / To practise how to pronounce them.
2. In a notebook.
3. Because it will help me to remember them.
4. In English or my own language.
5. To help me to understand how to use the word.
6. Think of situations where I can use the word.

4
1. f
2. g
3. a
4. d
5. b
6. e

5
1. called
2. like
3. How do
4. between
5. wrong/not right
6. opposite
7. does
8. explain

6 *possible answers*:
1. What does this word mean?
2. How do you spell this word?
3. How do you say this in English?
4. Could you explain this word?
5. What's the opposite of this word?
6. What's this called in English?

Unit 5

1
1 e	3 b
2 i	4 h

5 a	7 d
6 f	8 g

2 explanation; description; guess; instruction; invention; practice; education

3
1 repeat
2 homework
3 guess
4 practise
5 compared
6 do; forgot
7 made; up
8 described

4
1 text
2 paragraph
3 dialogue
4 activities
5 an essay
6 context
7 discussion
8 simple

5
1 revise
2 looked; up
3 conversation
4 exercises
5 dialogue
6 activity
7 simple
8 essay

6 *possible answers, from Hungary*:
1 Twice a day. I usually read the news in the morning and in the evening, or sometimes I read something for my English class.
2 Yes, because looking up words in a dictionary would take a long time.
3 Not very often – only when I am preparing for an exam.
4 Only before tests. I know I should do it more regularly but I don't have time for that.
5 Discussing things in groups in class, and watching videos or my favourite series outside class.
6 I like listening to dialogues several times. It helps me with pronunciation and understanding conversation in English.
I think they help if I know a word already and hear it again.

Unit 6

1
1 eight
2 twenty
3 sixty-seven
4 fifty
5 thirty-five
6 six
7 thirteen
8 seventy-two
9 twenty-four
10 eighty-nine

2
1 about/around a hundred euros
2 about/around ten lessons
3 about/around thirty years
4 about/around forty students
5 about/around fifty dollars
6 about/around eighty people
7 about/around seventy pounds
8 about/around twenty chairs

3
1 twenty-nine
2 seventy-seven
3 sixty-three
4 thirty-one
5 twenty-four
6 forty-five

5
1 two hundred
2 three hundred and forty
3 one thousand five hundred
4 two thousand six hundred and fifty
5 seven thousand
6 42,500

6
1 a/one thousand
2 five thousand and fifty-six
3 eleven thousand three hundred and one
4 a/one million
5 two thousand five hundred
6 three hundred and twenty-five thousand
7 a/one billion
8 two thousand

7
1 They said it was thousands of dollars.
2 It's about/around fifty minutes.
3 There are thousands (of them).
4 I bought about/around twenty books.
5 We want to grow hundreds of trees.
6 There are millions of people with this problem.

Unit 7

1
1 nine fifteen
2 ten twenty-five
3 three thirty-five
4 six forty-five
5 five fifty
6 seven twenty
7 two thirty
8 four forty

2
1 (a) quarter past seven
2 half past nine
3 twenty-five to twelve
4 ten to four
5 five to nine
6 three minutes past one
7 (a) quarter to three
8 seventeen minutes past four

3
1 At five past eight.
2 At eight forty-five/(a) quarter to nine.
3 At two minutes past nine.
4 At nine thirty-five/twenty-five to ten.
5 At ten past ten.

4 *possible answers for England*:
1 They usually open at 9.00 and they close at 5.00.
2 Supermarkets usually open at 8.00, and other shops usually open at 9.00 or 9.30. They usually close between 5.30 and 7.00.
3 Restaurants in England are often open all day from 12.00 p.m. to 10.00 p.m.
4 Most schools start at 8.30 or 9.00 and finish at 3.00. Most people start work at 9.00 a.m. and finish at 5.00 p.m.
5 I have lunch at about 12.30.
6 I have dinner at around 7.00 p.m.

5
1 S	4 S	7 S	10 S
2 D	5 S	8 D	11 D
3 S	6 D	9 S	12 S

6
1 just
2 almost/nearly
3 at
4 midday/noon
5 in
6 at
7 all
8 almost/nearly
9 just
10 all

7
1 at midday
2 in the morning
3 all day
4 in the evening
5 all evening
6 at midnight
7 at night
8 almost/nearly 8.00
9 just before

Unit 8

1
1 Monday, Tuesday, Wednesday, Thursday, Friday, Saturday, Sunday
2 spring, summer, autumn, winter
3 January, February, March, April, May, June, July, August, September, October, November, December

3
1 Tuesday
2 September
3 summer
4 December
5 Saturday
6 April
7 February
8 winter
9 Thursday
10 July

4 *possible answers:*
1 September.
2 I like spring because it's light and the trees and plants start to grow.
3 Friday, because it's nearly the weekend.
4 I go and see my family, and we have a big lunch together.
5 New Year's Day is a holiday. My family and I go for a long walk.
6 May 1st is a public holiday for people who work, and in March or April we have Easter Sunday.

5
1 third
2 twentieth
3 fifth
4 first
5 eighth
6 sixteenth
7 fourteenth
8 thirteenth
9 second

6
1 April the tenth/the tenth of April
2 March the fourth/the fourth of March
3 April the seventeenth/the seventeenth of April
4 March the twenty-first/the twenty-first of March
5 April the eleventh/the eleventh of April
6 April the sixth/the sixth of April
7 March the thirty-first/the thirty-first of March
8 April the twenty-third/the twenty-third of April

7
1 February the third/the third of February
2 July the fourth/the fourth of July
3 December the tenth/the tenth of December
4 August the twelfth/the twelfth of August
5 January the fifteenth/the fifteenth of January
6 twenty twenty-two/two thousand and twenty-two
7 May the twenty-first/the twenty-first of May

8 November the thirtieth/the thirtieth of November
9 April the twenty-second/the twenty-second of April
10 twenty fifteen/two thousand and fifteen
11 *your answer*
12 *your answer*

Unit 9

1
1 F – I got back six days ago.
2 T
3 F – I paid it **two** days ago.
4 T
5 F – I was in **Moscow**.
6 F – I'm going to the cinema **this evening**.
7 T
8 F – I'm seeing Scott in **five** days.
9 T
10 T

2
1 ago
2 diary
3 night
4 this
5 appointment
6 next

3
1 I went to the cinema
2 I had a meeting/I went to Wheeler's café
3 I stayed at Will's/I went to Will's
4 I've got a doctor's appointment
5 It's Callum's birthday
6 I'm seeing my parents/Mum and Dad for lunch

4
1 since
2 for
3 for
4 for
5 since
6 since

5
1 just
2 while
3 ever
4 since
5 recently
6 yet
7 ever
8 recently; for

6
1 yet
2 already
3 just
4 recently
5 ever
6 yet
7 while
8 since

Unit 10

1 **Two:** feet, ears, knees, shoulders, legs, hands, ankles, arms

2
1 shoulder
2 stomach
3 neck
4 bottom
5 blood
6 teeth
7 finger

3
1 skin
2 nose
3 back
4 chin
5 face
6 head/hand
7 teeth
8 chest
9 blood
10 brain
11 bottom
12 stomach

4 1 S 6 D
2 S 7 S
3 D 8 D
4 S 9 D
5 S 10 S

5 1 arm 4 neck
2 bottom 5 eyes/ears
3 foot 6 leg/knee

6 1 eye 8 skin
2 toes 9 leg
3 finger 10 blood
4 bottom 11 heart
5 hair 12 brain
6 tooth/teeth 13 bone
7 waist 14 body

Unit 11

1 1 F – 'average height' means not tall and not short.
2 F – 'quite thin' means not very thin, but thinner than average.
3 T
4 T
5 F – the answer to 'How much does he weigh' is 60kg (for example).
6 T
7 F – 'average weight' means not heavy and not slim.
8 F – 'slim' is more positive than 'thin'.
9 T
10 F – 'height' describes how tall somebody is, 'weight' describes how heavy somebody is.

2 1 height 6 weighs
2 slim 7 short
3 fat 8 lost
4 quite 9 much
5 put on 10 quite

3 1 T
2 F – she's got blonde hair.
3 F – it's long.
4 F – the young man is handsome/good-looking.
5 T
6 F – The woman's got fair hair.
7 T
8 T
9 F – he's middle aged.
10 F – it's grey.

4 1 pretty 10 handsome
2 dark 11 grey
3 smile 12 blonde
4 features 13 beautiful
5 teenager 14 attractive
6 good-looking 15 teenage
7 straight 16 fair
8 beard 17 curly
9 middle-aged 18 good-looking

5 *possible answers*:
I'm a middle aged woman with short dark curly hair. I'm quite attractive.
I think all of the young people are attractive, but I don't like beards. The middle-aged man has a nice smile, but I think he's put on weight.

Unit 12

1 1 lie down 5 sit down
2 fall over 6 get on
3 ride 7 run
4 stand up

2 1 dance
2 sit down; lie down
3 fall over
4 ride
5 get on

3 1 stand up 6 jumped
2 walk 7 rode
3 climb 8 ran; fell
4 dance 9 got off; on
5 lie down/sit down

4 1 a door
2 a ball
3 a book
4 a person
5 a dictionary
6 a pencil
7 a bicycle

5 1 pick up a cup 1; drop a cup 1
2 pick up a TV 2; turn on a TV 1
3 break a bottle 1; open a bottle 2
4 pull a person 1 or 2; carry a person 2
5 throw a ball 1; catch a ball 1 or 2
6 drop a ruler 1; break a ruler 2
7 carry a door 2; close a door 1
8 pick up a baby 1 or 2; hold a baby 1 or 2

6 1 closed/shut
2 picked up; put ... down
3 dropped
4 pulled; carried/pushed
5 gave; held
6 threw
7 carry

Unit 13

1 1 I need some personal information.
2 Where do you come from?
3 What do you do?
4 What is your postcode?
5 How old are you?
6 Where is the receptionist from?

2 1 Where do you come from?
2 Where in Poland exactly?
3 What do you do?
4 What's your address?
5 How old are you?

3
1 first
2 from
3 Whereabouts
4 What's
5 postcode
6 do
7 married
8 old

4 *possible answers*:

ABOUT YOU
Gomez.
Alicia.
I'm from Spain.
Sevilla.
It's Gaspar Perez 27 Sta Clara, Sevilla.
41007.
I'm a history teacher.
Yes, I am.
I'm 34.

5
1 F – 'perfect' means so good it cannot be better.
2 I
3 F – 'improve' means become better.
4 T
5 F – a language course is a number of lessons. Your language level is how good you are at the language.
6 T
7 F – 'how long?' means 'how much time?'
8 T

6
1 improving
2 level
3 can communicate very well
4 abroad
5 planning
6 great/wonderful
7 progress/improvement
8 help (people)

7 *possible answers*:
1 I'm elementary level.
2 It's difficult, and I can only understand a little.
3 Yes, I want to improve for my job, and my girlfriend is English.
4 Yes, slowly.
5 Yes, to England to visit my girlfriend's family.
6 Yes, I'd like a job in London to improve my English.

Unit 14

1
1 daughter
2 nephew
3 niece
4 sister-in-law
5 cousin
6 grandparents
7 husband
8 grandmother
9 uncle
10 aunt
11 relatives

2

MALE	FEMALE	MALE	FEMALE
father	mother	brother-in-law	sister-in-law
brother	sister	grandfather	grandmother
husband	wife	grandson	granddaughter
nephew	niece	cousin	cousin
relative	relative	parent	parent
son	daughter	uncle	aunt

3 *your own answers*

4
1 F – they are married.
2 T
3 F – he's older than Karen.
4 T
5 T
6 F – Luke is Amy's boyfriend.
7 F – there are 5 in Damon's family.
8 T
9 T
10 F – Luke is Damon's brother.

5
1 I was born in 2001.
2 We spend a lot of time together.
3 My girlfriend is older than me.
4 There are six of us in my family.
5 I am the youngest in my family.
6 I've got an older brother and a younger sister. OR an older sister and a younger brother.

6 *possible answers*:
1 There are five of us.
2 1999.
3 I've got two sisters: one is three years older than me, and the other is two years younger than me.
4 I spend a lot of time with my younger sister because she goes out with my best friend, Ben.
5 No, my older sister is married and lives with her husband.

Unit 15

1
1 nice
2 funny
3 clever
4 strange
5 friendly
6 patient
8 laugh
9 relaxed

2
1 unfriendly
2 intelligent
3 stupid
4 clever/intelligent
5 funny
6 patient
7 relaxed

3 1 laugh
    2 like; fun; strange
    3 What; kind; clever/intelligent

4 *possible answers*:
    My mother is very kind.
    My cousin Lucia is very friendly.
    My teacher Mrs Amato is very patient with me.
    Dino, my boyfriend, is good fun.
    My friend Alicia is very intelligent.
    Mr Fideo, my neighbour upstairs, is quite strange.

5 1 D   2 D   3 S   4 D   5 S

6 1 T
    2 F – they're completely different.
    3 T
    4 T
    5 F – Sophie's quite lazy.
    6 T
    7 F – she's tidy.
    8 F – it didn't matter.

7 1 own
    2 life
    3 share
    4 matter
    5 competely/really
    6 other

8 *possible answers*:
    1 I'm very tidy, but my wife is really untidy.
    2 I'm hard-working some of the time!
    3 Yes, I'm really quiet. I don't like a lot of noise.
    4 No, I'm not very serious.
    5 Yes, I've got a lot of friends and I go out quite often.
    6 No, I don't.

Unit 16

1 get to know somebody, ex-boyfriend, get married, go out with somebody, have a baby, romantic relationship

2 1 They had a baby last year.
    2 They separated in January.
    3 We have a very good relationship.
    4 How did you get to know your boyfriend?/ How did your boyfriend get to know you?
    5 They were together for three years.
    6 I went out with him for six months.

3 1 got; wife
    2 got; together
    3 couple
    4 out; separated
    5 ex-
    6 divorced; partner/girlfriend; get

4 1 D   2 S   3 S   4 D   5 D   6 S

5 1 advice
    2 each
    3 old; known
    4 get
    5 met
    6 known; see
    7 meeting
    8 flatmate; best, personalities

6 *possible answers*:
    1 A man called Noah.
    2 About 20 years.
    3 At work.
    4 About once a week, because we don't work together now.
    5 He's good fun and we laugh at the same things.
    6 Yes, he gives me good advice if I have a problem. I'm not as good at giving advice as he is.

Unit 17

1 1 angry   4 scared   7 afraid
    2 worried   5 embarrassed 8 surprised
    3 bored   6 unhappy   9 excited

2 1 emotions   4 scared
    2 bored   5 in love
    3 sad   6 embarrassed

3 1 worried
    2 surprised
    3 excited
    4 felt; embarrassed
    5 happy
    6 bored
    7 afraid/scared
    8 love
    9 emotions/feelings

4 1 upset/bad/unhappy
    2 nervous
    3 thirsty
    4 hungry
    5 in pain
    6 pleased
    7 sorry

5 1 nervous   5 argument; argue
    2 tired   6 sorry
    3 pleased   7 thirsty
    4 pain   8 upset; crying

6 *possible answers*:
    1 I felt tired when I got up this morning.
    2 I felt nervous before my exam last week.
    3 I felt hungry an hour ago.
    4 I felt thirsty during the night.
    5 I argued with my boyfriend on Saturday.
    6 I was in pain last week when I fell over.
    7 I cried a couple of weeks ago when I saw a very sad film.
    8 I felt pleased when I finished work on Friday afternoon.

Unit 18

1
1	2020	6	midnight
2	Friday	7	the autumn
3	April	8	winter
4	the morning	9	lunchtime
5	4.00	10	the evening

2
1	at	3	in	5	On	7	in	9	At
2	at	4	in	6	in	8	at	10	on

3 *possible answers:*
I get up **at** seven o'clock.
I study English **on** Tuesday and Thursday evenings.
I go swimming **in** the summer.
I usually go out with friends **at** the weekend.
I watch TV **in** the evenings.
I go to bed **at** about eleven o'clock.
My birthday is **on** 6th June.
I was born **in** 1997.
We have public holidays **on** Christmas Day, **on** New Year's Day, **on** May Day (in early May), and several other days.

Unit 19

1
1 trees
2 motorway
3 river
4 shop
5 church
6 gate
7 mountain
8 field
9 building

2
1	under	4	towards	7	out of
2	into	5	past	8	down
3	up	6	through	9	across

3
1 across/over/under
2 across/over
3 through
4 along
5 past

4 *your own answers*

Unit 20

1
1	in	8	on
2	on	9	on
3	at	10	in
4	in	11	on
5	in	12	at
6	on	13	on
7	in	14	at

2
1	in	5	on
2	in	6	in
3	on	7	at
4	on	8	at; at; in

3 *possible answers:*
1 I live in a town.
2 I live in a house.
3 Yes, it's the River Ebro.
4 My bedroom is on the first floor.
5 I've got lots of pictures and lights on the wall.
6 Yes, I do.
7 Yes, but not often.
8 At school.

4
1 T
2 T
3 T
4 F – the people are in front of the garage.
5 T
6 F – the gate is between the house and the garage.
7 F – the children are in front of Mum and Dad.
8 T
9 T
10 T

5
1	next to	5	near
2	in front of	6	in front of
3	in front of	7	next to
4	between	8	behind

6 *possible answers:*
1 There's another house.
2 There's a garden and a hill.
3 Another house.
4 No, there aren't.
5 My parents' bedroom.
6 The dining room.
7 A bathroom.
8 Yes, a tree.

Unit 21

1
1 night
2 pencil
3 book
4 apple
5 milk
6 sky
7 mountain

2
1 at the top
2 at the back
3 at the bottom
4 At first
5 at the front
6 at the end
7 in the middle
8 in the end
9 on the other side
10 At the start/beginning
11 At first; In the end

3 AT: least, the same time, the time, the moment
ON: holiday, the phone, time
IN: fact, prison, hospital

4 1 at the same time
2 on holiday
3 at the moment
4 in hospital
5 At least
6 on time
7 at school/university

5 1 at the time
2 in hospital
3 at least
4 by the end of
5 in prison
6 in fact
7 at university
8 on his phone

Unit 22

1 1 good at
2 I agree.
3 depends on
4 bored with
5 Do you ask your parents for money?
6 care about
7 live with
8 interested in speaking

2 1 thank; present/gift
2 cares
3 depends
4 spent
5 interested
6 ask

3 1 with   4 for   7 at
2 for   5 on   8 with
3 in   6 about   9 with

4 *possible answers*:
I live with my wife.
I sometimes ask my parents for advice, but I don't think I depend on them.
No, I never ask them for money.
Yes, I usually agree with them.
No, I don't spend much on clothes.
I don't really care about making money, but I would quite like a bit more.
I almost always thank people for presents.
I'm interested in sailing, photography and going to the theatre.
I'm quite good at photography, and I'm good at my job.
I get bored with things like housework.

5 1 f   2 a   3 e   4 b   5 g   6 d

6 1 at   4 about   7 about
2 for   5 on   8 of
3 for   6 for   9 of

7 1 based   3 pay   5 applied
2 heard   4 noticed   6 think

8 *possible answers*:
Yes, I listen to the radio when I have my breakfast.
No, that's not true. I don't like social media.
No, that's not true. I usually notice what people are wearing.
Yes, I like films based on true stories.
I like furniture made of wood very much.
I don't like waiting for buses. I don't take taxis, so I don't pay for them.
I applied for a job in the summer and I got it.
I think about the future a lot, more than the past.

Unit 23

1 1 D   3 D   5 S
2 S   4 D   6 D

2 1 get **up**
2 have a **shower**
3 get **dressed**
4 I **arrive** at
5 I **finish/leave** work
6 I **have/eat** dinner
7 go **to** bed
8 usually **sleep**
9 daily **routine** is

3 1 get   5 arrive at/get to
2 have   6 dinner
3 have/eat   7 go
4 leave   8 sleep

4 *possible answers*:
1 I get dressed before I have breakfast.
2 Yes, before breakfast.
3 In the kitchen.
4 I leave home at about 7.15.
5 I get to work at 8.00.
6 I have dinner with my husband.
7 I go to bed at about 11.30.
8 I sleep for about six or seven hours a night.

5 1 Do you often do the shopping?
2 He is never late for school.
3 We sometimes get up early and play tennis.
4 Do you always go shopping at the weekend?
5 Martha often goes out during the week.
6 I see my sister once or twice a week.

6 1 stay   4 go   7 during
2 go   5 do   8 once
3 play   6 at   9 twice

7 *possible answers*:
1 F – I **sometimes** play tennis in the summer, but in the winter too.
2 F – In my family, I **often** do the shopping, or my sister does.
3 F – I **never** go for a long walk during the week.
4 F – I **often** play video games at the weekend.
5 F – I **often** have dinner with my family.
6 F – **At the weekend**, I go out a lot.
7 T
8 F – I **sometimes** go shopping with a friend.

Unit 24

1
1 jacket
2 trousers
3 jumper
4 button
5 coat
6 T-shirt
7 dress
8 pocket
9 jeans
10 tie
11 shirt
12 skirt
13 shorts
14 sweater

2
1 Megan
2 Enzo
3 Osman
4 Milla
5 Megan
6 Enzo
7 Milla
8 Osman
9 Milla, Enzo and Megan
10 Kim
11 Enzo and Osman
12 Milla, Osman, Kim, Megan
13 Enzo and Megan
14 no

3 WHOLE BODY: suit, dress, coat, uniform
ABOVE THE WAIST: top, tie, T-shirt, shirt, jumper
BELOW THE WAIST: trousers, skirt, shorts, jeans

4
1 skirts; dresses
2 put your coat on
3 trousers; jeans
4 hot
5 a uniform
6 an item of clothing

5
1 D
2 S
3 D
4 S
5 D
6 S
7 D
8 D
9 D

6 *possible answers*:
1 I'm wearing a blue T-shirt, a pair of jeans and a jacket.
2 It was Sunday, so I wore a dress. I also put my coat on when I went out.
3 I wear jeans and sweaters a lot at the weekends, but if I'm going out, I often wear a skirt and top, or a dress.
4 I don't go to parties very often, but I usually wear a dress.
5 Yes. I worked in a restaurant when I was younger and I wore a uniform. I didn't like it!

Unit 25

1
1 T
2 F – glasses are made of glass, plastic or metal.
3 T
4 F – you can carry an umbrella.
5 T
6 T
7 T
8 F – people usually wear one scarf.

2
1 socks
2 hat
3 ring
4 boots/socks
5 tights/socks
6 glasses
7 scarf
8 watch
9 umbrella
10 handbag

3
1 S
2 D
3 S
4 D
5 S
6 S
7 D
8 S

4
1 Give me the sock.
2 not possible
3 I've got one pair of trainers.
4 Where's my glove?
5 She's got my scarf.
6 Where is my shoe?
7 not possible
8 not possible

5 a gold necklace; a watch; a pair of leather boots; a pair of trainers; a pair of gloves; a leather belt; a pair of tights; a plastic ring

6 *possible answers*:
1 I always wear a watch, a ring and a necklace.
2 I never wear socks or a hat.
3 Yes, I wear them a lot.
4 I wear glasses for reading and I often wear sunglasses when I'm driving.
5 I wear jewellery every day and I always wear a watch, but I take it off when I go to bed. I never wear a hat. I sometimes wear a scarf in the winter.

Unit 26

1 red, green, pink, purple, orange, grey, dark blue, cream, brown, light blue, black, yellow, white

2
1 purple
2 light blue
3 green
4 pink
5 grey
6 dark blue
7 brown
8 cream
9 colours

3
1 uncomfortable
2 expensive
3 small
4 long
5 cheap
6 comfortable

4
1 a short blue skirt
2 comfortable brown shoes
3 a large orange handbag
4 a long red skirt
5 uncomfortable red shoes
6 an expensive purple tie
7 a small green handbag

5
1 S
2 S
3 D
4 D
5 S
6 S
7 D
8 S

6
1 take/am/'m
2 style
3 wrong
4 take
5 fit; too
6 look/are
7 size; too
8 great/lovely/nice; great/lovely/nice
9 fit; too
10 right
11 appearance

Unit 27

1 1 T
2 F – the total is £60.
3 F – you have got enough.
4 T
5 F – they cost the same.
6 T
7 T

2 1 cash   6 -dollar
2 purse   7 dollars
3 credit card   8 total
4 coins   9 enough
5 cost   10 each

3 *possible answers*:
1 Yes, I usually have about €80. I need it because I often buy food when I'm out.
2 I keep it in my purse. Sometimes I just have money in my pocket.
3 Yes, I have enough for a coffee and a book, but not jewellery.
4 If I'm not buying many things, I pay in cash, but if I buy a lot, I pay by debit card.

4 1 price   6 online
2 spend   7 earn
3 saved   8 sold
4 won   9 bill
5 price   10 off

5 1 bought   3 sold   5 won
2 spent   4 earned   6 saved

6 1 online   5 sale
2 bills   6 earn/spend
3 free   7 products
4 price   8 prize

7 *possible answers*:
1 Yes, I sometimes buy books online.
2 No, I don't. I usually use my debit card.
3 It's usually free, yes.
4 It's about £1.
5 No, I don't like sales very much.
6 No, in general they earn less than men.
7 They buy DVDs and books, I think.
8 Yes, I won a prize at school – it was an art book.

Unit 28

1 1 chemist's   5 medicine
2 pharmacy   6 clothes shop
3 department store   7 present
4 shopping centre   8 electrical store

2 bookshop, department store, clothes shop, pharmacy, supermarket, electrical store, furniture shop, everything, medicine, except

3 1 ~~toyshop~~   4 ~~fruit and vegetable shop~~
2 ~~gift shop~~   5 ~~music shop~~
3 ~~furniture shop~~   6 ~~chemist's~~

4 *possible answers*:
1 baker's/supermarket
2 toy shop/department store/shopping centre/gift shop
3 gift shop/department store/shopping centre/music shop
4 music shop/shopping centre
5 chemist's/pharmacy/supermarket
6 shoe shop/department store
7 furniture shop/department store
8 clothes shop/department store
9 electrical store/shopping centre/department store

5 1 two things
2 to
3 the shoes on
4 of two things
5 personal
6 online
7 shop
8 the price
9 somebody's face

6 1 d   3 h   5 e   7 c
2 a   4 g   6 b

7 1 prefer   5 try; on
2 choose   6 online
3 service   7 sales
4 particular   8 touch

8 *possible answers*:
1 I like both of them, but I prefer small shops for meat and fish.
2 No, it's difficult to choose. I often make mistakes.
3 Yes, it is.
4 I prefer comfortable shoes.
5 No, sometimes I buy clothes online and try them on at home. I can always send them back.
6 I prefer to go to the shops, but sometimes it's easier and cheaper online.
7 The sales are usually in January, and also in the summer.
8 Yes, I like to touch clothes.

Unit 29

1 1 recipe
2 memory
3 diary
4 camera
5 possession

2 1 camera   5 voice
2 recipes   6 diary
3 possessions   7 recordings
4 gun   8 memory

3 1 any more   5 gun
2 tool   6 voice
3 recipe   7 belongs
4 memories   8 possessions

4 *possible answers:*
1 I've got some very old books that belonged to my grandfather, and my father's watch.
2 Yes, I really enjoyed school. I had a lot of friends, and the teachers were very good.
3 I use the camera on my mobile phone because I always have it with me.
4 I've got a recording of my mother and sister on my phone. They're singing and laughing.

5 1 F – Clothes are made of material.
2 T
3 T
4 F – an alarm clock is usually made of plastic or metal.
5 T
6 T
7 F – if something is unusual, you don't see it often, or it doesn't happen often.
8 F – an electric fan is useful if it's very hot.
9 T

6 1 I use my mobile as an **alarm** clock in the mornings.
2 My desk is made of **wood** and is very old.
3 What **shape** is the table? ~ I think it's round.
4 He's got a very **unusual** alarm clock – it's made of wood.
5 The garden chairs are made of white **plastic** and they're very hard.
6 A computer is made of **metal** and plastic.
7 What do you call the **device** that turns the TV on and off?

7 *possible answers:*
1 My dining room table is round.
2 No, I use a real alarm clock.
3 My desk is made of wood, and the computer, keyboard and printer are plastic and metal. There are some pencils made of wood too. And the lamp is made of plastic, I think.
4 Yes, I've got a digital TV.
5 I use an electric fan in the summer.

Unit 30

1 1 S   3 S   5 D   7 S
     2 D   4 D   6 S   8 D

2 1 No   5 No
     2 Yes   6 Yes
     3 Yes   7 No
     4 Yes   8 No

3 1 found/discovered   5 killed
     2 area/part   6 crimes
     3 named   7 series/number
     4 attacked   8 alive

4 1 D   3 D   5 D   7 D
     2 S   4 D   6 S   8 S

5 1 find   4 think
     2 team/group   5 people
     3 important   6 happens

6 1 late   5 major
     2 statement   6 believe
     3 danger   7 happen
     4 searching   8 public

Unit 31

1 1 What's   8   feel
     2 's got   9   feel
     3 feel   10 a common
     4 've got   11 's
     5 a headache   12 flu
     6 Has   13 haven't got
     7 healthy   14 Has he got

2 1 cough; unhealthy
     2 temperature
     3 matter; well; toothache
     4 stomach ache
     5 sick
     6 flu
     7 health
     8 illness; common
     9 cold

3 1 S   2 D   3 S   4 D   5 D   6 D

4 1 F – If you get better, you feel less ill.
     2 F – A couple of weeks is about 2 weeks.
     3 T
     4 F – If you don't sleep for a week, you feel weak.
     5 T
     6 T
     7 F – You should keep warm if you have flu.
     8 F – If you stay in bed, you don't get up.
     9 T
     10 T

5 1 stayed
     2 couple
     3 get better/improve
     4 advice
     5 tablets/pills
     6 should
     7 chemist's/pharmacy
     8 rest
     9 keep
     10 getting
     11 weak

Unit 32

1 1 hurts/hurt *(present or past both possible)*
     2 cut
     3 accident
     4 broken
     5 drugs
     6 injury
     7 pain
     8 cut
     9 serious

2 1 She had a pain in her arm.
2 He had a serious injury.
3 I hit my head on the door.
4 I knocked my head on the wall.
5 I burnt my mouth on the hot soup.
6 She cut her foot on the broken glass.
7 My arm hurts a lot.
8 The doctor gave me some drugs for the pain.
9 I broke / have broken a bone in my ankle.

3 1 broken
2 drugs
3 pain(s)
4 your
5 burnt/cut

4 *possible answers*:
1 I broke my arm when I was 10. I fell over at the swimming pool.
2 No, I haven't.
3 Sometimes, if I work at the computer for too long.
4 Last week. I cut my finger when I was cutting vegetables.
5 Yes, I often burn my hands and fingers in the kitchen, but nothing serious.

Unit 33

1 1 S   3 D   5 D   7 S
   2 D   4 S   6 D   8 D

2 1 Yes   3 Yes   5 No   7 No
   2 No   4 No   6 Yes   8 No

3 1 anywhere
2 nowhere
3 somewhere
4 everywhere
5 nowhere
6 somewhere
7 anywhere
8 somewhere

4 1 2,000
2 the Sahara Desert
3 two billion years old
4 the Pacific Ocean
5 Siberia, in Russia
6 Yes, a few places.

Unit 34

1 1 g<u>o</u>vernment
2 dis<u>as</u>ter
3 env<u>i</u>ronment
4 disap<u>pe</u>ar
5 des<u>tro</u>y

2 1 increasing
2 disappearing
3 government
4 build
5 destroying
6 land

3 1 increases
2 government
3 disaster
4 land
5 environment
6 disappears
7 destroy
8 extreme

4 1 recycle
2 energy
3 gas
4 coal
5 petrol
6 electricity
7 develop
8 cause

5 1 F – Pollution is a bad thing.
2 T
3 T
4 T
5 F – You can't see gas.
6 T
7 F – If you develop something, you make it.
8 T
9 F – Pollution is bad for fish and animals.
10 T

6 1 f   2 d   3 g   4 a   5 c   6 b

7 *possible answers*:
1 We use gas and electricity.
2 Electricity is more expensive – about double the cost of gas. I think coal is cheap, but people don't use it a lot now.
3 Yes, it's very bad in the centre of the city.
4 It's the buses, cars and lorries, and some industry too.
5 Yes, I recycle bottles, paper, cardboard and plastic every week.

Unit 35

1 1 Chi<u>nese</u>
2 Hun<u>ga</u>rian
3 <u>Ger</u>man
4 <u>I</u>talian
5 Japa<u>nese</u>
6 Ca<u>na</u>dian
7 Ko<u>re</u>an
8 E<u>gyp</u>tian

2 1 T
2 T
3 F – They speak Thai.
4 T
5 F – They speak English.
6 T
7 T
8 F – They speak French, Italian or German.

3 1 Britain
2 Europe
3 North
4 continent
5 South/Latin
6 Africa/Asia
7 the Middle East
8 Asia
9 continent

4 1 Italy, C
2 Hungary, C
3 Mexico, C
4 Swiss, N
5 China, C
6 Czech, N
7 Egypt, C
8 Spanish, N
9 Brazil, C
10 Turkey, C
11 Greek, N
12 French, N
13 Germany, C
14 Russia C
15 Argentinian, N
16 Portugal, C

5
1. Poland
2. Brazilian
3. Russia
4. Russian
5. Polish
6. Japanese
7. Korean
8. Turkish
9. Italian
10. Chinese
11. Spain
12. Australian

6 -ian: Argentinian, Australian, Brazilian, Canadian, Egyptian, Hungarian, Indian, Russian
-ish: British, Polish, Spanish, Turkish
-an: American, German, Korean, Mexican
-ese: Chinese, Japanese, Portuguese

7 *your own answers*

Unit 36

1
1. river
2. mountain
3. coast
4. high
5. long
6. border
7. Ocean, east
8. major
9. north
10. enormous
11. popular

2
1. famous
2. huge
3. west
4. north
5. ocean
6. long; long
7. beach
8. popular

3 *possible answers about Britain (England, Scotland and Wales)*:
1. London, in the south of England/Britain.
2. Manchester, Liverpool, Birmingham, Edinburgh, Glasgow and Cardiff.
3. No.
4. The River Severn, in south-west England (290 kilometres).
5. Ben Nevis, in Scotland.
6. Trafalgar Square, Buckingham Palace, The Tower of London, Edinburgh Castle, The Lake District, Stonehenge, etc.

4 1 S   2 D   3 S   4 D   5 D   6 S

5 SIZE: a small village, a large city, a small town
LOCATION: on the coast, on the River Duero, south-west of the capital
POPULATION: over two million, just under 50,000, about 3,000
INTERESTING FACTS: famous for its modern buildings, mobile phone industry, a warm climate, city full of culture

6
1. of
2. in
3. of
4. on
5. population
6. industry
7. ancient
8. climate

7 *possible answer*:
Bath is a medium-sized town, 170 km west of London, in the south-west of England. It's on the River Avon. It has a population of just under 100,000. It is a famous tourist city in England, with lots of ancient buildings, including the Roman Baths and many museums. It is cool and wet in winter and quite warm in summer.

Unit 37

1
1. c
2. i
3. h
4. j
5. b
6. e
7. a
8. f
9. g

2
1. raining
2. sunny/bright
3. snows
4. windy
5. weather
6. cloudy
7. icy
8. blowing

3
1. a bit
2. a lot of
3. a lot
4. a bit of
5. a bit
6. a lot
7. a bit
8. a lot of

4
1. showers
2. Suddenly
3. clear
4. minutes
5. strong
6. changes

5
1. There was heavy rain last night.
2. The weather in Spain is better than here.
3. There was a shower in the afternoon.
4. The weather changes every day.
5. It's dry today.
6. We had a storm.
7. There are clear skies.
8. It snows all the time in winter.

6 *possible answers, from India*:
1. Not, really! We get some rain occasionally in spring.
2. We get snowfall only in a few parts of the country, up in the hill stations.
3. We have horrible hot and dusty summers!
4. Yes, most parts of my country have dry winters, however it rains in the southern parts!
5. No, we don't have heavy rains in spring unless they are hail storms.
6. Yes, some parts of the country get strong winds and in fact dust storms in summers. Some parts get strong winds during monsoons!

Unit 38

1 whale, elephant, bear, lion, sheep, monkey, cat, mouse, fly

2 PETS: cat, dog
FARM ANIMALS: cow, horse, pig
INSECTS: fly, bee
WILD ANIMALS: elephant, tiger, lion, bear

3
1. most
2. lion
3. whale
4. son
5. hair
6. tiger
7. wild

4 *(Other answers may be possible.)*
1. people
2. horses/elephants
3. sea
4. insects
5. fly
6. mice
7. farms
8. zoo
9. wings

5 1 pets
　　2 farmer; farm
　　3 wild
　　4 both
　　5 insect
　　6 zoo
　　7 wings
　　8 both

6 1 **four legs**: lion, tiger, elephant, horse, sheep, cow, pig, cat, dog, mouse, bear (but some people say 2)
　　2 **two legs**: bird, monkey, bear (but some people say 4)
　　3 **six legs**: bee, fly
　　4 **no legs**: snake, whale

7 *possible answers, from the Czech Republic*:
　　1 Yes, I have a cat.
　　2 Yes, in the zoo, and also in a forest.
　　3 I'm afraid of spiders.
　　4 Cows, pigs, sheep, hens and goats.
　　5 Probably. I like going to zoos.
　　6 No.

Unit 39

1 1 taught
　　2 put
　　3 let
　　4 brought
　　5 bought
　　6 sang
　　7 spent
　　8 drove
　　9 spoke
　　10 held
　　11 spelt/spelled
　　12 rang
　　13 sat
　　14 burnt/burned

2 1 swam; began
　　2 wrote; drove
　　3 bought; thought
　　4 sent; built
　　5 put; cut
　　6 got; fell

3 *possible answers*:
　　1 I swam a kilometre.
　　2 He forgot my homework.
　　3 She sent the letter to the lawyer.
　　4 He lent me his bike.
　　5 She put them in the cupboard.
　　6 He fell on the stairs.
　　7 She lost 100 euros.
　　8 They ran three kilometres.

4 1 swam
　　2 caught
　　3 rode; rode
　　4 cut/broke/burnt; hurt
　　5 drove
　　6 wrote/sent
　　7 cost
　　8 came/got
　　9 rang
　　10 bought
　　11 began
　　12 woke (up)

5 1 driven
　　2 ridden
　　3 cut
　　4 won/lost/spent
　　5 spoken
　　6 hit/hurt
　　7 broken
　　8 fallen

possible answers:
　1 Yes, I drove my brother's car last summer. I was quite scared.
　2 No, I haven't.
　3 Yes, I cut my hair very badly when I was a child.
　4 Yes, I have. I spent a large sum of money to buy a house.
　5 No, I haven't.
　6 No, I haven't.
　7 Yes, I have. I broke my arm last year.
　8 Yes, I have. I fell from a tree when I was six years old.

Unit 40

1 1 She's got blue eyes.
　　2 They've got a small dog.
　　3 I haven't got a smartphone.
　　4 He hasn't got any money.
　　5 Have you got any sisters?
　　6 Has she got a flat in town?
　　7 They haven't got a shop now.
　　8 Have they got a big office?

2 1 Has she got any children?
　　2 They've got a lovely garden.
　　3 Has she got long hair?
　　4 My sister hasn't got/doesn't have a boyfriend.
　　5 Have you got a computer?/Do you have a computer?
　　6 We haven't got any friends here./We don't have any friends here.

3 1 got
　　2 Do
　　3 Have
　　4 Do
　　5 Have
　　6 Do

4 *possible answers*:
　　1 Yes, I have. I use it to go to college.
　　2 Yes, I do. It's an Apple.
　　3 Yes, they have. His name's Barney.
　　4 No, they don't.
　　5 Yes, I've got the *Oxford Essential Dictionary*.
　　6 Yes, I do. I've got an American friend, and a German friend who speaks excellent English.

5

	GROUP 1	GROUP 2	GROUP 3	GROUP 4	GROUP 5
	rest	breakfast	bath	swim	holiday
	break	lunch	shower	run	weekend
		dinner	wash	walk	journey

6 1 walk/look
　　2 drink
　　3 dinner
　　4 swim
　　5 rest
　　6 journey

7 1 eat
　　2 walk/run
　　3 break
　　4 look/walk
　　5 time/day
　　6 weekend
　　7 holiday/time
　　8 bath

Unit 41

1 1 What does his wife do?
    2 His company makes software programs./
       His software company makes programs.
    3 Why does English make you tired?
    4 I want to do Spanish at school next year./
       Next year I want to do Spanish at school.
    5 Is this jumper made of wool?
    6 What did you do last night?

2 1 made   5 made
    2 do   6 made
    3 do   7 do
    4 makes   8 make

3 *possible answers*:
    1 Cars and pianos are made in the UK.
    2 I make little bags for friends.
    3 Music makes me cry, and sometimes films as
       well.
    4 I did maths, English, French, German, History,
       Geography, Chemistry, Physics, Biology and PE.
    5 I'll probably watch TV after dinner.
    6 I went shopping, saw an exhibition at an art
       gallery, and had dinner in a restaurant with
       friends.

4 *your own answers*

5 1 done   5 did
    2 do   6 made
    3 make   7 make
    4 made   8 make

6 1 e   2 f   3 b   4 a   5 c

7 1 make   5 do
    2 make   6 make
    3 make   7 do
    4 do

8 *possible answers*:
    1 Yes, always.
    2 Yes, usually when I'm speaking.
    3 No, they're very quiet.
    4 Not a lot.
    5 Yes, very often.
    6 No, not really, but I don't want to be poor.
    7 No, not always. It depends how important
       something is.

Unit 42

1 1 Did you get my message?
    2 He gets angry if you're late.
    3 We got home late last night.
    4 It's getting cold.
    5 I got three letters today.
    6 Where did you get that bag?
    7 He needs to get a job.
    8 Do you want to get a/the train?

2 1 receive   5 receive
    2 become   6 buy
    3 arrive   7 be given
    4 become   8 travel

3 *possible answers*:
    1 getting cold
    2 get here/home/back
    3 get them
    4 get a/the bus
    5 get one
    6 get it.
    7 getting late.
    8 get a bus/taxi
    9 got a good mark/grade
   10 get every day/week

4 *possible answers*:
    1 I get the bus every day.
    2 It doesn't get very cold in my country.
    3 I get around/about 10 texts every day.
    4 I got a new skirt.
    5 You can get information about my town from
       the internet.

Unit 43

1 1 1   3 4   5 5   7 4
    2 2   4 3   6 1   8 5

2 1 see   5 watch
    2 watch   6 see
    3 see/watch   7 saw
    4 see   8 saw/watched

3 1 see   5 see
    2 watch   6 see
    3 see/watch   7 see
    4 saw/watched

4 *possible answers*:
    1 No, I can't see very well without glasses
       because my eyes are bad. When I'm driving,
       I have to wear them.
    2 Yes, I watch him often – it's lovely to watch him.
    3 I always watch the news and sports.
    4 I saw a programme yesterday about Iran –
       it was very interesting.
    5 I see her every week.
    6 I see them every day.
    7 Yes, it's difficult because it has a lot of
       meanings.

Unit 44

1 1 control   4 cause
    2 promise   5 copy
    3 over

2 1 H   2 M   3 H   4 H and M   5 H   6 M

3 1 cost   6 surprise
    2 fighting   7 smell
    3 control   8 dreaming
    4 promised   9 caused
    5 chat   10 sleep

4 1 I had a dream about you.
2 Did he make a comment on the report?
3 She made a promise to help me.
4 Does this soap have a nice smell?
5 They gave him a surprise.
6 I must send/write a reply to Jilly's letter. / I must send/write Jilly a reply.
7 Did you give Mo a call?
8 I had a look at her newspaper.
9 Could you make a copy of this?
10 He gave me a smile this morning.

5 *possible answers*:
1 I sometimes dream about people in my family who I don't see very often. It's strange.
2 Travelling by train costs a lot of money in the UK.
3 Some cheese has a very strong smell. And my dog has a strong smell too, but I don't mind it!
4 The fact that people are extremely rich or extremely poor causes a lot of problems.
5 It surprises me that people have such different ideas about politics.
6 The world can't control the internet. It's very good in some ways, but dangerous in others.

Unit 45

1 1 ✓
2 ✓
3 butter/some butter
4 ✓
5 bread/some bread
6 ✓
7 olive oil/some olive oil
8 rice/some rice
9 jam/some jam
10 ✓
11 cheese/some cheese/a piece of cheese

2 1 pasta 5 pasta
2 cheese 6 chocolates
3 cake 7 Butter
4 rice 8 biscuits

3 *your own answers*

4 1 a 3 b 5 e
2 g 4 c 6 f

5 1 Could I have twelve eggs, please?
2 Do you need a bag?
3 Have you got any French cheese?
4 How much pasta do you need?
5 That's just over half a kilo.
6 How many oranges do you need?

6 1 got; many
2 have; much; grams; all
3 Could/Can; just; That's;
4 ready; need

Unit 46

1 grapes, lemon, nuts, strawberries, pineapple, pear, orange, peach, apple

2 1 oranges
2 lemons
3 peaches
4 pineapples
5 bananas
6 nuts

3 1 Bananas
2 Oranges
3 Pineapples
4 Nuts
5 Sweet
6 Grapes
7 Strawberries
8 Peaches
9 fruit

4 *your own answers*

5 1 peas 7 beans
2 onion 8 cucumber
3 pepper 9 mushroom
4 potato 10 tomato
5 cabbage 11 garlic
6 lettuce 12 carrot

6 1 T 6 T
2 T 7 T
3 F 8 F
4 T 9 F
5 F 10 T

7 *possible answers (for Britain)*:
cabbage: Yes, but not much.
mushrooms: Yes, a lot.
red peppers: Yes, but not much.
fresh tomatoes: Yes, a lot.
frozen peas: Yes, a lot.
cooked onions: Yes, a lot.
fresh cucumber: Yes, a lot.
lettuce: Yes, a lot.
frozen carrots: Yes, but not much.
beans: Yes, a lot.
cold potatoes: Yes, but not much.
garlic: Yes, but not much.

Unit 47

1 1 F – They don't eat meat or fish.
2 T
3 F – It's a type of bird.
4 F – You get bacon from pigs.
5 T
6 T
7 F – Squid is a type of seafood.
8 F – Pig is an animal.
9 T
10 F – You get ham from pigs.

2
1	beef	6	squid
2	ham	7	bacon
3	tuna	8	sausages
4	duck	9	pork
5	crab	10	prawns

3
1 Pork, because it's a type of meat, not an animal.
2 Lamb, because it isn't from a pig.
3 Tuna, because it's a fish, not a type of meat.
4 Vegetarian, because it's not a type of meat, fish or seafood.
5 Cow, because it's an animal, not a type of meat.
6 Salmon, because it's a fish.

4 *possible answers:*
1 I like beef but it's expensive so I don't eat it very often.
2 I don't eat squid. It's very difficult to buy where I live.
3 I eat a lot of salmon.
4 I don't like crab so I don't eat it.
5 I like tuna.
6 I eat prawns, often with pasta.
7 I don't like duck – I prefer to see ducks swimming.
8 I like lamb.

Unit 48

1
1	3	3	6	5	3	7	1
2	3	4	6	6	2	8	3

2
1	fork	10	white
2	spoon	11	bottle
3	plate	12	beer
4	bowl	13	salt
5	bottle	14	black pepper
6	fizzy water	15	bottles
7	glasses	16	oil
8	wine	17	vinegar
9	red		

3 *possible answers, from China:*
On restaurant tables in my country we usually have chopsticks, bowls, spoons, cups or glasses, and a pot of tea or a bottle of water. We have dishes for food. We sometimes have plates, napkins, and pepper, too.

We don't usually have knives, forks, salt, vinegar, white wine, red wine, beer, or fizzy water.

We never have oil on the table.

Unit 49

1
1 It's boiled rice.
2 The potatoes are fried.
3 A cheese sauce.
4 The first course was salad.
5 Did you have ice cream?
6 There was fruit for dessert.
7 I had tomato soup.
8 How was the apple pie?

2
1 F – You eat ice cream with a spoon.
2 T
3 T
4 F – You eat soup in chips in different bowls.
5 T
6 T
7 F – People don't have cream on pizza.
8 T
9 T
10 F – Apple pie is a dessert.

3
1	sauce	5	course
2	pie	6	cream
3	fried	7	boiled
4	soup		

4 *possible answer:*
I'd like the soup for the starter, and then duck with orange sauce and boiled potatoes for the main course. Then for the dessert, I'd like apple pie with cream.

5
1	some more	7	of course
2	to order	8	the
3	another	9	I'll
4	meal	10	certainly
5	all right	11	waiter
6	tuna instead	12	without

6
1 have
2 without
3 course
4 or still
5 some
6 Certainly/Sure/Of course
7 'll
8 bill
9 sure/certainly/of course

Unit 50

1 crisps / snack / cheese sandwich / cake / toasted sandwich
tea with lemon / drink / black coffee / fizzy drink / orange juice

2
1 F – Ice is frozen water.
2 T
3 T
4 F – Hot chocolate is a drink.
5 T
6 T
7 F – You can have a drink or a snack in a café.
8 T
9 F – Crisps are not sweet.
10 T

3
1	bread	7	fizzy/alcoholic/hot
2	sandwich	8	pub
3	chocolate	9	white
4	ice	10	black
5	coffee/tea	11	juice
6	drink(s)	12	tea/coffee

4 *your own answers*

5
1	S	3	D	5	S	7	S	9	D
2	S	4	S	6	D	8	D	10	S

6 B I'd like two toasted ham sandwiches, please.
   A Is that to have here or take away?
   B To have here, please.
   A Is that everything?
   B Can I get two teas, please?
   A It will be a couple of minutes.
     Please take a seat.

7 1 Can I **have/get** a tea with lemon, please?
   2 To drink here or **take** away?
   3 To **drink/have** here.
   4 Would you **like** brown bread?
   5 Yes, **please**.
   6 OK, anything **else**?
   7 **No**, thanks.
   8 Fine. It will be a couple **of** minutes.
   9 **Take/Have** a seat, please.

Unit 51

1
1	to	5	ride	
2	car	6	both are correct	
3	both are correct	7	both are correct	
4	on	8	coach	

2
1	rides	5	motorbike	
2	coach	6	foot	
3	lorries/trucks	7	vehicles	
4	underground/car/ train	8	vans/a van	

3 *possible answers*:
   1 Yes, I can. I learnt to drive when I was 18.
   2 When I was about 7 or 8, I think.
   3 I usually go by bus, but I can also get a train. I can't walk – it's too far.
   4 No, I can't and I wouldn't like to.
   5 Yes, it's excellent. It's not expensive and it's very clean and safe.
   6 Yes, I sometimes go by coach, for example if I'm going to a football match.

4
1	traffic	5	speed limit	
2	rush hour	6	a quiet road	
3	main road	7	motorway	
4	miles per hour			

5 1 busy; hour
   2 main
   3 far
   4 get; unfortunately
   5 journey

6 *possible answers for a driver in Britain*:
   1 Yes. Sometimes there's too much traffic, but often there are accidents or bad weather.
   2 70 miles an hour.
   3 Not very often. I prefer smaller, slower roads.
   4 Yes, we do.
   5 7.30 a.m – 9.30 a.m. and again between 4.30 p.m. and 6.30 p.m.
   6 I went to Brighton by car a few weeks ago. It's about 130 miles. Unfortunately, there was a lot of traffic and the roads were very busy, so it took about four hours.

Unit 52

1 get off the bus; How long does it take?; the next stop; It doesn't take long; Excuse me.

2 1 Does the 24 stop outside the post office?
   2 Where do I get off for the cinema?
   3 Does the 24 go to the park?
   4 How often does the 24 run?
   5 Which is the last stop for the 16?
   6 How many stops is it to the railway station?
   7 Excuse me, which bus do I get to the school?
   8 How long does it take to the railway station?

3
1	Yes, it does.	5	The railway station.
2	At the next stop.	6	Five.
3	No, it doesn't.	7	The 16 or the 24.
4	Every ten minutes.	8	Fifteen minutes.

4
1	routes	7	timetable
2	stop	8	run
3	next	9	every
4	last	10	takes
5	get off	11	outside/near
6	goes	12	long

5 *possible answers*:
   1 Yes, at the end of the road.
   2 The 9 and the 15.
   3 The town centre or the airport.
   4 One runs every 15 minutes, the other every half hour.
   5 Sometimes to the town centre, but I don't get the bus very often.
   6 About six.
   7 About twenty minutes.

Unit 53

1 1 a fast train
   2 get off the train
   3 the (train) fare
   4 the 7 o'clock train
   5 a seat
   6 at a railway station/train station
   7 the timetable
   8 a carriage

2
1 fare
2 coach/carriage
3 missed
4 get/take
5 last
6 get on
7 waited
8 timetable
9 for
10 slow
11 journey

3
1 seat
2 change
3 return
4 direct
5 passengers
6 London
7 office
8 train
9 there

4
1 change
2 leaves
3 platform
4 gets
5 take/get
6 to
7 single
8 return
9 book/reserve

5 *possible answers*:
1 Last Thursday.
2 A return.
3 I went to Oxford for a meeting.
4 It was £10.50.
5 No, I didn't have time.
6 I had to change at Didcot.

Unit 54

1
1 The bookshop is opposite ~~of~~ the hotel.
2 Go straight on and keep ~~to~~ going.
3 Is there a cinema near ~~from~~ here?
4 It's on your left ~~side~~.
5 Turn ~~to~~ left and go straight on.
6 It's the third ~~road~~ turning on the right. (*also possible*: It's the third road ~~turning~~ on the right.)
7 Where's the ~~most~~ nearest post office?

2
1 D   2 S   3 S   4 S   5 D   6 D

3
1 Excuse me. How do I get to the museum?
2 Go along here and turn left.
3 Excuse me. Is there a post office near here?
4 It's the third turning on the right.
5 Excuse me. Do you know the way to the station?
6 Cross the road at the traffic lights.

4
1 turning
2 much
3 left/right/corner
4 me
5 road/river
6 going
7 on
8 here
9 way
10 lights

5 Conversation 1
1 get
2 straight
3 turning
4 left
5 much
6 problem

Conversation 2
1 Excuse
2 near
3 along
4 take
5 turning
6 right
7 opposite
8 thanks
9 That's

6 *possible answers*:
1 Go straight on, then turn left into Frith Street, and the hotel is on the next corner on your right.
2 Go straight on, then turn left into Frith Street. Take the first turning on the right and keep going. The museum is on your left.
3 Yes, go straight on, and take first turning on your right/turn right. The post office is on the corner.

Unit 55

1
1 f   4 b   7 d
2 h   5 i   8 a
3 j   6 e   9 c

2
1 in a road
2 in a restaurant
3 in a school
4 in a shop window
5 on a drinks machine
6 in a hotel window
7 near the sea
8 in a bank

3
1 signs/notices
2 notice/sign
3 sale
4 allowed
5 let
6 gap
7 closed/shut; open
8 feed
9 Mind
10 toilets

4
1 no parking
2 entrance/no exit
3 no smoking
4 keep off the grass
5 out of order
6 please do not feed the animals
7 allowed
8 queue here
9 danger
10 keep right

5 NO exit/smoking
PLEASE queue here
MIND the gap, your head
KEEP right/left

Unit 56

1
1 S   4 D   7 S
2 D   5 S   8 D
3 D   6 D   9 S

2
1 art gallery, museum, palace, church and a castle
2 market
3 library
4 museum, palace, castle, art gallery and church
5 park
6 tower
7 post office
8 bridge
9 church (or castle or palace)
10 buildings
11 places

3 *possible answers*:
1 False. No, there are three or four.
2 Yes, there is. I go there about once a month.
3 Yes, we have both.
4 Yes, there are two big parks and several small ones.
5 Most of them are.
6 False. No, there's a market every Saturday.
7 Yes, there is.
8 False. No, it's a lovely place to live.

4 1 noisy   5 safe
   2 lots   6 dirty
   3 view   7 There's
   4 opinion   8 pollution

5 Yes: 2, 3, 6, 7
   No: 1, 4, 5, 8

6 1 opinion   5 crowds
   2 dangerous   6 clean
   3 do   7 pollution
   4 busy/crowded   8 quiet

Unit 57

1 own, produce, grow

2 1 F – There are cows in the field.
   2 T
   3 T
   4 T
   5 T
   6 T
   7 T
   8 F – There aren't a lot of trees near the farmer.
   9 F – The farmer grows fruit and keeps cows.
   10 F – The lake isn't in the valley.

3 1 valley; hill   5 fields
   2 lake   6 own
   3 grass   7 farming
   4 gate   8 grow; produce

4 *possible answers*:
1 I live on a hill.
2 No, there isn't, but there's a river near my home.
3 Yes, in my garden.
4 Yes, I can, at the end of the garden.
5 Yes, there are some on the hill.
6 I own two dogs.
7 Yes, it is.
8 Farmers produce a lot of milk and cheese. They also grow vegetables and wheat.

5 1 a   2 f   3 g   4 b   5 c   6 d

6 1 water   5 natural
   2 Fresh   6 creative
   3 area   7 pick
   4 earth   8 nature

7 *possible answers*:
1 Yes, I often do in the summer.
2 Yes. I grow strawberries and raspberries, and I pick them from June to September.
3 Yes, I grow a lot of plants outside, but nothing inside.
4 Fresh air is really important. I like to see wild flowers in the countryside. The beauty of nature makes me feel happier. I like to see areas with plants in town; it brings more colour to the streets.

Unit 58

1 1 Anna and Rob   8 the second floor
   2 on the top floor   9 on the first floor
   3 Lucy   10 the lift; the stairs
   4 on the top floor   11 You put the key in
   5 the roof   the lock to open
   6 8   the door.
   7 front door

2 1 lift   9 top floor
   2 apartment
   3 ground floor   **3** 1 floor
   4 front door   2 ground
   5 steps   3 neighbours
   6 neighbour   4 lift; stairs
   7 roof   5 steps
   8 stairs   6 key

4 *possible answers*:
1 I live in an apartment on the second floor.
2 There's another flat and the person who looks after the building lives there.
3 An older lady called Dona Angeles is my neighbour, and a married couple live on the top floor.
4 It's got stairs, no lift.
5 No, there are no steps to the front door.
6 Yes, you have to open the door with a key.

5 view / modern / living room / hall / kitchen / home / dining room / upstairs / bedroom / parking / bathroom

6 1 living   6 views   11 bedrooms
   2 bathroom   7 hall   12 bathrooms
   3 view   8 kitchen   13 parking
   4 park   9 study   14 outside
   5 outside   10 Upstairs   15 inside

7 *possible answers*:
1 Most houses have two or three floors, but there are some very tall, old houses which have five floors.
2 Yes, they've got the same rooms, but in some houses there's an extra room for the washing machine.
3 A lot of houses in the modern part of the town have parking, but in the old part, parking is a big problem.

4 There are a lot of houses in the countryside, and just outside the centre of cities there are houses too.

5 Sometimes a very good garden makes a house a bit more expensive. A view of the sea will often make a house more expensive too.

Unit 59

1 1 S 3 S 5 D 7 S
     2 D 4 D 6 S

2 1 washing machine   8 turn; on/off
     2 dishwasher; sink   9 rubbish
     3 cupboard   10 empty
     4 bin   11 tap
     5 oven   12 equipment
     6 fridge   13 cooker
     7 full

3 *possible answers*:
We've got lots of cupboards, a sink and taps, an oven, a fridge, a washing machine, a bin, and a lot of kitchen equipment.
We haven't got a dishwasher.

4 1 prepare   4 clean
     2 homework   5 look after
     3 do   6 have to

5 1 feed   5 do; housework
     2 do; washing   6 did; homework
     3 task   7 look after
     4 washing up   8 have to

6 *possible answers*:
In my home, my husband and I both do some housework.
He does the washing up.
I do the washing.
He cooks the dinner.
I clean the kitchen.
I do the ironing.
We probably both do the same number of everyday tasks because we both have full-time jobs – and also, he's better at cooking than I am.

Unit 60

1 GROUP A: seat, suitcase, table, sheet
GROUP B: picture, Portuguese, match, nature, furniture
GROUP C: international, dictionary

2 1 f   3 h   5 g   7 c
     2 i   4 a   6 b   8 e

3 1 wardrobe   7 pieces of furniture
     2 sheets   8 wooden
     3 wall   9 table
     4 suitcase   10 national
     5 lamp   11 international
     6 space   12 a few

4 *possible answer*:
I'm Lucy, and I live at home with my family. There's a bed with sheets, a table and a lamp on it. I've got a wardrobe in a corner of the room and a comfortable chair to sit on. I've got lots of pictures of my family and friends on the wall. I've got a suitcase on top of the wardrobe. The furniture is all wooden and it's a really nice room.

5 1 do; a brush   5 washbasin
     2 have   6 towel; have
     3 puts on   7 bath
     4 shave   8 brush; mirror

6 1 bath   7 put on
     2 towel   8 teeth
     3 mirror   9 wash
     4 hair   10 brush/do
     5 clean/brush   11 shave
     6 mirror/washbasin   12 razor

7 1 teeth
     2 hair
     3 mirror
     4 brush
     5 make-up; put ...on
     6 have; razor; electric razor

8 *possible answers*:
     1 I brush them after breakfast.
     2 Twice a day.
     3 Lots of times!
     4 Yes, I do.
     5 I only wear it sometimes.
     6 My husband shaves every morning with a razor.

Unit 61

1 1 armchair   5 window   9 television
     2 carpet   6 fire   10 curtain
     3 floor   7 sofa   11 clock
     4 light   8 shelf   12 telephone

2 1 F – There are two windows.
     2 T
     3 T
     4 T
     5 T
     6 T
     7 T
     8 F – There are two corners.
     9 T
     10 F – There are four curtains.
     11 T
     12 T
     13 F – There are two shelves.
     14 T

3 1 phone/telephone   7 light
     2 sofa; armchair   8 shelf
     3 curtains   9 carpet
     4 clock   10 corner
     5 fan   11 window
     6 fire

4 *possible answers*:
1 I've got a sofa, an armchair and a small table in my living room.
2 I've got a TV.
3 I've got a carpet on the floor and a telephone on a shelf.

Unit 62

1
1 uncertain
2 unlucky
3 irregular
4 correct
5 unnecessary
6 unhealthy
7 correct
8 impolite

2
1 polite
2 informal
3 a regular
4 lucky
5 unnecessary
6 impolite
7 uncertain
8 unhealthy

3
1 polite
2 Irregular
3 informal
4 unlucky
5 uncertain/unsure
6 unhealthy
7 rude
8 unnecessary

4 *possible answers*:
1 Yes, my neighbours are all lovely.
2 That's true.
3 Yes, most of them are interesting.
4 No, I'm usually lucky – the weather is good.
5 That's true.
6 That's true.
7 That's true, but I sometimes text people when I'm having a meal.
8 That's probably true, but I like to have a shower every day.

Unit 63

1
1 No 3 No 5 Yes 7 Yes 9 No
2 Yes 4 Yes 6 No 8 Yes 10 No

2
1 strong
2 awake
3 poor
4 low
5 wide
6 alive
7 light

3
1 hard
2 weak
3 rich
4 dead
5 high
6 light
7 narrow
8 asleep
9 poor
10 soft

4 Words that are ticked: useless, common, different, general, media, useful, similar
Other words: specific, unusual, tradition

5
1 T
2 T
3 F – A traditional building is not modern in style.
4 F – An unusual event doesn't happen a lot.
5 T
6 F – A useless thing won't help you.
7 T
8 F – A lazy person doesn't work hard.
9 F – It's usually light in the middle of the day.
10 T

6
1 general
2 useful
3 light
4 unusual
5 traditional
6 hardworking
7 useless

7 *possible answers*:
It's unusual for me to get colds and flu.
I prefer modern houses.
I prefer a dark room.
We enjoy similar things.
I think social media is both positive and negative.
I don't like specific holiday plans.
Sometimes it's useful to know about history.
They think I'm quite hardworking.

Unit 64

1
1 only
2 still
3 especially
4 only
5 even
6 still

2
1 He's 75 and he **still** plays tennis.
2 It's nice there, **especially** in the morning.
3 There are **only** three students in the class.
4 He **even** works on Sundays./He works, **even** on Sundays.
5 She's **still** at university.
6 Rio is big, but Sao Paolo is **even** bigger.

3
1 Only
2 still
3 especially
4 only
5 Even
6 especially
7 still
8 even

4
1 both answers are correct
2 really
3 both answers are correct
4 really
5 both answers are correct
6 quite
7 both answers are correct
8 really

5
1 extremely/really
2 rather/pretty
3 a bit
4 very/really
5 a little
6 quite/pretty
7 very/extremely
8 rather/pretty

6 *possible answers*:
1 slow/unfriendly
2 handsome/attractive/friendly/nice
3 enjoyed it/hated it
4 lonely/bored/unhappy
5 interesting/good
6 late
7 friendly/nice
8 lazy

Unit 65

1
1 slowly
2 badly
3 angrily
4 late
5 clearly
6 happily
7 well
8 hard
9 easily
10 quietly
11 correctly
12 fast

2
1 I write very clearly.
2 My cousin sings well.
3 My boss works hard.
4 Lola drives carefully.
5 Robina answered the questions correctly.
6 Julio doesn't pronounce words clearly.
7 Miriam did the exercise easily.
8 Amina works very fast.
9 My little boy reads slowly.
10 She spoke to Sam angrily.

3
1 late
2 loudly
3 clearly/slowly
4 badly
5 carefully
6 hard

4 *possible answers:*
1 I never arrive late; I always arrive at the right time.
2 My father speaks very loudly.
3 Yes, she does.
4 I think I drive well.
5 Yes, I have to think carefully.
6 Sometimes I relax a little, but usually I work hard.

Unit 66

1
1 D
2 S
3 S
4 D
5 S
6 D
7 S

2
1 PE/physical education
2 literature
3 history
4 geography
5 art
6 languages
7 chemistry
8 computer science
9 biology
10 design and technology
11 physics
12 arts subjects
13 science subjects

3 *possible answers:*
1 I was good at English literature.
2 I was quite good at geography.
3 I was bad/terrible at maths.
4 I didn't study biology, physics or chemistry after the age of 15.
5 The subject I liked most was English literature.
6 The subject I hated most was physics.

Unit 67

1
2 g
3 b
4 e
5 a
6 f
7 d

2
1 leave
2 get/find
3 carry on/continue/ stay
4 options
5 either
6 or
7 training

3
1 uniform
2 leave
3 get/find; training
4 carry on/continue/ stay
5 at

4 *possible answers, from Kenya:*
0 Children in Kenya start school when they are between 5 and 7.
1 Yes, the children usually wear a uniform.
2 They can leave school at the age of 18.
3 At this age, they do more training at university or at a college.
4 Yes, they stay in school since they will not have completed high school education until they complete Form Four at the age of 18.
5 They can go to university or a college to get training for their future career or a particular job, for example working as a doctor.

5
1 no
2 five
3 two
4 A (for biology)
5 E (for maths)
6 Grade C (a pass)

6
1 take/do
2 do
3 well; grade/mark
4 results
5 badly; failed
6 worst

7 *possible answers:*
1 Most of my lessons were 50 minutes.
2 Yes, quite hard.
3 I took important exams at 16 and 18.
4 I took nine exams when I was 16, and four exams when I was 18.
5 Yes, fortunately I did.
6 Biology is my best subject.

Unit 68

1
1 do
2 term
3 write
4 last
5 library
6 do
7 Unfortunately
8 After
9 takes

2
1 degree; in
2 research
3 fortunately
4 again
5 essay; took
6 last
7 bookshop
8 unfortunately

3 *possible answers, from Mexico:*
1 Here in Mexico, the course lasts five years.
2 Unfortunately, only 16%.
3 Unfortunately, most students don't do that.
4 Between four or five months.
5 It is not always possible.

4
1 S
2 D
3 S
4 D
5 S
6 S
7 D

5
1 doctor
2 engineer
3 architect
4 lawyer
5 lecturer
6 designer
7 journalist
8 businessman

6
1 professor
2 law
3 manager
4 journalist
5 lectures
6 business
7 reporter
8 engineering
9 science
10 businesswoman

7 *your own answers*

Unit 69

1
1 job
2 shop assistant
3 nurse
4 long
5 clothes
6 hasn't
7 employee
8 boss
9 dentist
10 Models
11 builder
12 in the police

2
1 D 3 S 5 D 7 S
2 S 4 D 6 S

3
1 a pilot, a dentist, a teacher
2 a dentist, a nurse, a fashion designer,
   a hairdresser, a builder, a chef, a soldier,
   a pilot, a cleaner, a lorry driver, a shop assistant
3 a pilot, a teacher (a maths teacher),
   a businessman/woman, a builder
4 unemployed
5 a nurse, a soldier, a police officer/policeman/
   policewoman, a pilot, a chef, a dentist
6 a secretary, a cleaner, a businessman/businesswoman

4
1 secretary
2 a pilot
3 a hairdresser
4 the boss
5 a fashion designer
6 a model
7 a teacher
8 a chef
9 company

5 *possible answers:*
1 My friend Lucia is a secretary.
2 Carlo is a chef at the pizzeria.
3 Christelle is my hairdresser.
4 My friend Marissa is a teacher.
5 I don't know anyone who is a taxi driver.
6 Mr Ranelli is my dentist.
7 My mum is a businesswoman.
8 My uncle is the boss in a small factory.

Unit 70

1
1 long hours
2 an office
3 advertising
4 work for
5 does he earn
6 hours a day
7 an American airline
8 earn much
9 a year
10 ten to six

2
1 hospital; in
2 company; salary; a
3 long; from; to
4 earn
5 in; army
6 for; airline
7 advertising
8 manages;
   manager

3 *possible answers:*
1 I'm a reporter.
2 I work for a local newspaper.
3 I work in an office, but I go out and talk to people.
4 I work long hours, often 10 or 12 hours a day.
5 No, we don't earn very much.

4
1 e 2 f 3 b 4 a 5 d

5
1 We discussed our problems.
2 I have a meeting this afternoon.
3 She spends a lot of time travelling.
4 Could you organize the meeting?
5 My job involves using a computer.
6 I met her for the first time last week.

6
1 clients
2 discuss
3 project
4 designing
5 involves
6 organize
7 send
8 reports
9 colleagues
10 spend

Unit 71

1
She offered me the job. 7
I went for an interview. 5
I posted it. 4
I decided to apply. 2
I saw an advertisement for a job. 1
I accepted the job. 8
I filled in the form. 3
The interviewer asked me questions. 6

2
1 offered
2 post
3 interview
4 fill
5 training
6 applying
7 experience
8 accept
9 advertisement/advert/ad
10 interviewer

3 *possible answers:*
1 I've applied for two jobs: a teaching job and a
   job in advertising.
2 I had interviews for both jobs.
3 My training for the teaching job was a one-year
   teacher training course.
4 I filled in a form for my interview.
5 I'd like to work with young people, especially
   helping them with sports activities.

Unit 72

1
1 Yes
2 No
3 Yes
4 Yes (usually)
5 No
6 Yes
7 Yes
8 No

2
1 He's at work today.
2 This is such a good book.
3 Stand up when she enters the room.
4 The film was so long.
5 She's part of a small group.
6 This is such a difficult job.

3
1 worries
2 whole
3 so
4 enter
5 such
6 charities; parts
7 support
8 amazing/incredible

4 *possible answers*:
1 It was quite good and I enjoyed the work.
2 Yes, I was worried about arriving on time and wearing the right clothes.
3 Yes, they were very friendly and the boss was amazing.
4 Yes, there were three of us and we all worked and had lunch together.

Unit 73

1 1 keyboard   4 menu   7 screen
   2 window   5 tablet   8 printer
   3 laptop   6 mouse   9 program

2 1 laptop/tablet   6 program
   2 screen   7 document/window
   3 menu   8 mouse
   4 printer   9 keep
   5 tablet

3 *possible answers*:
1 No, I haven't. I've got an Apple Mac.
2 Yes, I've got a printer and I use it nearly every day.
3 I haven't got a laptop, but I've got a tablet and I keep it in the kitchen.
4 Yes, I've got thousands. They're mostly of friends and family.
5 I prefer a PC because it has a bigger screen and keyboard.

4 save, move, type, remove, replace, close

5 h, e, d, c, f, a, b, g (*also possible*: h, e, f, d, c, b, a, g)

6 1 lines   6 save
   2 careful   7 replace; with
   3 copies   8 cut
   4 file   9 types
   5 print/make   10 closed

Unit 74

1 1 ~~reply~~
   2 ~~the internet~~
   3 ~~document~~
   4 ~~a reply~~
   5 ~~the internet~~

2 1 Did you **get/receive** …
   2 The letter **got** lost …
   3 Have you **replied** to …
   4 … not **on** the internet
   5 … jamie **at** gmail dot com
   6 Could you **email/send/post** …
   7 I need to **check** …
   8 … send it by **post/email**
   9 … sue 1 at gmail **dot** com

3 A   B   C
   1 sent   4 receive/get   6 reply
   2 letter   5 reply   7 on
   3 lost   8 internet

4 website, virus, recognize, online

5 1 S   3 D   5 D   7 D
   2 S   4 D   6 D   8 S

6 1 videos   5 virus
   2 passwords   6 search
   3 blog   7 click; recognize
   4 websites   8 contains

7 *possible answers*:
1 Yes, I do, usually music videos.
2 No, never.
3 No, I haven't.
4 I use the BBC website, Wikipedia, and the Arsenal football website.
5 No, it hasn't.
6 Yes, a lot.
7 No, I don't because it's dangerous.
8 I don't open it. I delete it.

Unit 75

1 1 S   3 S   5 D   7 S
   2 D   4 S   6 S

2 1 message; rang;   5 phone; messaged
     answer   6 make
   2 number   7 message
   3 call; busy; phone   8 mobile; double
   4 wrong

3 *possible answers*:
1 Phone: Double three eight, nine seven four. Mobile: oh double seven double oh, nine double oh, six, eight four.
2 My mother and my sister.
3 Yes, I do. I message my friends all the time.
4 Hello?
5 No, not very often.

4 *correct answers*:
1 Oh, hello, is that Jackie?
2 Just a moment …
3 Speaking.
4 Oh hello, how are you?
5 I'm sorry, he's out.
6 OK, I'll call back later.
7 Yes, bye.

5 **Conversation 1**   8 speak to
   1 speaking   9 just a
   2 This is   10 get
   3 in/there
   4 please   **Conversation 3**
   5 at the moment   11 Is that
   6 call/phone/ring;   12 speaking
     back   13 it
   7 bye/goodbye

   Conversation 2

6 *a possible answer, from Poland:*
The phrases we use in Polish for answering the phone are quite different. We have a special word for *hello* on the phone: *halo*. Instead of *Speaking*, we say *Słucham*, which means literally 'I'm listening', and we use *Mówi Marisa* ('Marisa is speaking') for *It's Marisa*. When we ask for someone, we can say either *Czy to Marisa?* (which is basically the same as in English) or *Czy zastałam/zastałem Marisę?* (literally, 'Have I got hold of Marisa?').

Unit 76

1
1 owner
2 visitor
3 traveller
4 winner
5 instructor
6 driver
7 television/TV actor
8 factory worker

2 radio listener, film actor, bus driver, driving instructor, office worker, English teacher

3
1 visitors
2 owner
3 race/competition
4 driver
5 workers
6 listeners
7 readers
8 speaker
9 winner
10 teacher

Unit 77

1
1 flying
2 shopping
3 camping
4 spelling
5 sightseeing
6 understanding
7 teaching
8 driving

2 *your own answers*

3 writing English, painting pictures, sleeping in a tent, listening to music, playing football, learning languages, buying clothes, cooking meals

4 *possible answers:*
1 Writing English is quite difficult.
2 Painting pictures is not something I do.
3 Sleeping in a tent is not something I enjoy.
4 Listening to music is something I do a lot.
5 Playing football is something I used to do.
6 Learning languages is fun.
7 Buying clothes is boring for me.
8 Cooking meals is something I do every day.

Unit 78

1
1 ce<u>le</u>brate; cele<u>bra</u>tion
2 des<u>cribe</u>; des<u>crip</u>tion
3 pre<u>dict</u>; pre<u>dic</u>tion
4 de<u>cide</u>; de<u>ci</u>sion
5 <u>or</u>ganize; organi<u>za</u>tion
Note that the stress in nouns falls on the syllable before the last syllable.

2
1 invention
2 celebration
3 description
4 solution
5 prediction
6 organization

3
1 decision, decided
2 solve, solution
3 description
4 celebrate
5 invented
6 organizing; organization
7 predicted
8 inventions

4

VERB	NOUN	VERB	NOUN
move	*movement*	discover	*discovery*
succeed	success	*think*	thought
arrange	*arrangement*	argue	*argument*
choose	*choice*	complain	*complaint*

5
1 an argument
2 complaint
3 thought
4 success
5 arrangements
6 discovery

6
1 complaint
2 choose
3 choice
4 argue
5 argument
6 succeed
7 success
8 thoughts

7 *possible answers:*
1 No, I haven't. My neighbours are very quiet.
2 No, I like to think about it carefully.
3 Yes, we could choose between Spanish and German, for example.
4 No, never.
5 No, I haven't.
6 No, I'm not interested in business.
7 No, family is the most important thing for me.
8 Yes, a lot.

Unit 79

1 <u>bath</u>room   <u>rail</u>way station   <u>first</u> floor
<u>add</u>ress book   <u>bus stop</u>   <u>phone</u> number
<u>dish</u>washer   capital <u>letter</u>   <u>police</u> officer

2
1 a bathroom
2 a dining room
3 a bus stop
4 a DJ (disc jockey)
5 a railway station
6 an art gallery
7 an address book
8 a dishwasher

3
1 number
2 officer
3 jockey
4 mark
5 tense; participle
6 floor
7 stop
8 phrasal
9 full
10 capital

4 department store, sports centre, ticket office, traffic lights, swimming pool, credit card, public transport, high street

5
1 public
2 credit
3 birthday
4 identity
5 high
6 traffic
7 park
8 machine
9 office
10 sales/shop; department

6
1 identity
2 centre
3 credit
4 pool
5 birthday
6 store

7 *possible answers*:
1 Yes, I have an identity card for work. It's got my name and a photo on it.
2 No, I don't.
3 Yes, I do. I use it for shopping.
4 No, I don't.
5 I don't send birthday cards. I email or call people to wish them a happy birthday.
6 Yes, I do. I usually buy clothes.

Unit 80

1 1 A   2 B   3 A   4 B   5 A   6 A

2 1 I hate chocolate.
2 They don't like doing homework very much.
3 He doesn't like speaking English very much.
4 I quite like shopping.
5 She doesn't like driving.
6 I don't mind working at night.

3 1 love/like   5 hate
2 all   6 like
3 mind   7 quite/really
4 really   8 at

4 *possible answers*:
1 Yes, I like going to the cinema too.
2 I quite like classical music, especially Bach and Vivaldi.
3 I love shopping – I go with my friends and we have a good time.
4 I don't mind driving, but it's not exciting.
5 I don't mind writing emails to my friends, but sometimes it's boring writing emails for work.
6 I love watching TV.
7 No, I hate housework.
8 I quite like talking on the phone to my friends.

5 1 I enjoy watching TV.
2 I'm not interested in politics.
3 My favourite film is *Star Wars*.
4 She prefers reading to writing.
5 He's an amazing boss.
6 Was the party good fun?
7 It's a boring programme.
8 Singing is enjoyable.

6 1 fun   5 interesting
2 prefer   6 enjoy
3 favourite   7 incredible
4 interested   8 modern

7 *possible answers*:
1 Yes, it's good fun.
2 I prefer fish.
3 I love Rio de Janeiro: it's a very exciting city.
4 No, I'm not interested in jazz.
5 Yes, I do. I read books and watch history programmes a lot.
6 I enjoy walking in the countryside with my dog.
7 No, the restaurants where I live aren't very good.
8 I prefer old houses.

Unit 81

1 **Inside your home**: play computer games; do a lot of drawing; collect stamps

2 1 g   2 b   3 a   4 f   5 c   6 d

3 1 does   6 goes
2 collects   7 play
3 play   8 watches
4 go   9 go
5 do   10 does

4 *possible answers*:
I do a lot of travelling, I go out with friends a lot, I watch TV, I do a lot of cooking.
I would like to go to the gym and play the guitar.
I'm not interested in fishing, camping, computer games, golf, drawing or painting.

5 1 S   2 D   3 D   4 S   5 S   6 D

6 1 ✓
2 False. Kolya is a good singer.
3 False. Kolya plays the guitar.
4 False. There are various clubs in schools.
5 ✓
6 False. Natasha is quite good at dancing.
7 False. Computers and collecting things are popular hobbies.
8 False. Older people like repairing cars.

7 1 hobby   5 song
2 popular   6 at
3 various   7 repairing
4 singer

8 *possible answers*:
0 Yes, I'm a member of a swimming club.
1 I love making things like clothes, and I also enjoy painting.
2 Young people particularly like sports of all kinds, but gaming is also very popular.
3 I have various hobbies.
4 I am in a singing group, but if I sing alone, my voice isn't very good.
5 I can sing 'Human' by Rag and Bone Man.
6 I'm good at making things for the house: cushions, for example.
7 Yes, I often break things, so it's a good thing I like repairing things.

Unit 82

1 ice hockey, motor racing, table tennis, American football, basketball

2 1 game   5 do
2 skiing   6 bit/lot
3 racing   7 players; team
4 go   8 goal

3 **INSIDE A BUILDING**: basketball, ice hockey, running, swimming, table tennis, tennis
OUTSIDE A BUILDING: American football, baseball, football/soccer, motor racing, running, skiing, swimming, tennis

4 *possible answers*:
1 I play a bit of football and basketball with friends.
2 I play tennis every week and go skiing in the winter.
3 I watch football, rugby and tennis on TV.
4 Football is the most popular sport in Britain, but swimming, cycling, motor racing, rugby and cricket are also popular.

5
1 match/game
2 against
3 to
4 scored
5 nil
6 beat
7 won
8 draw
9 against

6
1 match/game
2 against
3 lost
4 drew; with/against
5 time
6 points
7 beat
8 scored
9 won (or lost)
10 leading
11 score

7 *possible answers*:
Manchester City beat Arsenal 2-0. Sterling scored just before half-time, and Aguero scored the second goal in the 78th minute.

Unit 83

1
1 concert
2 orchestra
3 pianist
4 audience
5 perform
6 opera singer
7 performance

2
1 classical
2 pianist
3 violinist
4 orchestra
5 musical instruments
6 performance
7 audience
8 performed/played
9 pieces
10 by

3 *possible answers*:
1 I don't go to classical music concerts very often because they're quite expensive.
2 *La Bohème* by Puccini, *The Magic Flute* by Mozart, the *Eroica Symphony* by Beethoven and *Swan Lake* by Tchaikovsky
3 I learnt to play the piano as a child, but I don't play now.
4 No.
5 The guitar.

4
1 made
2 not good
3 cheaper
4 go
5 are able to
6 like

5
1 tour
2 live
3 album
4 hit
5 records/albums/CDs
6 musician
7 performer
8 festival
9 recorded
10 ability

6 *possible answers*:
1 I really like Radiohead.
2 I do both.
3 Yes, I saw them at Glastonbury.
4 *In Rainbows*.
5 Yes, they do.
6 No, but they have popular albums.

Unit 84

1 science   violent   exciting   crime

2
1 thriller
2 comedy
3 action film
4 science fiction
5 cartoon
6 love story
7 horror film

3
1 sort
2 adventure/action
3 kind
4 romantic
5 horror
6 funny
7 type

4
1 romantic
2 violent
3 scary
4 funny

5
1 F – He's an actor.
2 T
3 T
4 T
5 F – It's a woman.
6 T
7 F – He's a director.

6
1 about
2 brilliant
3 in
4 stars
5 hero
6 actor
7 director
8 on
9 Let's

7 *possible answers*:
1 I like thrillers and action films.
2 It was a Polish film called *Cold War*.
3 It was on at our local cinema.
4 Joanna Kulig and Tomasz Kot.
5 Pawel Pawlikowski.
6 It's about two Polish people after the Second World War. It's a love story with an unhappy ending.

Unit 85

1
1 in
2 the
3 on
4 out
5 on
6 programme
7 –
8 of
9 a newspaper
10 of
11 crime

2
1 watch; saw/watched
2 believe/think; none
3 news; happened
4 listen; heard/listened to
5 paper/newspaper
6 on; drama
7 to
8 programme

3 *your own answers*

4
1 D
2 S
3 D
4 D
5 S
6 S
7 S
8 D
9 S

5
1 magazines
2 reports
3 events
4 disasters
5 wars
6 opinion(s)
7 journalists/reporters
8 celebrities

6 *possible answers*:
1 This week, Greta Thunberg spoke to the US Congress about climate change.
2 In the last five years, the UK had a referendum on leaving the EU or not.
3 I buy a newspaper on Saturdays, but during the rest of the week I usually get news from the TV, the radio and the internet.
4 The meerkat adverts (for Compare the Market) on TV are not new now, but I think they are still popular.
5 Jon Snow is a famous TV news reporter in the UK.

Unit 86

1
1 F – Non-fiction is about real things, fiction is not about real events.
2 T
3 T
4 F – If you are in trouble, it's bad.
5 T
6 T
7 F – A novel is a story.
8 T
9 F – If you create something, you make it or make it happen.
10 T

2
1 series/number
2 novels
3 character
4 detective
5 created
6 rules
7 trouble
8 solves

3 *possible answers, from Poland*:
1 Olga Tokarczuk is a famous author who writes novels.
2 Bieguni (Flights) is a novel by Olga Tokarczuk.
3 Korona królów (Crown of Kings) is a popular series on TV.
4 King Kazimierz is one of the main characters in Korona królów.
5 Eberhard Mock is a famous detective in fiction.
6 I sometimes ride a bike on a zebra crossing.

4
1 same, mainly
2 mostly, home
3 realize, fine
4 achieve, receive
5 butter, publish
6 variety, another
7 blue, including
8 recent, see

5
1 with you
2 know it
3 good
4 lots of different things
5 is
6 short
7 mainly
8 more information

6
1 past; mostly/mainly
2 including
3 realized
4 published
5 variety
6 tried; achieved

Unit 87

1 1 g   2 d   3 f   4 b   5 a   6 c

2
1 flight
2 accommodation
3 booked/arranged
4 might
5 foreign
6 checked
7 packed
8 suitcase

3 *possible answers*:
1 Yes, I always book a long time before I travel because it's often cheaper.
2 Usually I do if I'm travelling with all the family. If I'm alone, I often don't.
3 No, I don't.
4 Yes, always. I need to know what I have.
5 No, never, but I know I should do.

4
1 No
2 Yes
3 No
4 Yes
5 No
6 Yes
7 No

5 1 d   3 a   5 e
2 f   4 b

6
1 available
2 single/double
3 double/single
4 en suite
5 dear
6 matter
7 a
8 include
9 afraid
10 extra
11 parking
12 details

Unit 88

1
1 went on
2 recommend
3 excellent
4 tourists
5 definitely
6 stay
7 tourism
8 chat

2 1 excellent 5 staying
  2 helpful 6 recommend
  3 tourists 7 definitely/certainly
  4 guests

3 1 stay
  2 service
  3 chat
  4 recommend
  5 tourists

4 *possible answers*:
  1 One night.
  2 Yes, quite good.
  3 Yes, I did.
  4 Yes, definitely/certainly.
  5 No, it's a business hotel.

5 1 g 3 f 5 b
  2 a 4 d 6 e

6 1 sign 5 serve
  2 leave 6 change
  3 call/take 7 collect
  4 pay 8 check

7 1 key 3 serve 5 out
  2 until/till 4 have; have 6 call

Unit 89

1 1 board 5 airport
  2 check-in 6 hand luggage
  3 boarding card 7 airline
  4 aeroplane 8 security

2 boarding pass; hand luggage; board the plane;
  check-in desk; ticket machine

3 1 passengers; check-in
  2 reach
  3 boarding; luggage; check
  4 gate; board/get on
  5 airports
  6 print; machine
  7 luggage

4 *possible answers*:
  1 No, I use different airlines.
  2 Yes, I do.
  3 No, the first thing I do is check in, then I have
    a coffee.
  4 Yes, of course.
  5 No, it doesn't matter to me.
  6 Yes, I do.

5 1 You get on the plane.
  2 You fasten your seat belt.
  3 The plane takes off.
  4 Flight attendants provide drinks.
  5 The plane lands.
  6 You get off the plane.
  7 Someone checks your passport.
  8 You collect your luggage.
  9 You leave the airport.

6 1 departure 7 landed
  2 board/get on 8 arrival
  3 fasten 9 checked
  4 takes off 10 collect
  5 flight 11 leave
  6 provide

7 *possible answers*:
  1 I'm fine, but my wife is very nervous.
  2 I eat some of it, but it's usually terrible.
  3 I'm excited.
  4 I always try to travel with just hand luggage.

Unit 90

1 *possible answers*:
  They used to go to Hyères on holiday.
  They used to get a bus to Hyères.
  They used to stay in an apartment.
  He used to go swimming.
  She used to sit on the beach.
  She used to read on the beach.
  They used to have lunch in the apartment.
  They used to have dinner in one of the restaurants.
  They used to relax after lunch.
  She used to write postcards.
  He used to go out on a boat.

2 1 couple
  2 beach
  3 boat
  4 rocks
  5 relax
  6 flew
  7 used

3 1 We **used** to stay 4 my dad, **while** my mum
  2 a couple **of** weeks 5 lots of **postcards**
  3 **used** to swim 6 a **typical** day

4 *possible answers*:
  1 We went to several places: sometimes the south
    coast of England and sometimes to a couple of
    places in Spain.
  2 A couple of weeks.
  3 Yes, I went on a boat in England a couple of
    times – I enjoyed it.
  4 I like being active – swimming and doing other
    sports.

5 1 go 5 guided
  2 guidebook 6 take
  3 go on 7 round
  4 visit 8 an ideal

6 1 photos 7 tour
  2 went; guide 8 visit
  3 got; map/ 9 gets
    guidebook 10 round; take
  4 sightseeing 11 ideal/perfect
  5 guided; prefer 12 look
  6 guidebook

7 *possible answers:*
1 Yes, I usually get a map from the tourist information office.
2 I sometimes buy a guidebook but not often.
3 No, but I sometimes go on bus tours.
4 Yes, generally I prefer to go sightseeing on my own.
5 Yes, almost always.
6 Yes, I spend most of my time looking round.
7 No, I don't take lots of photos but my wife does.
8 Not often, but it sometimes happens.
9 My ideal place for a sightseeing holiday is Venice.

Unit 91

1 1 Hello, nice to meet you.
2 Max, this is Emma. (or Emma, this is Max.)
3 Bye. Hope to see you again. (OR Hope to see you again. Bye.)
4 Goodbye. Nice to meet you. (OR Nice to meet you. Goodbye.)

2 1 introduce
2 shake
3 greet (*also possible*: meet)
4 Introductions
5 welcome
6 greetings

3 1 Hello/Hi; Nice/Good; meet
2 again; Bye/Goodbye
3 this; meet you; welcome
4 Hope/Good; Bye/Goodbye

4 1 See you tomorrow.
2 He's very well.
3 What's the matter?
4 See you later.
5 See you soon.
6 How are things?
7 Give my love to Suki.
8 I've got to go now.
9 That's fine.

5 things; Fine/Very well; matter;'ve got to; dear; give my love; will

6 well; fine/good; how's; good/fine
Anyway; 've got to; later; that's; then

Unit 92

1 1 How often do you go there?
2 What sort of music do you like?
3 What does he do?
4 How long have you lived there?
5 What type of films do you watch?
6 Who does this belong to?
7 What's his flat like?
8 Why do you like her?

2 a 4   c 7   e 6   g 2
   b 5   d 1   f 3

3 1 often; once/twice   5 belong
2 Whose; mine   6 kind/sort/type
3 What   7 idea
4 Yeah/Yes   8 long

4 1 What   5 nearest
2 long   6 seeing
3 time   7 Which
4 many   8 far

5 1 far   5 Which
2 close/shut 6 nearest
3 many   7 What
4 worth   8 recommend

6 *possible answers:*
1 I live in Sevilla, in Spain.
2 I have lived here twenty-five years.
3 The Alcazar Palace and the Cathedral.
4 About a kilometre.
5 There are many, but my favourite is Egana Oriza.
6 It's only a few hundred metres.

Unit 93

1 1 you; me; course
2 bring; please; problem
3 Could (*also possible*: Can); afraid
4 polite
5 responses
6 take; bring
7 make
8 requests; polite
9 put

2 *possible answers:*
1 A Could/Can you finish this exercise for homework, please?
   B Yes, sure.
2 A Luca, can/could you change places with Maria, please?
   B Yes, no problem.
3 A Could/Can you bring your notebook tomorrow, please?
   B I'm afraid I can't.
4 A Can/Could you lend me a pencil, please?
   B Yes, sure.
5 A Could you take these books to the library, please?
   B I'm afraid I can't. I have to leave now.
6 A Could/Can you finish the/your essay by Monday?
   B Yes, sure.

3 *possible answers*:
1 Is it **all right** if I use this dictionary?
2 **Do you mind** if I make a coffee?
3 **Could** I stay for another ten minutes?/**Is it OK/ all right if/Do you mind if** I stay another ten minutes?
4 Is it OK **if I** close the window?
5 Can **I borrow** your book?
6 Yes, **sure/no problem/go ahead/that's fine.**
7 I'm **afraid** I need it.
8 Yes, **of course/no problem/go ahead/that's fine.**

4 1 Do you mind if I go at one o'clock today, please?
2 Could I borrow a piece of paper, please?/ Could you lend me a piece of paper, please?
3 Is it OK if I go to the toilet?
4 Is it all right if I sit in a different seat?
5 Can you lend me a pen, please?/ Can I borrow a pen, please?

5 Go ahead.; No problem.; Of course.; That's fine.; I'm afraid I need it.

Unit 94

1 1 S   2 D   3 D   4 S   5 S   6 D

2 1 Would you **like** to come round later?
2 Yes, I'd love **to.**
3 Do you want to **go** out for dinner?
4 That **sounds** lovely.
5 I've just got an **invitation** to a party.
6 I'm afraid **I can't.**
7 That **would** be nice.
8 Do you want **to** come to a party?
9 I'm **sorry,** but I'm busy tonight.
10 Ben **invited** me to lunch on Saturday.

3 1 Would you like to go out for a meal?
~ Yes, great!
2 Do you want to come round for a coffee?
~ I'm afraid I can't.
3 Would you like to come to a party tomorrow?
~ Yes, that sounds lovely.
4 Do you want to go out for a coffee?
~ I'd love to, but I'm going to the gym.

4 dialogue 1
What shall we do this weekend?
The weather's nice, so
what about going to the beach?
Yes, that's a good idea.
And maybe we could take the train.
Fine. Shall we get the tickets online?
I'd prefer to get them at the station.

dialogue 2
Where shall we go tomorrow?
What about a nice meal at home?
I think I'd prefer to go out.
But it's going to rain.
OK, then let's order a pizza.
OK, fine.

5 1 What **shall** we do this evening?
2 Do you have a **suggestion**?
3 What about **going** to see a film?
4 I'd prefer **to** go by train.
5 Yes, **that's** a good idea.
6 Where **shall** we go tomorrow?

6 1 B What about going to the theatre?
A I'm not sure about that.
2 A What shall we do on Saturday?
B Perhaps we could go out for a meal.
A OK, let's do that.
3 A Where shall we go this afternoon?
B Let's go to a museum.
A Yeah, that's a good idea.

Unit 95

1 1 Do you want something to eat?
2 No thanks.
3 I'm fine, thanks.
4 Would you like something to eat?
5 Let me help you.
6 Thank you very much.
7 Thanks. Could I have a coffee?

2 1 help; please   4 let; worry
2 offer   5 refused
3 need; Thanks   6 accept

3 1 Would you like a drink?/Would you like something to drink?
Yes, please. Could I have some water?
2 Do you need some/any help?
No, I'm fine, thanks./No, don't worry, thanks.
3 Would you like something to eat?
Thanks./Yes, please. Could I have an apple?
4 Let me help you.
No, don't worry.

4 1 f   3 i   5 d   7 g
2 a   4 h   6 e   8 b

5 1 That's   5 mind
2 I'm   6 sorry; polite
3 forgotten; right   7 broken; worry
4 very/really/so;   8 rude
matter

6 1 so, really
2 it doesn't matter; that's all right; never mind; don't worry
3 when you:
feel bad about something
feel sad about something
want somebody to repeat something

Unit 96

1
1. <u>cer</u>tainly
2. im<u>po</u>ssible
3. possi<u>bi</u>lity
4. <u>de</u>finitely
5. <u>like</u>ly
6. <u>pro</u>bably
7. per<u>haps</u>

2
1. D   3. D   5. D   7. D
2. S   4. S   6. S   8. S

3
1. I'**ll** probably …
2. … likely **to** come …
3. … think **so**.
4. … hope **not**.
5. … there's **a** chance …
6. I **may/might** see …

4
1. probably; may/might
2. definitely; probably; likely
3. wedding; certainly
4. chance
5. attend; likely; may/might
6. possibility; so
7. maybe; certain; probably
8. impossible

5 *possible answers:*
1. I hope so.
2. I'll probably go out with my friends.
3. No, I'm definitely going out on Sunday.
4. I might do a bit of work.
5. I'll probably watch some sport in the evening.
6. I don't think I'm likely to spend a lot.
7. Yes, I'm definitely going to see my family for lunch on Sunday.
8. Maybe. I'm not sure.

Unit 97

1
1. ✗ it's **also** near the park
2. ✗ he understands Greek **too**
3. ✓
4. ✗ and **also** washed the car
5. ✓
6. ✗ and there's a park near the house **as well**

2
1. I often eat ice cream/cake and I also like cake/ ice cream.
2. I enjoy watching TV, and I go to the cinema a lot too.
3. I can speak English/German and I can understand German/English as well.
4. I read a lot of books and I also listen to music.
5. I play football and I watch it on TV as well.
6. I drive and I walk a lot too.

3 'True' or 'false' as correct for you.

4
1. He went to bed late, but he couldn't sleep.
2. People don't like her very much. However, she's very kind.
3. Although the food was terrible, the service was good./The food was terrible, although the service was good.
4. It was snowing, but we still decided to go out.
5. We lost our dog. However, we found it after an hour.
6. Although I wore a coat, I was still cold.
7. I watched the whole programme. I didn't enjoy it, though.
8. We had a big lunch. However, Jason was still hungry.

5
1. I was really hungry, but I had to wait until 10.00 for dinner.
2. I was last in the queue. However, I only had to wait five minutes.
3. I was very cold. However, someone lent me a jacket.
4. I was very frightened, but someone held my hand.
5. I was late for the party. However, everybody was still there.
6. I was really tired. However, I stayed at work to finish the job.

6 *possible answers:*
1. I didn't like it.
2. we (still) went out.
3. it was very friendly.
4. she (still) went to work.
5. she didn't pass the exam.
6. when I got there, it was closed.

Unit 98

1
1. because of   5. so
2. to   6. in order to
3. because   7. so
4. as a result

2
1. (in order) to   5. because
2. so   6. so
3. because of   7. (in order) to
4. As a result   8. as a result/so

3 *possible answers:*
1. because of the weather.
2. in order to work.
3. so I was late for work.
4. and as a result I didn't get to work until 9.30.
5. because I went out with friends in the evening.
6. so I was tired the next day.

4
1. Secondly   4. First of all
2. After that   5. then
3. Finally   6. Before that

5 *possible answers*:
1 Firstly, you make the pasta sauce. Secondly, you boil the pasta. Finally, you add the sauce to the pasta.
2 First of all, I did a degree in History. After that, I trained to be a teacher, and finally, I got a teaching job in Liverpool.
3 First of all, we left our home in Rome. Then we stayed in Munich for a week. After that, we spent the second week in Heidelberg. Finally we flew back to Rome.
4 First I made a shopping list. Then I went to the market. After that I came home and had a cup of tea. Finally, I cooked the dinner
5 Firstly, I had a shower, then I got dressed. After that, I had breakfast and finally, I rang for a taxi and left home.

6 *possible answer*:
First of all, I took a train to Bristol and met my friend, Sue. After that, we went for a walk by the river in the sunshine. Then we went to a café and had lunch which was delicious. And finally, we went to her flat and had a cup of coffee with her brother.

Unit 99

1 1 out   5 up
       2 up   6 up
       3 over   7 off
       4 out

2 1 out   4 down   7 off
       2 up   5 down   8 over
       3 up   6 up   9 up

3 *possible answers*:
1 I would like to give up sweets.
2 I grew up in London.
3 I feel afraid.
4 I don't often go out in the evenings. When I do, I go to dinner with my friends.

4 1 Take it off.   5 Take them off.
       2 Put it on.   6 Give it up.
       3 Turn it on.   7 Turn them on.
       4 Put them on.   8 Put it on.

5 1 correct   5 correct
       2 correct   6 correct
       3 turn **it** on   7 put **it** on
       4 take **it** off   8 correct

6 1 go back   4 take off
       2 carry on   5 go up
       3 go away   6 wake up

Unit 100

1 1 d   2 c   3 b   4 f   5 a   6 e

2 1 go
       2 out
       3 in
       4 back
       5 ready/dressed/changed
       6 get

3 1 dressed   4 sleep
       2 ready   5 better
       3 changed   6 get

4 *possible answers*:
1 I get dressed before I have breakfast.
2 No, I get ready very quickly.
3 Yes, I usually get changed. I put my jeans on.
4 Yes, sometimes.
5 Yes, I hope so.
6 Yes, we get lots of tourists where I live.

5 the rest of the time; hurry up; let me know; I guess so; come on; well done; right now

6 1 nothing
       2 like
       3 away/now; hurry
       4 Guess; Wow; done
       5 after
       6 guess/suppose; let
       7 else

7 1 The bar was busy so we went somewhere else.
       2 Could you let me know later?
       3 Who is going to take care of the children?
       4 Hurry up, Sacha!
       5 Do you feel like going out?
       6 Penny is here. Everyone else went out.

下列单词中有些已在单元标题中出现，我们默认学习者已经掌握。

classroom
family
hotel
learn
money
number
restaurant
school
sport
university
weather

下列单词包括部分语法用词和常见词汇，我们默认学习者已经掌握。

adult
anyone
artist
ball
be
boy
cannot
cent
chart
child
class
cup
dancer
diet
difficult
everybody
future
girl
he
hello
her
hey
him
his
I
imagine
important
interest
it
its
join
life
list
local
man
me

metre
must
my
no
no one
nobody
object
or
our
page
paint
people
period
person
quick
quickly
real
room
scientist
second (= unit of time)
section
she
show
skill
slow
somebody
someone
something
student
talk
tell
that
the
theatre
their
them
they
title
today
tonight
topic
understand
us
we
woman
yes
you
young
your
yourself

Word list 单词总表

本表中的部分单词、短语标有欧洲语言共同参考框架（CEFR）等级，这些单词选自 Oxford **3000**。注意：单词或短语后标注的数字是单元序号，而非页码。

a bit （用作 *adv*）稍微，有点儿 A2 37
a bit (+ *adj*) 稍微，有点儿 A2 37, 64
a bit (of sth) 小量，少量（某物）B1 37
a couple (of sth) 几个／件（某物）A2 31, 50, 90
a day/week, etc. 每天／周，等 70
a few 一些 A1 60
a little 少许，少量 A1 64
a lot (of sth) 大量（某物）A1 37
a night 见 **£90 a night** 每晚90英镑 87
ability /əˈbɪləti/ 能力 A2 83
about /əˈbaʊt/ 大约 A1 6
about /əˈbaʊt/ A1 见 **it's about …** 关于…… 84
above /əˈbʌv/ 在……上方 A1 20
abroad /əˈbrɔːd/ 到国外，在国外 A2 13
accept /əkˈsept/ 接受 A2 71, 95
accessory /əkˈsesəri/ 配饰 25
accident /ˈæksɪdənt/ 意外 A1 32
accommodation /əˌkɒməˈdeɪʃn/ 住处 B1 87
achieve /əˈtʃiːv/ 实现，完成 A2 86
across /əˈkrɒs/ 从一边到另一边，横过 A1 19
act /ækt/ *v* 表演 A2 76
action film 动作片 84
active /ˈæktɪv/ 忙碌的，活跃的 A2 15
activity /ækˈtɪvəti/ 活动 A1 5
actor /ˈæktə(r)/ （男）演员 A1 76, 84
actress /ˈæktrəs/ 女演员 A1 84
actually /ˈæktʃuəli/ 事实上 A2 21
ad /æd/ 广告 A1 71, 85
address /əˈdres/ *n* 地址 A1 13
address book 通讯录 79
adjective /ˈædʒɪktɪv/ 形容词 2
adventure film 冒险片 84
adverb /ˈædvɜːb/ 副词 2
advert /ˈædvɜːt/ 广告 71, 85
advertisement /ədˈvɜːtɪsmənt/ 广告 A2 71, 85
advertising /ˈædvətaɪzɪŋ/ 广告业 A2 70
advice /ədˈvaɪs/ 建议 A1 16, 31
afraid (of sth/sb) 害怕（某事／物／人）A1 17
afraid /əˈfreɪd/ 见 **I'm afraid (not)** 很遗憾（不行）A2 87, 93
afraid /əˈfreɪd/ 见 **I'm afraid I can't** 很遗憾，我不能 A2 94
Africa /ˈæfrɪkə/ 非洲 35
after that 然后，之后 98
afternoon /ˌɑːftəˈnuːn/ A1 见 **in the afternoon** 在下午 7
again /əˈgen/ 再一次 A1 68
against /əˈgenst/ 对阵 A2 82
age /eɪdʒ/ A1 见 **at the age of** 在……岁 A1 67
ago /əˈgəʊ/ 以前 A1 9
agree with (sb) 同意（某人）A1 22

air /eə(r)/ A1 见 **fresh air** 新鲜空气 A1 57
airline /ˈeəlaɪn/ 航空公司 A2 70, 89
airport /ˈeəpɔːt/ 机场 A1 89
alarm clock 闹钟 29
album /ˈælbəm/ 专辑 B1 83
alcoholic drinks 酒精饮料 50
alive /əˈlaɪv/ 活着的 A2 30, 63
all (of sth) （某事／物的）全部 A1 85
all day A1 **/morning/afternoon/evening** 整天／整个上午／整个下午／整晚 7
all right 可接受的，满意的 A2 49, 93
all the time 总是 A2 37
allow /əˈlaʊ/ 允许 A2 55
almost /ˈɔːlməʊst/ 几乎 A2 7
alone /əˈləʊn/ 独自 15
along /əˈlɒŋ/ 沿着 A2 19
already /ɔːlˈredi/ 已经 A2 9
also /ˈɔːlsəʊ/ 同样 A1 97
although /ɔːlˈðəʊ/ 虽然 A2 97
always /ˈɔːlweɪz/ 一直 A1 23
a.m. 上午 7
amazing /əˈmeɪzɪŋ/ 令人惊喜的 A1 72, 80
American football 美式橄榄球 82
American /əˈmerɪkən/ 美国人 35
ancient /ˈeɪnʃənt/ 老旧的 A2 36
and /ənd/ 和 A1 97
and so on 等等 B1 3
angrily /ˈæŋgrəli/ 生气地 A2 65
angry /ˈæŋgri/ 生气的 A1 17, 65
animal /ˈænɪml/ 动物 A1 38, 47
ankle /ˈæŋkl/ 脚踝 A2 10
another /əˈnʌðə(r)/ 又一，再一 A1 49
answer (the phone) 接（电话）A1 75
any more 再也 A2 29
anything else? 还要别的什么吗？A1 50
anyway /ˈeniweɪ/ （用于结束对话或转换话题）反正 A2 91
anywhere /ˈeniweə(r)/ 在任何地方 A2 33
apartment /əˈpɑːtmənt/ 公寓 A1 58
appearance /əˈpɪərəns/ 外观 A2 26
apple /ˈæpl/ 苹果 A1 46
apply for sth 申请某事／物 A2 22, 71
appointment /əˈpɔɪntmənt/ 预约，约定 B1 9
April /ˈeɪprəl/ 四月 A1 8
Arabic /ˈærəbɪk/ 阿拉伯语 35
architect /ˈɑːkɪtekt/ 建筑师 A2 68
architecture /ˈɑːkɪtektʃə(r)/ 建筑 A2 68
area /ˈeəriə/ 地区，场地 A1 30, 57
Argentina /ˌɑːdʒənˈtiːnə/ 阿根廷 35
Argentinian /ˌɑːdʒənˈtɪniən/ 阿根廷人 35
argue /ˈɑːgjuː/ 争论 A2 17, 78

argument /ˈɑːgjumənt/ 争论 A2 17, 78
arm /ɑːm/ 手臂 A1 10
armchair /ˈɑːmtʃeə(r)/ 扶手椅 61
army /ˈɑːmi/ 陆军 A2 70
around /əˈraʊnd/ 大约 A1 6
arrange /əˈreɪndʒ/ 安排 A2 78, 87
arrangement /əˈreɪndʒmənt/ 安排 A2 78
arrival /əˈraɪvl/ 到达, 抵达 B1 89
arrive (at a place) 到达, 抵达 (某地) A1 23, 53, 89
art /ɑːt/ 艺术 A1 66
art gallery 美术馆 56, 79
article /ˈɑːtɪkl/ 文章 A1 85
arts subjects 文科 66
as a result 因此 A2 98
as well 也 A2 97
Asia /ˈeɪʒə/ 亚洲 35
ask sb for sth 向某人要某物 A1 22
asleep /əˈsliːp/ 睡着 A2 63

at /ət/
(a place) 在 (某处) A1 20
(a time) 在 (某时间或时刻) A1 18
(= @) A1 74
all /ɔːl/ 一点也, 完全 80
breakfast, etc. 在早餐等时 A1 18
Christmas /ˈkrɪsməs/ 在圣诞节 18
first /fɜːst/ 首先 A2 21
least /liːst/ 至少 A2 21
midnight /ˈmɪdnaɪt/ 在午夜 7, 18
New Year 在新年 18
night /naɪt/ 在夜里 7, 18
school /skuːl/ 在上学 A1 21
(the age of sth) 在 (……岁) A2 67
the back of sth 在某物的后面 21
the beginning/start of sth 在某事/物的开头 A1 21
the bottom of sth 在某物的底部 21
the end of sth 在某事/物的结尾 A1 21
the front of sth 在某物的前面 21
the moment 此刻 A1 18, 21, 75
the same time 与此同时 A1 21
the time 当时 A2 21
the top of sth 在某物的顶部 A2 21
the weekend 在周末 A1 18, 23
university /ˌjuːnɪˈvɜːsəti/ 在上大学 A1 21
work /wɜːk/ 在上班 A1 72
attack /əˈtæk/ 攻击 A2 30
attend /əˈtend/ 出席 A2 96
attractive /əˈtræktɪv/ 吸引人的 A2 11
audience /ˈɔːdiəns/ 观众 A2 83
August /ˈɔːgəst/ 八月 A1 8
aunt /ɑːnt/ 姨母, 姑母 A1 14
Australia /ɒˈstreɪliə/ 澳大利亚 35
Australian /ɒˈstreɪliən/ 澳大利亚人 35
author /ˈɔːθə(r)/ 作者 A2 86
autumn /ˈɔːtəm/ 秋季 A1 8
available /əˈveɪləbl/ 可获得的 A2 87

average /ˈævərɪdʒ/ 平均的 A2 11
awake /əˈweɪk/ 醒着的 63
away /əˈweɪ/ A1 见 go away 走开 99
away /əˈweɪ/ 见 right away 此刻, 立刻 100
awful /ˈɔːfl/ 糟糕的 A2 26
baby /ˈbeɪbi/ A1 见 have a baby 生孩子 16
back /bæk/ 背部 A1 10
backache /ˈbækeɪk/ 背痛, 腰痛 31
bacon /ˈbeɪkən/ 培根, 咸猪肉 47
bad /bæd/ 难受的 17; 差的 A1 67
bad at sth 不善于 (做某事) A1 66
badly /ˈbædli/ 糟糕地 A2 65
bag /bæg/ 包, 书包 A1 1, 45
baker's /ˈbeɪkə(r)z/ 面包房 28
banana /bəˈnɑːnə/ 香蕉 A1 46
band /bænd/ 乐队 A1 83
bank account 银行账户 27
bar (of chocolate) (巧克力) 条 B1 45
bar /bɑː(r)/ 酒吧 A2 50
base sth on sth 以某事/物为某事/物的基础 B1 22
baseball /ˈbeɪsbɔːl/ 棒球 A2 82
basketball /ˈbɑːskɪtbɔːl/ 篮球 82
bath /bɑːθ/ 浴缸; 洗澡 A1 60
bathroom /ˈbɑːθruːm/ 浴室 A1 58, 79

be /biː/
able to do sth 能够做某事 A2 83
born /bɔːn/ 出生 A1 14
divorced /dɪˈvɔːst/ 离婚 A2 16
from /frəm/ 来自 A1 13
sick /sɪk/ 呕吐 A1 31
the same as sth 与某事/物相同 A1 3
together /təˈgeðə(r)/ 处于恋爱关系 A1 16
beach /biːtʃ/ 海滩 A1 36, 90
beans /biːnz/ 豆 A2 46
bear /beə(r)/ 熊 A2 38
beard /bɪəd/ 胡须 11
beat /biːt/ v 击败 A2 82
beautiful /ˈbjuːtɪfl/ 美丽的 A1 11
because /bɪˈkɒz/ 因为 A1 98
because of sth/sb 因为某事/物/人 A1 98
become /bɪˈkʌm/ 成为 A1 16
bed /bed/ 床 A1 60
bedroom /ˈbedruːm/ 卧室 A1 58
bee /biː/ 蜜蜂 B1 38
beef /biːf/ 牛肉 A2 47
beer /bɪə(r)/ 啤酒 A1 48
before that 在此之前 A1 98
begin /bɪˈgɪn/ 开始 A1 39
beginning /bɪˈgɪnɪŋ/ A1 见 at the beginning of sth 在某事/物的开头 A1 21
behind /bɪˈhaɪnd/ 在……后面 A1 20
believe /bɪˈliːv/ 相信 A1 30, 85
belong to sb 属于某人 A2 29, 92
below /bɪˈləʊ/ 在……下方 A1 20
belt /belt/ 皮带 A2 25

best /best/ A1 见 (the) best 最佳(的) 67
best friend 最好的朋友 16
better (than) (比……)更好 A1 37
better /ˈbetə(r)/ A2 见 get better 好转 A2 31
between /bɪˈtwiːn/ 在……之间 A1 20
bicycle /ˈbaɪsɪkl/ 自行车 A1 51
big /bɪg/ 大的 A1 26
bike /baɪk/ 自行车 A1 51
bill /bɪl/ 账单 A1 27, 49, 88
billion /ˈbɪljən/ 十亿 A2 6
bin /bɪn/ 垃圾箱 A2 59
biology /baɪˈɒlədʒi/ 生物学 A2 66
bird /bɜːd/ 鸟 A1 38
birthday /ˈbɜːθdeɪ/ 生日 A1 8
birthday card 生日贺卡 79
biscuit /ˈbɪskɪt/ 饼干 A2 45
bit /bɪt/ A2 见 a bit (of sth) 些许(某物) B1 37, 64
black /blæk/ 黑色 A1 26
black coffee 黑咖啡, 清咖 50
black pepper 黑胡椒 48
blog /blɒg/ 博客 A1 74
blonde /blɒnd/ 金黄色的 A1 11
blood /blʌd/ 血 A1 10
blow /bləʊ/ 吹, 刮 A2 37
blue /bluː/ 蓝色 A1 26
board /bɔːd/ v (= get on) 登(飞机, 船, 等) B1 89
board /bɔːd/ n 板, 牌 A2 1
board pen 白板笔 1
boarding pass/card 登机(船)牌 89
boat /bəʊt/ 小船 A1 90
body /ˈbɒdi/ 身体 A1 10
body /ˈbɒdi/ A1 见 a dead body 一具尸体 30
boil /bɔɪl/ 煮沸 A2 49
boiled /bɔɪld/ 煮过的 A2 49
bone /bəʊn/ 骨头 A2 10
book /bʊk/ v 预约, 预定 A2 53, 87
bookshop /ˈbʊkʃɒp/ 书店 28, 68
boots /buːts/ 靴子 A1 25
border /ˈbɔːdə(r)/ 边界 B1 36
bored /bɔːd/ 厌倦的 A1 17, 80
bored with sth 对某事/物感到厌倦 A1 22
boring /ˈbɔːrɪŋ/ 无聊的 A1 80
born /bɔːn/ A1 见 be born 出生 A1 14
borrow /ˈbɒrəʊ/ 借用 A2 93
boss /bɒs/ 老板 A2 69
both (of sb/sth) 两者都 A1 38
bottle /ˈbɒtl/ 瓶子 A1 48
bottom /ˈbɒtəm/ 臀部 B1 10
bowl /bəʊl/ 碗 A2 48
box /bɒks/ 盒子 A1 45
boyfriend /ˈbɔɪfrend/ 男朋友 A1 14, 16
brain /breɪn/ 脑 A2 10
Brazil /brəˈzɪl/ 巴西 35
Brazilian /brəˈzɪliən/ 巴西人 35
bread /bred/ 面包 A1 45
bread (white/brown) (白/黑)面包 50

break /breɪk/ 折断, 打破 A1 12, 32, 39, 95
break a rule 违规 86
breakfast /ˈbrekfəst/ 早餐 A1 23
bridge /brɪdʒ/ 桥 A2 56
bright /braɪt/ 晴朗的 A2 37
brilliant /ˈbrɪliənt/ 极好的 A2 84
bring /brɪŋ/ 带来 A1 39, 93
Britain /ˈbrɪtn/ 英国 35
broken /ˈbrəʊkən/ 断的 A2 32
brother /ˈbrʌðə(r)/ 兄弟 A1 14
brother-in-law /ˈbrʌðə(r) ɪn ˈlɔː/ 内兄/弟, 姐/妹夫, 连襟 14
brown /braʊn/ 棕色 A1 26
brown bread 黑面包 50
brush /brʌʃ/ n, v 梳子, 刷子; 梳, 刷 A2 60
build /bɪld/ 建造 A1 34, 39
builder /ˈbɪldə(r)/ 建筑工人 69
building /ˈbɪldɪŋ/ 建筑物 A1 56, 70
burn /bɜːn/ 烧伤 A1 32, 39
bus /bʌs/ 公共汽车 A1 51
bus driver 公交司机 69
(bus) stop (公交)车站 52, 79
business studies 商科 68
businessman /ˈbɪznəsmæn/ (男)商人 A2 68, 69
businesswoman /ˈbɪznəswʊmən/ 女商人 68, 69
busy /ˈbɪzi/ 繁忙的, 忙碌的 A1 51, 56, 94
busy /ˈbɪzi/ (= telephone) (电话)占线的 B1 75
but /bət/ 但是 A1 97
butter /ˈbʌtə(r)/ 黄油 A1 45
button /ˈbʌtn/ 纽扣 A2 24
buy /baɪ/ 购买 A1 27, 39
by /baɪ/ A1 见 a book by Tolstoy 托尔斯泰写的一本书 83
by the end of sth 到某事结束前 A2 21
bye /baɪ/ 再见 A1 75, 91
cabbage /ˈkæbɪdʒ/ 卷心菜 46
café /ˈkæfeɪ/ 咖啡馆 A1 50
cake /keɪk/ 蛋糕 A1 45, 50
call /kɔːl/ n, v 通话; 打电话给某人 A1 44, 75, 88
call sb back 再打电话给某人 75
called /kɔːld/ 被称作 A1 4
camera /ˈkæmərə/ 照相机 A1 29
camping /ˈkæmpɪŋ/ 露营 A2 77, 81
Can I get … ? 可以给我……吗? 50
Can I have … ? 可以给我……吗? 50
Can I/you … ? 我能不能……? /能不能请你……? 93
Canada /ˈkænədə/ 加拿大 35
Canadian /kəˈneɪdiən/ 加拿大人 35
capital /ˈkæpɪtl/ 首都 A1 36
capital letter 大写字母 8, 79
car /kɑː(r)/ 汽车 A1 51
car park 停车场 A1 79
care about sb/sth 关心某人/事/物 A2 22
career /kəˈrɪə(r)/ 事业 A1 69
careful /ˈkeəfl/ 细心的 A2 73
carefully /ˈkeəfli/ 细心地 A2 65, 73

carpet /ˈkɑːpɪt/ 地毯 A2 61

carriage /ˈkærɪdʒ/ （列车）车厢 C1 53

carrot /ˈkærət/ 胡萝卜 A1 46

carry /ˈkæri/ 提 A1 12, 25

carry on (with sth) 继续（做某事） A2 67, 99

cartoon /kɑːˈtuːn/ 动画片 A2 84

cash /kæʃ/ 现金 A2 27

castle /ˈkɑːsl/ 城堡 A2 56

cat /kæt/ 猫 A1 38

catch (an illness) 染上（疾病） B1 31, 39

catch (a ball) 接住（球） A2 12, 39

cause /kɔːz/ n, v 原因；导致 A2 34, 44

CD /ˌsiː ˈdiː/ 光碟 A1 1, 83

CD player 激光唱片机 1

celebrate /ˈselɪbreɪt/ 庆祝 78

celebration /ˌselɪˈbreɪʃn/ 庆祝（活动） 78

celebrity /səˈlebrəti/ 名人 85

century /ˈsentʃəri/ 世纪 A1 18

certain /ˈsɜːtn/ 确定的 A2 62, 96

certainly /ˈsɜːtnli/ 当然 A2 49, 88, 96

chair /tʃeə(r)/ 椅子 A1 1

chance /tʃɑːns/ A2 见 a good chance 较大的可能性 96

change /tʃeɪndʒ/ (= become different) 改变 A1 37

change (money) 兑换（货币） A1 88

change (trains) 换乘（列车） A2 53

change places 换座 93

character /ˈkærəktə(r)/ A2 见 main character 主角 86

charity /ˈtʃærəti/ 慈善机构 A2 72

chat /tʃæt/ v, n 闲聊 A2 44, 88

cheap /tʃiːp/ 便宜的 A1 26

check /tʃek/ 查看 A1 74, 87, 89

check in （酒店）登记入住，（机场）办理登机 A2 88, 89

check-in /ˈtʃek ɪn/ 登机手续办理 89

check-in desk 值机柜台 89

check out （酒店）办理退房 A2 88

cheese /tʃiːz/ 奶酪 A1 45

chef /ʃef/ 主厨 A2 69

chemist's /ˈkemɪsts/ 药店 28, 31

chemistry /ˈkemɪstri/ 化学 A2 66

chest /tʃest/ 胸部 B1 10

chicken /ˈtʃɪkɪn/ 鸡 A1 47

chin /tʃɪn/ 下巴 10

China /ˈtʃaɪnə/ 中国 35

Chinese /ˌtʃaɪˈniːz/ 中国人；汉语 35

chips /tʃɪps/ 薯条 A2 49

chocolate /ˈtʃɒklət/ 巧克力 A1 45

choice /tʃɔɪs/ 选择 A2 28, 78

choose /tʃuːz/ 选择 A1 28, 78

Christmas Day 圣诞日 8

church /tʃɜːtʃ/ 教堂 A2 56

cinema /ˈsɪnəmə/ 电影院 A1 84

circle /ˈsɜːkl/ n 圆圈 A2 29

circle /ˈsɜːkl/ v 圈出 A2 3

city /ˈsɪti/ 城市 A1 36

classical music 古典乐 83

clean /kliːn/ adj 干净的 A2 56

clean /kliːn/ v 清洁 A1 59

clean (your teeth) 使……干净（刷牙） A1 60

cleaner /ˈkliːnə(r)/ 清洁工 69

clear (sky) 晴朗的（天空） A2 37

clearly /ˈklɪəli/ 清楚地 A2 65

clever /ˈklevə(r)/ 聪明的 A2 15

click on sth 点击某物 B1 74

client /ˈklaɪənt/ 客户 B1 70

climate /ˈklaɪmət/ 气候 A2 36

climb /klaɪm/ 爬，攀登 A1 12

clock /klɒk/ 时钟 A1 29, 61

close /kləʊz/ v 关闭；歇业 A1 12, 73, 92

close friend 密友 16

closed /kləʊzd/ 歇业的 A2 55

clothes /kləʊðz/ 衣服，穿着 A1 24

clothes shop 服装店 28

clothing /ˈkləʊðɪŋ/ 服装（统称） A2 24

cloud /klaʊd/ 云 A2 37

cloudy /ˈklaʊdi/ 多云的 37

club /klʌb/ 社团 A1 81

coach /kəʊtʃ/ (= bus) 长途汽车 A2 51

coach /kəʊtʃ/ (= in train) （列车）车厢 53

coal /kəʊl/ 煤 B1 34

coast /kəʊst/ 海岸 36

coat /kəʊt/ 外套 A1 24

coffee /ˈkɒfi/ 咖啡 A1 50

coin /kɔɪn/ 硬币 B1 27

cold /kəʊld/ adj 寒冷的 A1 37

cold /kəʊld/ n 感冒 A1 31

colleague /ˈkɒliːg/ 同事 A2 70

collect (stamps, etc.) 收集（邮票，等） A2 81

collect /kəˈlekt/ (= go and get sth) 领取 B1 88, 89

college /ˈkɒlɪdʒ/ 职业学校 A1 67

colour /ˈkʌlə(r)/ 颜色 A1 26

column /ˈkɒləm/ 栏 A2 3

come /kʌm/ 来 A1 39

come from somewhere 来自某地 A1 13

Come on! 赶快！ A2 100

come round 拜访 23, 94

comedy /ˈkɒmədi/ 喜剧 A2 84

comfortable /ˈkʌmftəbl/ 舒适的 A2 26

comma /ˈkɒmə/ 逗号 6

comment /ˈkɒment/ n 评论 A2 44

comment /ˈkɒment/ v 评论 B1 44

common /ˈkɒmən/ 常见的 A1 31, 63

communicate /kəˈmjuːnɪkeɪt/ 交流 A2 13

community /kəˈmjuːnəti/ 社区 A2 71

company /ˈkʌmpəni/ 公司 A1 69

compare (sth with sth) （将某事／物与某事／物）比较 A1 5, 28

competition /ˌkɒmpəˈtɪʃn/ 竞赛 A2 76

complain /kəmˈpleɪn/ 投诉 A2 78

complaint /kəmˈpleɪnt/ 投诉 B1 78

complete /kəmˈpliːt/ v 完成 A1 3

completely different 截然不同 15

computer games 电脑游戏 81

disaster /dɪˈzɑːstə(r)/ 灾难 **A2** 34, 85

disc jockey 音乐节目主持人；打碟师 79

discover /dɪˈskʌvə(r)/ 发现 **A2** 30, 78

discovery /dɪˈskʌvəri/ 发现 **A2** 30, 78

discuss /dɪˈskʌs/ 讨论 **A1** 5, 70

discussion /dɪˈskʌʃn/ 讨论 **A2** 5

dish /dɪʃ/ 碟, 盘 **A1** 48

dishwasher /ˈdɪʃwɒʃə(r)/ 洗碗机 59, 79

dislike /dɪsˈlaɪk/ 厌恶 **B1** 80

divorced /dɪˈvɔːst/ 离婚的 **A2** 16

DJ /ˈdiː dʒeɪ/ 音乐节目主持人；打碟师 79

do /duː/

(= have a job or study sth) 从事；学习 **A1** 13, 41

(an activity) 做（事）**A1** 41, 82

a course 读课程 68

a degree (in sth) 攻读（某专业的）学位课程 68

an exam 参加考试 67

an exercise 做练习题 5, 41

badly /ˈbædli/ 表现糟糕 67

exercise /ˈeksəsaɪz/ 锻炼 41

homework /ˈhəʊmwɜːk/ 做作业 5, 41, 67

research /rɪˈsɜːtʃ/ 进行研究 68

the housework 做家务 41, 59

the ironing 熨衣服 59

the shopping 购物 41

a sport 运动 82

the washing 洗衣服 59

the washing up 刷洗餐具 59

well /wel/ 表现出色 **A2** 67

you know the way to … ? 你认不认识去……的路？54

you mind if I … ? 倘若我……你不介意吧？93

you want to … ? 你想不想做……？94

you want … ? 你想不想要……？95

your best 尽力 41

your hair 梳头 60

doctor /ˈdɒktə(r)/ 医生 **A1** 68

document /ˈdɒkjumənt/ 文件 **A2** 73

dog /dɒg/ 狗 **A1** 38

dollar /ˈdɒlə(r)/ 美元 **A1** 27

don't mind 不在意，无所谓 80

don't worry 别担心 95

door /dɔː(r)/ **A1** 见 **front door** 前门 58

dot /dɒt/ 点 **B2** * 74

double /ˈdʌbl/ 成双的 **A2** 4, 75

double room 双人间 87

down /daʊn/ 向下 **A1** 19

download (music) *v* 下载（音乐）**A2** 83

downstairs /ˌdaʊnˈsteəz/ 顺楼梯而下, 在楼下 **A1** 58

draw with/against sb 与某人打平 82

drawing /ˈdrɔːɪŋ/ 绘画 **A2** 81

dream /driːm/ *n, v* 梦；做梦 **A2** 44

dress /dres/ 连衣裙 **A1** 24

drink /drɪŋk/ *v* 喝 **A1** 39

drink /drɪŋk/ *n* 饮料 **A1** 50

drive /draɪv/ 驾驶 **A1** 39, 51, 76

driver /ˈdraɪvə(r)/ 司机 **A1** 69, 76

driving /ˈdraɪvɪŋ/ 开车 **A2** 77

drop /drɒp/ 使落下 **A2** 12

drug /drʌg/ 药物 **A2** 32

dry /draɪ/ 干燥的 **A2** 37

duck /dʌk/ 鸭子 47

during (the week) 在（工作日）期间 **A1** 23

DVD player 数字影碟播放机 61

each /iːtʃ/ 各个 **A1** 27

each other 互相 **A1** 15, 16

ear /ɪə(r)/ 耳朵 **A1** 10

early /ˈɜːli/ 早的 **A1** 23

earn /ɜːn/ 挣钱 **A2** 27, 70

earth /ɜːθ/ 泥土 **B1** 57

Earth /ɜːθ/ **A2** 见 **planet Earth** 行星地球 84

easily /ˈiːzəli/ 轻松地 65

east /iːst/ *n, adj* 东方；向东的；东部的 **A1** 36

easy /ˈiːzi/ 轻松的 **A1** 65

eat /iːt/ 吃 **A1** 47

education /ˌedʒuˈkeɪʃn/ 教育 **A2** 67

e.g. 例如 3

egg /eg/ 蛋 **A1** 45

Egypt /ˈiːdʒɪpt/ 埃及 35

Egyptian /iˈdʒɪpʃn/ 埃及人 35

eight /eɪt/ 八 **A1** 6

eighteen /ˌeɪˈtiːn/ 十八 **A1** 6

eighteenth /ˌeɪˈtiːnθ/ 第十八 8

eighth /eɪtθ/ 第八 8

eighty /ˈeɪti/ 八十 **A1** 6

either … or 要么……要么…… **A2** 67

electric fan 电风扇 29

electric razor 电动剃须刀 60

electrical store 电器商店 28

electricity /ɪˌlekˈtrɪsəti/ 电 **A2** 34

electronic mail 电子邮件 74

elephant /ˈelɪfənt/ 大象 **A1** 38

eleven /ɪˈlevn/ 十一 **A1** 6

eleventh /ɪˈlevnθ/ 第十一 8

else /els/ **A1** 见 **everyone else** 其他所有人 **A2**, **somewhere/nothing else** 其他地方/别无他物 100

email /ˈiːmeɪl/ *n, v* 电子邮件；（给……）发电子邮件 **A1** 44, 74

embarrassed /ɪmˈbærəst/ 尴尬的 **B1** 17

emotions /ɪˈməʊʃnz/ 情绪 **B1** 17

employ /ɪmˈplɔɪ/ 雇用 **A2** 69

employee /ɪmˈplɔɪiː/ 雇员 **A2** 69

employer /ɪmˈplɔɪə(r)/ 雇主 **A2** 69

empty /ˈempti/ *adj* 空的 **A2**；*v* 清空 **B1** 59

en suite 卧室带浴室的 87

end /end/ **A1** 见 **at/by the end of sth** 在某事/物的结尾 **A1** 21

end /end/ **A1** 见 **in the end** 最终 **A2** 21

energy /ˈenədʒi/ 能量 **A2** 34

engineer /ˌendʒɪˈnɪə(r)/ 工程师 **A2** 68

engineering /ˌendʒɪˈnɪərɪŋ/ 工程学 **B1** 68

England /ˈɪŋglənd/ 英格兰 35

first of all 首先 A2 98

firstly /ˈfɜːstli/ 第一 A2 98

fish /fɪʃ/ 鱼 A1 47

fishing /ˈfɪʃɪŋ/ 钓鱼 A2 81

fit /fɪt/ 合身 26

five /faɪv/ 五 A1 6

fizzy water 气泡水 48, 49

fizzy drink 碳酸饮料 50

flat /flæt/ *adj* 平的 A2 29

flat /flæt/ *n* 公寓 A1 58

flatmate /ˈflætmeɪt/ 合住公寓者 16

flight /flaɪt/ 航班 A1 87

flight attendant 空乘人员 89

floor /flɔː(r)/ 地板 A1 61

flower /ˈflaʊə(r)/ 花 A1 57

flu /fluː/ 流感 A2 31

fly /flaɪ/ *n* (= insect) 苍蝇 A2 38

fly /flaɪ/ *v* 坐飞机出行 A1 87, 90

flying /ˈflaɪɪŋ/ 坐飞机出行 A2 77

follow (instructions) 遵照（指示）A2 5

food /fuːd/ 食物 A1 45, 50

foot /fʊt/ (*pl* **feet**) 脚（复数feet）A1 10

football /ˈfʊtbɔːl/ 足球 A1 82

for /fə(r)/ 达（表示动作或情况持续的时间）A1 9

for example 比如 A1 3

foreign /ˈfɒrən/ 外国的 A2 87

forest /ˈfɒrɪst/ 森林 A1 33

forget /fəˈget/ 忘记 A1 5, 39, 95

fork /fɔːk/ 叉子 A2 48

form /fɔːm/ 表格 A1 71

formal /ˈfɔːml/ 正式的 A2 3, 62

fortunately /ˈfɔːtʃənətli/ 幸运的是 A2 68

forty /ˈfɔːti/ 四十 A1 6

four /fɔː(r)/ 四 A1 6

fourteen /ˌfɔːˈtiːn/ 十四 A1 6

fourteenth /ˌfɔːˈtiːnθ/ 第十四 8

fourth /fɔːθ/ 第四 8

France /frɑːns/ 法国 35

free /friː/ 免费的 A2 27

French /frentʃ/ 法国人；法语 35

fresh /freʃ/ 新鲜的 A2 46

fresh air 新鲜空气 57

Friday /ˈfraɪdeɪ/ 星期五 A1 8

fridge /frɪdʒ/ 冰箱 A2 59

fried /fraɪd/ 油炸的 B1 49

friend /frend/ A1 见 **best friend** 最好的朋友 A1 16

friendly /ˈfrendli/ 友好的 A1 15

from /frəm/ 见 **be from** 来自 13

from … to 从……到…… A1 70

front /frʌnt/ A1 见 **at the front of** 在……前部 21

front /frʌnt/ A1 见 **in front of sth** 在……前方 A1 20

front door 前门 58

frozen /ˈfrəʊzn/ 冰冻的 B1 46

fruit /fruːt/ 水果 A1 46

fruit and vegetable shop 蔬果店 28

fry /fraɪ/ 油炸 B1 49

full /fʊl/ 满的 A1 59

full stop 句号 79

fun /fʌn/ 乐趣 A1 15, 80

funny /ˈfʌni/ 滑稽的，好笑的 A1 15, 84

furniture shop 家具店 28

furniture /ˈfɜːnɪtʃə(r)/ 家具 A2 60

game /ɡeɪm/ A1 见 **play a game** 玩游戏，进行比赛 23, 81, 82

gap /ɡæp/ 空隙 A2 55

garden /ˈɡɑːdn/ 花园 A1 57

gardening /ˈɡɑːdnɪŋ/ 园艺 81

garlic /ˈɡɑːlɪk/ 蒜 46

gas /ɡæs/ 天然气 A2 34

gate /ɡeɪt/ 大门，栅栏门 A2 57

gate /ɡeɪt/ (= at an airport) 登机口 A2 89

general /ˈdʒenrəl/ 大体的 A2 63

geography /dʒiˈɒɡrəfi/ 地理 A1 66

German /ˈdʒɜːmən/ 德国人；德语 35

Germany /ˈdʒɜːməni/ 德国 35

get /ɡet/ A1 39

(= arrive at/in somewhere) 到达 A1 23, 42, 51, 53

(= be given) 得到 A1 42, 67, 74

(= become) 变成 A2 42

(= buy) 购买 A1 42

(= fetch) 去拿来 A1 100

(= travel by sth) 搭乘 A1 42, 52, 53

见 **we/you get** (= there are) 表示存在或发生 100

back /bæk/ (= return) 返回 A2 100

better /ˈbetə(r)/ 好转 A2 31, 100

changed /tʃeɪndʒd/ 换（衣服）100

divorced /dɪˈvɔːst/ 离婚 14

dressed /drest/ 穿衣服 23, 100

in /ɪn/ (= arrive) 到达 B2 100

lost /lɒst/ 迷路 A2 74, 90

married /ˈmærɪd/ 结婚 A1 14, 16

on/off (a train, plane, bus, etc.) 上／下（火车、飞机、公共汽车，等）A1 12, 52, 53, 89

on (well) with sb 与某人（和睦）相处 B1 16

out (of sth) 离开（某物）A2 100

ready /ˈredi/ 做好准备 A1 45, 100

sb (= go and find) 找某人来接电话 A1 75

there /ðeə(r)/ 到那里 A1 51

to know sb 与某人渐渐熟识 B1 16, 100

to sleep 入睡 100

to work 去上班 23

up /ʌp/ 起床 A1 23

gift /ɡɪft/ 礼物 A2 22, 28

gift shop 礼品店 28

girlfriend /ˈɡɜːlfrend/ 女朋友 A1 14, 16

give /ɡɪv/ A1 12

my love to sb 向某人问好 91

sb advice 给某人建议 16

sb a call 给某人打电话 44

sb a smile 对某人微笑 44

sb a surprise 给某人惊喜 44
　　sth up 放弃某事/物 A2 99
glass (of sth) 一杯（某物）A1 48
glasses /ˈglɑːsɪz/ 眼镜 A1 25
gloves /glʌvz/ 手套 B1 25

go /gəʊ/ A1 52

+ -ing A1 82
　　across (the road, a bridge) 通过（道路、桥）19
　　ahead /əˈhed/ (= yes, of course) 开始吧（表示允许）B1 93
　　along (the road) 沿着（道路）走 19
　　along here 沿着（这条路）直行 54
　　and get 去拿来 A2 100
　　away /əˈweɪ/ 走开 A2 99
　　back /bæk/ 返回 A1 99
　　camping /ˈkæmpɪŋ/ 去露营 81
　　by car 乘汽车去 51
　　down (the stairs) 走（楼梯）下去 19
　　down /daʊn/ (= decrease) 下降 A2 99
　　fishing /ˈfɪʃɪŋ/ 去钓鱼 81
　　for (a walk/swim) 去（散步、游泳）A2 23
　　home /həʊm/ 回家 A1 23
　　into (a house, etc.) 进入（房屋，等）A1 19
　　on a guided tour 跟着导游去旅行 90
　　on a trip 去旅行 88
　　on foot 步行去 51
　　over (a bridge) 从（桥）上穿过 19
　　out /aʊt/ 外出；外出娱乐 A1 23, 99
　　out for sth 为了某事/物外出 94
　　out of (a house, etc.) 离开（房屋，等）19
　　out (with sb) （与某人）外出 81
　　out with sb (= have a relationship) 与某人约会 16
　　past (a church, etc.) 路过（教堂，等）19
　　shopping /ˈʃɒpɪŋ/ 去购物 23
　　sightseeing /ˈsaɪtsiːɪŋ/ 去观光 90
　　straight on 径直向前走 54
　　through (a gate) 穿过（大门）19
　　to bed 就寝 A1 23
　　towards (a hill, etc.) 朝（小山，等）前行 19
　　under (a bridge) 从（桥）底下过 19
　　up (the stairs) 走（楼梯）上去 19
　　up /ʌp/ (= increase) 上升 A2 99
　　on holiday 去度假 87
goal /gəʊl/ 进球 A2 82
gold /gəʊld/ 金子 A2 25
golf /gɒlf/ 高尔夫 A2 81
good /gʊd/ 好的 A1 67
good at sth 善于做某事 A1 22, 66, 81
good chance 较大的可能性 96
good fun 很有趣 15
good to meet you 很高兴见到你 91
good-looking /ˌgʊdˈlʊkɪŋ/ 好看的 11
goodbye /ˌgʊdˈbaɪ/ 再见 A1 75
government /ˈgʌvənmənt/ 政府 A2 34
grade /greɪd/ 等第 B1 67
gram /græm/ 克 45

granddaughter /ˈgrændɔːtə(r)/ （外）孙女 14
grandfather /ˈgrænfɑːðə(r)/ （外）祖父 A1 14
grandmother /ˈgrænmʌðə(r)/ （外）祖母 A1 14
grandparents /ˈgrænpeərənts/ （外）祖父母 A1 14
grandson /ˈgrænsʌn/ 孙子，外孙 14
grapes /greɪps/ 葡萄 46
grass /grɑːs/ 草 A2 57
great /greɪt/ 好极的 A1 13, 26, 94
great fun 非常有趣 15
Great Britain 英国 35
Greece /griːs/ 希腊 35
Greek /griːk/ 希腊人；希腊语 35
green /griːn/ 绿色 A1 26
green pepper 青椒 46
greet /griːt/ 问候 A2 91
greeting /ˈgriːtɪŋ/ 问候 n 91
grey /greɪ/ 灰色 A1 11, 26
ground floor 底楼 58
group /gruːp/ (= musical) 乐团 83
grow /grəʊ/ 种植 A1 57
grow up 长大 A1 99
guess /ges/ n, v 猜测 A1 5
Guess what? 你猜怎么着？A1 100
guess /ges/ A1 见 I guess so 我想是的 A2 100
guest /gest/ 宾客 A2 88
guide /gaɪd/ n 向导 A2 90
guidebook /ˈgaɪdbʊk/ 旅游指南 90
guided tour 跟着导游的旅行 90
guitar /gɪˈtɑː(r)/ 吉他 A1 81
gun /gʌn/ 枪 A2 29
gym /dʒɪm/ 健身房 A1 81
hair /heə(r)/ 头发 A1 10
hairdresser /ˈheədresə(r)/ 理发师 69
half /hɑːf/ 一半 A1 45
half past (one, etc.) 半点（一点半，等）7
half-time /ˌhɑːf ˈtaɪm/ 中场休息时间 82
hall /hɔːl/ 门厅 A2 58
ham /hæm/ 火腿 47
hand /hænd/ 手 A1 10
hand luggage 随身行李 89
handbag /ˈhændbæg/ 手提包 25
handsome /ˈhænsəm/ 英俊的 11
happen /ˈhæpən/ 发生 A1 30, 85
happily /ˈhæpɪli/ 高兴地 A2 65
happy /ˈhæpi/ 高兴的 A1 17
hard /hɑːd/ adj (= difficult) 困难的 A1 65
hard /hɑːd/ adj (= not soft) 坚硬的 A2 63
hard /hɑːd/ adv (= a lot) 大量地 A1 65, 67
hardworking /ˌhɑːdˈwɜːkɪŋ/ 刻苦的 15, 63
hat /hæt/ 帽子 A1 25
hate /heɪt/ 厌恶 A1 80

have /həv/ A1 40

(= eat/drink) 吃，喝 A1 50
　　a good/great day 祝你度过愉快的一天 40
　　a good/great time 玩得开心 40

a good/great weekend/holiday/journey 周末／
假期／旅途快乐 40
a baby 生孩子 16
a bath 洗澡 40
a break 休息一下 40
a chat 聊一聊 44
a dream 做梦 44
a drink /sth to eat 喝饮料／吃东西 40
a fight 打斗 44
a guess 猜一猜 5
a look (at sth) 看一看（某物） 40, 44
an argument 争论 78
a rest 休息一下 40
a run 跑步 40
a seat 就座 50
a shave 刮胡子 60
a sleep 睡一觉 44
a (nice) smell 有气味（闻起来香） 44
a swim 游泳 40
a thought 有一个想法 78
a wash 洗（澡／脸／手, 等） 40, 60
a shower 洗澡 23, 40
a walk 散步 40
breakfast /ˈbrekfəst/ 吃早餐 23, 40
got (an illness) 染上（疾病） 31
got (family) 有（家人） 14
got /ɡɒt/ 拥有 A1 40, 45
got to do sth 不得不做某事 A2 91
dinner /ˈdɪnə(r)/ 吃晚餐 23, 40
lunch /lʌntʃ/ 吃午餐 23, 40
to do 不得不做 59, 88

head /hed/ 头 A1 10
headache /ˈhedeɪk/ 头痛 A2 31
health /helθ/ 健康 A1 31
healthy /ˈhelθi/ 健康的 A1 31, 62
hear /hɪə(r)/ 听 A1 85
hear about sth 听说某事／物 A2 22
heart /hɑːt/ 心脏 A2 10
heavy /ˈhevi/ (= not light) 重的 A2 63
heavy rain 大雨 37
height /haɪt/ 身高 A2 11
help /help/ v 帮助 A1 4, 13, 95
help /help/ n 帮助 A1 95
helpful /ˈhelpfl/ 有用的 A2 88
here /hɪə(r)/ A1 见 go along here 沿此路直行 54
here /hɪə(r)/ A1 见 over here 在这里 53
hero /ˈhɪərəʊ/ 男主角 A2 84
heroine /ˈherəʊɪn/ 女主角 84
hi /haɪ/ 你好 A1 91
high /haɪ/ 高的 A1 63
high /haɪ/ A1 见 3,000m high 3000米高 36
high street 主要商业街 B1 79
hill /hɪl/ 小山 A2 57
Hindi /ˈhɪndi/ 印地语 35
history /ˈhɪstri/ 历史 A1 66
hit /hɪt/ v 碰撞 A2 32, 39

hit /hɪt/ n 风行一时的事物 A2 83
hobby /ˈhɒbi/ 爱好 A1 81
hold /həʊld/ 抱住 A2 12, 39
holiday /ˈhɒlədeɪ/ 假期 A1 87
home /həʊm/ 家 A1 58
homework /ˈhəʊmwɜːk/ 家庭作业 A1 5, 41, 59
hope /həʊp/ A1 见 I hope so / I hope not 希望/并非
如此 96
hope to see you again 希望能再见到你 91
horror film 恐怖片 84
horse /hɔːs/ 马 A1 38
hospital /ˈhɒspɪtl/ 医院 A1 70
hot /hɒt/ 热的 A1 37
hot chocolate 巧克力热饮 50
hour /ˈaʊə(r)/ 小时 A1 70
house /haʊs/ 房屋 A1 58
housework /ˈhaʊswɜːk/ 家务 41, 59

how /haʊ/

are things? 过得怎么样？ 91
are you? 你好吗？ A1 91
do I get to … ? 去……该怎么走？ 54
do you do? 你好 91
do you say … ? ……怎么说？ 4
far /fɑː(r)/ 多远 51, 92
long /lɒŋ/ 多久 A1 13, 52, 68, 92
many /ˈmeni/ 多少 A1 45, 92
much /mʌtʃ/ 多少；多少钱 A1 44, 45, 92
often /ˈɒfn/ 多长时间一次 A1 92
old /əʊld/ 多大年纪 13
tall /tɔːl/ 多高 11
however /haʊˈevə(r)/ 然而 A1 97
huge /hjuːdʒ/ 巨大的 A2 36
human /ˈhjuːmən/ 人 A2 33
hundred /ˈhʌndrəd/ 一百 A1 6
Hungarian /hʌŋˈɡeəriən/ 匈牙利人；匈牙利语 35
Hungary /ˈhʌŋɡəri/ 匈牙利 35
hungry /ˈhʌŋɡri/ 饥饿的 A1 17
hurry up 赶快 100
hurt /hɜːt/ 伤害 A2 32, 39
husband /ˈhʌzbənd/ 丈夫 A1 14, 16

I /aɪ/

don't think so 我不这样认为 96
guess so 我想是的 A2 100
hope so 希望如此 96
hope not 希望不要 96
suppose so 我想是的 100
think so 我想是的 A2 96
'd like 我想要 50
'd love to 我很乐意 94
'll have (when ordering) （用于点餐）我要 49
'm afraid (not) 很遗憾（不行） A2 87, 93
'm afraid I can't 很遗憾, 我不能 94
'm fine, thanks 我很好, 谢谢 95
'm not sure 我不确定 94

'm sorry but ... 很抱歉，但…… 94
'm sorry I'm late 抱歉，我迟到了 95
ice /aɪs/ (= weather) 冰 A1 37
ice /aɪs/ (= in a drink) 冰块 A1 50
ice cream 冰淇淋 A1 49
ice hockey 冰球 82
icy /ˈaɪsi/ 冰冷的 37
idea /aɪˈdɪə/ 想法 A1 92
idea /aɪˈdɪə/ A1 见 that's a great idea 好主意 94
ideal /aɪˈdiːəl/ 理想的 A2 90
identity card 身份证 79
if /ɪf/ A1 见 Do you mind if / Is it OK if ... ?
倘若……你介意吗? / ……可以吗? 93
ill /ɪl/ 生病的, 不舒服的 A2 31
illness /ˈɪlnəs/ 疾病 A2 31
immediately /ɪˈmiːdiətli/ 立即 A2 23
impolite /ˌɪmpəˈlaɪt/ 不礼貌的 62
impossible /ɪmˈpɒsəbl/ 不可能的 A2 62, 96
improve /ɪmˈpruːv/ 完善 A1 13, 31
improvement /ɪmˈpruːvmənt/ 完善 B1 13

in /ɪn/

(a place) 在(某地) A1 20
(sth with walls or sides) 在某物的内部 A1 20
(= at home) 在家 A2 75
(a big area) 位于(面积大的地区) A1 20
2020, etc. 在2020年, 等 A1 18
(ten) days (十)天内 A1 9
fact /fækt/ 事实上 A1 21, 86
front of sth 在某物的前方 A1 20
hospital /ˈhɒspɪtl/ 住院 A2 21
January, etc. 在一月, 等 A1 18
love /lʌv/ 恋爱中 A2 17
order to do sth 为了做某事 B1 98
pain /peɪn/ 处于痛苦中 17, 32
prison /ˈprɪzn/ 坐牢 A2 21
the back of sth 在某物的后部 21
the end 最终 A2 21
the middle of sth 在某物的中部 21
the morning, etc. 在上午, 等 A1 18
the (news)paper 刊登在报纸上 85
the past 过去 A1 86
(the) spring, etc. 在春天, 等 A1 18
trouble /ˈtrʌbl/ 遇到麻烦 86
include /ɪnˈkluːd/ 包括 A1 87
included /ɪnˈkluːdɪd/ 包含在内的 A2 87
including /ɪnˈkluːdɪŋ/ 其中包括 A2 86
increase /ɪnˈkriːs/ n, v 增加 A2 34
incredible /ɪnˈkredəbl/ 难以置信的 A2 72, 80
indefinite article 不定冠词 2
India /ˈɪndiə/ 印度 35
Indian /ˈɪndiən/ 印度人 35
industry /ˈɪndəstri/ 行业 A2 36
informal /ɪnˈfɔːml/ 非正式的 A2 3, 62
information /ˌɪnfəˈmeɪʃn/ 信息 A1 13, 74
injury /ˈɪndʒəri/ 伤害 A2 32

insect /ˈɪnsekt/ 昆虫 A2 38
inside /ˌɪnˈsaɪd/ 在……里面 A2 10, 58
instead /ɪnˈsted/ 作为替代 A2 49
instruct /ɪnˈstrʌkt/ 指导 C1 76
instructions /ɪnˈstrʌkʃnz/ 指示 A2 5
instructor /ɪnˈstrʌktə(r)/ 指导者 A2 76
instrument /ˈɪnstrəmənt/ (= musical) 乐器 A2 83
intelligent /ɪnˈtelɪdʒənt/ 智慧的 A2 15
interested (in sth) (对某事 / 物)感兴趣的 A1 22, 80
interesting /ˈɪntrəstɪŋ/ 有趣的 A1 80
international /ˌɪntəˈnæʃnəl/ 国际的 A2 60
internet /ˈɪntənet/ 互联网 A1 74
interview /ˈɪntəvjuː/ n, v 面试 A1 71
interviewer /ˈɪntəvjuːə(r)/ 面试官 71
into /ˈɪntə/ 到……里面 A1 19
introduce sb (to sb) (给某人)介绍某人 A1 91
introduction /ˌɪntrəˈdʌkʃn/ 介绍 A2 91
invent /ɪnˈvent/ 编造; 创造 A2 5, 78
invention /ɪnˈvenʃn/ 发明 A2 78
invitation /ˌɪnvɪˈteɪʃn/ 邀请 A2 94
invite /ɪnˈvaɪt/ 邀请 A2 94
involve /ɪnˈvɒlv/ 包含 A2 70
Ireland /ˈaɪələnd/ 爱尔兰 35
ironing /ˈaɪənɪŋ/ 熨烫 59
irregular /ɪˈreɡjələ(r)/ 不规则的 2, 62
Is it OK / all right if ... ? 如果……可以吗? 93
Is that everything? 还要别的吗? 50
Is that ... ? (= on the phone) (通话中)是……吗? 75
Is there ... near here? 这里附近有……吗? 54
island /ˈaɪlənd/ 岛屿 A1 33
it doesn't matter 没关系 87, 95
IT manager 信息技术主管 68
Italian /ɪˈtæljən/ 意大利人; 意大利语 35
Italy /ˈɪtəli/ 意大利 35
item of clothing 衣物 24
jacket /ˈdʒækɪt/ 夹克衫 A1 24
jam /dʒæm/ 果酱 A2 45
January /ˈdʒænjuəri/ 一月 A1 8
Japan /dʒəˈpæn/ 日本 35
Japanese /ˌdʒæpəˈniːz/ 日本人; 日语 35
jazz /dʒæz/ 爵士乐 A2 80
jeans /dʒiːnz/ 牛仔裤 A1 24
jewellery /ˈdʒuːəlri/ 珠宝 A2 25
job /dʒɒb/ 职业 A1 13, 67, 69
journalism /ˈdʒɜːnəlɪzəm/ 新闻学 B2* 68
journalist /ˈdʒɜːnəlɪst/ 记者 A2 68, 85
journey /ˈdʒɜːni/ 旅行 A1 51, 53
juice /dʒuːs/ A1 见 orange juice 橙汁 50
July /dʒuˈlaɪ/ 七月 A1 8
jump /dʒʌmp/ 跳 A2 12
jumper /ˈdʒʌmpə(r)/ 针织套衫 24
June /dʒuːn/ 六月 A1 8
just /dʒʌst/ 刚才 A1 9
just a moment 稍等一下 75
just before / after 就在……之前 / 后 7
just over / under 刚好高 / 低于…… 36, 45

keep /ki:p/ 存放 A1 73

keep a record of sth 记录某事/物 4

keep /ki:p/ A1 见 keep warm 保暖 31

keep going 径直向前走 54

keep left/right 靠左/右行驶 55

keep off 不要靠近 55

key /ki:/ 钥匙 A1 58, 88

keyboard /ˈki:bɔ:d/ 键盘 B1 73

kill /kɪl/ 杀死 A2 30

kilo (gram) 千克 45

kilometre /ˈkɪləmi:tə(r)/ 千米, 公里 A1 36

kilometres (per hour) （每小时所行）公里数 51

kind /kaɪnd/ 善良的 B1 15

kind /kaɪnd/ A1 见 What kind of … ? 是哪一种……?
84, 92

kitchen /ˈkɪtʃɪn/ 厨房 A1 58

knee /ni:/ 膝盖 A2 10

knife /naɪf/ 刀 A2 48

knock /nɒk/ 敲击 B1 32

know /nəʊ/ 认识 A1 4, 16

Korean /kəˈri:ən/ 韩国人, 朝鲜人；韩语, 朝鲜语 35

kph /ˌkeɪ pi: ˈeɪtʃ/ 每小时所行公里数 51

lake /leɪk/ 湖 A2 57

lamb /læm/ 羔羊 47

lamp /læmp/ 灯 A2 60

land /lænd/ v 着陆 A2 89

land /lænd/ n 陆地 A1 34

landline /ˈlændlaɪn/ 固定电话 75

language /ˈlæŋgwɪdʒ/ 语言 A1 35, 66

laptop /ˈlæptɒp/ 笔记本电脑 A2 73

large /lɑ:dʒ/ 大的 A1 26

last (stop) 最后的（终点站） A1 52, 53

last /lɑ:st/ v 持续 A2 68

last year A1 /week/night, etc. 去年/上周/昨晚, 等 9

late /leɪt/ adv, adj 迟, 晚 A1 23, 65

late /leɪt/ A1 见 in your late thirties 在你三十七、
八岁时 30

later /ˈleɪtə(r)/ A1 见 see you later 回头见 91

Latin America 拉丁美洲 35

laugh /lɑ:f/ 笑 A1 15

law /lɔ:/ 法律 A2 68

lawyer /ˈlɔ:jə(r)/ 律师 A2 68

lazy /ˈleɪzi/ 懒惰的 A2 15, 63

lead /li:d/ v 领先 B1 82

leather /ˈleðə(r)/ 皮革 B1 25

leave /li:v/ 离开 A1 53, 89

leave a message 留言 75

leave home 离家 23

leave school 毕业离校 67

leave sth somewhere 把某物落在某地 88

lecture /ˈlektʃə(r)/ 讲座 A2 68

lecturer /ˈlektʃərə(r)/ 讲师 68

left /left/ (= not right) 朝左边 A1 54

leg /leg/ 腿 A1 10

lemon /ˈlemən/ 柠檬 A2 46, 50

lend /lend/ 出借 A2 39, 93

lesson /ˈlesn/ 课 A1 67

let /let/ 允许 A1 39, 55

let me … 请让我…… A2 95

let sb know 告诉某人 A2 100

let's /lets/ 让我们 84

letter /ˈletə(r)/ 信件 A1 74

lettuce /ˈletɪs/ 生菜 46

level /ˈlevl/ 等级 B1 13

library /ˈlaɪbrəri/ 图书馆 A1 56, 68

lie down 躺下 12, 99

lift /lɪft/ 电梯 A2 58

light /laɪt/ (= not heavy) 轻的 A2 63

light /laɪt/ n 灯 A1 61

light blue 浅蓝色 26

like /laɪk/ (= similar to) prep 与……相似 A1 4

like /laɪk/ v 喜欢 A1 80, 81

like /laɪk/ A1 见 What's he/she like? 他/她是个什么
样的人? 15

likely (to) 很可能 A2 96

line /laɪn/ (= of a phone) 电话线路 A2 75

line /laɪn/ (= of writing) 字行 A1 73

link /lɪŋk/ 链接 A2 74

lion /ˈlaɪən/ 狮子 A1 38

listen /ˈlɪsn/ 听 A1 22, 76, 85

listener /ˈlɪsənə(r)/ 听者 A2 76

literature /ˈlɪtrətʃə(r)/ 文学 B1 66

little /ˈlɪtl/ 小的 A1 26

live /lɪv/ (= happening now) 现场的 B1 83

live with sb 与某人一起生活 A1 22

living room 客厅 A1 58

lock /lɒk/ 锁 A2 58

long /lɒŋ/ (= not short) 长的 A1 11, 26

long /lɒŋ/ A1 见 20km long 20公里长 36

long hours 长时间 70

look /lʊk/ n 看 A2 44

look /lʊk/ v 看 A1 44

look nice/great, etc. 看上去不错/很好, 等 26

look after sth/sb 料理某事/物, 照顾某人 59, 100

look at sb/sth 看着某人, 查看某事/物 A1 22, 74

look round 参观 90

look sth up 查询某事/物 A2 5, 99

lorry /ˈlɒri/ 卡车 A2 51

lorry driver 卡车司机 69

lose (to sb) 被（某人）打败 A1 39, 82, 95

lose weight 减肥 11

lost /lɒst/ A2 见 get lost A2; be lost 丢失, 迷路 74, 90

loudly /ˈlaʊdli/ 响亮地 A2 65

love /lʌv/ v 热爱 A1 80

love /lʌv/ n 爱情 A1 17

love story 爱情片 84

lovely /ˈlʌvli/ 优美的; 极好的 A2 11, 26, 94

low /ləʊ/ 低的, 矮的 A2 63

lucky /ˈlʌki/ 幸运的 A2 62

luggage /ˈlʌgɪdʒ/ 行李 89

lunch /lʌntʃ/ A1 见 have lunch 吃午餐 23, 40

machine /məˈʃi:n/ 机器 89

made of sth 由某物制成 22

magazine /ˈmæɡəˈziːn/ 杂志 85

main character 主角 86

main course 主菜 49

main road 主干道 51

mainly /ˈmeɪnli/ 主要地 **B1** 86

major /ˈmeɪdʒə(r)/ 主要的；重要的；大的 **A2** 30, 36

make /meɪk/

(= produce/create) 制造 **A1** 41

(= produce a change) 使……变得 **A1** 41

a call 打电话 75, 88

a choice 做选择 78

a comment 评论 44

a complaint 投诉 78

a copy 复印 44, 73

a decision 做决定 41

a discovery 发现 78

a mistake 犯错 **A2** 41

an arrangement 安排 78

a noise 发出噪声 41

a promise 承诺 44

money /ˈmʌni/ 赚钱 **A2** 41

sense /sens/ 讲得通 **A2** 41

sure /ʃʊə(r)/ 确保 **A2** 93

the bed 铺床 41

sth up 编造某事 **B1** 5

make-up /ˈmeɪk ʌp/ 化妆品 **B2*** 60

manage /ˈmænɪdʒ/ 管理 **A2** 70

manager /ˈmænɪdʒə(r)/ 经理 **A2** 70

manner /ˈmænə(r)/ 方式 **A2** 65

many /ˈmeni/ **A1** 见 how many 多少 **A1** 45, 92

map /mæp/ 地图 **A1** 90

March /mɑːtʃ/ 三月 **A1** 8

mark /mɑːk/ n 分数 **B1** 67

market /ˈmɑːkɪt/ 市场 **A1** 56

married /ˈmærid/ 已婚的 **A1** 13

match /mætʃ/ n 比赛 **A1** 82

match /mætʃ/ v 配对 **A1** 3

material /məˈtɪəriəl/ 材料 **A2** 29

mathematics /ˌmæθəˈmætɪks/ 数学 **A2** 66

maths /mæθs/ 数学 **A2** 66

matter /ˈmætə(r)/ **A2** 见 it doesn't matter 没关系 15, 87, 95

matter /ˈmætə(r)/ **A2** 见 What's the matter? （用于询问情况）怎么了？ 31

May /meɪ/ 五月 **A1** 8

may /meɪ/ 也许 **A2** 96

maybe /ˈmeɪbi/ 也许 **A1** 94, 96

meal /miːl/ 一餐 **A1** 49

mean /miːn/ 表示……的意思 **A1** 4

meaning /ˈmiːnɪŋ/ 意思 **A1** 4

meat /miːt/ 肉 **A1** 47

media /ˈmiːdiə/ 媒体 **A2** 85

medical /ˈmedɪkl/ 医疗的 **A2** 31

medicine /ˈmedsn/ 药物 **A2** 28, 68

meet /miːt/ (= for the first time) 遇见 **A1** 16, 70

meet /miːt/ (= go somewhere and wait for sb) 迎接 **A1** 16

meeting /ˈmiːtɪŋ/ 会议 **A1** 70

member /ˈmembə(r)/ 成员 **A1** 30

memory /ˈmeməri/ 记忆 **A2** 29

menu /ˈmenjuː/ (= in a restaurant) （饭店）菜单 **A1** 49

menu /ˈmenjuː/ (= on a computer) （计算机）菜单 **A1** 73

message /ˈmesɪdʒ/ n 消息；短信 **A2** 74, 75

message /ˈmesɪdʒ/ v 给……发短信 75

metal /ˈmetl/ 金属 **A2** 29

metre high ……米高 36

Mexican /ˈmeksɪkən/ 墨西哥人 35

Mexico /ˈmeksɪkəʊ/ 墨西哥 35

mice /maɪs/ (= animal) 老鼠（复数） **A1** 38

mice /maɪs/ (of a computer) 鼠标（复数） 73

midday /ˌmɪdˈdeɪ/ 中午 7

middle-aged /ˈmɪdlˈeɪdʒd/ 中年的 11

Middle East 中东 35

midnight /ˈmɪdnaɪt/ 午夜 **A1** 7

might /maɪt/ 也许 **A2** 87, 96

miles per hour, mph 每小时所行英里数 51

milk /mɪlk/ 牛奶 **A1** 45, 50

million /ˈmɪljən/ 百万 **A1** 6

mind /maɪnd/ **A2** 见 Do you mind if … ? 倘若……你不介意吧？ 93

mind /maɪnd/ **A2** 见 I don't mind 我无所谓 80

mind /maɪnd/ (= be careful) 当心 **B1** 55

mine /maɪn/ 我的 **A2** 92

minus /ˈmaɪnəs/ 减 6

minutes past/to 过/差几分钟 7

mirror /ˈmɪrə(r)/ 镜子 **A2** 60

miss (a train) 错过（列车） **A1** 53

missing /ˈmɪsɪŋ/ 缺失的 **A2** 3

mistake /mɪˈsteɪk/ **A1** 见 make a mistake **A2** 犯错 3, 41

mobile phone 手机 **A1** 29, 75

mobile number 手机号码 75

model /ˈmɒdl/ 模特 **A2** 69

modern /ˈmɒdn/ 现代的；新式的 **A1** 36, 58, 63, 80

moment /ˈməʊmənt/ **A1** 见 at the moment **A1** 当时 18, 21, 75

moment /ˈməʊmənt/ **A1** 见 just a moment 稍等一下 75

Monday /ˈmʌndeɪ/ 星期一 **A1** 8

monkey /ˈmʌŋki/ 猴子 **A2** 38

month /mʌnθ/ 月份 **A1** 8

moon /muːn/ 月亮 **A2** 7

more /mɔː(r)/ **A1** 见 any more 再也（不） 29

more /mɔː(r)/ **A1** 见 some more 再来一些 49

morning /ˈmɔːnɪŋ/ **A1** 见 in the morning **A1** 在上午 7

most (of sth) （某事/物的）大部分 **A1** 85

mostly /ˈməʊstli/ 主要地 **A2** 86

mother /ˈmʌðə(r)/ 母亲 **A1** 14

motor racing 赛车 82

motorbike /ˈməʊtəbaɪk/ 摩托车 51

motorcycle /ˈməʊtəsaɪkl/ 摩托车 A2 51

motorway /ˈməʊtəweɪ/ 高速公路 51

mountain /ˈmaʊntən/ 山 A1 36

mouse /maʊs/ (pl mice) (= animal) 老鼠 (单数) A1 38

mouse /maʊs/ (pl mice) (= of a computer) 鼠标 (单数) A1 73

mouth /maʊθ/ 嘴 A1 10

move /muːv/ 移动 A1 73, 78

movement /ˈmuːvmənt/ 移动 A2 78

movie /ˈmuːvi/ 电影 A1 84

much /mʌtʃ/ A1 见 how much A1 多少；多少钱 44, 45

much /mʌtʃ/ A1 见 thanks very much 十分感谢 54, 95

mum /mʌm/ 妈妈 A1 14

museum /mjuˈziːəm/ 博物馆 A1 56

mushroom /ˈmʌʃrʊm/ 蘑菇 46

music shop 音像店 28

musical instrument 乐器 83

musician /mjuˈzɪʃn/ 音乐家 A2 83

name /neɪm/ v 说出……的名字 A1 30

narrow /ˈnærəʊ/ 狭窄的 A2 63

national /ˈnæʃnəl/ 国家的 A2 60

nationality /ˌnæʃəˈnæləti/ 民族 35

natural /ˈnætʃrəl/ 自然的 A1 57

nature /ˈneɪtʃə(r)/ 自然 A2 57

near /nɪə(r)/ 附近的；在……附近 A1 20, 52, 54

nearest /ˈnɪə(r)ɪst/ 最近的 54, 92

nearly /ˈnɪəli/ 将近 A2 7

necessary /ˈnesəsəri/ 必要的 A2 62

neck /nek/ 脖子 A2 10

necklace /ˈnekləs/ 项链 25

need /niːd/ v 需要 A1 45, 95

negative /ˈneɡətɪv/ 消极的 A1 63

neighbour /ˈneɪbə(r)/ 邻居 A1 58

nephew /ˈnefjuː/ 侄子，外甥 14

nervous /ˈnɜːvəs/ 紧张的 A2 17

never /ˈnevə(r)/ 从不 A1 23

never mind 没关系 95

new /njuː/ 新的 A1 80

news /njuːz/ A1 见 the news 新闻报道 A1 85

New Year's Day 元旦 8

newspaper /ˈnjuːzpeɪpə(r)/ 报纸 A1 85

next (stop) 下一 (站) A1 52, 53

next to 紧邻 A1 20

next week/Thursday/year, etc. 下周/下周四/明年，等 A1 9

nice /naɪs/ 不错的 A1 15, 26

nice to meet you 很高兴见到你 91

niece /niːs/ 侄女，外甥女 14

night /naɪt/ A1 见 at night 在夜里 7, 18

night /naɪt/ A1 见 last night 昨天夜里 9

nil /nɪl/ 零 82

nine /naɪn/ 九 A1 6

nineteen /ˌnaɪnˈtiːn/ 十九 A1 6

ninety /ˈnaɪnti/ 九十 A1 6

nineteenth /ˌnaɪnˈtiːnθ/ 第十九 8

ninth /naɪnθ/ 第九 8

no problem 没问题 A1 54, 93

no smoking 禁止吸烟 55

no, thanks / thank you 不需要, 谢谢 50, 95

no vacancies 没有空房 55

noise /nɔɪz/ 噪音 A2 56

noisy /ˈnɔɪzi/ 吵闹的 A2 56

non-fiction /ˌnɒn ˈfɪkʃn/ 非虚构作品 86

none (of sth) 毫无 (某事/物) A2 85

noon /nuːn/ 正午 7

normally /ˈnɔːməli/ 通常 A2 23

north /nɔːθ/ n, adj 北方；向北的；北部的 A1 36

North America 北美洲 35

north-east /ˌnɔːθ ˈiːst/ 东北 36

north-west /ˌnɔːθ ˈwest/ 西北 36

Northern Ireland 北爱尔兰 35

nose /nəʊz/ 鼻子 A1 10

not bad 不错 91

not sure 不确定 4

note /nəʊt/ (= money) 纸币 B1 27

notebook /ˈnəʊtbʊk/ 笔记本 B2* 1, 4

nothing else 别无他物 100

notice /ˈnəʊtɪs/ n 告示 A2 1, 55

notice /ˈnəʊtɪs/ v 注意到 A2 22

noticeboard /ˈnəʊtɪsbɔːd/ 公告牌 1

noun /naʊn/ 名词 2

novel /ˈnɒvl/ 小说 A2 86

November /nəʊˈvembə(r)/ 十一月 A1 8

now /naʊ/ A1 见 right now 此刻；立刻 A1 100

nowhere /ˈnəʊweə(r)/ 哪里都不 A2 33

number /ˈnʌmbə(r)/ (= phone) 电话号码 A1 75

nurse /nɜːs/ 护士 A1 69

nuts /nʌts/ 坚果 A2 46

o'clock /əˈklɒk/ ……点钟 A1 7

ocean /ˈəʊʃn/ 海洋 A2 36

October /ɒkˈtəʊbə(r)/ 十月 A1 8

of course 当然 A1 49, 93

off /ɒf/ B1 见 50% off 半价 27

offer /ˈɒfə(r)/ n, v 提供 A2 71, 95

office /ˈɒfɪs/ 办公室 A1 70

often /ˈɒfn/ 时常 A1 23

oh /əʊ/ (= zero) 零 75

oh! /əʊ/ （表示惊奇、痛苦等情绪）啊，唉！ A1 91

Oh dear! 我的天啊！ A2 87, 91

oil /ɔɪl/ 油 A2 48

OK /əʊˈkeɪ/ A1 见 Is it OK if … ? ……可以吗？ 93

OK /əʊˈkeɪ/ A1 见 that's OK 没问题 54

old /əʊld/ 旧的，年代久远的 A1 58, 80

old friend 老朋友 A2 16

older than 比……年纪大 14

oldest /ˈəʊldɪst/ 见 the oldest 年纪最大的 14

olive oil 橄榄油 45

olive /ˈɒlɪv/ 油橄榄 45

on /ɒn/

1st January, etc. 在1月1日，等 A1 18

foot /fʊt/ 徒步 51

his/her, etc. mobile 他／她在用手机通话 21
holiday /ˈhɒlədeɪ/ 度假中 A1 21, 87
Monday, etc. evening 在星期一等晚上 A1 18
my/your, etc. own 单独，独自 B1 15
(something long/flat) 在（平或长的物体）上 A1 20
the coast 在沿海地区 A2 20
the corner 在拐角处 54
the ground/first/second/top floor 在底／二／三／顶楼 58
the phone 在打电话 A1 21, 75
the river 在河面上 20
the road 在道路上 20
the side of sth / the other side 在某物的（另）一边；在某事的（另）一方面 A2 21
the table 在桌上 20
the wall 在墙上 A2 20
time /taɪm/ 准时 A2 21
tour /tʊə(r)/ 巡回演出中 83
TV A1 / the radio 在电视／台（节目）中 85
your right/left 在你的右／左手边 54
once /wʌns/ A1 见 once a A1 (week) 每（周）一次 23
one /wʌn/ 一 A1 6
onion /ˈʌnjən/ 洋葱 A1 46
online /ˌɒnˈlaɪn/ 在线的 A1 27, 28, 74
only /ˈəʊnli/ 仅仅 A1 64
open /ˈəʊpən/ 打开；开张 A1 12, 92
open (a document) 打开（文件） A1 73
opera singer 歌剧演唱家 83
opinion /əˈpɪnjən/ 意见 A1 56, 85
opposite /ˈɒpəzɪt/ 反义词；在……对面 A1 3, 4, 20, 54
option /ˈɒpʃn/ 选项 A2 67
orange /ˈɒrɪndʒ/ (= colour) 橙色 A1 26
orange /ˈɒrɪndʒ/ (= fruit) 橙，橘 A1 46
orange juice 橙汁 50
orchestra /ˈɔːkɪstrə/ 管弦乐队 B2 * 83
order /ˈɔːdə(r)/ v 点（菜） A1 49
order /ˈɔːdə(r)/ A1 见 Are you ready to order? 现在可以点菜吗？ 49
organization /ˌɔːɡənaɪˈzeɪʃn/ 组织 A2 78
organize /ˈɔːɡənaɪz/ 组织 A2 70, 78
other /ˈʌðə(r)/ A1 见 each other 互相 A1 15, 16
out /aʊt/ (= not at home) 外出 A1 75
out loud 出声地 4
out of (a place) 离开（某地） A1 19
out of order 出故障 55
outside /ˌaʊtˈsaɪd/ (= in front of sth) 在……前 A2 52
outside /ˌaʊtˈsaɪd/ (= not inside) 在……外面 A2 58
oven /ˈʌvn/ 烤箱 A2 59
over /ˈəʊvə(r)/ (= direction) 穿过 A1 19
over /ˈəʊvə(r)/ (= more than) 超过 A1 36
over here 在这里 53
over there 在那里 A1 53
overweight /ˌəʊvəˈweɪt/ 超重的 11
own /əʊn/ 见 on my own 单独 B1 15
own /əʊn/ v 拥有 A2 57, 76
owner /ˈəʊnə(r)/ 拥有者 A2 57, 76

pack /pæk/ 打包，装箱 A2 87
pain /peɪn/ 疼痛 A2 32
painting /ˈpeɪntɪŋ/ 画油画 A1 77, 81
pair /peə(r)/ A1 见 a pair of shoes 一双鞋 25
palace /ˈpæləs/ 宫殿 A2 56
paper /ˈpeɪpə(r)/ 报纸 A1 85
paragraph /ˈpærəɡrɑːf/ 段落 A1 5
parent /ˈpeərənt/ 父／母亲 A1 14
park /pɑːk/ 公园 A1 56
park /pɑːk/ v 停（车） A1 58
parking /ˈpɑːkɪŋ/ 停车（位） A2 55, 58, 87
part of speech 词性 2
part of sth 某事／物的一部分 A1 72
particular /pəˈtɪkjələ(r)/ 特定的 A2 28
partner /ˈpɑːtnə(r)/ 伴侣 A1 16
party /ˈpɑːti/ 聚会 A1 94
pass (an exam) 通过（考试） A2 67
passenger /ˈpæsɪndʒə(r)/ 乘客 A2 53, 89
passport /ˈpɑːspɔːt/ 护照 A1 87
password /ˈpɑːswɜːd/ 密码 B2 * 74
past /pɑːst/ (= direction) 经过 A2 19
past /pɑːst/ A1 见 half past 半点 7
past participle 过去分词 2, 79
past simple 一般过去式 2
past tense 过去时 79
pasta /ˈpæstə/ 意大利面 45, 48
patient /ˈpeɪʃnt/ 耐心的 B2 15
pay /peɪ/ 支付 A1 27, 88
pay attention 注意 A2 5
pay for sth 为某事／物付费 A1 22
PC /ˌpiː ˈsiː/ (= personal computer) 个人计算机 73
PE /ˌpiː ˈiː/ (= Physical Education) 体育 66
peace /piːs/ 和平 A2 85
peach /piːtʃ/ 桃子 46
pear /peə(r)/ 梨 46
peas /piːz/ 豌豆 46
pen /pen/ （钢）笔 A1 1
pencil /ˈpensl/ 铅笔 A1 1
pepper /ˈpepə(r)/ (= black pepper) （黑）胡椒粉 A1 48
pepper /ˈpepə(r)/ 见 red/green pepper 红／青辣椒 46
per cent 百分之…… A2 27
perfect /ˈpɜːfɪkt/ 完美的 A1 13, 90
perform /pəˈfɔːm/ 演出 A2 83
performance /pəˈfɔːməns/ 演出 B1 83
performer /pəˈfɔːmə(r)/ 表演者 83
perhaps /pəˈhæps/ 也许 A2 94, 96
permission /pəˈmɪʃn/ 许可 A2 93
personal /ˈpɜːsənl/ (= for one person) 针对个人的 A1 28
personal (information) 个人（信息） 13
personal computer 个人电脑 73
personality /ˌpɜːsəˈnæləti/ 个性 A2 16
pet /pet/ 宠物 A2 38
petrol /ˈpetrəl/ 汽油 A2 34
pharmacy /ˈfɑːməsi/ 药房 28, 31
phone /fəʊn/ n, v 电话；打电话 A1 29, 61, 75
phone /fəʊn/ A1 见 on the phone 在打电话 A1 21, 75

phone number 电话号码 **A1** 75, 79

phone sb back 再打电话给某人 75

photo /ˈfəʊtəʊ/ 照片 **A1** 73, 90

photograph /ˈfəʊtəɡrɑːf/ 照片 **A1** 73

phrasal verb 短语动词 79

phrase /freɪz/ 短语 **A1** 2

physical education 体育 66

physics /ˈfɪzɪks/ 物理 **A2** 66

pianist /ˈpiːənɪst/ 钢琴家 83

piano /piˈænəʊ/ 钢琴 **A1** 83

pick /pɪk/ 采摘 **B1** 57

pick sth up 举起某物 **A2** 12

picture /ˈpɪktʃə(r)/ 照片 **A1** 60

pie /paɪ/ 馅饼 49

piece /piːs/ 片, 块 **A1** 45

piece /piːs/ **A1** 见 a piece of furniture 一件家具 60

piece /piːs/ **A1** 见 a piece of music 一首乐曲 83

piece /piːs/ **A1** 见 a piece of paper 一张纸 1

pig /pɪɡ/ 猪 **A1** 38, 47

pill /pɪl/ 药片 **B2** * 31

pilot /ˈpaɪlət/ 飞行员 **A2** 69

pineapple /ˈpaɪnæpl/ 菠萝 46

pink /pɪŋk/ 粉色 **A1** 26

pizza /ˈpiːtsə/ 披萨 49

place /pleɪs/ 地点, 场所 **A1** 56

plan (to do) sth 计划 (做) 某事 **A1** 13

plan /plæn/ n, v 计划 **A1** 30

plane /pleɪn/ 飞机 **A1** 89

planet /ˈplænɪt/ 行星 **A2** 84

plant /plɑːnt/ n 植物 **A1**

plant /plɑːnt/ v 种植 **A2** 57

plastic /ˈplæstɪk/ 塑料 **A2** 25, 29

plate /pleɪt/ 盘子 **A2** 48

platform /ˈplætfɔːm/ 站台 **A2** 53

play (a game) 玩 (游戏); 进行 (比赛) **A1** 23, 81, 82

play (an instrument) 演奏 (乐器) **A1** 81

player /ˈpleɪə(r)/ 参赛选手 **A1** 82

please /pliːz/ (用于礼貌地请求某人做某事) 请 **A1** 45, 50, 55

pleased /pliːzd/ 满意的 **A2** 17

plus /plʌs/ 加 **B1** 6

p.m. /ˌpiːˈem/ 午后 7

pocket /ˈpɒkɪt/ 口袋 **A2** 24

point /pɔɪnt/ 得分 **A2** 82

Poland /ˈpəʊlənd/ 波兰 35

police officer 警官 **A2** 69, 79

policeman /pəˈliːsmən/ (男) 警员 **A1** 69

policewoman /pəˈliːswʊmən/ 女警员 69

Polish /ˈpəʊlɪʃ/ 波兰人; 波兰语 35

polite /pəˈlaɪt/ 礼貌的 **A2** 62, 93, 95

pollution /pəˈluːʃn/ 污染 **A2** 34, 56

poor /pɔː(r)/ 贫穷的 **A1** 63

popular /ˈpɒpjələ(r)/ 受欢迎的 **A1** 36, 81

population /ˌpɒpjuˈleɪʃn/ 人口 **A2** 36

pork /pɔːk/ 猪肉 47

Portugal /ˈpɔːtʃʊɡl/ 葡萄牙 35

Portuguese /ˌpɔːtʃʊˈɡiːz/ 葡萄牙人; 葡萄牙语 35

positive /ˈpɒzətɪv/ 积极的 **A1** 63

possessions /pəˈzeʃnz/ 财产, 所有物 **A2** 29

possibility /ˌpɒsəˈbɪləti/ 可能性 **A2** 96

possible /ˈpɒsəbl/ 可能的 **A1** 62, 96

post office 邮局 **A1** 56

post /pəʊst/ n, v 邮寄 **A1** 71, 74

postcard /ˈpəʊstkɑːd/ 明信片 90

postcode /ˈpəʊstkəʊd/ 邮编 13

potato /pəˈteɪtəʊ/ 土豆 **A1** 46

pound /paʊnd/ 英镑 **A1** 27

practice /ˈpræktɪs/ n 练习 **A1** 5

practise /ˈpræktɪs/ v 练习 **A1** 5

prawn /prɔːn/ 对虾 47

predict /prɪˈdɪkt/ 预测 **A2** 78

prediction /prɪˈdɪkʃn/ 预测 **B1** 78

prefer to do sth 宁可做某事 **A1** 28, 90, 94

prefer (X to Y) (相比Y) 更喜欢 (X) **A1** 28, 80

prepare /prɪˈpeə(r)/ 准备 **A1** 59

preposition /ˌprepəˈzɪʃn/ 介词 2

present /ˈpreznt/ 礼物 **A1** 22, 28

pretty /ˈprɪti/ (= attractive) 漂亮的 **A1** 11

pretty /ˈprɪti/ (= quite) 相当 **A1** 64

price /praɪs/ 价格 **A1** 27

print /prɪnt/ 打印 **A2** 73, 89

printer /ˈprɪntə(r)/ 打印机 **A2** 73

prison /ˈprɪzn/ **A2** 见 in prison 坐牢 **A2** 21

prize /praɪz/ 奖品 **A2** 27

probably /ˈprɒbəbli/ 很可能 **A1** 96

problem /ˈprɒbləm/ **A1** 见 no problem 没问题 **A1** 54, 93

produce /prəˈdjuːs/ 生产 **A2** 57

product /ˈprɒdʌkt/ 产品 **A1** 27

professor /prəˈfesə(r)/ 教授 **A2** 68

program /ˈprəʊɡræm/ 程序 **A1** 73

programme /ˈprəʊɡræm/ 节目 **A1** 85

progress /ˈprəʊɡres/ 进步 **A2** 13

project /ˈprɒdʒekt/ 项目 **B1** 70

promise /ˈprɒmɪs/ n, v 承诺 **A2** 44

pronoun /ˈprəʊnaʊn/ 代词 2

pronounce /prəˈnaʊns/ 发音 **A2** 4

pronunciation /prəˌnʌnsiˈeɪʃn/ 发音 4

provide /prəˈvaɪd/ 提供 **A2** 89

pub /pʌb/ 酒吧 **A2** 50

public /ˈpʌblɪk/ **A2** 见 the public 公众 30

public transport 公共交通 **A2** 51

publish /ˈpʌblɪʃ/ 出版 **A2** 86

pull /pʊl/ 拉 **A2** 12

purple /ˈpɜːpl/ 紫色 **A1** 26

purpose /ˈpɜːpəs/ 目的 **A2** 29

purse /pɜːs/ (尤指女式) 钱包 27

push /pʊʃ/ 推 **A2** 12

put /pʊt/ **A1** 39

on make-up 上妆 60

on weight 增重 11

Saturday /ˈsætədeɪ/ 星期六 A1 8

sauce /sɔːs/ 调味汁 A2 49

Saudi Arabia 沙特阿拉伯 35

Saudi /ˈsaʊdi/ 沙特阿拉伯人 35

sausage /ˈsɒsɪdʒ/ 香肠 47

save (money) 节省（钱）A2 27

save /seɪv/ (= on a computer) 保存（文件）A2 73

say /seɪ/ 表达 A1 4

say sorry 道歉 95

scared (of sth/sb) （对某事／物／人）感到害怕 A2 17

scarf /skɑːf/ 围巾 25

scary /ˈskeəri/ 恐怖的 A2 84

school /skuːl/ 学校 A1 67

science fiction 科幻 A2 84

science (subjects) 理科 66

sci-fi /ˈsaɪ faɪ/ 科幻 84

score /skɔː(r)/ n, v 比分；得分 A2 82

Scotland /ˈskɒtlənd/ 苏格兰 35

screen /skriːn/ 屏幕 A2 73

sea /siː/ 大海 A1 90

seafood /ˈsiːfuːd/ 海鲜 47

search /sɜːtʃ/ n, v 搜寻 A2 30

search (for sth) (= on a computer) （用电脑）搜索（信息）A2 74

season /ˈsiːzn/ 季节 A2 8

seat /siːt/ 座位 A2 50, 53

seat belt 安全带 89

second /ˈsekənd/ 第二 A1 8

second floor 三楼（底楼以上的二楼）58

secondly /ˈsekəndli/ 其次 A2 98

secretary /ˈsekrətri/ 秘书 A2 69

security /sɪˈkjʊərəti/ 安检区 B1 89

see /siː/ (= notice) 看见 A1 43

see /siː/ (= watch a film/TV) 观看（电影／电视）A1 43, 85

see /siː/ (= find out about sth) 弄清 A1 43

see /siː/ (= visit/spend time with sb) 拜访 A1 16, 43

see /siː/ (= understand) 理解 B1 43

see you A1 (later/soon/then) 回头见 91

sell /sel/ 售卖 A1 27

send /send/ 发送 A1 39, 70, 74

send an email 发送电子邮件 44

send a reply 回复 44

sentence /ˈsentəns/ 句子 A1 2

separate /ˈseprət/ 分居；分手 B1 16

September /sepˈtembə(r)/ 九月 A1 8

series /ˈsɪəriːz/ (on TV, etc.) 系列节目 A2 86

series /ˈsɪəriːz/ (of events, etc.) 系列 B1 30

serious /ˈsɪəriəs/ (= not fun) 严肃的 A2 15

serious /ˈsɪəriəs/ (= very bad) 严重的 A2 32

serve /sɜːv/ 提供 A2 28, 88

service /ˈsɜːvɪs/ 服务 B1 28, 88

seven /ˈsevn/ 七 A1 6

seventeen /ˌsevnˈtiːn/ 十七 A1 6

seventeenth /ˌsevnˈtiːnθ/ 第十七 8

seventh /ˈsevnθ/ 第七 8

seventy /ˈsevnti/ 七十 A1 6

shake hands 握手 91

Shall we …? 要不我们……？94

shape /ʃeɪp/ 形状 A2 29

share a flat 合住公寓 15

shave /ʃeɪv/ n 剃须，修面 60

sheep /ʃiːp/ 绵羊 A1 38, 47

sheet /ʃiːt/ 被单 A2 60

shelf /ʃelf/ 架子 B1 61

shine /ʃaɪn/ 照耀 B1 37

shirt /ʃɜːt/ 衬衫 A1 24

shoe /ʃuː/ 鞋子 A1 25

shoe shop 鞋店 28

shop /ʃɒp/ n 商店 A1 28

shop assistant 营业员 45, 69, 79

shop online 在线购物 28, 74

shopping /ˈʃɒpɪŋ/ A1 见 go shopping / do the shopping 去购物 23, 28, 41, 77

shopping centre 购物中心 28, 79

short /ʃɔːt/ (= not tall) 矮的 A1 11

short /ʃɔːt/ (= not long) 短的 A1 11, 26

short form 缩写 3

shorts /ʃɔːts/ 短裤 24

should /ʃəd/ 应该 A1 31

shoulder /ˈʃəʊldə(r)/ 肩膀 A2 10

shower /ˈʃaʊə(r)/ (= in a bathroom) 淋浴；花洒 A1 23, 60

shower /ˈʃaʊə(r)/ (= light rain) 阵雨 B1 37

shut /ʃʌt/ adj 歇业的 A2 55

shut /ʃʌt/ v 关闭；歇业 A2 12, 39, 92

sick /sɪk/ A1 见 be/feel sick 呕吐／想呕吐 31

sightseeing /ˈsaɪtsiːɪŋ/ 见 go sightseeing 去观光 77, 90

sign /saɪn/ n (= notice) 标识 A2 55

sign /saɪn/ v (= write your name) 签名 A2 88

silver /ˈsɪlvə(r)/ 银 A2 25

similar /ˈsɪmələ(r)/ 相似的 A1 63

simple /ˈsɪmpl/ 简单的 A2 5

since /sɪns/ 自从 A2 9

sing /sɪŋ/ 唱 39, 81

singer /ˈsɪŋə(r)/ 歌手 A1 81

single (ticket) 单程票 53

single /ˈsɪŋgl/ (= not married) 单身的 A2 13

single room 单人间 87

sink /sɪŋk/ n 洗碗槽 59

sister /ˈsɪstə(r)/ 姐妹 A1 14

sister-in-law /ˈsɪstər ɪn lɔː/ 嫂子，弟媳，妯娌 14

sit /sɪt/ 坐 A1 39

sit down 坐下 A1 12, 99

site /saɪt/ (= website) 网站 A2 74

situation /ˌsɪtʃuˈeɪʃn/ 情况 A1 4

six /sɪks/ 六 A1 6

sixteen /ˌsɪksˈtiːn/ 十六 A1 6

sixteenth /ˌsɪksˈtiːnθ/ 第十六 8

sixth /sɪksθ/ 第六 8

sixty /ˈsɪksti/ 六十 A1 6

size /saɪz/ 尺寸 A2 26

skiing /ˈskiːɪŋ/ 滑雪 A2 82

skin /skɪn/ 皮肤 A2 10

skirt /skɜːt/ 裙子 **A1** 24

sky /skaɪ/ 天空 **A2** 37

sleep /sliːp/ v 睡觉 **A1** 23, 44

sleep /sliːp/ n 睡觉 **A1** 44

slim /slɪm/ 苗条的 11

slow train 慢行列车 53

slowly /ˈsləʊli/ 慢慢地 **A2** 65

small /smɔːl/ 小的 **A1** 26

smartphone /ˈsmɑːtfəʊn/ 智能手机 75

smell /smel/ n, v 气味；有……气味 **A2** 44

smile /smaɪl/ n, v 微笑 **A2** 11, 44

smoking /ˈsməʊkɪŋ/ 吸烟 **A2** 77

smoking /ˈsməʊkɪŋ/ **A2** 见 no smoking 禁止吸烟 55

snack /snæk/ 零食 50

snake /sneɪk/ 蛇 **A1** 38

snow /snəʊ/ n, v 雪；下雪 **A1** 37

so conjunction 所以 **A1** 98

so … (that) adverb (= for emphasis) 如此……（以至于……）
A1 72

soap /səʊp/ 肥皂 **A2** 60

soccer /ˈsɒkə(r)/ 足球 **A2** 82

social life 社交生活 15

social media 社交媒体 63

socks /sɒks/ 袜子 **A2** 25

sofa /ˈsəʊfə/ 沙发 61

soft /sɒft/ 软的 **A2** 63

software designer 软件设计师 68

soldier /ˈsəʊldʒə(r)/ 士兵 **A2** 69

solution /səˈluːʃn/ 解决方案 **A2** 78, 86

solve /sɒlv/ 解决 **A2** 78, 86

some (of sth) （某事／物的）部分 **A1** 45, 85

some more 再要一些 49

sometimes /ˈsʌmtaɪmz/ 有时 **A1** 23

somewhere /ˈsʌmweə(r)/ 在某地 **A2** 33

somewhere else 其他地方 100

son /sʌn/ 儿子 **A1** 14

song /sɒŋ/ 歌曲 **A1** 81

soon /suːn/ **A1** 见 see you soon 回头见 91

sorry /ˈsɒri/ **A1** 见 (so/very/really) sorry （非常）
抱歉 17, 94, 95

sorry /ˈsɒri/ **A1** 见 sorry I'm late 对不起，我来晚了 95

sort /sɔːt/ **A2** 见 What sort of … ? 哪一类……？ 84, 92

sound /saʊnd/ **A1** 见 that sounds lovely 听起来
不错 94

soup /suːp/ 汤 **A1** 49

source /sɔːs/ 来源 **A2** 34

south /saʊθ/ n, adj 南方；向南的；南部的 **A1** 36

South America 南美洲 35

South Korea 韩国 35

south-east /ˌsaʊθ ˈiːst/ 东南 36

south-west /ˌsaʊθ ˈwest/ 西南 36

soy sauce 酱油 49

space /speɪs/ [U] 空间 **A1** 60

Spain /speɪn/ 西班牙 35

Spanish /ˈspænɪʃ/ 西班牙人；西班牙语 35

speak /spiːk/ 说话 **A1** 39, 76

speaker /ˈspiːkə(r)/ 说话者 **A2** 76

speaking /ˈspiːkɪŋ/ （通话中）是我 75

special /ˈspeʃl/ 特殊的 **A1** 8

specific /spəˈsɪfɪk/ 具体的 **A2** 63

speed limit 限速 51

spell /spel/ 拼写 **A1** 4, 39

spelling /ˈspelɪŋ/ 拼写 **A1** 77

spend money (on sth) 花钱（买某物） 22, 27, 39

spend time doing sth 花时间做某事 **A1** 70

spend time with sb 与某人相处 14, 39

spider /ˈspaɪdə(r)/ 蜘蛛 **A2** 38

spoon /spuːn/ 勺 **A2** 48

sports centre 体育中心 79

spring /sprɪŋ/ 春季 **A1** 8

square /skweə(r)/ (= shape) 方形 **A2** 29

square /skweə(r)/ (= in a town) 广场 **A2** 56

squid /skwɪd/ 鱿鱼 47

stairs /steə(r)z/ 楼梯 **A2** 58

stand up 站起来 **A1** 12, 99

star /stɑː(r)/ n 主角 **A1** 84

star /stɑː(r)/ v 担任主角 **A2** 84

start school 开始上学 67

starter /ˈstɑːtə(r)/ 开胃菜 49

statement /ˈsteɪtmənt/ 声明 **A1** 30

station /ˈsteɪʃn/ 车站 **A1** 53

stay /steɪ/ v 暂住，留宿 **A1** 88

stay /steɪ/ n 暂住，留宿 **A2** 88

stay at school 继续求学 67

stay in 待在家里 **A1** 23

stay in bed 卧床 31

steps /steps/ 台阶 **A2** 58

still water 不含碳酸气的水 49

still /stɪl/ (= continuing) 仍旧 **A1** 64, 97

stomach /ˈstʌmək/ 胃 **A1** 10

stomach ache 胃痛 31

stop /stɒp/ n 车站 **A1** 52

storm /stɔːm/ 暴风雨 **A2** 37

story /ˈstɔːri/ **A1** 见 love story 爱情片 84

straight /streɪt/ 直的 **A1** 11

strange /streɪndʒ/ 奇怪的 **A2** 15

strawberry /ˈstrɔːbəri/ 草莓 46

stress /stres/ 强调 **B2** 30

strong /strɒŋ/ (= not weak) 强壮的 **A1** 31, 63

strong (wind) 强劲的（风） **A2** 37

study /ˈstʌdi/ n 书房 **B1** 58

stupid /ˈstjuːpɪd/ 愚蠢的 **A2** 15

style /staɪl/ 风格 **A1** 26

subject /ˈsʌbdʒɪkt/ 学科 **A1** 66

subway /ˈsʌbweɪ/ 地铁 51

succeed /səkˈsiːd/ 成功 **A2** 78

success /səkˈses/ 成功 **A1** 78

such … (that) 如此……（以至于……） **A2** 72

suddenly /ˈsʌdənli/ 突然地 **A2** 37

sugar /ˈʃʊɡə(r)/ 糖 **A1** 45

suggest /səˈdʒest/ 建议 **A2** 94

suggestion /səˈdʒestʃən/ 建议 **A2** 94

suit /suːt/ 套装 A2 24
suitcase /ˈsuːtkeɪs/ 手提箱 60, 87
summer /ˈsʌmə(r)/ 夏季 A1 8
sun /sʌn/ 太阳 A1 37
sunny /ˈsʌni/ 阳光明媚的 37
Sunday /ˈsʌndeɪ/ 星期日 A1 8
sunglasses /ˈsʌnglɑːsɪz/ 墨镜 25
supermarket /ˈsuːpəmɑːkɪt/ 超市 A1 28
support /səˈpɔːt/ v 支持 A2 72
suppose /səˈpəʊz/ A2 见 I suppose so 我想是的 100
sure /ʃʊə(r)/ (= certain) 确信 A1 4, 62
sure /ʃʊə(r)/ (= of course) （表示同意）当然 A2 49, 93
surname /ˈsɜːneɪm/ 姓 13
surprise /səˈpraɪz/ n, v 惊喜；使感到惊讶 A2 44
surprised /səˈpraɪzd/ 感到惊讶的 A2 17
surprising /səˈpraɪzɪŋ/ 令人惊讶的 A2 72
sweet /swiːt/ 甜的 A2 46
swim /swɪm/ v 游泳 A1 39
swim /swɪm/ n 游泳 B1 23
swimming /ˈswɪmɪŋ/ 游泳 A1 82
swimming pool 游泳池 A1 79
Swiss /swɪs/ 瑞士人 35
Switzerland /ˈswɪtsələnd/ 瑞士 35
symbol /ˈsɪmbl/ 符号 A2 3
synonym /ˈsɪnənɪm/ 近义词 3
system /ˈsɪstəm/ 系统 A2 67
T-shirt /ˈtiː ʃɜːt/ T恤 A1 24
table /ˈteɪbl/ (= furniture) 桌子 A1 1, 60
table /ˈteɪbl/ (= diagram) （一览）表 A2 3
table tennis 乒乓球 82
tablet /ˈtæblət/ (= computer) 平板电脑 A2 73
tablet /ˈtæblət/ (= medicine) 药片 B1 31

take /teɪk/

size 12, etc. 穿12号，等 26
(time) /taɪm/ 需要……时间 A1 68
(= carry) 拿走 A1 93
a message 捎口信 75
an exam 参加考试 67
a photo 拍照 90
a seat 就座 50
away /əˈweɪ/ 外带 50
care of sb/sth 照顾某人，料理某事/物 A2 100
off /ɒf/ (= leave) 起飞 A2 89, 99
place /pleɪs/ 进行 A2 30
sth off (= remove) 脱下某物 A2 24, 99
the bus/train 搭乘公共汽车/火车 51, 53
见 how long does it take? 需要多久? 52
见 take the first/second, etc. turning 在第一/二个路口等拐弯 54

tall /tɔːl/ 高的 A1 11
tap /tæp/ 水龙头 B2 * 59
task /tɑːsk/ 任务 59
taste /teɪst/ 有……味道 A2 46
taxi /ˈtæksi/ 出租车 A1 51
taxi driver 出租车司机 69

tea /tiː/ 茶 A1 50
teach /tiːtʃ/ 讲授 A1 39, 76
teacher /ˈtiːtʃə(r)/ 教师 A1 68, 69, 76
teaching /ˈtiːtʃɪŋ/ 讲授；当教师 A2 77
team /tiːm/ 队伍 A1 82
technology /tekˈnɒlədʒi/ 技术 A2 66
teenage /ˈtiːneɪdʒ/ 青少年的 A2 11
teenager /ˈtiːneɪdʒə(r)/ （13至19岁的）青少年 A1 11
teeth /tiːθ/ 牙齿（复数） A1 10
telephone /ˈtelɪfəʊn/ 电话 A1 29, 61
television /ˈtelɪvɪʒn/ 电视 A1 61
temperature /ˈtemprətʃə(r)/ 温度 A2 31
ten /ten/ 十 A1 6
tennis /ˈtenɪs/ 网球 A1 23, 82
tent /tent/ 帐篷 B1 81
tenth /tenθ/ 第十 8
term /tɜːm/ 学期 A2 68
terrible /ˈterəbl/ 糟糕的 A1 26
terrible at sth 很不擅长做某事 66
test /test/ v 测试 A1 3
text /tekst/ n 文本；短信 A1 5, 73, 75
Thai /taɪ/ 泰国人；泰语 35
Thailand /ˈtaɪlænd/ 泰国 35
than /ðən/ （引出比较的第二部分）比 A1 14
thank sb (for sth) （因为某事）感谢某人 22
thanks a lot 非常感谢 95
thanks very much 非常感谢 54
that would be lovely 那太好了 94
that's a great idea 好主意 94
that's all right 没关系 95
that's all, thanks 就这些，谢谢 45, 50
that's fine 没问题 45, 93
that's OK 没问题 54
the army 陆军 70
the best 最好的 67
the news 新闻报道 85
the oldest 最年长的 14
the rest 剩余部分 100
the same 相同的 3
the worst 最差的 67
the youngest 最年轻的 14
then /ðen/ 然后 A1 98
there are five of us 我们总共五个人 14
there's lots / a lot / nothing to do 有许多事要做/没有事情做 56
thin /θɪn/ 瘦的 A2 11
thing /θɪŋ/ 事物 A1 4
think /θɪŋk/ 想，考虑 A1 39, 78
think about/of sth 考虑，想到某事/对某事有特定的想法 A1 22
think /θɪŋk/ A1 见 I think so 我想是的 A2 / I don't think so 我不这么认为 96
third /θɜːd/ 第三 A1 8
thirsty /ˈθɜːsti/ 口渴的 A1 17
thirteen /ˌθɜːˈtiːn/ 十三 A1 6
thirteenth /ˌθɜːˈtiːnθ/ 第十三 8

thirtieth /ˈθɜːtiəθ/ 第三十 8

thirty /ˈθɜːti/ 三十 A1 6

this evening/weekend/morning A1, etc. 今天晚上 /
本周末 / 今天上午, 等 9

This is … (= on the phone) （通话中）我是…… A1 75

This is … (= introducing sb) （介绍某人）这位是……
A1 91

though /ðəʊ/ 虽然 B1 97

thought(s) /θɔːt(s)/ 想法 A2 78

thousand /ˈθaʊznd/ 一千 A1 6

three /θriː/ 三 A1 6

thriller /ˈθrɪlə(r)/ 惊悚片 84

through /θruː/ 穿过 A1 19

throw /θrəʊ/ 扔 A2 12

Thursday /ˈθɜːzdeɪ/ 星期四 A1 8

tick /tɪk/ 给……打钩 3

ticket /ˈtɪkɪt/ 票子 A1 53

ticket machine 售票机 89

ticket office 售票处 53, 79

tidy /ˈtaɪdi/ 整洁的 A2 15

tie /taɪ/ 领带 A2 24

tiger /ˈtaɪgə(r)/ 老虎 38

tights /taɪts/ 紧身裤, 连裤袜 25

time /taɪm/ A1 见 on time 准时 A2 21

timetable /ˈtaɪmteɪbl/ 时刻表 52, 53

tired /ˈtaɪəd/ 疲惫的 A1 17

to /tu/ (= purpose) 为了 A1 98

toasted sandwich 烤三明治 50

toe /təʊ/ 脚趾 B1 10

together /təˈgeðə(r)/ 在一起 A1 14

together /təˈgeðə(r)/ A1 见 be together 处于恋爱
关系 16

toilet /ˈtɔɪlət/ 厕所 A1 55, 60

tomato /təˈmɑːtəʊ/ 番茄 A1 46

tomorrow morning 明天上午 9

too /tuː/ (= excessive) 过于, 太 A1 26

too /tuː/ (= also) 也 A1 97

tool /tuːl/ 工具 A2 29

tooth (pl teeth) 牙齿（复数teeth） A1 10

toothache /ˈtuːθeɪk/ 牙痛 31

toothbrush /ˈtuːθbrʌʃ/ 牙刷 60

top /tɒp/ (= clothes) 上衣 A2 24

top /tɒp/ (= highest) （排名）最高的 A2 82

top floor 顶楼 58

total /ˈtəʊtl/ 总数, 总额 B1 27

touch /tʌtʃ/ 触摸 A2 28

tour /tʊə(r)/ A2 见 go on a guided tour 跟着导游去
旅行 90

tourism /ˈtʊərɪzəm/ 旅游业 A2 88

tourist /ˈtʊərɪst/ 游客 A1 88

towards /təˈwɔːdz/ 朝着 A2 19

towel /ˈtaʊəl/ 毛巾 A2 60

tower /ˈtaʊə(r)/ 塔 A2 56

town /taʊn/ 城镇 A1 36

town centre 城镇中心 A1 79

toy /tɔɪ/ 玩具 A2 28

toy shop 玩具店 28

tradition /trəˈdɪʃn/ 传统 A2 63

traditional /trəˈdɪʃənl/ 传统的 A2 63

traffic /ˈtræfɪk/ 路上行驶的车辆 A1 51

traffic lights 交通信号灯 54, 79

train /treɪn/ 列车 A1 53

train driver 列车司机 69

train station 列车站 53, 79

trainers /ˈtreɪnə(r)z/ 运动鞋 A2 25

training /ˈtreɪnɪŋ/ 培训 A2 67, 71

travel /ˈtrævl/ 旅行 A1 76

traveller /ˈtrævələ(r)/ 旅客 A2 76

travelling /ˈtrævəlɪŋ/ 旅行 81

tree /triː/ 树 A1 57

trip /trɪp/ 旅行 A1 88

trouble /ˈtrʌbl/ 麻烦 A2 86

trousers /ˈtraʊzəz/ 裤子 A1 24

truck /trʌk/ 卡车 A2 51

true /truː/ 对的 A1 3

try /traɪ/ 尝试 A1 86

try sth on 试穿某物 28

Tuesday /ˈtjuːzdeɪ/ 星期二 A1 8

tuna /ˈtjuːnə/ 金枪鱼（肉） 47

Turkey /ˈtɜːki/ 土耳其 35

Turkish /ˈtɜːkɪʃ/ 土耳其人；土耳其语 35

turn left/right 向左 / 右转 54

turn sth on/off 打开 / 关闭某物 A2 59, 99

turning /ˈtɜːnɪŋ/ 见 take the second turning 在第二个
路口拐弯 54

TV /ˌtiːˈviː/ 电视 A1 61

twelfth /twelfθ/ 第十二 8

twelve /twelv/ 十二 A1 6

twentieth /ˈtwentiəθ/ 第二十 8

twenty /ˈtwenti/ 二十 A1 6

twenty-first /ˌtwenti ˈfɜːst/ 第二十一 8

twenty-one /ˌtwenti ˈwʌn/ 二十一 6

twenty-second /ˌtwenti ˈsekənd/ 第二十二 8

twenty-third /ˌtwenti ˈθɜːd/ 第二十三 8

twenty-three /ˌtwenti ˈθriː/ 二十三 6

twenty-two /ˌtwenti ˈtuː/ 二十二 6

twice /twaɪs/ 两次 A1 23, 92

two /tuː/ 二 A1 6

type /taɪp/ A1 见 What type of … ? 哪一类……?
47, 84, 92

type /taɪp/ v 打字 B1 73

typical /ˈtɪpɪkl/ 典型的 A2 90

UK /ˌjuːˈkeɪ/ 英国 35

umbrella /ʌmˈbrelə/ 伞 A1 25

uncertain /ʌnˈsɜːtn/ 不确定的 62

uncle /ˈʌŋkl/ 叔父, 伯父 A1 14

uncomfortable /ʌnˈkʌmftəbl/ 不舒服的 26

under /ˈʌndə(r)/ (= below) 在……下面 A1 19

under /ˈʌndə(r)/ (= less than) 少于 A1 36

underground /ˌʌndəˈgraʊnd/ 地铁 51

underline /ˌʌndəˈlaɪn/ 在……下划线 3

understanding /ˌʌndəˈstændɪŋ/ 理解 A2 77

unemployed /ˌʌnɪmˈplɔɪd/ 无业的 **B1** 69

unfortunately /ʌnˈfɔːtʃənətli/ 不幸地，遗憾地 **A2** 51, 68

unfriendly /ʌnˈfrendli/ 不友善的 15

unhappy /ʌnˈhæpi/ 不高兴的 **A2** 17

unhealthy /ʌnˈhelθi/ 不健康的 31, 62

uniform /ˈjuːnɪfɔːm/ 制服，校服 **A2** 24, 67

unit /ˈjuːnɪt/ 单位，单元 **A2** 72

United Kingdom 英国（大不列颠及北爱尔兰联合王国）35

United States (of America) 美国（美利坚合众国）35

unlucky /ʌnˈlʌki/ 倒霉的 62

unnecessary /ʌnˈnesəsəri/ 不必要的 **B1** 62

unsure /ʌnˈʃʊə(r)/ 不确定的 62

untidy /ʌnˈtaɪdi/ 凌乱的 15

until /ənˈtɪl/ 直到 **A1** 88

unusual /ʌnˈjuːʒuəl/ 反常的 **A2** 29, 63

up /ʌp/ 向上 **A1** 19

up to (an age) 直到（某一年龄）**B1** 67

upset /ʌpˈset/ 不安的 **B1** 17

upstairs /ˌʌpˈsteəz/ 顺楼梯而上，在楼上 **A1** 58

use /juːz/ *v* 使用 **A1** 4

used to 过去常常 **A2** 90

useful /ˈjuːsfl/ 有用的 **A1** 63

useless /ˈjuːsləs/ 无用的 **B2**＊63

usually /ˈjuːʒuəli/ 通常 **A1** 23

vacancy /ˈveɪkənsi/ 空房 55

valley /ˈvæli/ 山谷 **A2** 57

van /væn/ 厢式货车 **A2** 51

variety /vəˈraɪəti/ 各种各样 **A2** 86

various /ˈveəriəs/ 各种各样的 **B1** 81

vegetable /ˈvedʒtəbl/ 蔬菜 **A1** 46

vegetarian /ˌvedʒəˈteəriən/ 素食者 47

vehicle /ˈviːəkl/ 车辆 **A2** 51

verb /vɜːb/ 动词 2

very /ˈveri/ 非常 **A1** 26, 64

very well 很好 91

video /ˈvɪdiəʊ/ 视频 **A1** 74

view /vjuː/ (= opinion) 看法 **A2** 56

view /vjuː/ (= what you can see) 视野 **A2** 58

village /ˈvɪlɪdʒ/ 村庄 **A1** 36

vinegar /ˈvɪnɪɡə(r)/ 醋 48

violent /ˈvaɪələnt/ 暴力的 **B1** 84

violin /ˌvaɪəˈlɪn/ 小提琴 83

violinist /ˌvaɪəˈlɪnɪst/ 小提琴手 83

virus /ˈvaɪrəs/ (= illness) 病毒 **A2** 31

virus /ˈvaɪrəs/ (= on a computer) （计算机）病毒 **A2** 74

visit /ˈvɪzɪt/ *n, v* 访问，拜访 **A1** 76, 90

visitor /ˈvɪzɪtə(r)/ 访客 **A1** 76

vocabulary /vəˈkæbjələri/ 词汇 5

voice /vɔɪs/ 声音 **A2** 29

vomit /ˈvɒmɪt/ 呕吐 31

waist /weɪst/ 腰 10

wait for sth 等待某事／物 **A1** 22, 53

waiter /ˈweɪtə(r)/ 服务员 **A1** 49

wake up 醒来 **A1** 23, 39, 99

Wales /weɪlz/ 威尔士 35

walk /wɔːk/ 行走 **A1** 12

wall /wɔːl/ 墙 **A1** 60

wallet /ˈwɒlɪt/ 钱包 27

want /wɒnt/ **A1** 见 Do you want to … ? 你想去……吗? 94

want /wɒnt/ **A1** 见 Do you want … ? 你想要……吗? 95

war /wɔː(r)/ 战争 **A2** 85

war film 战争片 84

wardrobe /ˈwɔːdrəʊb/ 衣柜 60

warm /wɔːm/ 温暖的 **A1** 37

wash /wɒʃ/ **A1** 见 wash the dishes 洗盘子 59

wash /wɒʃ/ *n* 清洗 **A2** 60

washbasin /ˈwɒʃbeɪsn/ （固定在浴室墙上的）洗脸盆 60

washing /ˈwɒʃɪŋ/ 洗衣服 **A2** 59

washing machine 洗衣机 59, 79

washing-up /ˌwɒʃɪŋ ˈʌp/ 刷洗餐具 59

watch /wɒtʃ/ *n* 手表 **A1** 25

watch /wɒtʃ/ *v* 观看 **A1** 43, 81, 85

water /ˈwɔːtə(r)/ *n* 水 **A1** 48

water /ˈwɔːtə(r)/ *v* 给……浇水 **B1** 57

way /weɪ/ 路线 **A1** 54

way out 出口 55

weak /wiːk/ 虚弱的 **A2** 31, 63

wear /weə(r)/ 穿戴 **A1** 24, 25

website /ˈwebsaɪt/ 网站 **A1** 74

wedding /ˈwedɪŋ/ 婚礼 **A2** 96

Wednesday /ˈwenzdeɪ/ 星期三 **A1** 8

week /wiːk/ **A1** 见 last/next week 上／下周 9

weekday /ˈwiːkdeɪ/ 工作日 23

weekend /ˌwiːkˈend/ 周末 **A1** 9, 23

weigh /weɪ/ 重…… **B1** 11

weight /weɪt/ 体重 **A2** 11

welcome /ˈwelkəm/ *adj, v* 受欢迎的；欢迎 **A1** 91

welcome *n* 迎接 **A2** 91

well /wel/ 出色地 **A1** 65

well /wel/ (= not ill) 身体好的 **A1** 31

Well done! 做得好! 100

west /west/ *n, adj* 西方；向西的；西部的 **A1** 36

wet /wet/ 潮湿的 **A2** 37

whale /weɪl/ 鲸 38

what /wɒt/ **A1** 92

about … ? （提出建议）……怎么样? **A1** 94

can I get you? 你想要什么? 50

do you do? (= what's your job?) 你是做什么工作的? 13, 69, 92

kind/sort/type of … ? 哪一种……? 84, 92

time is it? 现在几点? 7

time/when … ? 什么时候……? 92

would you like? 你想要什么? 50

's on? 什么片子正在上映? 84

's sth like? （询问意见）某事／物怎么样? 15, 92

's the matter? 出了什么事? 31, 91

's the time? 现在几点? 7

's the weather like? 天气怎么样? 37

's your job? 你是做什么工作的? 13, 69

when /wen/ 何时 **A1** 92

13个带*单词来自 Oxford **5000**。

adj	adjective
adv	adverb
[C]	(of a noun) countable
inf	informal
n	noun
OPP	opposite
pl	plural
pp	past participle
pt	past tense
sing	singular
sb	somebody
sth	something
SYN	synonym
[U]	(of a noun) uncountable
v	verb

English text originally published as Oxford Word Skills (Elementary Vocabulary) by Oxford University Press, Great Clarendon Street, Oxford © Oxford University Press 2020

英语原版 Oxford Word Skills (Elementary Vocabulary) 由牛津大学出版社出版
© Oxford University Press 2020

This Chinese Translation Edition published by Shanghai Translation Publishing House by arrangement with Oxford University Press (China) Ltd for distribution in the mainland of China only and not for export therefrom

本中文翻译版由牛津大学出版社授权上海译文出版社出版,仅在中国大陆地区发行,不得出口到其他地区(包括中国香港、澳门和台湾)

Copyright © Oxford University Press (China) Ltd and Shanghai Translation Publishing House 2023

牛津大学出版社(中国)有限公司,上海译文出版社有限公司 2023

Oxford is a registered trademark of Oxford University Press

Oxford 是牛津大学出版社的注册商标

Shanghai Translation Publishing House has made some changes to the original work in order to make this edition more appropriate for readers in the mainland of China

上海译文出版社对原书进行了个别修改,使其更符合中国大陆读者的需要

图字: 09-2021-790 号

图书在版编目(CIP)数据

牛津英语词汇:初级:第二版/(英)鲁思·盖尔恩斯(Ruth Gairns),(英)斯图亚特·雷德曼(Stuart Redman)著;孙欣祺译. —上海:上海译文出版社,2023.8
书名原文:Oxford Word Skills (Elementary Vocabulary)
ISBN 978-7-5327-9379-2

Ⅰ.①牛… Ⅱ.①鲁… ②斯… ③孙… Ⅲ.①英语-词汇-自学参考资料 Ⅳ.①H313

中国国家版本馆 CIP 数据核字(2023)第 115140 号

牛津英语词汇(初级)(第二版)

[英]鲁思·盖尔恩斯 [美]斯图亚特·雷德曼 著
孙欣祺 译
责任编辑/陆亚平 装帧设计/柴昊洲

上海译文出版社有限公司出版、发行
网址:www.yiwen.com.cn
201101 上海市闵行区号景路 159 弄 B 座
苏州市越洋印刷有限公司印刷

开本 787×1092 1/16 印张 16.25 字数 541,000
2023 年 10 月第 1 版 2023 年 10 月第 1 次印刷
印数:0,001—6,000 册

ISBN 978-7-5327-9379-2/H·1583
定价:68.00 元